1972

APOCALYPSE

APOCALYPSE

DOMINANT CONTEMPORARY FORMS

Edited by **JOE DAVID BELLAMY**
Mansfield State College

J. B. LIPPINCOTT COMPANY
PHILADELPHIA   NEW YORK   TORONTO

ISBN-O-397-47203-X
Library of Congress Catalog Card Number: 74-37655

COPYRIGHTS AND ACKNOWLEDGMENTS

HOLLIS ALPERT, "The Graduate Makes Out," from *Saturday Review,* July 6, 1968. Copyright © 1968 by Saturday Review, Inc.

ROGER ANGELL, "Life in These Now United States," from *A Day in the Life of Roger Angell* by Roger Angell. Copyright © 1969 by Roger Angell. All rights reserved. Reprinted by permission of The Viking Press, Inc.

ROGER ANGELL, "Your Horoscope: More Unsolicited Guidance from Out There," from *A Day in the Life of Roger Angell* by Roger Angell. Copyright © 1969 by Roger Angell. All rights reserved. Reprinted by permission of The Viking Press, Inc.

ROBERT ARDREY, "African Genesis," from *African Genesis* by Robert Ardrey. Copyright © 1961 by Literat S.A. Reprinted by permission of Atheneum Publishers.

MICHAEL J. ARLEN, "Marshall McLuhan and the Technological Embrace," from *Living-Room War* by Michael J. Arlen. Copyright © 1967 by Michael J. Arlen. All rights reserved. Reprinted by permission of The Viking Press, Inc.

JOAN BAEZ, "Child of Darkness," copyright © 1966 by Joan Baez. From *Daybreak* by Joan Baez. Reprinted by permission of the publisher, The Dial Press. Originally published in *Esquire.*

JOE DAVID BELLAMY, "An Interview with Robert Boles," copyright © 1970 by Joe David Bellamy. Reprinted by permission. Parts of this interview originally appeared in *Black Academy Review,* vol. I, no. 1 (Spring, 1970), and in *December,* vol. XII, nos. 1–2.

JOE DAVID BELLAMY, "The Human Zoo: Justifiable Speculation," copyright © 1972 by Joe David Bellamy.

DANIEL BERRIGAN, "The Breaking of Men and the Breaking of Bread," from the Introduction by Daniel Berrigan from *Prison Journals of a Priest Revolutionary* by Philip Berrigan, compiled and edited by Vincent McGee. Copyright © 1970 by Philip Berrigan. Reprinted by permission of Holt, Rinehart and Winston, Inc.

For my father
Orin Ross Bellamy
and for
Milton Goldberg

■ CONTENTS

Contents

■ CONTENTS BY FORM

PREFACE

A POCALYPSE: *Dominant Contemporary Forms* is a collection of diverse prose forms in contemporary idioms, chosen for their relevance to crucial (apocalyptical) contemporary issues and (potentially apocalyptical) phenomena, and chosen also for their relation to age-old human dilemmas, situations, miseries, celebrations. It is designed to stimulate a student's writing, reading, and thinking, (1) by providing provocative examples of *live* prose types; (2) by considering the differences, similarities, and interrelatedness of the dominant contemporary prose forms; and (3) by emphasizing the flexible *organic nature* of the medium, the necessity for *human responses* to any subject, and the *relation* of these responses to the process of writing itself.

Thematically. The book reflects the urgency felt by most thinking people regarding the topics considered and is calculated to motivate apathetic or slow-blooming persons toward states of increased awareness and searching. Repeatedly but implicitly, it poses for consideration the question: What is the nature of man? It offers a variety of loaded (but not unlikely) answers to such a question; attempts to consider ways in which man will either adapt to the demands of the natural world or exterminate himself; and considers the specific characteristics of some of those demands as well as the nature of exciting new pleasures or horrible doom that awaits as a consequence of his decisions and behavior.

Rhetorically. Any book in the area of composition that offers contemporary selections—and therefore does make a kind of tacit critical assessment of existing forms—must acknowledge the diversity and the astounding vitality of current nonfiction as well as the impracticality of attempting to contain this vitality in tight little molds. The essay is by no means dead. It is, in fact, undergoing a veritable renaissance and evolution. Some dazzling writers are in the process of pushing this evolution forward, shaping significant innovations in nonfiction forms.

Apocalypse: Dominant Contemporary Forms attempts to offer a judicious sampling of such writers while employing an ordering principle based upon *what exists* rather than upon a historical or arbitrarily imposed concept of types. This seems especially necessary because many of the old forms—those often given as examples for students to model their work after—are either obsolete or never really existed. No pro-

fessional writer would consider writing such essays these days. No publication would want to publish them. Although it may indeed be useful to discuss, say, the "informative essay," it is also useful to point out that very few *purely* informative essays actually exist—that the tag "informative" may help to define one's purpose in an essay but is basically inaccurate when referring to the essay's form.

Students may be fruitfully encouraged to understand, through practice and discussion, the validity of the analytic approach, in which composition may be discussed as a series of processes, as an interaction of categories such as description, exposition, narrative, argument; but students also need to be strongly urged—as they are in this book—to think about form as a synthesis of all these elements. They should be urged especially to think about whole compositions in terms of their relationships to the dominant contemporary forms, which is also to think about the possible practical applications of their writing by working under the assumption that their writing may well be more than a series of classroom exercises, that it may, in fact, have some influence, sooner or later, on the world outside the classroom.

A rudimentary premise in this book is that *persons* write (and read) essays, that is, that good writing (and remarkable style) is most likely to emerge from a personal response, from an emotional as well as an intellectual engagement with the subject matter, rather than from an effort to apply abstract principles to hypothetical writing situations. This idea comes from the conviction that a close relationship exists between human thought processes and emotional responses—and the process of writing (and reading).

A distinguishing feature of *Apocalypse: Dominant Contemporary Forms* is its treatment of the growing use of fictional techniques in the writing of nonfiction and the nature of the revolution in the writing of nonfiction which a general awareness of this relationship has engendered. An exploration of this relationship can be tremendously stimulating to composition students, many of whom owe their only previous interest in the subject to their attraction for fiction.

Selections. In addition to having been chosen for relevance, general excellence, and idiomatic qualities, selections have also been chosen: (1) for their clarity in illustrating the formal principles raised by the discussion questions at the end of each selection; (2) to be *within the reach*— in terms of reading difficulty—of the average college student; (3) for some diversity in length but especially for their proximity in length to essays students will presumably be writing; (4) for diversity of subject matter and point of view; (5) to include many never anthologized previously; (6) to include formally diverse selections, in many instances, by the same writer; (7) to ascend formally according to a scale of increasing difficulty, so that the student gains practice in forms closest to him and easiest to execute before moving on to more rigorous types and combinations.

Selections are arranged so that each thematic section contains a range of nonfiction types, as well as a fictionlike selection, a story, or a portion of a novel, which dramatizes (although not didactically) some aspect of the theme under consideration.

I would like to thank the following people for helping to make this book possible: Don Mahan and Reynolds Price, for their influence; Dr. John E. Saveson, Dean Charles H. Holmes, and President Lawrence Park, of Mansfield State College, for their encouragement; Nina Berglund, Victor Klopp, and James Simonis, for library help; Sharon Clark, Beth Edwards, Donna Ronchi, and Elysse Frank, for typing help; Kathleen R. Evans, for her help; Richard Heffron of the J. B. Lippincott Company, for his advice and forbearance; my mother, Beulah Bellamy, for her help; my daughter Lael, for use of her room and typewriter and bookshelf; my son Sam, for his occasional emendations to the text at five in the morning; and my wife, Connie Arendsee Bellamy, for her general grooviness.

JOE DAVID BELLAMY

Mansfield, Pennsylvania
January, 1972

PART ONE.

INTRODUCTION

THE ACCELERATION of change brought about by the technological revolution has clearly produced crises of values in all our major institutions, although perhaps the technological revolution, in itself, is not enough to account for the plight of the human species in this last third of the twentieth century.

To answer the question of how we arrived at this state of affairs requires a response of mind-boggling magnitude and complexity. But some effort to come to terms with this plight seems absolutely necessary if we are to have any chance of surviving it, much less of improving it.

The selections in the following three subject areas provide jumping-off points for a consideration of some of the main aspects of our plight, from the present explosive potential for violence within the United States to that symbol and embodiment of ultimate global apocalypse—The Bomb—the blinding annihilation that inevitably awaits us if we fail to understand ourselves and solve our problems. Related to these considerations are some recent anthropological theories that purport to help man understand his historical penchant for violent aggression—personal, national, or global—by examining the nature of his origins and his "million hard years" of evolution.

It seems self-evident that our present crisis—as a people—is in many ways unlike anything we have faced previously. Differences in value systems and life-styles have obviously existed before. Inequalities in the distribution of wealth, generational friction, and racial inharmony are not new. But the distinctness of the various battle lines, the numbers angrily marshaled to one side of any issue or the other, the bizarre shapes of the participants, the bitterness, the intolerance, the disparity in different people's concepts of the failure or success of our institutions together represent a social phenomenon of unprecedented proportion and with unprecedented potential for mass violence.

The historical scars and landmarks are already highly visible reference points: Kent State and Jackson State, Watts, movies like *Easy Rider* and *Medium Cool* that explored and dramatized some facet of the polarization process, the 1968 Democratic National Convention in Chicago, where the travesty of democratic principles of the convention itself and the police-instigated bloodletting of multitudes in the streets were witnessed live and in color in living rooms across the nation.

Books like *The Making of a Counter Culture* and *The Greening of America,* which offer more or less plausible explanations of the causes and characteristics of the polarization process, became national best sellers and generated vehement controversy.

Is our failure to live peacefully the result of a failure of our institutions or the failure of human nature, or both? Recent discoveries and speculation in the fields of archaeology and ethology (the scientific study of animal behavior) offer some interesting perspectives on this question.

Perhaps the primary assumption of much of contemporary anthropological thinking is: Since man's present state of civilization is compara-

3

tively recent, if we want to learn something about the nature of man, we must look at the characteristics he evolved which stood him in good stead for the million or so years prior to the last ten thousand years. As Alvin Toffler mentions in *Future Shock,* even if only the last 50,000 years are used as a measure, of the 800 lifetimes stretching back over those 50,000 years, fully 650 were spent in caves, and only in the last six lifetimes have masses of people been exposed to the printed word. Biologically, many anthropologists are saying, man remains essentially the simple tribal animal he was in the cave, making the best now of a very new and peculiar situation where many of his deepest and surest instincts no longer have survival value.

The question of what sort of "simple tribal animal" prehistoric man really was is obviously crucial, and not all authorities agree. But some startling new speculation is going on. To summarize: In the century following Darwin, most anthropologists held that man had arisen from a benign, nonaggressive forest ape. Then, within the last few decades, evidence began to accumulate from Leakey, Dart, and others to substantiate the theory that man's ancestor was, in fact, a creature known as *Australopithecus africanus,* a carnivore and a predator who owed his ascendancy to one talent above all others: his affinity for and skillful use of weapons. Robert Ardrey comments in *African Genesis,* "Far from the truth lay the antique assumption that man had fathered the weapon. The weapon, instead, had fathered man. The mightiest of predators had come about as the logical conclusion to an evolutionary transition. With his big brain and his stone handaxes, man annihilated a predecessor who fought only with bones. And if all human history from that date has turned on the development of superior weapons, then it is for very sound reason. It is for genetic necessity. We design and compete with our weapons as birds build distinctive nests." The implications of such a theory are shocking. Are we, in fact, doomed by our inheritance to lives of violence?

Other aspects of this approach—through an effort to understand early man and pre-man—are worth considering. Desmond Morris maintains that some of our major social problems arise out of an inability to adjust to the situation of no longer knowing personally each member of our communities because "as a species we were not [and are not] biologically equipped to cope with a mass of strangers masquerading as members of our tribe."

Although an evaluation of the anthropological perspective may seem to produce a preponderance of evidence of the bleakness of man's future on the planet, most experts find some cause for cautious optimism in the well-established adaptability of "the naked ape." Konrad Lorenz, the distinguished naturalist, has described the various means (through ritualization of aggression, for instance) that other species have developed to control their destructive drives in the interests of the survival of the species as a whole. He suggests that the human species may be able to survive as well, in spite of incredible odds, if we learn to ritualize our aggressions through every possible means and thus stop killing each other, in Vietnam, in Detroit, on college campuses, and elsewhere.

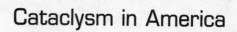

Cataclysm in America

THEODORE ROSZAK (b. 1933) is professor of history at California State College at Hayward. He has published numerous articles in such magazines as *The Nation* and the *New American Review* and was editor of *The Dissenting Academy* (1968). In *The Making of a Counter Culture* he examines the origins and nature of the youth culture and shows how its ideals have "helped call into question the conventional scientific world view and in so doing [have] set about undermining the foundations of the technocracy."

TECHNOCRACY'S CHILDREN

BEYOND the parental default, there are a number of social and psychic facts of life that help explain the prominence of the dissenting young in our culture. In a number of ways, this new generation happens to be particularly well placed and primed for action.

Most obviously, the society is getting younger — to the extent that in America, as in a number of European countries, a bit more than 50 per cent of the population is under twenty-five years of age. Even if one grants that people in their mid-twenties have no business claiming, or letting themselves be claimed for the status of "youth," there still remains among the authentically young in the thirteen to nineteen bracket a small nation of twenty-five million people. (As we shall see below, however, there is good reason to group the mid-twenties with their adolescent juniors.)

But numbers alone do not account for the aggressive prominence of contemporary youth. More important, the young seem to *feel* the potential power of their numbers as never before. No doubt to a great extent this is because the market apparatus of our consumer society has devoted a deal of wit to cultivating the age-consciousness of old and young alike. Teen-agers alone control a stupendous amount of money and enjoy much leisure; so, inevitably, they have been turned into a self-conscious

7

market. They have been pampered, exploited, idolized, and made almost nauseatingly much of. With the result that whatever the young have fashioned for themselves has rapidly been rendered grist for the commercial mill and cynically merchandised by assorted hucksters — *including* the new ethos of dissent, a fact that creates an agonizing disorientation for the dissenting young (and their critics). . . .

The force of the market has not been the only factor in intensifying age-consciousness, however. The expansion of higher education has done even more in this direction. In the United States we have a college population of nearly six million, an increase of more than double over 1950. And the expansion continues as college falls more and more into the standard educational pattern of the middle-class young. Just as the dark satanic mills of early industrialism concentrated labor and helped create the class-consciousness of the proletariat, so the university campus, where up to thirty thousand students may be gathered, has served to crystallize the group identity of the young — with the important effect of mingling freshmen of seventeen and eighteen with graduate students well away in their twenties. On the major campuses, it is often enough the graduates who assume positions of leadership, contributing to student movements a degree of competence that the younger students could not muster. When one includes in this alliance that significant new entity, the non-student — the campus roustabout who may be in his late twenties — one sees why "youth" has become such a long-term career these days. The grads and the non-students easily come to identify their interests and allegiance with a distinctly younger age group. In previous generations, they would long since have left these youngsters behind. But now they and the freshmen just out of high school find themselves all together in one campus community.

The role of these campus elders is crucial, for they tend to be those who have the most vivid realization of the new economic role of the university. Being closer to the technocratic careers for which higher education is supposed to be grooming them in the Great Society, they have a delicate sensitivity to the social regimentation that imminently confronts them, and a stronger sense of the potential power with which the society's need for trained personnel endows them. In some cases their restiveness springs from a bread-and-butter awareness of the basic facts of educational life these days, for in England, Germany, and France the most troublesome students are those who have swelled the numbers in the humanities and social studies only to discover that what the society really wants out of its schools is technicians, not philosophers. In Britain, this strong trend away from the sciences over the past four years continues to provoke annoyed concern from public figures who are not the least bit embarrassed to reveal their good bourgeois philistinism by loudly observing that the country is not spending its money to produce poets and Egyptologists — and then demanding a sharp cut in university grants and stipends.

Yet at the same time, these non-technicians know that the society cannot do without its universities, that it cannot shut them down or brutalize the students without limit. The universities produce the brains the technocracy needs; therefore, making trouble on the campus is making trouble in one of the economy's vital sectors. And once the graduate students—many of whom may be serving as low-level teaching assistants—have been infected with qualms and aggressive discontents, the junior faculty, with whom they overlap, may soon catch the fevers of dissent and find themselves drawn into the orbit of "youth". . . .

If we ask who is to blame for such troublesome children, there can be only one answer: it is the parents who have equipped them with an anemic superego. The current generation of students is the beneficiary of the particularly permissive child-rearing habits that have been a feature of our postwar society. Dr. Spock's endearing latitudinarianism (go easy on the toilet training, don't panic over masturbation, avoid the heavy discipline) is much more a reflection than a cause of the new (and wise) conception of proper parent-child relations that prevails in our middle class. A high-consumption, leisure-wealthy society simply doesn't need contingents of rigidly trained, "responsible" young workers. It cannot employ more than a fraction of untrained youngsters fresh out of high school. The middle class can therefore afford to prolong the ease and drift of childhood, and so it does. Since nobody expects a child to learn any marketable skills until he gets to college, high school becomes a country club for which the family pays one's dues. Thus the young are "spoiled," meaning they are influenced to believe that being human has something to do with pleasure and freedom. But unlike their parents, who are also avid for the plenty and leisure of the consumer society, the young have not had to sell themselves for their comforts or to accept them on a part-time basis. Economic security is something they can take for granted—and on it they build a new, uncompromised personality, flawed perhaps by irresponsible ease, but also touched with some outspoken spirit. Unlike their parents, who must kowtow to the organizations from which they win their bread, the youngsters can talk back at home with little fear of being thrown out in the cold. One of the pathetic, but, now we see, promising characteristics of postwar America has been the uppityness of adolescents and the concomitant reduction of the paterfamilias to the general ineffectuality of a Dagwood Bumstead. In every family comedy of the last twenty years, dad has been the buffoon.

The permissiveness of postwar child-rearing has probably seldom met A. S. Neill's standards—but it has been sufficient to arouse expectations. As babies, the middle-class young got picked up when they bawled. As children, they got their kindergarten finger paintings thumbtacked on the living room wall by mothers who knew better than to discourage incipient artistry. As adolescents, they perhaps even got a car of their own (or control of the family's), with all of the sexual privileges attending. They passed through school systems which, dismal as they all are in so many respects, have nevertheless prided themselves since World

9

War II on the introduction of "progressive" classes having to do with "creativity" and "self-expression." These are also the years that saw the proliferation of all the mickey mouse courses which take the self-indulgence of adolescent "life problems" so seriously. Such scholastic pap mixes easily with the commercial world's effort to elaborate a total culture of adolescence based on nothing but fun and games. (What else could a culture of adolescence be based on?) The result has been to make of adolescence, not the beginning of adulthood, but a status in its own right: a limbo that is nothing so much as the prolongation of an already permissive infancy.

To be sure, such an infantization of the middle-class young has a corrupting effect. It ill prepares them for the real world and its unrelenting if ever more subtle disciplines. It allows them to nurse childish fantasies until too late in life; until there comes the inevitable crunch. For as life in the multiversity wears on for these pampered youngsters, the technocratic reality principle begins grimly to demand its concessions. The young get told they are now officially "grown up," but they have been left too long without any taste for the rigidities and hypocrisies that adulthood is supposed to be all about. General Motors all of a sudden wants barbered hair, punctuality, and an appropriate reverence for the conformities of the organizational hierarchy. Washington wants patriotic cannon fodder with no questions asked. Such prospects do not look like fun from the vantage point of between eighteen and twenty years of relatively carefree drifting.

Some of the young (most of them, in fact) summon up the proper sense of responsibility to adjust to the prescribed patterns of adulthood; others, being incorrigibly childish, do not. They continue to assert pleasure and freedom as human rights and begin to ask aggressive questions of those forces that insist, amid obvious affluence, on the continued necessity of discipline, no matter how subliminal. This is why, for example, university administrators are forced to play such a false game with their students, insisting on the one hand that the students are "grown-up, responsible men and women," but on the other hand knowing full well that they dare not entrust such erratic children with any power over their own education. For what can one rely upon them to do that will suit the needs of technocratic regimentation?

The incorrigibles either turn political or drop out. Or perhaps they fluctuate between the two, restless, bewildered, hungry for better ideas about grown-upness than GM or IBM or LBJ seem able to offer. Since they are improvising their own ideal of adulthood—a task akin to lifting oneself by one's bootstraps—it is all too easy to go pathetically wrong. Some become ne'er-do-well dependents, bumming about the bohemias of America and Europe on money from home; others simply bolt. The FBI reports the arrest of over ninety thousand juvenile runaways in 1966; most of those who flee well-off middle-class homes get picked up by the thousands each current year in the big-city bohemias, fending off malnutrition and venereal disease. The immigration departments of

Europe record a constant level over the past few years of something like ten thousand disheveled "flower children" (mostly American, British, German, and Scandinavian) migrating to the Near East and India— usually toward Katmandu (where drugs are cheap and legal) and a deal of hard knocks along the way. The influx has been sufficient to force Iran and Afghanistan to substantially boost the "cash in hand" requirements of prospective tourists. And the British consul-general in Istanbul officially requested Parliament in late 1967 to grant him increased accommodations for the "swarm" of penniless young Englishmen who have been cropping up at the consulate on their way east, seeking temporary lodgings or perhaps shelter from Turkish narcotics authorities.

One can flippantly construe this exodus as the contemporary version of running off with the circus; but the more apt parallel might be with the quest of third-century Christians (a similarly scruffy, uncouth, and often half-mad lot) for escape from the corruptions of Hellenistic society: it is much more a flight *from* than *toward*. Certainly for a youngster of seventeen, clearing out of the comfortable bosom of the middle-class family to become a beggar is a formidable gesture of dissent. One makes light of it at the expense of ignoring a significant measure of our social health.

So, by way of a dialectic Marx could never have imagined, technocratic America produces a potentially revolutionary element among its own youth. The bourgeoisie, instead of discovering the class enemy in its factories, finds it across the breakfast table in the person of its own pampered children.

DISCUSSION QUESTIONS
SUGGESTIONS FOR WRITING

1. What are, in Roszak's estimation, the "social and psychic facts" that help explain the emergence and prominence of dissenting youth in our culture?

2. The modern informative magazine essay has many variations of tone, style, method, degree of formality or informality, etc. The informative magazine essay is mainly expository but may also use argumentation—the presentation of facts and evidence in some logical pattern—in order to prove a point. Other forms of persuasion, such as satire, eloquence, or invective, may be evident as well. Because of the usual hand-in-glove relationship of informative and persuasive elements, the distinctions between informative and persuasive essays per se should not be exaggerated. Can you find examples of information used to persuade? Of other methods of persuasion? Are there also examples of "pure" information?

3. *"Technocracy's Children" is a relatively formal example of the informative essay. Its language tends to be proper (i.e., formal, academic), its tone and intent serious. Such formal exposition usually requires a logical structure, a relatively strict pattern of development. What pattern of development is at work in this essay? Is it a logical structure?*

4. *Is there any evidence in the essay of a bias in favor of either the "counter culture" or of "the establishment"? Find examples of statements that praise or cast blame upon either group.*

CARSON

L. M. KIT CARSON (b. 1941) is a writer, film-maker, and frequent contributor to the *Evergreen Review, Esquire,* and other magazines. In this interview with Dennis Hopper, coauthor, director, and co-star of the Columbia film *Easy Rider,* the interviewer asks questions about the genesis, composition, and meaning of the film.

EASY RIDER:
A VERY AMERICAN
THING:
AN INTERVIEW
WITH
DENNIS
HOPPER

QUESTION: *How did this film start? With what? With whom?*

ANSWER: It started with Peter [Fonda] calling me on the telephone, saying he had an idea for a movie about two guys who smuggle cocaine, sell it, go across the country for Mardi Gras and get killed by a couple of duck-hunters because they have long hair. "Do you think it can make a movie?" And I said, "Yeh. I think it can make a great movie."

Q: *At what point did Terry Southern come into it?*

A: Terry Southern was an old friend of mine. I asked if we could use his name to get money; then, would he help us with it. He said, "Sure, I like the idea." So we got some cameras and people together, ran down and shot Mardi Gras first; then began the rest of the movie a month later.

Q: *Why'd you shoot on a split and backwards schedule like that?*

A: We wanted to use the real Mardi Gras and scheduled to shoot it. But Peter had gotten the wrong dates for Mardi Gras—we thought it was a month away. Suddenly we learned it was a week away. So we shot Mardi Gras without a script, without anything—with just what I had in my mind. I knew generally what I wanted the acid trip to be, and what I wanted from Mardi Gras.

Q: *How many days did it take to shoot Mardi Gras?*

A: We had five days at Mardi Gras. The acid trip was shot on two different days—half of one day, the whole of another day. This was fast, but I'd learned to squeeze, learned to work fast from television—how to move quickly and utilize your time. . . .

Q: *You shot in Los Angeles first after New Orleans?*

A: We were in Los Angeles for three weeks. We shot the commune, which was the only set we built, up on Topango Canyon outside the city. Then shot the interior of the whorehouse—which is really the inside of a friend's home. Then we shot four weeks cross-country. Whole movie: seven weeks including a week at Mardi Gras.

Q: *Elaborate on the way you handled the non-actors in the Southern café scene. It looked to me like the people in the booths had scriptcards on the table in front of them—they would refer to the cards, then look up and speak a line.*

A: Yeh, well, they weren't. They kept looking down because they were supposed to be playing dominoes. I never gave them the script. How I worked them? First of all, there was a man who preceded us into towns like that and got together people he thought would be right for the roles. I came into one village—Morganza, Louisiana—and looked at the people he'd chosen. I didn't care for them. And I saw a group of men standing over beside us doing the kind of joking that the guys in the café were to do. I said, "*Those* are the people I want." He said, "Well I don't know whether I can get them." And I said, "Those are the people I want." So he went over and asked them, and to his surprise they were more than happy to do it. Then I told these men that we had raped, killed a girl right outside of town; and there was nothing they could say about us in this scene that would be too nasty—I mean, they could say *anything* they wanted about us. (And they were pretty set in this frame of mind anyway.) All right. Then I gave them specific topics, things that were covered in the script: talk about long hair, is-it-a-boy-is-it-a-girl, the teeth I'm wearing around my neck, or Peter's black leather pants, or the sunglasses. Then I set up the camera in such a way that I could stop them: "Don't say that"; and isolate: "You say something about this." And the girls: I got them to flirting with one idea—they wanted a ride on the motorcycle. Because I wanted to get them outside. And because this flirting would aggravate the guys even more. So at first I just let them go at it, work their real feelings out. After watching a bit of this, I gave some definite lines: "Check the flag on that bike. Must be a bunch of Yankee queers." "You name it, I'll throw rocks at it." Those were lines from the script. But basically the scene, improvised and all, plays according to the *intention* of the café scene written in the script.

Q: *How long did this scene take to shoot?*

A: We shot it in half a day.

Q: *In regard to those cafe people: do you feel guilty of any indecency done to them?*

A: Do I feel that because of this film there's harm done to them personally?

Q: *Do you feel you violated them in any way?*

A: No, I don't believe that—well, you've got to understand that I believe that anything that is a creative act can be justified.

Q: *Murder included?*

A: Well, not quite that far, but almost. I don't know whether I violated them. But then we all violate. Still, there's an area in me where I hope I didn't hurt them because I happen to like those people. I didn't mean them any harm.

On the other hand, I know that if I'd come in there actually traveling across country alone, or if me, Peter, and Jack Nicholson had walked into that restaurant without a movie company behind us and those men had been sitting in there, we'd have been in a lot of trouble.

That's true—I know. I was in the Civil Rights March with King from Selma to Montgomery—it was crazy. There was one guy standing on the side of the road pissing on us. I mean, there he was with his cock in his hand pissing on nuns and priests, all over. And he was calling us white trash. Pissing on nuns and priests and rabbis and Protestants and all religious people in their uniforms, and on us—and calling us white trash. Crazy, you know: how can a man be pissing on people and calling *them* white trash? It doesn't make sense.

And I know that this time the only thing that stopped trouble was the fact that we were making a movie. And suddenly I could relate to these people as their director and they could relate to me.

Q: *Do you connect yourself to any actively political people today?*

A: I don't think anyone intelligent connects himself to anyone political today. The last time I mixed with politics was when I got kicked out of a SNCC meeting in the South because they were going into black power, and all the whites had to get out. Which was all right; they were right. They were going to take care of their people, and we should take care of our people—because our people were in just as much a mess as their people. Unfortunately, it's harder to take care of whites because a great mass of them don't think we have any real problems. When SDS went out to Newark a couple of years ago to the poor whites, the people said: "What are you trying to help us for? We're cool." And at the moment I don't think there's going to be any serious change in this attitude— most of us think, "I'm cool. *He's* the trouble." Until we have some sort of war. It'll have to be some kind of war because a lot of things need changing.

I think the movie says this—I mean, it creates this dangerous atmosphere. I know when we were making the movie, we could feel this: the whole country seemed to be burning up—Negroes, hippies, students. The country was on fire. And I meant to work this feeling into the symbols in the movie, like Peter's bike—Captain America's Great Chrome Bike—that beautiful machine covered with stars and stripes is

America. I'm not sure that people understand but that bike with all the money in the gas tank is America and we've got all our money in a gas tank — and that any moment we can be shot off it — BOOM — explosion — that's the end. We go up in flames. I mean, at the start of the movie, Peter and I do a very American thing — we commit a crime, we go for the easy money. We go for the easy money and then we're free. That's one of the big problems with the country right now: everybody's going for the easy money. I think Americans basically feel the criminal way is all right *if you don't get caught;* crime pays, *if* you get away with it. Not just obvious, simple crimes, but big corporations committing corporate crimes — swindling on their income tax, freezing funds abroad.

Q: *Are you saying that Peter in the movie represents America?*

A: Yeh. But more than that. Me and Peter are the Squire and his Knight, Sancho Panza and Don Quixote, also Billy the Kid and Wyatt Earp, *also* Captain America, the comic book hero, and his sidekick Bucky. I'm saying that Peter, as Captain America, is the Slightly Tarnished Lawman, is the sensitive, off-in-the-stars, the Great White Liberal who keeps saying, "Everything's going to work out," but doesn't do anything to help it work out. He goes to the commune, hears the people have been eating dead horses off the side of the road — does he break any of that fifty thousand out of his gas tank? What does he do? Nothing. "Hey, they're going to make it." Hey, the Negroes, the Indians, the Mexicans are going to make it. What does he do? He rides a couple of the girls over to another place because he's eating their food. *He does nothing.*

Finally he realizes this when he says, "We blew it." "We blew it" means to me that they could have spent that energy in something other than smuggling cocaine, could have done something other than help the society destroy itself.

Q: *All right. But I wonder whether this disfavor you've just explained toward Captain America comes across in the movie. I've seen the movie four times, and only the last time did I begin to pick up some ambivalence toward Captain America in the commune sequence. I'm asking you as a filmmaker, could you have made it more clear how you wanted us to feel about Captain America — just done it in that one sequence which, I think, is very crucial? Because when Captain America says, "They're going to make it," a lot of people get confused: "Does Hopper really believe that? That's bullshit. But sounds like he believes it."*

A: I don't think it comes through. I think Peter comes off as simply a Super Hero, or Super Anti-Hero. Bucky doesn't believe they're going to make it. Bucky says, "Hey man, they're not going to grow anything here. This is *sand.*"

Q: *Right, but you give Captain America the last line: "They're going to make it."*

A: Yeh. Doesn't Captain America always have the last line? "Go to Vietnam." I go to Vietnam. I don't question Captain America. I may be bitchy or carry on, but Captain America always has the last line. That's the way things are.

Q: *What do you think the moral effect of your film is going to be—for instance, what will happen when the scene in which Jack Nicholson smokes pot is shown at the Majestic Theatre in Dallas, Texas?*

A: I don't know. You do something and you do it for a lot of different reasons. I look at that scene on several levels. First, it's dishonest if those two guys on motorcycles don't smoke grass. It's ridiculous, unrealistic. You can't make a movie about these characters in the late 1960s and not have them turn on. And if they have a guy like Jack Nicholson around, they're going to turn him on. That's all, it's that simple, no propaganda intended. But the *main* reason I used pot in that scene was to give me a humorous handle for the Venusian speech— which I consider a very serious piece of work, heavy propaganda.

Q: *It succeeds as both.*

A: What I'm saying is, without that device of humor, people would get uptight, say, "Wh-what's he saying?" And this way nobody says, "What's he saying?" I've never had anybody say, "What are you saying in that scene?" And what we're saying is either an incredible lot of nonsense or an incredible lot of not-nonsense. So we made it funny, as in the Victorian period or other periods of oppression, when you wanted to say something hard to take, you always dressed it up as a folk ballad or a humorous little ditty that was sung in a tavern somewhere.

To get back to the moral effect of the scene—the only time a reaction really hit me, really hurt me: in Cannes, Omar Sharif's nineteen-year-old daughter came up—she'd never turned on before—and said that after the film she turned on. I said, "Oh, how'd you like it?" She said, "It didn't do anything for me." I said, "It's probably very difficult for anyone as frivolous as you to feel anything anyway." Because it hurt me, man. Because I didn't make that movie for her to use it as an excuse to turn on—I don't want any nineteen-year-old to go get high just because they see the movie. Look, I've been smoking grass for seventeen years—there've been bummers and good times. All in all, I'm glad I did it because smoking gave me some insight, some paranoia, some self-searching I wouldn't have had otherwise. But not everybody can handle it. And I did not make this movie to turn everybody in the country on to grass. I already assumed everybody was turned on or about to be turned on—without my movie.

Q: *You're prepared for some very righteous people to come raging up and saying, "What the hell are you trying to do?"*

A: Yeh, well I've had that. Right. In Cannes, we held a press conference after the film and UPI or one of those news services got up and said, "Why are you making a movie like this? Don't you realize how bad this is for the country? We have enough problems without you doing this terrible movie, etc." Then a young communist said, "Why did you make a movie for three hundred and seventy thousand dollars? Why didn't you make a 16mm. or 8mm. movie and give that money to the Cause? Why are you copping out, putting commercial music to this movie? Blah-blah." And I said, "You're only kidding yourself. If you make a propaganda film, art film, any film you feel has something to say—you *can* work small and show it to people who think like you already, dress like you, wear their hair like you, and you can all sit in a little room somewhere and look at your movie over and over. *Great.* But if you want to reach a large mass of people at this point in history, you *have* to deal with the people who are going to *release* your picture." And I also told the kid, "Hey, all I know is how to make movies. I don't know anything else. It took me fifteen years to raise three hundred and seventy thousand dollars. I'm not going to give it to the Cause— I am the Cause."...

Q: *The end shook me up quite a bit, probably because it seems so accidental.*

A: Not so accidental really. I believe that if Billy hadn't shot the finger to the guys in the truck, there wouldn't have been that existential moment when the guy decided to pull the trigger. It was action-reaction operating when they killed me. They killed Peter because they just didn't know what else to do—it was too complicated for them to work it out any other way. But I'm not denouncing the South in this ending: I say it was action provoking reaction. Businessmen have come up to me after the movie: "I like your movie, but I'm not the guys in the truck. You're saying I'm the guys in the truck." I'm not saying that. The guys in the truck and the guys on the motorcycles are both the same: criminals, victims of the climate of the country today.

DISCUSSION QUESTIONS
SUGGESTIONS FOR WRITING

1. An increasingly important form, the interview relies heavily on character interest to succeed. What aspects of Hopper's character are brought out in this interview which tend to fulfill the promise inherent in an interview with such a person? What sort of character is he?

2. Do Hopper's views tend to substantiate or contradict Roszak's interpretation as presented in The Making of a Counter Culture?

3. Aside from character or glamour interest, the interview also makes use, of course, of the interest we have in what an authority has to say on any particular subject — the ideal of getting-it-from-the-horse's-mouth. How do Hopper's remarks change your preconceptions about Easy Rider? *Should his remarks be taken as absolute or definitive?*

4. What is your reaction to Hopper's statement that "anything that is a creative act can be justified"?

REICH

CONSCIOUSNESS III: THE NEW GENERATION

CHARLES A. REICH (b. 1928) is professor of law at Yale University. In his controversial book *The Greening of America,* from which this selection is taken, he attempts to "analyze sympathetically" the youth culture that is "turning this country around."

BEGINNING with a few individuals in the mid-nineteen-sixties, and gathering numbers ever more rapidly thereafter, Consciousness III has sprouted up, astonishingly and miraculously, out of the stony soil of the American Corporate State. So spontaneous was its appearance that no one, not the most astute or the most radical, foresaw what was coming or recognized it when it began. It is not surprising that many people think it a conspiracy, for it was spread, here and abroad, by means invisible. Hardly anybody of the older generation, even the FBI or the sociologists, knows much about it, for its language and thought are so different from Consciousness II as to make it virtually an undecipherable secret code. Consciousness III is, as of this writing, the greatest secret in America, although its members have shouted as loudly as they could to be heard.

We must pause over the origins of Consciousness III, lest it seem too improbable and too transitory to be deemed as fundamental as Consciousness I and Consciousness II. One element in its origin has already been described: the impoverishment of life, the irrationality, violence, and claustrophobia of the American Corporate State. But how did this corporate machine, seemingly designed to keep its inhabitants perpetually on a treadmill, suddenly begin producing something altogether new and unintended? The new consciousness is the product of two interacting forces: the promise of life that is made to young Americans by all of our affluence, technology, liberation, and ideals, and the threat to that promise posed by everything from neon ugliness and boring jobs to the Vietnam War and the shadow of nuclear holocaust. Neither the promise nor the threat is the cause by itself; but the two together have done it.

The promise comes first. We have all heard the promise: affluence, security, technology make possible a new life, a new permissiveness, a new freedom, a new expansion of human possibility. We have all heard it, but to persons born after World War II it means something very different. Older people learned how to live in a different world; it is really beyond them to imagine themselves living according to the new promises. The most basic limitations of life—the job, the working day, the part one can play in life, the limits of sex, love and relationships, the limits of knowledge and experience—all vanish, leaving open a life that can be lived without the guideposts of the past. In the world that now exists, a life of surfing *is* possible, not as an escape from work, a recreation or a phase, but as a *life*— if one chooses. The fact that this choice is actually available is the truth that the younger generation knows and the older generation cannot know.

The promise is made real to members of the younger generation by a sense of acceptance about themselves. To older generations, particularly Consciousness II people, great issues were presented by striving to reach some external standard of personal attractiveness, popularity, ability at sports, acceptance by the group. Many lives, including some outstanding careers, were lived under the shadow of such personal issues; even late in life, people are still profoundly influenced by them. Of course the new generation is not free of such concerns. But to an astonishing degree, whether it is due to new parental attitudes, a less tense, less inhibited childhood, or a different experience during school years, these are not the issues which plague the younger generation. If the hero of *Portnoy's Complaint* is the final and most complete example of the man dissatisfied with the self that he is, the new generation says, "Whatever I am, I am." He may have hang-ups of all sorts, insecurities, inadequacies, but he does not reject himself on that account. There may be as many difficulties about work, ability, relationships, and sex as in any other generation, but there is less guilt, less anxiety, less self-hatred. Consciousness III says, "I'm glad I'm me."

The new generation has also learned lessons from technology, by being born with it, that the older generation does not know even though it invented technology. It is one thing to know intellectually that there is a Xerox machine that can copy anything, a pill that can make sexual intercourse safe, or a light motorcycle that can take two people off camping with ten minutes' preparation, but it is quite another thing to live with these facts, make use of them, and thus learn to live *by* them.

These experiences and promises are shared to some extent by the youth of every industrial nation, and the new consciousness is, as we know, not limited to the United States. But Consciousness III, the specifically American form, is not based on promise alone. A key word in understanding its origin is *betrayal*.

Older people are inclined to think of work, injustice and war, and of the bitter frustrations of life, as the human condition. Their capacity for outrage is consequently dulled. But to those who have glimpsed the real possibilities of life, who have tasted liberation and love, who have seen the promised land, the prospect of a dreary corporate job, a ranch-house life, or a miserable death in war is utterly intolerable. Moreover, the human condition, if that is what it is, has been getting steadily worse in the Corporate State; more and more life-denying just as life should be opening up. And hovering over everything is the threat of annihilation, more real and more terrifying to the young than to anyone else. To them, the discrepancy between what could be and what is, is overwhelming; perhaps it is the greatest single fact of their existence. The promise of America, land of beauty and abundance, land of the free, somehow has been betrayed.

They feel the betrayal in excruciatingly personal terms. Between them and the rich possibilities of life there intervenes a piercing insecurity—not the personal insecurity their parents knew, but a cosmic insecurity. Will the nation be torn apart by riots or war? Will their lives be cut short by death or injury in Vietnam? Will the impersonal machinery of the state—schools, careers, institutions—overwhelm them? Above all, will they escape an atomic holocaust (they were, as many people have pointed out, the generation of the bomb). Insecurity sharpens their consciousness and draws them together.

Parents have unintentionally contributed to their children's condemnation of existing society. Not by their words, but by their actions, attitudes, and manner of living, they have conveyed to their children the message "Don't live the way we have, don't settle for the emptiness of our lives, don't be lured by the things we valued, don't neglect life and love as we have." With the unerring perceptiveness of the child, their children have read these messages from the lifeless lives of their "successful" parents, have seen marriages break up because there was nothing to hold them, have felt cynicism, alienation, and despair in the best-kept homes of America. And will have none of it.

Kenneth Keniston, in *Young Radicals*, found that one of the most telling forces in producing the political ideals of the new generation is the contrast between their parents' ideals (which they accept) and their parents' failure to live these same ideals. Keniston found that young radicals show a *continuity* of ideals from childhood on; they simply stayed with them while their parents failed to.

We might add to this that our society, with its dogmatic insistence on one way of seeing everything, its dominating false consciousness, and its ever-widening gap between fact and rhetoric, invites a sudden moment when the credibility gap becomes too much, and invites cataclysmic consequences to the consciousness of a young person when that occurs. For so vehemently does the society insist that its "truth" be accepted wholly and undeviatingly down the line, and so drastic are the discrepancies once seen, that a single breach in the dike may bring a young person's entire conversion. All that is needed is to participate in one peace demonstration and find *The New York Times'* report of it inexcusably false, and the whole edifice of "truth" collapses. Such "conversions" are constantly seen on campuses today; a freshman arrives, his political views are hometown-Consciousness I, and suddenly he is radicalized. The fabric of manufactured "truth," spread taut and thin, breaches, and one breach leaves it irrevocably in tatters.

If a history of Consciousness III were to be written, it would show a fascinating progression. The earliest sources were among those exceptional individuals who are found at any time in any society: the artistic, the highly sensitive, the tormented. Thoreau, James Joyce, and Wallace Stevens all speak directly to Consciousness III. Salinger's Holden Caulfield was a fictional version of the first young precursors of Consciousness III. Perhaps there was always a bit of Consciousness III in every teen-ager, but normally it quickly vanished. Holden sees through the established world: they are "phonies" and he is merciless in his honesty. But what was someone like Holden to do? A subculture of "beats" grew up, and a beatnik world flourished briefly, but for most people it represented only another dead end. Other Holdens might reject the legal profession and try teaching literature or writing instead, letting their hair grow a bit longer as well. But they remained separated individuals, usually ones from affluent but unhappy, tortured family backgrounds, and their differences with society were paid for by isolation.

Unquestionably the blacks made a substantial contribution to the origins of the new consciousness. They were left out of the Corporate State, and thus they had to have a culture and life-style in opposition to the State. Their music, with its "guts," contrasted with the insipid white music. This way of life seemed more earthy, more sensual than that of whites. They were the first openly to scorn the Establishment and its values; as Eldridge Cleaver shows in *Soul on Ice*, and Malcolm X shows in his autobiography, they were radicalized by the realities of their situation. When their music began to be heard by white teen-agers through the medium of rock 'n' roll, and when their view of America became visible through the civil rights movement, it gave new impetus to the subterranean awareness of the beat generation and the Holden Caulfields.

The great change took place when Consciousness III began to appear among young people who had endured no special emotional conditions, but were simply bright, sensitive children of the affluent middle class. It is hard to be precise about the time when this happened. One chronology is based on the college class of 1969, which entered as freshmen in the fall of 1965. Another important date is the summer of 1967, when the full force of the cultural revolution was first visible. But even in the fall of 1967 the numbers involved were still very small. The new group drew heavily from those who had been exposed to the very best of liberal arts education—poetry, art, theatre, literature, philosophy, good conversation. Later, the group began to include "ordinary" middle-class students. In time there were college athletes as well as college intellectuals, and lovers of motorcycles and skiing as well as lovers of art and literature. But the core group was always white, well educated, and middle class.

Among today's youth, the phenomenon of "conversions" is increasingly common. It is surprising that so little has been written about these conversions, for they are a striking aspect of contemporary life. What happens is simply this: in a brief span of months, a student, seemingly conventional in every way, changes his haircut, his clothes, his habits, his interests, his political attitudes, his way of relating to other people, in short, his whole way of life. He has "converted" to a new consciousness. The contrast between well-groomed freshman pictures and the same individuals in person a year later tells the tale. The clean-cut, hard-working, model young man who despises radicals and hippies can become one himself with breathtaking suddenness. Over and over again, an individual for whom a conversion seemed impossible, a star athlete, an honor student, the small-town high school boy with the American Legion scholarship, transforms himself into a drug-using, long-haired, peace-loving "freak." Only when he puts on a headband and plays unexpectedly skillful touch football or basketball, or when a visitor to his old room back home catches sight of his honor society certificate, is his earlier life revealed.

As the new consciousness made youth more distinct, the younger generation began discovering itself as a generation. Always before, young people felt themselves tied more to their families, to their schools, and to their immediate situations than to "a generation." But now an entire culture, including music, clothes, and drugs, began to distinguish youth. As it did, the message of consciousness went with it. And the more the older generation rejected the culture, the more a fraternity of the young grew up, so that they recognized each other as brothers and sisters from coast to coast.

DISCUSSION QUESTIONS
SUGGESTIONS FOR WRITING

1. What are the central ideas of this selection?

2. Taken as a whole, is Reich's analysis a plausible explanation of the "generation gap" or of the "new polarization" or of "the war at home"? What techniques does the author use to persuade the reader of the plausibility of his thesis?

3. One critic of Reich's controversial book stated that it contains "uncritical admiration for just about every behavioral fad of the times." Can you find any evidence to substantiate this criticism?

4. An apparent contradiction that other critics have pointed out is that while Reich sees Consciousness III as the chief hope of the species, he seems to ignore the inherently parasitic dependence of Consciousness III upon Consciousness II or Consciousness I. These critics point out that much of the opportunity for Consciousness III is made possible by the labor of II or I, that Consciousness III is basically elitist, not self-sufficient, and therefore certainly not an important new hope for the future of the species, as Reich suggests. What is your reaction to this charge? What do you think Reich's reaction would be?

MAILER

THE SIEGE OF CHICAGO

NORMAN MAILER (b. 1923) became famous in 1948 with the publication of his best-selling novel about World War II, *The Naked and the Dead.* Now one of the best-known and most respected writers in America, he has turned more and more frequently in recent years — as in "The Siege of Chicago" — to nonfiction forms which blend journalism, "informal history," and the perceptions and imagination of a first-rate novelist in a distinctively Maileresque combination.

THEY were young men who were not going to Vietnam. So they would show every lover of war in Vietnam that the reason they did not go was not for lack of the courage to fight; no, they would carry the fight over every street in Old Town and the Loop where the opportunity presented itself. If they had been gassed and beaten, their leaders arrested on fake charges (Hayden, picked up while sitting under a tree in daylight in Lincoln Park, naturally protested; the resulting charge was "resisting arrest") they were going to demonstrate that they would not give up, that they were the stuff out of which the very best soldiers were made. Sunday, they had been driven out of the park, Monday as well, now Tuesday. The centers where they slept in bedrolls on the floor near Lincoln Park had been broken into by the police, informers and provocateurs were everywhere; tonight tear-gas trucks had been used. They were still not ready to give up. Indeed their militancy may have increased. They took care of the worst of their injured and headed for the Loop, picking up fellow demonstrators as they went. Perhaps the tear gas was a kind of catharsis for some of them, a letting of tears, a purging of old middle-class weakness. Some were turning from college boys to revolutionaries. It seemed as if the more they were beaten and tear-gassed, the more they rallied back. Now, with the facility for underground communication which seemed so instinctive a tool in their generation's equipment, they were on their way to Grant Park, en masse, a thousand of them, two thousand of them, there were conceivably as many as five thousand boys and girls massed in Grant Park at three in the morning, listening to speakers, cheering, chanting, calling across Michigan Avenue to the huge brooding facade of the Hilton, a block wide, over twenty-five stories high, with huge wings and deep courts (the better to multiply the number of windows with a view of the street and a view of Grant Park). The lights were on in hundreds of bedrooms in the Hilton, indeed people were sleeping and dreaming all over the hotel with the sound of young orators declaiming in the night below, voices rising twenty, twenty-five stories high, the voices clear in the spell of sound which hung over the Hilton. The Humphrey headquarters were here, and the McCarthy headquarters. Half the Press was quartered here, and Marvin Watson as well. Postmaster General and Presidential troubleshooter, he had come to bring some of Johnson's messages to Humphrey. His suite had a view of the park. Indeed two-thirds of the principals at the convention must have had a view early this morning, two and three and four A.M. of this Tuesday night, no, this Wednesday morning, of Grant Park filled across the street with a revolutionary army of dissenters and demonstrators and college children and McCarthy workers and tourists ready to take a crack on the head, all night they could hear the demonstrators chanting, "Join us, join us," and the college bellow of utter contempt, "Dump the Hump! Dump the Hump!" all the fury of the beatings and the tear-gassings, all the bitter disappointments of that recently elapsed bright spring when the only critical problem was who would make a better President, Kennedy or McCarthy (now all the dread of a future with Humphrey or Nixon). There was also the sense that police had now entered their lives, become an element pervasive as drugs and books and sex and music and family. So they shouted up to the windows of the Hilton, to the delegates and the campaign workers who were sleeping, or shuddering by the side of their bed, or cheering by their open window; they called up through the night on a stage as vast and towering as one of Wagner's visions and the screams of police cars joined them, pulling up, gliding away, blue lights revolving, lines of police hundreds long in their sky-blue shirts and sky-blue crash helmets, penning the demonstrators back of barriers across Michigan Avenue from the Hilton, and other lines of police and police fences on the Hilton's side of the street. The police had obviously been given orders not to attack the demonstrators here, not in front of the Hilton with half the Democratic Party watching them, not now at three in the morning—would anyone ever discover for certain what was to change their mind in sixteen hours?

Now, a great cheer went up. The police were being relieved by the National Guard. The Guard was being brought in! It was like a certificate of merit for the demonstrators to see the police march off and new hundreds of Guardsmen in khaki uniforms, helmets, and rifles take up post in place, army trucks coughing and barking and filing back and forth on Michigan Avenue, and on the side streets now surrounding the Hilton, evil-looking jeeps with barbed-wire gratings in front of their bumpers drove forward in echelons, and parked behind the crowd. Portable barbed-wire fences were now riding on Jeeps.

Earlier in the week, it had been relatively simple to get into the Hilton. Mobs of McCarthy workers and excited adolescents had jammed the stairs and the main entrance room of the lobby chanting all day, singing campaign songs, mocking every Humphrey worker they could recognize, holding station for hours in the hope, or on the rumor, that McCarthy would be passing through, and the cheers had the good nature and concerted rhythmic steam of a football rally. That had been Saturday and Sunday and Monday, but the police finally had barricaded the kids out of the lobby, and now at night covered the entrances to the Hilton, and demanded press passes, and room keys, as warrants of entry. The Hilton heaved and staggered through a variety of attacks and breakdowns. Like an old fort, like the old fort of the old Democratic Party, about to fall forever beneath the ministrations of its high shaman, its excruciated warlock, derided by the young, held in contempt by its own soldiers—the very delegates who would be loyal to Humphrey in the nomination and loyal to nothing in their heart—this spiritual fort of the Democratic Party was now housed in the literal fort of the Hilton staggering in place, all boilers working, all motors vibrating, yet seeming to come apart from the pressures on the street outside, as if the old Hilton had become artifact of the party and the nation. . . .

The kids were singing. There were two old standards which were sung all the time. An hour could not go by without both songs. So they sang "We Shall Overcome" and they sang "This Land Is Your Land," and a speaker cried up to the twenty-five stories of the Hilton, "We have the votes, you have the guns," a reference to the polls which had shown McCarthy to be more popular than Hubert Humphrey (yes, if only Rockefeller had run for the Democrats and McCarthy for the Republicans this would have been an ideal contest between a spender and a conservative) and then another speaker, referring to the projected march on the Amphitheatre next day, shouted, "We're going to march without a permit—the Russians demand a permit to have a meeting in Prague," and the crowd cheered this. They cheered with wild enthusiasm when one speaker, a delegate, had the inspiration to call out to the delegates and workers listening in the hundreds of rooms at the Hilton with a view of the park, "Turn on your lights, and blink them if you are with us. If you are with us, if you are sympathetic to us, blink your lights, blink your lights." And to the delight of the crowd, lights began to blink in the Hilton, ten, then twenty, perhaps so many as fifty lights were blinking at once, and a whole bank of lights on the fifteenth floor and the twenty-third floor went off and on at once, off and on at once. The

McCarthy headquarters on the fifteenth and the twenty-third were blinking, and the crowd cheered. Now they had become an audience to watch the actors in the hotel. So two audiences regarded each other, like ships signalling across a gulf of water in the night, and delegates came down from the hotel; a mood of new beauty was in the air, there present through all the dirty bandaged kids, the sour vomit odor of the Mace, the sighing and whining of the army trucks moving in and out all the time, the adenoids, larynxes, wheezes and growls of the speakers, the blinking of lights in the Hilton, yes, there was the breath of this incredible crusade where fear was in every breath you took, and so breath was tender, it came into the lungs as a manifest of value, as a gift, and the children's faces were shining in the glow of the headlights of the National Guard trucks and the searchlights of the police in front of the Hilton across Michigan Avenue. And the Hilton, sinking in its foundations, twinkled like a birthday cake.

DISCUSSION QUESTIONS
SUGGESTIONS FOR WRITING

1. What symbolic significance does Mailer attribute to the Hilton Hotel? How does this particular use of symbolism unify the piece? What irony is apparent in his final description of the hotel: "And the Hilton, sinking in its foundations, twinkled like a birthday cake"?

2. Like the good fiction writer he is, Mailer knows the dramatic importance of point of view in narrative. From whose point of view is this "informal history" told? What devices does Mailer use to establish sympathy for his point-of-view characters?

3. Some commentators have observed that contemporary history is more fantastic than fiction, that a fiction writer who would attempt to invent episodes of similar proportions in the realistic tradition could not help being accused of exaggeration or implausibility. Perhaps this explains why many fiction writers have turned to pure fantasy or surrealism and why other writers, such as Mailer, have turned to contemporary history for their subjects. Consider the fundamental differences between fiction and nonfiction writing. How is this selection from The Siege of Chicago *like fiction? How is it like nonfiction?*

4. Does Mailer's use of fictional techniques in this selection offer a clearer, more dramatic picture of the historical events recorded—or is this rather a distorted, one-sided, or overly subjective perspective? How would the traditional essay or news account be less distorted or more objective— if at all? What is an objective account? Is objectivity possible?

SMITH

VISIONS OF THE MILLENNIUM: DO YOU REALLY WANT TO BE RICH?

"ADAM SMITH" (b. 1930) is a pseudonym for a New York financial writer and veteran observer and commentator on the events and people of Wall Street. His work has appeared in *Life, New York,* and other magazines. As George J. W. Goodman (his real name), he has also written several novels. In the following selection he examines some of the ethical and psychological implications of the drive for affluence.

DO You Really Want to Be Rich?

It is part of the ethos of this country that you *ought* to be rich. You ought to be, unless you have taken some specific vow of poverty such as the priesthood, scholarship, teaching, or civil service, because money is the way we keep score. This feeling has been a long time in the making. It goes away sometimes in depressions, when briefly wealth becomes suspect and poverty is not dishonorable. The rest of the time, poverty is very close to criminal. The worst crimes a man can commit, other than the crimes of violence which for one with poverty would have to be considered irrational, are crimes against capital. A man can break most of the Commandments with impunity, but please, let him not go bust, that will get him ostracized faster than lying, fudging on his income taxes, cheating, adultery, and coveting all the oxes and asses there are.

In times of prosperity, the old feeling that you ought to be rich is very much in the air. It is not new. In a previous period of prosperity, just before the turn of the century, one of the most popular lectures in the country was Russell Conwell's "Acres of Diamonds." Those diamonds were wealth in your own backyard, and "every good man and woman ought to strive for it," thundered Conwell. "I say, get rich! Get rich!" In the same era, William Graham Sumner, a famous professor of Yale, wrote: "There is no reason, at the moment, why every American may not acquire capital by being industrious, prudent, and frugal, and thus become rich." And Bishop Lawrence, the doyen of the Episcopal Church, really did say, "In the long run, it is only to the man of morality that wealth comes. Godliness is in league with riches. Material prosperity makes the national character sweeter, more Christlike." So it is no wonder that when John D. Rockefeller was asked how he came by his vast fortune, he answered, "God gave me my money."

If God is truly on the side of the biggest bank accounts, there will be some who will be offended by the very idea that the management of money is a Game, even though Game these days has been dignified by game theory, mathematics, and computeering. Money, they would say, is serious business, no laughing matter, and certainly nothing that should suggest sport, frolic, fun, and play. Yet it may be that the Game element in money is the most harmless of all the elements present. Is it always to be this way?

Let us go back to the Master who gave us the aphorism, John Maynard Keynes, Baron of Tilton, and leave aside his revolutionary doctrines. For our purposes Keynes is not the Master because he changed the course of economic history. He is the Master because he started with nothing, set out to become rich, did so, part time, from his bed, as a player in the Game, and having become rich, had some thoughts that must be integral to any study of the Game. For what follows, we must acknowledge Keynes' own *General Theory* and *Essays in Persuasion*, and also the stimulating works on Keynes of Sir Roy Harrod and Robert L. Heilbroner.

Even second hand, through his biographers, a certain *joie de vivre* emerges. (None of the biographers mention Keynes' subterranean relationship with Lytton Strachey, and perhaps his proclivities are as irrelevant here as the later uses made of his theories.) Here was an economist and a Cambridge don, yet a man in the center of the Bloomsbury set that included the lights of English art and letters, who married the leading ballerina of Diaghilev's company. At the same time he was the chairman of a life insurance company and the darling of the avantgarde. He disdained inside information. Every morning he gathered his income statements and balance sheets and phoned his orders, using only his own knowledge and intuition, and after his phone calls he was ready for the business of the day. He not only made himself several million dollars, but he became Bursar of Kings College in Cambridge and multiplied its endowment by a factor of ten.

He was a pillar of stability in delicate matters of international diplomacy, but his official correctness did not prevent him from acquiring knowledge of other European politicians that included their mistresses, neuroses, and financial prejudices. He collected modern art long before it was fashionable to do so, but at the same time he was a classicist with the finest private collection of Newton's writings in the world. He ran a theater, and he came to be a Director of the Bank of England. He knew Roosevelt and Churchill and also Bernard Shaw and Pablo Picasso. He played bridge like a speculator, preferring a spectacular play to a sound contract, and solitaire like a statistician, noting how long it took for the game to come out twice running. And he once claimed that he had but one regret in life—he wished he had drunk more champagne.

(Mr. Heilbroner, who wrote that paragraph, is obviously another admirer.) And what did the Master think of the Game? All purposeful money-making impulses come from the thousands of years of economic scarcity. But wealth is not pursued solely as an answer to scarcity. "He that loveth silver shall not be satisfied with silver; nor he that loveth abundance with increase," wrote Koholeth, the Preacher, Ecclesiastes. What does the purposive investor seek? "Purposiveness," said Lord Keynes, "means that we are more concerned with the remote future results of our actions than with their own quality or their immediate effects on our own environment. The 'purposive' man is always trying to secure a spurious and delusive immortality for his acts by pushing his interest in them forward into time. He does not love his cat, but his cat's kittens; nor, in truth, the kittens, but only the kittens' kittens, and so on forward for ever to the end of cat-dom. For him jam is not jam unless it is a case of jam tomorrow and never jam today. Thus by pushing his jam always forward into the future, he strives to secure for his act of boiling it an immortality."

You know, in the end, that so deep-seated an impulse could not be merely the amusement that comes with a Game. The compounding of wealth, like the building of the City, is part of the much older game of life against death. The immortality is spurious because that particular wheel is fixed; you do have to lose in the end. That is the way the senior game is set up: You can't take it with you.

In a remarkably prophetic essay, "The Economic Possibilities for our Grandchildren," Keynes has some remarks that would seem to make him the king of the hippies, if hippies could read Keynes, the Master of the flowerchildren as well as of speculators. He said the problem of the future would be how to use the freedom from pressing economic cares "which science and compound interest will have won . . . to live wisely and agreeably and well." In this millennium, he wrote, "I see us free, therefore, to return to some of the most sure and certain principles of religion and traditional virtue—that avarice is a vice, that the exaction of usury is a misdemeanor, and the love of money is detestable—

> that those walk most truly in the paths of virtue and sane wisdom who take least thought for the morrow. We shall once more value ends above means and prefer the good to the useful. We shall honour those who can teach us how to pluck the hour and the day virtuously and well, the delightful people who are capable of taking direct enjoyment in things, the lilies of the field who toil not, neither do they spin.

In this millennium, wealth will no longer be of social import, morals will change, and "we shall be able to rid ourselves of many of the pseudo-moral principles which have hag-ridden us for two hundred years, by which we have exalted some of the most distasteful of human qualities into the position of the highest virtues. We shall be able to afford to dare to assess the money-motive at its true value:

The love of money as a possession—as distinguished from love of money as a means to the enjoyments and realities of life—will be recognised for what it is, a somewhat disgusting morbidity, one of those semi-criminal, semi-pathological propensities which one hands over with a shudder to the specialists in mental disease.

There. Now that you know, do you really want to be rich?

DISCUSSION QUESTIONS
SUGGESTIONS FOR WRITING

1. *How does the author's insight that "it is part of the ethos of this country that you ought to be rich" provide perspectives on the new polarization? Relate, for example, to Hopper's statements: "I'm not sure that people understand but that bike with all the money in the gas tank is America. . . ." "I mean, at the start of the movie, Peter and I do a very American thing—we commit a crime, we go for the easy money. . . ." "It took me fifteen years to raise three hundred and seventy thousand dollars. I'm not going to give it to the Cause—I am the Cause." Relate to Reich's: "In the world that now exists, a life of surfing is possible, not as an escape from work, a recreation or a phase, but as a life—if one chooses."*

2. *How is biographical material used in this piece for the purpose of persuasion? How does the author characterize John Maynard Keynes?*

3. *Do you agree with Keynes's formulation of "the problem" of the future—"how to use the freedom from pressing economic cares" which science and compound interest will have won . . . to live wisely and agreeably and well"? Does this sound like a summary of what Consciousness III is trying to do? Are the characters portrayed by Peter Fonda and Dennis Hopper in* Easy Rider *Consciousness III types? Do they live wisely, agreeably, and well?*

4. *What is the author's final attitude toward the acquisition of wealth—that it is something worth doing, that other values such as "living wisely" are more important, that the reader should decide for himself?*

BROWN

DIE NIGGER DIE!

H. RAP BROWN (b. 1943), former chairman of the Student Nonviolent Coordinating Committee (SNCC), has come to symbolize the ideology of black revolution. *Die Nigger Die,* a "political autobiography," is about the making of a revolutionary and a call to black people to be "the vanguard force" in the "struggle of oppressed people."

ONE of the basic problems any Black child has to deal with as he grows up is authority. First, there's the big white world that forces a white God and white Jesus on him and has him worshipping somebody that doesn't even look like him. There's that big white world telling him what's right and what's wrong and how to do and how not to do and all of it is designed to keep him oppressed, to keep him down. And all of that is reinforced by negro america, which is a mirror of the big white world and does the white world's job inside the Black community. Negro america becomes the official policeman for white america. You grow up and you're taught not to talk back to white people, not to look at white women, to be respectful, to speak so-called correct English, to grease and straighten your hair, to scrub your skin as white as you can.

At some point or another, the Black child begins to challenge this authority, both within negro america and the big white world when he confronts it. . . .

My rebellion against this authority occurred whenever I encountered negro america. When I entered Southern University in 1960, I was fifteen years old. I was in constant conflict with the administration. It was really like a plantation. The Presidency had been handed down from the father to the son, who should've died with his father. He was truly a white man's boy and didn't mind folks knowing it. This nigger was so bad, he powdered his face.

One time I remember Odetta came to do a concert. We were required to wear suits and ties to concerts and things like that. So we got all knotted up and went down and here came these white dudes from LSU with sport shirts and sneakers on. I stopped right at the door and started screaming and hollering on the Dean who was standing there. "Man, what's wrong with you? How you gon' let them boys in there?" But he pretended like he hadn't seen them white boys. "You saw it!" I yelled. "Don't come handing me that." I was making so much racket that he told me to meet him in his office the next day. I went and before he could say a word, I jumped down his throat again. I called him a whole bunch of names and he got mad and threatened to kick me out of school.

That showed me again where negro america was. They were scared not to love white people. He come trying to tell me, "Well, if they went in with sneakers on, that just shows their ignorance." I said, "Man, don't come telling me that. You could put on a tie and the finest suit in the world and they wouldn't let you in a concert at LSU. Don't run nothing like that down on me. Telling me that's their ignorance. That's your ignorance, muthafucka!"

Here was that question of authority again. If authority is to be used, it should not be a coercive type thing. After all, what dictates that a person can be put in an authoritative position over someone else? If it's experience, then respect should come from that, not authority. People should adhere to rules because they respect them and not because some position mandates that respect. Now if you raise a legitimate issue with a person and they respect it, then they're gonna adhere to it. It's like the principle of self-determination. But when you're in a certain position and you tell a cat to do something with no grounds for it, it provokes a type of rebellious behavior.

This occurs throughout america. In negro america, anything the teacher or the preacher or the doctor says is law. Not because it's right, but because of who said it. In white america, if the President or Senator Dipshit says it, no one challenges it. It can be wrong as hell, but everybody applauds anyway. I don't give a shit who says what. If the muthafucka is wrong, he's wrong.

My rebellion in its early stages was against authority which did nothing against the authority which was in charge of negroes—the white folks. Teachers, for example. I didn't respect 'em because I knew how they were around white folks. I didn't understand and still don't understand why people are so insecure that they can't talk out against certain things. If something didn't go right, they'd just lay back and say, "Well, it'll get better and things will improve. Ain't nothing I can do about it; it'll better itself." "The Lawd will fix it."

In this country, authority is a cover for wrong. I don't respect wrong and I don't respect authority that represents wrong. And old cracker ass Lightning Bug Johnson knows that's true, because I told him myself. Back in 1965, I was living in Washington, D.C., and I was Chairman of NAG, the Non-Violent Action Group. It was the time of the Selma March when people were beaten up on Pettis Bridge. We had a delegation to go to see Johnson. First we went to see Katzenbach. A negro minister said we don't want to take too many 'cause we don't want him to feel threatened. Katzenbach assumed the typical white attitude. I remember Lester McKinney was trying to raise a question and Katzenbach ignored him. So, I told Katzenbach that if he couldn't answer the man's question, then I didn't see what we were doing there.

The following day we were supposed to go see Humphrey, but we never did. The next day we went to see Johnson in this big conference room that had this conference table about two miles long. About 20 members comprised the delegation, white and negro. When we went in, everybody sat down and then Johnson came in. From the jump, the leader of the delegation who is now one of the boys in charge of Washington, D.C., went into his act. Soon as "the man" got there, he started grinning and laughing. He had this statement written out and he passed it across the table to Johnson. Johnson was arrogant as hell and mad 'cause we were there. His whole attitude was, "What you niggers doin' here takin' up my time." He pissed me off from the get. Well, he looked at the statement and didn't even read it. He just threw it back across the table. Threw it back! And this negro reached out and picked it up. Now if I'd been sitting next to this negro, I would've picked it up and thrown it back at that cracker and we would've had a war right there. But he took it.

After that, each member of the delegation introduced himself and said a few words. The dude from the NAACP got up and said, "Mr. President, it really is a pleasure to be here. This will be something that I'll be proud to tell my children and grandchildren about." Then came another fool and he said the same thing. Next came the dude from CORE and I thought, Well, I know he's supposed to be a militant, a bad dude, and he's gonna tell this cracker what's on his mind. He got up and said, "Good morning, Mr. President. It is a pleasure to be here."

Well, it was my time and I'm really pissed off by this time. It was obvious that everyone was tommin' and nobody was going to speak to the issue. So I started off by telling Johnson, "I'm not happy to be here and I think it's unnecessary that we have to be here protesting against the brutality that Black people are subjected to. And furthermore, I think that the majority of Black people that voted for you wish that they had gone fishing." While our negro leader had been talking about civil rights, Johnson had cut in on him and said, "Speaking of deprivation of rights, my two daughters couldn't sleep last night because of all that picketing noise out in front of the White House." So I told him, "I don't think anyone is interested in whether your daughters could sleep or not. We are interested in the lives of our people. Which side is the federal government on?" I looked around and the bootlickers were getting scared. Man, negroes were getting scared. Johnson's whole attitude changed.

The next day Drew Pearson (one of the many white authorities on negroes) said that I had treated Johnson with "ill abuse." But once Johnson's attitude changed it was easier then for other dudes to begin to talk. But the negroes still didn't raise the points that they should've. There were two white cats who halfway tore into Johnson's ass. When we came out, all them jive Toms and all them old white folks come running round telling me what a good job I had done and that it was good that I had done that. Those are the kind of friends you don't need!

To me, Johnson was a dude who used his position against people and I can't buy that. It's ridiculous. The President ain't nothing but another man. And Johnson was a big-eared, ugly, red-necked cracker. I looked at that muthafucka's ears. If he could learn to wiggle them he could fly. I ain't bullshitting. And when I was tearing into Johnson's ass, Humphrey, who is supposed to be a "liberal," was getting madder than a pimp with dogshit on his shoe. So, I looked at him and knew where he was at. The little red punk.

And to show the muthafuckas what I thought about the whole meeting, I stole some stuff out of the White House. I liberated everything I could! Sure did. Show you what I think of you, muthafuckas. I was trying to figure how to get a painting off the wall and put it under my coat. I figured it belonged to me anyway.

The whole concept of authority has to be redefined. People have to understand that individuals, not positions, merit respect. Negro america and white america assume that positions mandate respect. When this respect for position does not materialize, they begin to utilize force. This is why the Black world has rejected both negro america and white america and their ideas of authority.

DISCUSSION QUESTIONS
SUGGESTIONS FOR WRITING

1. A distinguishing characteristic of autobiography is that it allows the reader to confront the writer's resources of memory and to interpret the impact upon his personality of past events, as he has come to know and understand them after some passage of time. What is your interpretation of the impact on H. Rap Brown's life of the events recounted in this selection?

2. What is H. Rap Brown's point about authority and the need to redefine authority in America? Do you agree?

3. What methods does the author use to persuade the reader of the legitimacy or rightness of his thesis? Is he successful?

4. Just as in the writing of fiction, the writer of autobiography must create believable characters and establish sympathy for at least one of these characters—himself. H. Rap Brown characterizes himself as oppressed from birth, impatient with injustice and hypocrisy, courageous in speaking up to authority. What other elements of his behavior tend to help (or hinder) his effort to establish sympathy for himself, in your estimation?

KUNEN

SUMMER IN THE CITY AND OTHER DOWNS

JAMES SIMON KUNEN (b. 1948) wrote *The Strawberry Statement* while a sophomore at Columbia University "before, during, and after" the 1968 student rebellion there, in which he played an active role. Parts of the book appeared in *New York Magazine* and in *The Atlantic Monthly*.

Wednesday, June 19: I went to Washington, D.C., for the rich people's march in support of the Poor People's Campaign. You are supposed to come away from these affairs with a renewed commitment and sense of purpose. I came away with two girls' addresses and a slight tan.

Thursday, June 20: Went to court a second time to be told I must go a third time in September. That's good because when they start to nail us in the fall, the whole student body will be around to watch, and act.

Friday, June 21: I saw a good-looking, interesting, intelligent girl in the subway train and, of course, knew I would never see her again unless I said something. But I didn't really know what to say, and anyway I was dressed in a cruddy old sweatshirt. I mean, *wearing* a sweatshirt is fine, but I wasn't wearing it, I just happened to have it on. I could have cited the fantastic odds against our ever having been in the same place at the same time. We both got off at the same stop. Encouraged by fate in action, I asked her for a cigarette and tried to get her to know me, but she pointed out that she was waiting for someone and said good-bye before I was leaving. I said, "I'm writing a book. Look for yourself in it."

Monday, June 24: I wrote: "Morning—Cox Commission; Noon—Liberation School opens" on my calendar, but that is the extent of my acquaintance with either event. Getting up early is an incredible drag, or at least I should think it would be.

I would just like to point out that my pillow leaks feathers all over me. I always look like a tax collector who has just been run out of some rural community, probably on a rail.

Think I may get a car with my future writing money. Hate to sell out to materialism, but I'm happy in a car. Just driving, moving, rolling, streaming from one place. Not so much to someplace. But from somewhere, going away, being in between, going. Driving fast when certain songs are on. Sharing the road with other cars and wondering who's in them and where they're going. Parking is the antithesis of all this. I hate parking a car.

I walked about today. What happened to Manhattan should not happen to any island. Not to say that New York is all bad. It's mostly bad, but there are some good things. Central Park for instance. Central Park is one of the better places in the world. People don't go there specifically to be happy. They just go there. And once there they don't have anything particular to do, nowhere to hurry to go, and so they'll talk to you.

In the night I heard a radio discussion on Columbia. Judith Crist blamed the whole thing on "balmy spring nights." Said we "might as well be swallowing goldfish," which is untrue.

Another panelist said that a small hard-core group planned the action a year ago, which would be a lie, except that the guy believed it.

The moderator told an anecdote about a demonstrator with a sign reading "Down with Everything That's Up," and said that what we (oldies) are doing today is paying the penalty for years of permissiveness, which is true, if permissiveness means raising kids to think and not obey any authority that happens to come stomping along.

All concurred that we students "should be busy studying to be leaders instead of carping about things."

Tuesday, June 25: A girl called who had seen me on the tube. She sounded beautiful, so I assumed she wasn't.

She was. Long dark hair. Tall. Thin. Big almond eyes. Beautiful this. Beautiful that. I couldn't believe her.

A friend called me and I told him about the girl. He then called back and told me that he and his brother felt that she was a federal agent. I thought that was incredible, but then I also thought it would be incredible if she weren't a fed. "But look," I said, "there are too many flaming subversives at Columbia for the authorities to bother with me." "Yeah, but you're the one who's been *writing*," he said. I locked the door before going to bed.

Wednesday, June 26: Ate dinner with Archibald Cox, ex-Solicitor General of the United States and Chairman of the Fact-Finding Commission. He said the law is like anything else. It can be used for good or for bad. He also ingested food and breathed, and I liked him. I couldn't help it.

Just heard an obnoxious ad (a redundant statement) for Nehru suits. If you find a good way to live or just something that you like, they take it and buy and sell it and never know what it's worth, and make it worth nothing. You turn to the East, and you end up with "guru-vy Gimbels."

I can look forward to little things. Right now I'm looking forward to brushing my teeth with a brand-new tube of toothpaste I bought. The trick is not to think about how someday it inevitably will be bent and twisted up with hard, dry paste at the end. Live for the moment, man.

Thursday, June 27: I don't understand why our government has us fight the war. I don't know. Are they incredibly evil men, or are they stupid, or are they insane? How can Johnson sleep? How can he go to bed knowing that 25,000 American boys — and countless Vietnamese — have died because of his "policies." He obviously doesn't consider the Vietnamese to be people at all. They're strange, distant, numberless, and yellow, so perhaps he can't empathize with them, can't know their existence and their joys. But what about the Americans? He thinks perhaps that the war is not going well. Doesn't he realize that wars can't go well, that people always die in them and that's not well? Doesn't he know anything? Do statistics hide the truth and keep him from feeling? When I see statistics I practically throw up. I can never forget it. It's in me that my friends everyday hear gunfire and see others fall and hate the enemy. But when they see the ground spin up at them and feel the wetness of their own blood, whom do you think they hate then? These kids who were and were being and were going to be, suddenly finding that they will not be what they wanted or anything else, suddenly finding themselves ending. Won't know or do anything any more. Never see or be seen again. Whom do you suppose they hate? Don't the leaders know that? Couldn't they work out a better way to settle problems? Little boys fight, but by the age of *sixteen*, as irresponsible teens, *they* see that fighting doesn't prove anything. Young men hardly ever fight. Only when their countries do. So it's the countries which display incredibly juvenile behavior. Wars are silly. They're ludicrous. But they're real, extant, constant, present. Why don't countries just stop it? Just cut it out, that's all. We don't want any. They struggle tortuously to arrive at disarmament pacts. They tell everybody that arriving at peace is complex, difficult. Don't they see? It's not a question of state department negotiations or of treaties or international law. It's very simple. All that's necessary is for the leaders to see what they've always done and are doing and for once know and feel and get sick and stop. Nobody fight any more. Of course it's not that simple. But I must be stupid because it seems that simple to me.

It seems that simple to me, and that's not a generation gap, it's an idea difference, and a power gap. You've got the power. You make millions of people suffer. They're hungry and they've got nowhere to go and nothing to do for it. Well cut it out, will you? Just stop it.

If you won't stop it we'll stop you. I've got nothing to lose. You can have your cars and your hi-fi's and your pools and your nice schools. (Sometimes.) I'd like to pawn them off and use the money for schools and houses for the poor. I'd like to do that so I'd feel good. So I'd feel good.

Let's not put our country down. It happens that the United States is the scourge of the earth, but let's not put it down.

I have a mad desire to live.

Hey, do you know what Communists do? They fall in love and have babies sometimes. I swear to God. . . .

Sunday, June 30: . . . The roaches are a bit of a problem. We each have our areas. I have my corner, and they have the rest of the apartment. Except they always come into my corner.

Actually, the parallels between my roaches and the Viet Cong can hardly be ignored. There are seventeen parallels. Both my roaches and the V.C. are indigenous forces, are ignorant, ill-clad and underfed; they both drag away the bodies of their slain, come back no matter how many are killed, move by night, avoid prolonged engagements with the enemy, are not white, are fighting against people who are, have been fighting for generations, are of uncertain numbers, move via infiltration routes, are wily, are out-armed by the enemy, are contemptuous of death, are independent of outside control, are inscrutable, and are winning. . . .

Monday, July 1: . . . It occurred to me today, in a great flash of trying to think of something to write, that we could become a great country. What an opportunity! The field's wide open. There aren't any good countries. They're all bad, in varying degrees. We could become the first good country ever.

There used to be a dream for America. You know, the American dream? America was going to be different. Free. Good. Free and good. Of course they blew it right away. As soon as the Puritans came over they set up religious laws. But at least they clung to the dream. Until now. Now no one hopes for America to be different. I guess it was the dream that ruined the dream. People became convinced it was true, so they never made it true. People think the U.S.A. (a great-sounding, nice, informal name) is special, so we can do anything and it's okay (an American expression). People should wake up and dream again.

DISCUSSION QUESTIONS
SUGGESTIONS FOR WRITING

1. Is James Simon Kunen a Consciousness III type?

2. In the diary form the writer maintains a personal, chronological record of experiences that have some special meaning for him, usually allowing himself a greater range of freedom than if he were writing for an audience, although, clearly, some diaries, as well as variations of the diary form, have been written with an audience in mind, as was probably the case with Kunen. The implied intimacy of the diary form and the opportunity for character revelation are major aspects of its appeal. If the diarist offers information or insight into people or events of a period, such as the Columbia riots, in Kunen's case, the diary may also have historical appeal. What examples of intimacy, character revelation, or historical interest can you locate in this piece?

3. What techniques does Kunen use in his diary that he might just as well have used if he had been writing a novel, using a first-person narrator?

4. In what ways is Kunen a moralist? Point out examples of satire, eloquence, and invective used in service of his moral persuasions.

ROGER ANGELL
(b. 1920) is a frequent
contributor to *The New
Yorker*. Several of his
pieces are collected in his
recent book *A Day in the
Life of Roger Angell*.

LIFE IN THESE NOW UNITED STATES

(The "Reader's Digest" Is
Captured by the Enemy)

AMERICAN OLEOS

OFFICER BOB, who has directed traffic on our Main Street for as long as most of us can remember, saw a long-haired, typically "messy-looking" youth crossing against the lights one morning. He blew his whistle, stopping all traffic, and said, "Watch your step, Miss." When the teen-ager glared at him, the well-liked minion of the law smiled and said, "Oh, I beg your pardon. I thought you were a girl. You *look* like a girl."

"And you look like J. Edgar Hoover's grandmother in drag," shot back the youngster. He stepped closer to Officer Bob and said, "Listen, Fuzzhead, if you read anything besides *The Spanker's Monthly*, you'd know by now that hostility to unusual forms of male dress almost invariably conceals a repressed homosexuality, marked by hysteria and frequent episodes of enraged brutality. Likewise, if you could stop fondling the butt of that Smith & Wesson Police Special like some cornball Rod Steiger, you might notice that you've been wising off at the son of the First Selectman. My pop has his eye on you, Sturmbannführer, and you'd better, like, get on the stick."

The next morning, when the same young man appeared at Officer Bob's crossing, they had a briefer exchange. "Pig!" said the lad. "Punk!" muttered Officer Bob. That day, however, Officer Bob gave out forty-seven tickets for overtime parking, issued fourteen summonses to schoolchildren for loitering, and arrested an eighty-three-year-old grandmother for driving with a mud-spattered license plate. Now he is our town's Chief of Police. "I sure learned my lesson," says Officer Bob, twinkling. "The kids are where it's at." — Betty Birch (in the Iowa *Grunt*).

•

In addition to her duties as our school-bus driver and town clerk, my Great-Aunt Hannah, a widow, is a nudist. Every afternoon, rain or shine, she lies down on the glider on her front porch, as naked as a door-knob (See "Toward a More With-It Speech," P. 89. — *Ed*.), and reads

Sunshine and Health, in plain view of all the traffic on Elm Street. As you can imagine, this has caused some "talk," but over the years our town has learned to put up with her little ways. "If we just ignore her," said the Rev. Gantry, the Jansenist minister, "maybe she'll knock it off. Or catch a bad cold," he added, chuckling.

Last fall, Aunt Hannah's granddaughter, Esther-Mae, went off to college at State U., and a few weeks later Esther-Mae's picture appeared on the front page of the new undergraduate paper there; she was taking part in a Grape Strike Pageant, and she was as naked as a darning egg. (Very good! — *Ed.*) Now Esther-Mae has moved to the East Village, in New York, where we hear she has embarked on a profitable film career, and lots of the kids in our town have taken to spending the afternoons with Great-Aunt Hannah on the porch, where they eat cookies and look at her picture books. As my husband says, "It only shows to go you — you can't knock tolerance!" — Alice Leonowens (from *The Pharmacist's Retort*).

RAPPING OUT LOUD

I'VE discovered what's bugging my Dad — the F.B.I.! — Buddy Fliegelman, in the P.S. 92 *Grab-Bag.*

Marriage is a long sentence that begins with a proposition. — *The Christian Dentist.*

We had a prairie fire last summer, and by the time it was over the whole town was smoking grass. Get it? — Tom Beeber (Petunia, Colo.).

I can read my Dad like a book — and he wears a plain brown wrapper. — Buddy Fliegelman, *ibid.*

A BOY NAMED ERNESTO
Another Boring Story from Everyday Life

ONE afternoon, many years ago, a rich American was having his shoes shined on a sidewalk in Cienfuegos, a city in Cuba. The ragged local boy on his knees before him was working away with a will, humming a native song and making the shoecloth pop. The American removed his Panama hat and wiped the perspiration from his brow with a silk handkerchief, and then puffed with satisfaction on his Havana cigar. It had been a good day for him. He was a broker for the United Fruit Company, and that morning he had concluded a profitable deal with a corrupt landowner that would halve the wages for several thousand local sugar workers while simultaneously depriving them of their right ever to own bicycles. He had also arranged with the wily governor of the province to raise the tax on literacy — a plan that would swell the already bloated coffers of the infamous United Fruit monopoly. Yes indeed, it was a good day!

The boy finished his labors, and the American handed him a counterfeit peso.

"No teep, señor?" asked the lad, with an impudent grin.

"No 'teep,' Pedro," said the man, tousling his hair. "Sorry 'bout that. The sooner you greaseballs learn to stand on your own feet and give an honest day's work for an honest day's pay, the sooner us gringos will be hotfooting it to Switzerland with the last contents of your Treasury. *Comprende?*"

"*Si, señor*," piped the boy. "And *muchas gracias* for another valuable lesson in laissez-faire economics. I won't be needing your filthy lagniappe anymore, for I'm off for the Sierra Maestra." And he threw the lead coin in the man's face and strode away.

Only then did the American glance down and notice that the peasant lad had shined his nice white shoes with stove polish. He started after him with an oath, but the clever youngster had tied his shoelaces together, and the imperialist fell heavily to the pavement and fractured his pince-nez.

"*Ay, Chihuahua!*" cried the boy's mother, who had been watching this scene from the window of her slum. "Ernesto, come back! We will starve — and besides, you have forgotten to brush your teeth *con* Gleem!"

"I will be back, Mamacita, astride the wind of history!" cried the boy from the corner. "One day — I swear it to you, *madre mia* — this man's son will pin my likeness, in a giant poster, to the wall of his room at the Groton School!"

The ragged boy was right. Che Guevara was on his way!

PUT-ONS: THE BEST MEDICINE

ONE evening last autumn, second graders at the Vapid Falls, Minn., elementary school locked their principal, Mr. Forbush, in a mop closet and proceeded to wreck his office. They burned the school records and stuffed Mallomars into his dictating machine. They poured ink all over his checkbook, mucilage in his rubbers, and raspberry Kool-Aid in his box of cigars. They tore down his picture of President Harding and played kickball with his globe.

The next morning, after the school janitor had released him from the mop closet, Forbush went directly to the second-grade room. "O.K., kids," he said to the class. "I'm ready to talk turkey. Amnesty for demonstrators is guaranteed. Compulsory naps are abolished. What are your demands?"

The boys and girls looked at each other in astonishment. "What demands, Mr. Forbush?" piped up Billy Fraser at last. "Gee whiz, haven't you ever heard of Trick or Treat?"

"Holy mackerel, I forgot about Halloween!" Forbush cried, smacking himself on the forehead and laughing heartily. "The joke's on me, kids." Still chuckling, he expelled the entire class.

Hiram Warsaw, a nineteen-year-old Bronx dropout, grew tired of making obscene telephone calls one day. Instead, he looked up the name of the last man in the Manhattan telephone book and called him up. "Hello, Mr. Zzyzybyzynsky?" he said.

"Yes?" said Mr. Zzyzybyzynsky warily.

"I was just looking in the phone book and I noticed —"

"Yeah, I know, I *know!*" Mr. Zzyzybyzynsky shouted.

"Don't hang up!" Warsaw said. "Listen, I just saw you were the last name in the phone book and I thought I'd call you up, because my name is Aababonowicz and I'm the *first* man in the Manhattan book."

"No kidding?" said Zzyzybyzynsky, interested.

"Yeah, how *about* that!" Warsaw said. "I was thinking we ought to get together somewhere, Mr. Zzyzybyzynsky, and grok about our problems. I mean, we have a lot in common."

"Yeah, O.K., sure thing," said Mr. Zzyzybyzynsky eagerly. "Where shall we meet?"

"Oh, around the 'M's somewhere," said Warsaw, and hung up. The next day, in an inexplicable fit of ennui, he enlisted in the Marines for a four-year hitch.

NEW HOPE FOR LYCANTHROPY!

Thanks to the Treatment of a Courageous Backwoods Psychiatrist, Victims of America's Most Whispered-About Illness Are at Last Taking Their Place in Normal Society (condensed from *The Garageman's Almanac*).

WHEN Ralph Waldo Lupus, the only child of a wealthy Winnetka, Ill., couple, was about six months old, his mother first noticed that he had long gray hair growing on his palms, but the family pediatrician assured her (wrongly) that this minor oddity would soon "clear itself up." Little Ralph Waldo's boyhood was happy and unnotable — with one exception. Approximately once a month, at the time of the full moon, he would have no appetite for his breakfast. Questioned by Mrs. Lupus, he invariably reported that he felt "full" — rather as if he had eaten several large hamburgers, cooked very rare, during the night. He also told about experiencing vivid dreams of running about the countryside "dressed up like a big doggy." His mother decided he had been reading too many comic books, and thereafter "cracked down" on his reading matter.

For some years, life went along smoothly enough for this typical American family. The only cloud on the Lupuses' horizon was the curious fact that they seemed unable to keep any dogs or other pets on their estate. A series of watchdogs — an Airedale, three dachshunds, a bull terrier, and a large German shepherd — vanished, one by one, after a week or two in residence, always apparently running away during the night. At the same time, Mr. Lupus noted the gradual dwindling of his herd of angora rabbits. One morning, after the hired man had reported the theft or flight of the family's prize Merino ram, young Ralph Waldo, now fourteen, slept very late and then breakfasted on four Alka-Seltzers. Mr. Lupus, pleading a sudden business engagement, packed a bag and hurriedly left the house, never to return.

Alone, and by now deeply concerned about her son's appearance, which seemed to alternate rapidly between emaciation and sleek good health, Mrs. Lupus began a six-year medical odyssey to find diagnosis and treatment for her boy. Across the land, diagnosticians, psychiatrists, dentists, and nutritionists examined Ralph Waldo, and, noting only an unusually rangy musculature of the lower body, pronounced him healthy and normal. At last, depleted in spirit and pocketbook, Mrs. Lupus brought her son last year to the rustic clinic of psychiatrist Dr. Jakob Pretorius, in northern Manitoba. Dr. Pretorius, a small, white-haired man with extremely thick glasses, examined Ralph Waldo for an hour and then sat down for a private chat with Mrs. Lupus.

"Madam," he said bluntly, "I know what you suspect."

"You do?" said Mrs. Lupus, blenching.

"You believe your son to be a victim of lycanthropy. In plain words, you think he is a werewolf."

Mrs. Lupus nodded, her face suffused with shame. "At last, it's out in the open," she murmured.

"Which is half the battle," said the good Doctor. "Madam, I can help your son. I can even guarantee a cure. The fact is, Mrs. L., *there is no such thing as lycanthropy!* It exists only in the mind."

"But, Doctor—those howls in the night? Those scrabbling footsteps on the porch roof?"

"Only the wind," said Dr. Pretorius.

"Those sudden changes in appearance?"

"Psychosomatic. You see, your son *believes* he is a werewolf, and so, secretly, do you. You are both victims of a delusion more common than is suspected. Why, *why* must we still go on whispering about lycanthropy! When will we rid ourselves once and for all of this burden of superstition and fear that has come down to us from the Dark Ages? Madam, this is the twentieth century!"

Dr. Pretorius sent Mrs. Lupus back to Winnetka on the next train, having explained that he would lock himself alone in a small room with Ralph Waldo on the night of the next full moon, which was to fall two days later, and then merely awaken the young man at the proper time for "a good, long talk."

A week later, Ralph Waldo Lupus came home, a changed man. There was a new confidence in his step, a ruddy flush of health in his cheeks. Indeed, he seemed so well, so mature, that Mrs. Lupus quickly agreed when he asserted that he wished to seek his fortune in Chicago.

Unfortunately, Mrs. Lupus was not able to thank Dr. Pretorius. His associates have told her that he disappeared on the very night of Ralph Waldo's cure, leaving only his shoes, notebook, and worry beads in the room. They believe him to be suffering from amnesia, brought on by overwork. It is sad he can't see Ralph Waldo Lupus today—a fine young man snatched back by intelligent psychotherapy from a social stigma that now, thanks to Dr. Jakob Pretorius, will be rooted from the darkest places of the American unconscious. Mrs. Lupus visited her son recently and noted with pride that he had gained fifteen pounds and two inches in the past six months. He is a rookie in the Chicago Police Department, assigned to park patrol, and expects promotion shortly.

Coming Next Month:

Black Power: The Miracle of the Electric Eel
Playin' My Axe: Harold Stassen's New Career as a Rock Musician
Let's Get in God's Bag
From Pot to Hash: Confessions of a Short-Order Cook
Human Encounter Groups: New Hope for the Post Office?
The Friendly Lepers of Katmandu
Getting Busted: The Truth About Those Silicone Treatments
And other articles of heartening credulousness!

DISCUSSION QUESTIONS
SUGGESTIONS FOR WRITING

1. What aspects of contemporary American culture are satirized or parodied in "Life in These Now United States"?

2. What is lycanthropy, and what new hope is offered for its cure?

3. What characteristics such as plot similarities, methods of characterization, or narrative technique do these vignettes have in common?

4. What attitudes does Angell reveal toward authority, toward middle-class values, toward the United Fruit Company, toward medicine and psychoanalysis? Or is it impossible to say?

Man's Origins and Aggression

ROBERT ARDREY
(b. 1908) graduated from
the University of Chicago,
where he began studying
the sciences of man. For
years a successful play-
wright and screen writer,
Mr. Ardrey returned to the
study of man in 1955 on a
visit to Africa. The resulting series of books has included *African Genesis,
The Territorial Imperative,*
and *The Social Contract.*

AFRICAN GENESIS

CAIN'S CHILDREN

WHAT are the things that we know about man? How much have the natural sciences brought to us, so far, in the course of a silent, unfinished revolution? What has been added to our comprehension of ourselves that can support us in our staggering, lighten our burdens in our carrying, add to our hopes, subtract from our anxieties, and direct us through hazard and fog and predicament? Or should the natural sciences have stayed in bed?

We know above all that man is a portion of the natural world and that much of the human reality lies hidden in times past. We are an iceberg floating like a gleaming jewel down the cold blue waters of the Denmark Strait; most of our presence is submerged in the sea. We are a moonlit temple in a Guatemala jungle; our foundations are the secret of darkness and old creepers. We are a thriving, scrambling, elbowing city; but no one can find his way through our labyrinthine streets without awareness of the cities that have stood here before. And so for the moment let us excavate man.

What stands above the surface? His mind, I suppose. The mind is the city whose streets we get lost in, the most recent construction on a very old site. After seventy million years of most gradual primate en-largement, the brain nearly trebled in size in a very few hundreds of thousands of years. Our city is spacious and not lacking in magnificence, but it has the problems of any boom town. Let us dig.

We are Cain's children. The union of the enlarging brain and the carnivorous way produced man as a genetic possibility. The tightly packed weapons of the predator form the highest, final, and most immediate foundation on which we stand. How deep does it extend? A few million, five million, ten million years? We do not know. But it is the material of our immediate foundation as it is the basic material of our city. And we have so far been unable to build without it.

Man is a predator whose natural instinct is to kill with a weapon. The sudden addition of the enlarged brain to the equipment of an armed already-successful predatory animal created not only the human being but also the human predicament. But the final foundation on which we stand has a strange cement. We are bad-weather animals. The deposit was laid down in a time of stress. It is no mere rubble of carnage and cunning. City and foundation alike are compacted by a mortar of mysterious strength, the capacity to survive no matter what the storm. The quality of the mortar may hold future significance far exceeding that of the material it binds.

Let us dig deeper. Layer upon layer of primate preparation lies buried beneath the predatory foundation. As the addition of a suddenly enlarged brain to the way of the hunting primate multiplied both the problems and the promises of the sum total, man, so the addition of carnivorous demands to the non-aggressive, vegetarian primate way multiplied the problems and promises of the sum total, our ancestral hunting primate. He came into his Pliocene time no more immaculately conceived than did we into ours.

The primate has instincts demanding the maintenance and defence of territories; an attitude of perpetual hostility for the territorial neighbour; the formation of social bands as the principal means of survival for a physically vulnerable creature; an attitude of amity and loyalty for the social partner; and varying but universal systems of dominance to insure the efficiency of his social instrument and to promote the natural selection of the more fit from the less. Upon this deeply-buried, complex, primate instinctual bundle were added the necessities and the opportunities of the hunting life.

The non-aggressive primate is rarely called upon to die in defence of his territory. But death from territorial conflict is second among the causes of lion mortality in the Kruger reserve. The non-aggressive primate seldom suffers much beyond humiliation in his quarrels for dominance. The lion dies of such conflicts more than of all other causes. The forest primate suppresses many an individual demand in the interests of his society. But nothing in the animal world can compare with the organization and the discipline of the lion's hunting pride or the wolf's hunting pack.

We can only presume that when the necessities of the hunting life encountered the basic primate instincts, then all were intensified. Conflicts became lethal, territorial arguments minor wars. The social band as a hunting and defensive unit became harsher in its codes whether of amity or enmity. The dominant became more dominant, the subordinate more disciplined. Overshadowing all other qualitative changes, however, was the coming of the aggressive imperative. The creature who had once killed only through circumstance killed now for a living.

As we glimpsed in the predatory foundation of man's nature the mysterious strength of the bad-weather animal, so we may see in the coming of the carnivorous way something new and immense and perhaps more significant than the killing necessity. The hunting primate was free. He was free of the forest prison; wherever game roamed the world was his. His hands were freed from the earth or the bough; erect carriage opened new and unguessed opportunities for manual answers to ancient quadruped problems. His daily life was freed from the eternal munching; the capacity to digest high-calorie food meant a life more diverse than one endless meal-time. And his wits were freed. Behind him lay the forest orthodoxies. Ahead of him lay freedom of choice and invention as a new imperative if a revolutionary creature were to meet the unpredictable challenges of a revolutionary way of life. Freedom — as the human being means freedom — was the first gift of the predatory way.

We may excavate man deeply and ever more deeply as we dig down through pre-primate, pre-mammal, and even pre-land-life levels of experience. We shall pass through the beginnings of sexual activity as a year-around affair, and the consequent beginnings of the primate family. But all the other instincts will be there still deeper down: the instinct to dominate one's fellows, to defend what one deems one's own, to form societies, to mate, to eat and avoid being eaten. The record will grow dim and the outlines blurred. But even in the earliest deposits of our nature where death and the individual have their start, we shall still find traces of animal nostalgia, of fear and dominance and order.

Here is our heritage, so far as we know it today. Here is the excavated mound of our nature with *Homo sapiens'* boom town on top. But whatever tall towers reason may fling against the storms and the promises of the human future, their foundations must rest on the beds of our past for there is nowhere else to build.

Cain's children have their problems. It is difficult to describe the invention of the radiant weapon as anything but the consummation of a species. Our history reveals the development and contest of superior weapons as *Homo sapiens'* single, universal cultural preoccupation. Peoples may perish, nations dwindle, empires fall; one civilization may surrender its memories to another civilization's sands. But mankind as a whole, with an instinct as true as a meadow-lark's song, has never in a single instance allowed local failure to impede the progress of the weapon, its most significant cultural endowment.

Must the city of man therefore perish in a blinding moment of universal annihilation? Was the sudden union of the predatory way and the enlarged brain so ill-starred that a guarantee of sudden and magnificent disaster was written into our species' conception? Are we so far from being nature's most glorious triumph that we are in fact evolution's most tragic error, doomed to bring extinction not just to ourselves but to all life on our planet?

It may be so; or it may not. . . . But to reach such a conclusion too easily is to over-simplify both our human future and our animal past. Cain's children have many an ancestor beyond *Australopithecus africanus*, and many a problem beyond war. And the first of our problems is to comprehend our own nature. For we shall fashion no miracles in our city's sky until we know the names of the streets where we live.

WHO PECKS WHOM

Every organized animal society has its system of dominance. Whether it be a school of fish or a flock of birds or a herd of grazing wildebeest, there exists within that society some kind of status order in which individuals are ranked. It is an order founded on fear. Each individual knows all those whom he must fear and defer to, and all those who must defer to him. Self-awareness in the limited sense of consciousness of rank seems to have appeared at some very early moment in the evolution of living things.

Whether or not in such societies as the antelope herd every individual has a separate rank, we cannot yet say. Too little study has been done. In some societies there may be classes themselves ranked which an individual achieves or to which he is relegated. But determination of rank by birth is a characteristic of the insect world alone. Among the vertebrates, from fish to apes, status is competitively determined fairly early in the individual's lifetime. That rank is rarely lost, and rarely improved upon.

Dominance occurs when two or more animals pursue the same activity. It is a type of behaviour long-observed, since all animals — wild, captive, or domesticated — pursue it. But not until zoology turned its attention to the natural state did we begin to comprehend the unyielding fabric of dominance in the texture of animal societies. The social animal does not merely seek to dominate his fellows; he succeeds. And succeeding, he achieves a status in the eyes of the other. That status will be permanent; and oddly enough satisfying as a rule to all parties.

In the halls of science there are many doors, and the one with the sign that reads *Animal Dominance* is one that we have scarcely opened. We have learned much: that it is a force at least as old and as deep as territory; that like territory it benefits sex but stands independent of it; that among social animals it is universal, and among our primate family the source of society's most mysterious subtleties; and that among all animal sources of human behaviour, the instinct for status may in the end prove the most important. But while we may observe it, we still do not truly understand it. And that is why any new study of status in animal societies is apt to leave the most informed reader in a renewed state of stupefaction.

The jackdaw is an extremely intelligent bird who reaps the benefit ... of a highly organized social life. It is logical, I suppose, that any animal who gains so much from the deathless wisdom of society will see to it that his society operates with the least possible friction. Natural selection would so decree. But I still find my credulity strained by the subtleties of the jackdaw social order. And were Konrad Lorenz a less experienced observer, I should probably wind up in stolid disbelief.

Every male jackdaw has his number, as it were. From Number One to Number Last there is not the least vagueness in the hierarchical position of the individual male bird within a flock. That position is settled upon at an early date in life. Even in chickhood a shuffling about for status begins. Food may be abundant, but quarrels flourish. Somebody pecks somebody, and gets pecked back; somebody retreats. Gradually the timid, the weak, the irresolute fall; gradually the strong and the determined rise. Before too long rivalry of body and character has determined the exact social position of every male bird in the flock. And he will keep that position, most probably, for life. Lorenz never saw a case of change in status caused by discontent from below.

Every barnyard has its pecking order, as every farmer knows. Chickens like jackdaws establish a hierarchy. And the position of the individual chicken determines all pecking rights. Who may peck whom? No chicken may peck another ranking higher in the order. This is known in zoology as a straight-line hierarchy. The high-ranking chicken may peck left and right at the feeding pan; but there is always that lowly chicken who is pecked by all, and can peck no one in return.

As compared to the jackdaw the chicken is a crude sort of animal, and her barnyard society is an artificial thing. The jackdaw establishes his order of dominance not to nourish quarrels but to minimize them. The senseless autocrat of the barnyard may flourish her rank at every opportunity, and vent her anger on the lowliest. The high-ranking jackdaw rarely descends to such behaviour. If he enters a quarrel among the lowly, it is usually to settle it.

It seems to be a general rule of jackdaw conduct that while one may quarrel with one's hierarchical neighbours, one should not peck too far down the ranks. Number 4 may quarrel with Number 5 or Number 6, but Number 10 is out of bounds. Remarkably enough top jackdaws almost immediately upon achieving their lofty positions acquire a sense of social responsibility. Carpenter observed precisely the same response in rhesus monkeys. The high-ranking jackdaw stands aloof from flock disagreements. Numbers 1, 2 and 3 may have certain differences among themselves; they do not enter into differences with the masses. Occasionally such an aristocrat may enter a low-placed argument, but invariably he sides with the contestant bearing the lower number. It is as if intuitively he bears the weight of a balance of power. Lorenz can find no explanation for such conduct excepting in the prevalence of quarrels over nesting sites. By throwing his weight on the side of the lowest placed members of the flock, the jackdaw insures that all will find reasonably satisfactory nests.

Jackdaws mate for life, and like most birds who follow such a custom become engaged at an earlier date. Wild geese pair in the spring following birth, although sexual maturity does not come about for another year. And it is the same with jackdaws. The young males will have finished their status struggle when pairing begins and the jackdaw female promptly upon pairing assumes the social position of her male. His rights and restraints become her rights and restraints. Throughout all their lives, they will together defend that social position against any rare challenge. But should a female not secure a mate, then it becomes a sadder sort of story. She remains at the tail of all social things in a mournful, unclassified spot. She is last to the food and last to the shelter. She is pecked by the lowliest, snubbed by the least. No aristocrat descends to her defence, for she holds not even a minimum power to keep in balance; neither are there lesser jackdaws on whom she can vent her frustrations. One can well apprehend the jackdaw drive for status, even to gain the status of last in line, when one considers the fate of the sorry unnumbered. The spinster jackdaw has little to look forward to, not even the couch, someday, of the jackdaw analyst.

It was one of these sad, surplus females who revealed to Lorenz, through a train of circumstances, the full workings of the jackdaw social code.

Lorenz raised his flock from chicks. In the month before pairing and before rank order had been quite established one of the stronger males disappeared. At first Lorenz thought that the bird had gone off on an adventure and would return. But as weeks went by and he did not return, Lorenz checked the bird off as a probable victim of some watchful hawk. And he forgot him.

The flock proceeded with its social shakedown and the hierarchy was established. A strong, handsome young male secured the Number One position. Number Two argued for a while, then accepted his vice-presidential role. Distribution of rank moved quickly along until every male had a number. Then pairing proceeded. Just as worthy females in an individualist species look to territory as the mark of the eligible mate, so worthy females in a social species regard the male of high rank with special favour. Number One got a strong young female for his own, and together they made a handsome couple. On down the line the jackdaws paired, each male getting the approximate best that his rank could afford. And at the end of the line the completed pairing found two bedraggled females left over.

That was in the springtime. Mating would not take place for another year. The young jackdaw society settled down to the business of maturing: to the daily life of feeding and preening, of basking and growing, of praising one's fiancée and disparaging one's enemies. The top-ranking jackdaws found the aloofness proper to their aristocratic roles. The middle classes pecked at the lower classes, and the lower classes pecked at the unhappy spinsters. And then the vanished male returned. No hawk had got the strong young bird but only wanderlust. Where he had been Lorenz could not guess. But here he was, after almost six months' absence, returned to a society where order had already been established and pairing completed. The problem of rank came first in the prodigal's instincts. He fixed Number One with a bright, metallic stare.

There were few overt quarrels between the two birds. They ate together. They perched near each other. They looked at each other. It is Lorenz' opinion that the dominant relationship between two animals is established as much by the matching of energy, courage, and assurance as it is by strength. Perhaps the prodigal's adventures in far, desperate places had given him an assurance that no stay-at-home could match. Whatever were the determinants in the dignified struggle, there was little to observe. But by the second day it was all over: Number One had suddenly become Number Two, and the wanderer, Number One.

The problem of rank was settled; the problem of pairing remained. The new Number One assumed in the moment of his ascendancy all that aristocratic carriage which his eminence demanded. But he had no lady. He could not accept an appropriate consort from among the females already paired; jackdaws are faithful. The new Number One could take only one course, and he took it with dignity. He paired with one of the leftovers.

A female, we recall, takes the rank of her male. All in a happy hour the scrubby little female had become the President's wife. All in a happy hour the unwanted spinster from the wrong end of the pecking order had taken her place at the head. The glass slipper fitted; the pumpkin coach arrived. And all in a most miraculous hour from which jackdaw fairy-tales might well be spun the skimpy little Cinderella found her days as a drudge behind her, the days of being pecked upon never to be repeated, the time of being last to the food, last to the shelter, of being snubbed, scorned, pushed about, crowded out, undefended, unloved, feared by none and rejected by all—it was a time that could be forgotten forever. But did she forget it? She did not.

Romance is one thing, reality another. Number One's wife became the worst behaved nouveau in the history of jackdaw society. She snubbed, she flurried, she pushed about, she displayed her dreary plumage, fluttered her skinny wings, and pecked, and pecked, and pecked. In the moment of his ascendancy jackdaw instinct had directed her male to accept the aristocratic jackdaw role. But from the moment of her ascendancy all she apprehended were her rights. And she neglected none. It took her a year to settle down.

Only one factor of social behaviour, in Konrad Lorenz' opinion, was more significant than the rejected female's immediate, intuitive grasp of all those prerogatives to which her new rank entitled her. And that was the immediate and equally intuitive grasp, on the part of every jackdaw, of the new social situation which each now faced. The creature whom all had pecked could now be pecked by none. Her flauntings were unnecessary. Her pecking and her posturing might appease those frustrations acquired through the long unhappy months, but they were quite unneeded to impress others with the grandeur of her new estate. From the hour of her ascendancy, every jackdaw by oldest instinct knew his new place, and hers. She was Number One.

DISCUSSION QUESTIONS
SUGGESTIONS FOR WRITING

1. Critics of Ardrey's thesis that "the weapon . . . fathered the man," or that "we design and compete with our weapons as birds build distinctive nests," out of "genetic necessity," have argued that this is nothing more than a recasting of the doctrine of original sin, a new sort of Calvinism. Does this criticism seem valid to you?

2. What methods does Ardrey use generally to dramatize the succession of information he provides? Which of the methods of persuasion — argument, satire, eloquence, invective — does Ardrey resort to most frequently in African Genesis? *Provide examples of the types identified.*

3. What is social or animal dominance? Speculate over possible evolutionary reasons why it seems to have appeared so early in the evolution of living things.

4. If Ardrey's thesis is true — that the progress of the weapon is man's most significant cultural achievement — must "the city of man therefore perish in a blinding moment of universal annihilation"?

THE
NAKED APE:
ORIGINS

DESMOND MORRIS
(b. 1928) is a zoologist
and former curator of
mammals at the London
Zoo. He is now director of
the Institute of Contemporary Arts. His books in-
clude: *The Biology of Art,
The Mammals;* and with
his wife, Ramona: *Men
and Snakes, Men and
Apes,* and *Men and Pan-
das.* In the following selection the author traces the
evolution of "the naked
ape" and offers several
alternative theories as to
the manner in which the
naked ape became rela-
tively hairless.

. . . The primate group, to which our naked ape belongs, arose originally from primitive insectivore stock. These early mammals were small, insignificant creatures, scuttling nervously around in the safety of the forests, while the reptile overlords were dominating the animal scene. Between eighty and fifty million years ago, following the collapse of the great age of reptiles, these little insect-eaters began to venture out into new territories. There they spread and grew into many strange shapes. Some became plant-eaters and burrowed under the ground for safety, or grew long, stilt-like legs with which to flee from their enemies. Others became long-clawed, sharp-toothed killers. Although the major reptiles had abdicated and left the scene, the open country was once again a battlefield.

Meanwhile, in the undergrowth, small feet were still clinging to the security of the forest vegetation. Progress was being made here, too. The early insect-eaters began to broaden their diet and conquer the digestive problems of devouring fruits, nuts, berries, buds and leaves. As they evolved into the lowliest forms of primates, their vision im-proved, the eyes coming forward to the front of the face and the hands developing as food-graspers. With three-dimensional vision, mani-pulating limbs and slowly enlarging brains, they came more and more to dominate their arboreal world.

Somewhere between twenty-five and thirty-five million years ago, these pre-monkeys had already started to evolve into monkeys proper. They were beginning to develop long, balancing tails and were increasing considerably in body size. Some were on their way to becoming leaf-eating specialists, but most were keeping to a broad, mixed diet. As time passed, some of these monkey-like creatures became bigger and heavier. Instead of scampering and leaping they switched to brachiating — swinging hand over hand along the underside of the branches. Their tails became obsolete. Their size, although making them more cumbersome in the trees, made them less wary of ground-level sorties.

Even so, at this stage — the ape phase — there was much to be said for keeping to the lush comfort and easy pickings of their forest of Eden. Only if the environment gave them a rude shove into the great open spaces would they be likely to move. Unlike the early mammalian explorers, they had become specialized in forest existence. Millions of years of development had gone into perfecting this forest aristocracy, and if they left now they would have to compete with the (by this time) highly advanced ground-living herbivores and killers. And so there they stayed, munching their fruit and quietly minding their own business.

It should be stressed that this ape trend was for some reason taking place only in the Old World. Monkeys had evolved separately as advanced tree-dwellers in both the Old and the New World, but the American branch of the primates never made the ape grade. In the Old World, on the other hand, ancestral apes were spreading over a wide forest area from western Africa, at one extreme, to south-eastern Asia at the other. Today the remnants of this development can be seen in the African chimpanzees and gorillas and the Asian gibbons and orangutans. Between these two extremities the world is now devoid of hairy apes. The lush forests have gone.

What happened to the early apes? We know that the climate began to work against them and that, by a point somewhere around fifteen million years ago, their forest strongholds had become seriously reduced in size. The ancestral apes were forced to do one of two things: either they had to cling on to what was left of their old forest homes, or, in an almost biblical sense, they had to face expulsion from the Garden. The ancestors of the chimpanzees, gorillas, gibbons and orangs stayed put, and their numbers have been slowly dwindling ever since. The ancestors of the only other surviving ape — the naked ape — struck out, left the forests, and threw themselves into competition with the already efficiently adapted ground-dwellers. It was a risky business, but in terms of evolutionary success it paid dividends.

The naked ape's success story from this point on is well known, but a brief summary will help, because it is vital to keep in mind the events which followed if we are to gain an objective understanding of the present-day behaviour of the species.

Faced with a new environment, our ancestors encountered a bleak prospect. They had to become either better killers than the old-time carnivores, or better grazers than the old-time herbivores. We know today that, in a sense, success has been won on both scores; but agriculture is only a few thousand years old, and we are dealing in millions of years. Specialized exploitation of the plant life of the open country was beyond the capacity of our early ancestors and had to await the development of advanced techniques of modern times. The digestive system necessary for a direct conquest of the grassland food supply was lacking. The fruit and nut diet of the forest could be adapted to a root and bulb diet at ground level, but the limitations were severe. Instead of lazily reaching out to the end of the branch for a luscious ripe fruit, the vegetable-seeking ground ape would be forced to scratch and scrape painstakingly in the hard earth for his precious food.

His old forest diet, however, was not all fruit and nut. Animal proteins were undoubtedly of great importance to him. He came originally, after all, from basic insectivore stock, and his ancient arboreal home had always been rich in insect life. Juicy bugs, eggs, young helpless nestlings, treefrogs and small reptiles were all grist to his mill. What is more, they posed no great problems for his rather generalized digestive system. Down on the ground this source of food supply was by no means absent and there was nothing to stop him increasing this part of his diet. At first, he was no match for the professional killer of the carnivore world. Even a small mongoose, not to mention a big cat, could beat him to the kill. But young animals of all kinds, helpless ones or sick ones, were there for the taking, and the first step on the road to major meat-eating was an easy one. The really big prizes, however, were poised on long, stilt-like legs, ready to flee at a moment's notice at quite impossible speeds. The protein-laden ungulates were beyond his grasp.

This brings us to the last million or so years of the naked ape's ancestral history, and to a series of shattering and increasingly dramatic developments. Several things happened together, and it is important to realize this. All too often, when the story is told, the separate parts of it are spread out as if one major advance led to another, but this is misleading. The ancestral ground-apes already had large and high-quality brains. They had good eyes and efficient grasping hands. They inevitably, as primates, had some degree of social organization. With strong pressure on them to increase their prey-killing prowess, vital changes began to take place. They became more upright—fast, better runners. Their hands became freed from locomotion duties—strong, efficient weapon-holders. Their brains became more complex—brighter, quicker decision-makers. These things did not follow one another in a major, set sequence; they blossomed together, minute advances being made first in one quality and then in another, each urging the other on. A hunting ape, a killer ape, was in the making.

It could be argued that evolution might have favoured the less drastic step of developing a more typical cat- or dog-like killer, a kind of cat-ape or dog-ape, by the simple process of enlarging the teeth and nails into savage fang-like and claw-like weapons. But this would have put the ancestral ground-ape into direct competition with the already highly specialized cat and dog killers. It would have meant competing with them on their own terms, and the outcome would no doubt have been disastrous for the primates in question. (For all we know, this may actually have been tried and failed so badly that the evidence has not been found.) Instead, an entirely new approach was made, using artificial weapons instead of natural ones, and it worked.

From tool-using to tool-making was the next step, and alongside this development went improved hunting techniques, not only in terms of weapons, but also in terms of social co-operation. The hunting apes were pack-hunters, and as their techniques of killing were improved, so were their methods of social organization. Wolves in a pack deploy themselves, but the hunting ape already had a much better brain than a wolf and could turn it to such problems as group communication and co-operation. Increasingly complex manoeuvres could be developed. The growth of the brain surged on.

Essentially this was a hunting-group of males. The females were too busy rearing the young to be able to play a major role in chasing and catching prey. As the complexity of the hunt increased and the forays became more prolonged, it became essential for the hunting ape to abandon the meandering, nomadic ways of its ancestors. A home base was necessary, a place to come back to with the spoils, where the females and young would be waiting and could share the food. This step . . . has had profound effects on many aspects of the behaviour of even the most sophisticated naked apes of today.

So the hunting ape became a territorial ape. His whole sexual, parental and social pattern began to be affected. His old wandering, fruit-plucking way of life was fading rapidly. He had now really left his forest of Eden. He was an ape with responsibilities. He began to worry about the prehistoric equivalent of washing machines and refrigerators. He began to develop the home comforts — fire, food storage, artificial shelters. But this is where we must stop for the moment, for we are moving out of the realms of biology and into the realms of culture. The biological basis of these advanced steps lies in the development of a brain large and complex enough to enable the hunting ape to take them, but the exact form they assume is no longer a matter of specific genetic control. The forest ape that became a ground ape that became a hunting ape that became a territorial ape has become a cultural ape. . . .

•

. . . When we first encountered this strange species we noted that it had one feature that stood out immediately from the rest, when it was placed as a specimen in a long row of primates. This feature was its naked skin, which led me as a zoologist to name the creature 'the naked ape'. We have since seen that it could have been given any number of suitable names: the vertical ape, the tool-making ape, the brainy ape, the territorial ape, and so on. But these were not the first things we noticed. Regarded simply as a zoological specimen in a museum, it is the nakedness that has the immediate impact, and this is the name we will stick to, if only to bring it into line with other zoological studies and remind us that this is the special way in which we are approaching it. But what is the significance of this strange feature? Why on earth should the hunting ape have become a naked ape?

Unfortunately fossils cannot help us when it comes to differences in skin and hair, so that we have no idea as to exactly when the great denudation took place. We can be fairly certain that it did not happen before our ancestors left their forest homes. It is such an odd development that it seems much more likely to have been yet another feature of the great transformation scene on the open plains. But exactly how did it occur, and how did it help the emerging ape to survive?

This problem has puzzled experts for a long time and many imaginative theories have been put forward. One of the most promising ideas is that it was part and parcel of the process of neoteny. If you examine an infant chimpanzee at birth you will find that it has a good head of hair, but that its body is almost naked. If this condition was delayed into the animal's adult life by neoteny, the adult chimpanzee's hair condition would be very much like ours.

It is interesting that in our own species this neotenous suppression of hair growth has not been entirely perfected. The growing foetus starts off on the road towards typical mammalian hairiness, so that between the sixth and eighth months of its life in the womb it becomes almost completely covered in a fine hairy down. This foetal coat is referred to as the lanugo and it is not shed until just before birth. Premature babies sometimes enter the world still wearing their lanugo, much to the horror of their parents, but, except in very rare cases, it soon drops away. There are no more than about thirty recorded instances of families producing offspring that grow up to be fully furred adults.

Even so, all adult members of our species do have a large number of body hairs — more, in fact, than our relatives the chimpanzees. It is not so much that we have lost whole hairs as that we have sprouted only puny ones. (This does not, incidentally, apply to all races — negroes have undergone a real as well as an apparent hair loss.) This fact has led certain anatomists to declare that we cannot consider ourselves as a hairless or naked species, and one famous authority went so far as to say that the statement that we are 'the least hairy of all the primates is, therefore, very far from being true; and the numerous quaint theories that have been put forward to account for the imagined loss of hairs are, mercifully, not needed.' This is clearly nonsensical. It is like saying that because a blind man has a pair of eyes he is not blind. Functionally, we are stark naked and our skin is fully exposed to the outside world. This state of affairs still has to be explained, regardless of how many tiny hairs we can count under a magnifying lens.

The neoteny explanation only gives a clue as to how the nakedness could have come about. It does not tell us anything about the value of nudity as a new character that helped the naked ape to survive better in his hostile environment. It might be argued that it had no value, that it was merely a by-product of other, more vital neotenous changes, such as the brain development. But as we have already seen, the process of neoteny is one of differential retarding of developmental processes. Some things slow down more than others—the rates of growth get out of phase. It is hardly likely, therefore, that an infantile trait as potentially dangerous as nakedness was going to be allowed to persist simply because other changes were slowing down. Unless it had some special value to the new species, it would be quickly dealt with by natural selection.

What, then, was the survival value of naked skin? One explanation is that when the hunting ape abandoned its nomadic past and settled down at fixed home bases, its dens became heavily infested with skin parasites. The use of the same sleeping places night after night is thought to have provided abnormally rich breeding-grounds for a variety of ticks, mites, fleas and bugs, to a point where the situation provided a severe disease risk. By casting off his hairy coat, the den-dweller was better able to cope with the problem.

There may be an element of truth in this idea, but it can hardly have been of major importance. Few other den-dwelling mammals—and there are hundreds of species to pick from—have taken this step. Nevertheless, if nakedness was developed in some other connection, it might make it easier to remove troublesome skin parasites, a task which today still occupies a great deal of time for the hairier primates.

Another thought along similar lines is that the hunting ape had such messy feeding habits that a furry coat would soon become clogged and messy and, again, a disease risk. It is pointed out that vultures, who plunge their heads and necks into gory carcasses, have lost the feathers from these members; and that the same development, extended over the whole body, may have occurred among the hunting apes. But the ability to develop tools to kill and skin the prey can hardly have preceded the ability to use other objects to clean the hunters' hair. Even a chimpanzee in the wild will occasionally use leaves as toilet paper when in difficulties with defecation.

A suggestion has even been put forward that it was the development of fire that led to the loss of the hairy coat. It is argued that the hunting ape will have felt cold only at night and that, once he had the luxury of sitting round a camp fire, he was able to dispense with his fur and thus leave himself in a better state for dealing with the heat of the day.

Another, more ingenious theory is that, before he became a hunting ape, the original ground ape that had left the forests went through a long phase as an aquatic ape. He is envisaged as moving to the tropical sea-shores in search of food. There he will have found shellfish and other sea-shore creatures in comparative abundance, a food supply much richer and more attractive than that on the open plains. At first he will have groped around in the rock pools and the shallow water, but gradually he will have started to swim out to greater depths and dive for food. During this process, it is argued, he will have lost his hair like other mammals that have returned to the sea. Only his head, protruding from the surface of the water, would retain the hairy coat to protect him from the direct glare of the sun. Then, later on, when his tools (originally developed for cracking open shells) became sufficiently advanced, he will have spread away from the cradle of the sea-shore and out into the open land spaces as an emerging hunter.

It is held that this theory explains why we are so nimble in the water today, while our closest living relatives, the chimpanzees, are so helpless and quickly drown. It explains our streamlined bodies and even our vertical posture, the latter supposedly having developed as we waded into deeper and deeper water. It clears up a strange feature of our body-hair tracts. Close examination reveals that on our backs the directions of our tiny remnant hairs differ strikingly from those of other apes. In us they point diagonally backwards and inwards towards the spine. This follows the direction of the flow of water passing over a swimming body and indicates that, if the coat of hair was modified before it was lost, then it was modified in exactly the right way to reduce resistance when swimming. It is also pointed out that we are unique amongst all the primates in being the only one to possess a thick layer of sub-cutaneous fat. This is interpreted as the equivalent of the blubber of a whale or seal, a compensatory insulating device. It is stressed that no other explanation has been given for this feature of our anatomy. Even the sensitive nature of our hands is brought into play on the side of the aquatic theory. A reasonably crude hand can, after all, hold a stick or a rock, but it takes a subtle, sensitized hand to feel for food in the water. Perhaps this was the way that the ground ape originally acquired its super-hand, and then passed it on ready-made to the hunting ape. Finally, the aquatic theory needles the traditional fossil-hunters by pointing out that they have been singularly unsuccessful in unearthing the vital missing links in our ancient past, and gives them the hot tip that if they would only take the trouble to search around the areas that constituted the African coastal sea-shores of a million or so years ago, they might find something that would be to their advantage.

Unfortunately this has yet to be done and, despite its most appealing indirect evidence, the aquatic theory lacks solid support. It neatly accounts for a number of special features, but it demands in exchange the acceptance of a hypothetical major evolutionary phase for which there is no direct evidence. (Even if eventually it does turn out to be true, it will not clash seriously with the general picture of the hunting ape's evolution out of a ground ape. It will simply mean that the ground ape went through a rather salutary christening ceremony.)

An argument along entirely different lines has suggested that, instead of developing as a response to the physical environment, the loss of hair was a social trend. In other words it arose, not as a mechanical device, but as a signal. Naked patches of skin can be seen in a number of primate species and in certain instances they appear to act as species recognition marks, enabling one monkey or ape to identify another as belonging to its own kind, or some other. The loss of hair on the part of the hunting ape is regarded simply as an arbitrarily selected characteristic that happened to be adopted as an identity badge by this species. It is of course undeniable that stark nudity must have rendered the naked ape startlingly easy to identify, but there are plenty of other less drastic ways of achieving the same end, without sacrificing a valuable insulating coat.

Another suggestion along the same lines pictures the loss of hair as an extension of sexual signalling. It is claimed that male mammals are generally hairier than their females and that, by extending this sex difference, the female naked ape was able to become more and more sexually attractive to the male. The trend to loss of hair would affect the male, too, but to a lesser extent and with special areas of contrast, such as the beard.

This last idea may well explain the sex differences as regards hairiness but, again, the loss of body insulation would be a high price to pay for a sexy appearance alone, even with subcutaneous fat as a partial compensating device. A modification of this idea is that it was not so much the appearance as the sensitivity to touch that was sexually important. It can be argued that by exposing their naked skins to one another during sexual encounters, both male and female would become more highly sensitized to erotic stimuli. In a species where pair-bonding was evolving, this would heighten the excitement of sexual activities and would tighten the bond between the pair by intensifying copulatory rewards.

Perhaps the most commonly held explanation of the hairless condition is that it evolved as a cooling device. By coming out of the shady forests the hunting ape was exposing himself to much greater temperatures than he had previously experienced, and it is assumed that he took off his hairy coat to prevent himself from becoming over-heated. Superficially this is reasonable enough. We do, after all, take our jackets off on a hot summer's day. But it does not stand up to closer scrutiny. In the first place, none of the other animals (of roughly our size) on the open plains have taken this step. If it was as simple as this we might expect to see some naked lions and naked jackals. Instead they have short but dense coats. Exposure of the naked skin to the air certainly increases the chances of heat loss, but it also increases heat gain at the same time and risks damage from the sun's rays, as any sun-bather will know. Experiments in the desert have shown that the wearing of light clothing may reduce heat loss by curtailing water evaporation, but it also reduces heat gain from the environment to 55 per cent of the figure obtained in a state of total nudity. At really high temperatures, heavier, looser clothing of the type favoured in Arab countries is a better protection than even light clothing. It cuts down the in-coming heat, but at the same time allows air to circulate around the body and aid in the evaporation of cooling sweat.

Clearly the situation is more complicated than it at first appears. A great deal will depend on the exact temperature levels of the environment and on the amount of direct sunshine. Even if we suppose that the climate was suitable for hair loss — that is, moderately hot, but not intensely hot — we still have to explain the striking difference in coat condition between the naked ape and the other open-country carnivores.

There is one way we can do this, and it may give the best answer yet to the whole problem of our nakedness. The essential difference between the hunting ape and his carnivore rivals was that he was not physically equipped to make lightning dashes after his prey or even to undertake long endurance pursuits. But this is nevertheless precisely what he had to do. He succeeded because of his better brain, leading to more intelligent manoeuvring and more lethal weapons, but despite this such efforts must have put a huge strain on him in simple physical terms. The chase was so important to him that he would have to put up with this, but in the process he must have experienced considerable overheating. There would be a strong selection pressure working to reduce this over-heating and any slight improvement would be favoured, even if it meant sacrifices in other directions. His very survival depended on it. This surely was the key factor operating in the conversion of a hairy hunting ape into a naked ape. With neoteny to help the process on its way, and with the added advantages of the minor secondary benefits already mentioned, it would become a viable proposition. By losing the heavy coat of hair and by increasing the number of sweat glands all over the body surface, considerable cooling could be achieved — not for minute-by-minute living, but for the supreme moments of the chase — with the production of a generous film of evaporating liquid over his air-exposed, straining limbs and trunk.

This system would not succeed, of course, if the climate were too intensely hot, because of damage to the exposed skin, but in a moderately hot environment it would be acceptable. It is interesting that the trend was accompanied by the development of a sub-cutaneous fat layer, which indicates that there was a need to keep the body warm at other times. If this appears to counterbalance the loss of the hairy coat, it should be remembered that the fat layer helps to retain the body heat in cold conditions, without hindering the evaporation of sweat when over-heating takes place. The combination of reduced hair, increased sweat glands, and the fatty layer under the skin appears to have given our hard-working ancestors just what they needed, bearing in mind that hunting was one of the most important aspects of their new way of life.

So there he stands, our vertical, hunting, weapon-toting, territorial, neotenous, brainy, Naked Ape, a primate by ancestry and a carnivore by adoption, ready to conquer the world. But he is a very new and experimental departure, and new models frequently have imperfections. For him the main troubles will stem from the fact that his culturally operated advances will race ahead of any further genetic ones. His genes will lag behind, and he will be constantly reminded that, for all his environment-moulding achievements, he is still at heart a very naked ape.

DISCUSSION QUESTIONS
SUGGESTIONS FOR WRITING

1. What reasons might Morris have had for his posture of objectivity about the naked ape, his pretense of speaking about a creature of some peculiar "other" species?

2. One reviewer referred to reading The Naked Ape *as an "ego-shrinking" experience. How would you characterize your reactions to it?*

3. What theories are offered of the origin and evolutionary purpose of the naked ape's nakedness?

4. Since scientists may never be able to provide conclusive empirical evidence for any particular theory of how the naked ape lost his hair, what good does it do to speculate about such a subject?

JOE DAVID BELLAMY (b. 1941) teaches writing and literature in the Pennsylvania State College system at Mansfield State College. He attended Duke University, Antioch College, and the University of Iowa Writers Workshop and has published fiction, poetry, and nonfiction in *The Atlantic Monthly, Wisconsin Review, Chicago Review,* and elsewhere. The following review of Morris's *The Human Zoo* is intended both as an introduction to the ideas raised by that book and as a means of gaining critical perspective on the author's methods in his work in general.

THE HUMAN ZOO: JUSTIFIABLE SPECULATION

PERHAPS we should be suspicious of a zoologist (former curator of mammals at the London Zoo) who proposes to see so much of our lives as analogous to a zoo situation—just as we might be suspicious of a Freudian psychologist who wishes to explain every human experience according to Freudian principles, or a Marxist literary critic who wishes to judge all works of art in terms of whether or not they succeed in aiding the struggle of the proletariat.

Perhaps we should be doubly suspicious when such a man seems to answer all our most pressing problems and to explain many contemporary phenomena in the same terms—from the audience hysteria at the appearance of rock groups like the Beatles to a biological explanation for student riots.

Like many a successful popularizer before him, Desmond Morris is a master at cleverly intermingling scientific data with "human interest" material. At times, he seems to be virtually coining a whole new eclectic metaphysical system from his favorite hypotheses.

In spite of these shortcomings, however, Desmond Morris's *The Hu-*

man Zoo does contain many apparently valid observations and thought-provoking interpretations that, in many cases, may cause the reader to want to forget its limitations in return for the startling, if one-sided, view of himself it has to offer.

In *The Human Zoo*, just as in his earlier best seller, *The Naked Ape*, Desmond Morris uses an extended metaphor to compare man to his animal relatives—and to speculate about human behavior, physiology, and culture on the basis of an ongoing series of comparisons between humans and animals. In *The Naked Ape* this metaphor was concerned with the peculiarity of man's hairlessness in relation to all other species of monkeys and apes. In *The Human Zoo* the central metaphor turns on the similarities between the human species in the present state of civilization and numerous animal species, *not* in their natural habitats, but in states of captivity. Under normal conditions, Morris points out,

> wild animals do not mutilate themselves, masturbate, attack their off-spring, develop stomach ulcers, become fetishists, suffer from obesity, form homosexual pair-bonds, or commit murder. . . . The zoo animal in a cage [however] exhibits all these abnormalities that we know so well from our human companions.

A major premise of *The Human Zoo* is not only that man is basically "an animal," or rather "a naked ape self-named *Homo sapiens*," but also that he is "biologically . . . still [a] simple tribal animal." In this Morris sees a particularly telling explanation for the apparent contemporary bewilderment and disorientation of the species—the profound shock of the "almost instantaneous" speed (in evolutionary terms) of the human advance from a hunting and food-gathering way of life, for which man was most suited by "a million hard years" of evolution, through rapid stages of agricultural development and the domestication of animals, to the present staggering level of technological sophistication and population expansion.

The eventual abandonment of the ancient social patterns of the tribe —characterized by localized, interpersonal interaction and a strong sense of tribal identity—was (and still is) a terrifically difficult adaptation for such a tribal hunter-gatherer to make, in Morris's view. The simple tribesman no longer knew personally each member of his community, and "as a species we were not biologically equipped to cope with a mass of strangers masquerading as members of our tribe." The transformation to the present "super-tribal" state called for drastic adjustments, strenuous new competition, new conditioning—and led to the stress of anomie and overcrowding, sexual aberrations, mass-scale war and violence, previously unheard-of atrocities—in a nutshell, the whole zoo syndrome.

It also led to what Morris calls the "stimulus struggle" of our super-tribal condition, "a specialty of the urban animal." Being of the type of animals which have evolved no single, specialized survival device, man has had to become "the supreme opportunist," the type of creature which can never stop exploring and investigating its environment for whatever advantage it might have to offer—who has, in fact, evolved a nervous system that cannot tolerate inactivity or absence of stimulation. Super-tribal man, released from the demands of living for survival alone, is obliged by his biological constitution to seek out other means to secure the optimum amount of stimulation from his environment. Whereas his super-tribal development has the advantage of allowing for individual *choice* of the method of stimulation, its disadvantages are clear. Super-tribal man constantly struggles to avoid boredom on the one hand and excessive stress on the other; but even if he manages to find a golden mean, substitutes for real survival activity sometimes seem meaningless because they are inevitably substitutes—no matter how he tends to look at them.

The subject of "super-sex" is treated with all the frankness and attention to detail one would expect from the author who gave us in his previous book a fully detailed clinical account of coitus as if from "the unbiased eyes of a hovering Martian." Here the treatment is perhaps overzealous—ranging from an examination of the "no fewer than ten major categories" of super-tribal sex to speculations about the course of European history if Hitler or Napoleon had had normally formed genitals. One curious detail is his description of an "ancient [stone] phallus that reputedly towered to the height of three hundred and sixty feet [and was] covered in pure gold." The reader is left to ponder the magnificence (or monstrosity) of the human imagination—without the least hint as to the site or possible creators of such a piece of stonework.

Morris describes in another chapter the manner in which the normal struggle for social dominance, or status-seeking, a characteristic of all mammal groups, expanded into the "nightmare of super-status" as man reached the super-tribal state. The essential feature of the status struggle in nature, according to Morris, is that it is based on the *personal* relationships of the individuals inside the social group. For the primitive human tribesman the problem was therefore a comparatively simple one. But when the tribes grew into super-tribes and relationships became increasingly impersonal, the problem of the status "rat-race" became agonizing. A situation developed comparable to the "behavioral sink," where, if an animal group becomes too large or the available space too small, dominance battles rage uncontrollably, the leaders suffer intolerable strain, the weakest members of the group are hounded to their deaths, and the rituals of display and counterdisplay degenerate into bloody violence. Among other problems generated by this state of affairs is the prevalence of "hundreds of thousands of would-be leaders with no real hope of leading . . . throughout the length and breadth of our massive communities." The dominance frustration that permeates the super-tribal culture explains, for Morris, the widespread addiction to fictional and athletic violence as well as the irrational redirecting of aggression toward substitutes such as dogs, children, or subordinates.

> Our super-tribesman, neglecting his family to drag himself one more rung up the social ladder, gloating over the brutalities in his books and films, kicking his dogs, beating his children, persecuting his underlings, torturing his victims, killing his enemies, giving himself stress diseases and blowing his brains out, is not a pretty sight. He has often boasted about being unique in the animal world, and on this score he certainly is.

In spite of the costliness of "our relentless social progress," Morris does not see all the consequences as cause for pessimism. He seems bent, in fact, upon communicating his sense of wonder concerning the weird course our species has taken and — wisely — reserves judgment on its outcome. Man's push to civilization is, he believes, "the most exciting game the world has ever seen." Although typical of the author's occasional glibness or fascination with banal comparisons, it is a relief to note that he avoids resorting to a facile primitivism. (Although simplified, his view of primitive societies seems reasonably factual, not mythic or idyllic.) His self-avowed purpose in this book is to "show the increasing price we have to pay for indulging . . . our powerful inventive, exploratory urges . . . and the ingenious ways in which we contrive to meet that price." This is done with the hope that "if we can understand better the true nature of the players, it should be possible to make the game even more rewarding, without . . . becoming more dangerous and, ultimately, disastrous for the whole species."

One can hardly quibble with such a goal. In spite of the exaggeration of his all-embracing metaphor of the zoo, Morris's basic premise is solid enough — that a great deal can be learned about man's nature by scrutinizing (or even by speculating about) his evolutionary history.

> . . . Somewhere in all that mass of wires, cables, plastics, concrete, bricks, metal and glass . . . , there is an animal, a human animal, a primitive tribal hunter, . . . desperately struggling to match his ancient inherited qualities with his extraordinary situation.

If certain aspects of Morris's work are highly speculative, it is also true that we have very little to go on in reconstructing our ancient inheritance. Surely speculation of this kind should have a place, both in helping to break ground for future experimentation and discovery and, even more so, in helping us to imagine areas of our past and characteristics of our deepest natures that may never be touched upon in any other way.

DISCUSSION QUESTIONS
SUGGESTIONS FOR WRITING

1. What aspects of The Human Zoo *does the reviewer hold up for questioning? Which does he approve of?*

2. Note the descriptive function of the review as well as its analytical and judgmental characteristics and the manner in which these aspects overlap. Cite examples of the use of description as it implies judgment of the work. What is the final judgment of the work?

3. At what point (if any) does the reviewer suggest that the analogy between zoo and urban life may break down?

4. Why does the reviewer seem to feel that "speculation" of this type should have a place? Does he imply that the imaginative projections of The Human Zoo *are possibly more valuable than the verifiable facts provided in it?*

CAPOTE

IN
COLD BLOOD

TRUMAN CAPOTE (b. 1924) became a prominent figure in the American literary establishment with the publication of his precocious first novel, *Other Voices, Other Rooms. In Cold Blood* is his ninth book and represents the outcome of his long-standing desire to make a contribution toward the establishment of a serious new literary form, which he has labeled the "non-fiction novel."

. . . "Up till then he hadn't been able to see us very good. I think what he saw hit him hard. Dick says, 'Now, sir, all we want you to do is show us where you keep that safe.' But Mr. Clutter says, 'What safe?' He says he don't have any safe. I knew right then it was true. He had that kind of face. You just knew whatever he told you was pretty much the truth. But Dick shouted at him, 'Don't lie to me, you sonofabitch! I know goddam well you got a safe!' My feeling was nobody had ever spoken to Mr. Clutter like that. But he looked Dick straight in the eye and told him, being very mild about it — said, well, he was sorry but he just didn't have any safe. Dick tapped him on the chest with the knife, says, 'Show us where that safe is or you're gonna be a good bit sorrier.' But Mr. Clutter — oh, you could see he was scared, but his voice stayed mild and steady — he went on denying he had a safe.

"Sometime along in there, I fixed the telephone. The one in the office. I ripped out the wires. And I asked Mr. Clutter if there were any other telephones in the house. He said yes, there was one in the kitchen. So I took the flashlight and went to the kitchen — it was quite a distance from the office. When I found the telephone, I removed the receiver and cut the line with a pair of pliers. Then, heading back, I heard a noise. A creaking overhead. I stopped at the foot of the stairs leading to the second floor. It was dark, and I didn't dare use the flashlight. But I could tell there was someone there. At the top of the stairs, silhouetted against a window. A figure. Then it moved away. . . ."

"For all I knew, maybe it was somebody with a gun. But Dick wouldn't even listen to me. He was so busy playing tough boy. Bossing Mr. Clutter around. Now he'd brought him back to the bedroom. He was counting the money in Mr. Clutter's billfold. There was about thirty dollars. He threw the billfold on the bed and told him, 'You've got more money in this house than that. A rich man like you. Living on a spread like this.' Mr. Clutter said that was all the cash he had, and explained he always did business by check. He offered to write us a check. Dick just blew up—'What kind of Mongolians do you think we are?'—and I thought Dick was ready to smash him, so I said, 'Dick. Listen to me. There's somebody awake upstairs.' Mr. Clutter told us the only people upstairs were his wife and a son and daughter. Dick wanted to know if the wife had any money, and Mr. Clutter said if she did, it would be very little, a few dollars, and he asked us—really kind of broke down— please not to bother her, because she was an invalid, she'd been very ill for a long time. But Dick insisted on going upstairs. He made Mr. Clutter lead the way.

"At the foot of the stairs, Mr. Clutter switched on lights that lighted the hall above, and as we were going up, he said, 'I don't know why you boys want to do this. I've never done you any harm. I never saw you before.' That's when Dick told him, 'Shut up! When we want you to talk, we'll tell you.' Wasn't anybody in the upstairs hall, and all the doors were shut. Mr. Clutter pointed out the rooms where the boy and girl were supposed to be sleeping, then opened his wife's door. He lighted a lamp beside the bed and told her, 'It's all right, sweetheart. Don't be afraid. These men, they just want some money.' She was a thin, frail sort of woman in a long white nightgown. The minute she opened her eyes, she started to cry. She says, talking to her husband, 'Sweetheart, I don't have any money.' He was holding her hand, patting it. He said, 'Now, don't cry, honey. It's nothing to be afraid of. It's just I gave these men all the money I had, but they want some more. They believe we have a safe somewhere in the house. I told them we don't.' Dick raised his hand, like he was going to crack him across the mouth. Says, 'Didn't I tell you to shut up?' Mrs. Clutter said, 'But my husband's telling you the God's truth. There isn't any safe.' And Dick answers back, 'I know goddam well you got a safe. And I'll find it before I leave here. Needn't worry that I won't.' Then he asked her where she kept her purse. The purse was in a bureau drawer. Dick turned it inside out. Found just some change and a dollar or two. I motioned to him to come into the hall. I wanted to discuss the situation. So we stepped outside. . . . We were just outside the door, where we could keep an eye on them. But we were whispering. I told Dick, 'These people are telling the truth. The one who lied is your friend Floyd Wells. There isn't any safe, so let's get the hell out of here.' But Dick was too ashamed to face it. He said he wouldn't believe it till we searched the whole house. He said the thing to do was tie them all up, then take our time looking around. You couldn't argue with him, he was so excited. The glory of having everybody at his mercy, that's what excited him. Well, there was a bathroom next door to Mrs. Clutter's room. The idea was to lock the parents in the bathroom, and wake the kids and put them there, then bring them out one by one and tie them up in different parts of the house. And then, says Dick, after we've found the safe, we'll cut their throats. Can't shoot them, he says—that would make too much noise. . . ."

"Dick stood guard outside the bathroom door while I reconnoitered. I frisked the girl's room, and I found a little purse—like a doll's purse. Inside it was a silver dollar. I dropped it somehow, and it rolled across the floor. Rolled under a chair. I had to get down on my knees. And just then it was like I was outside myself. Watching myself in some nutty movie. It made me sick. I was just disgusted. Dick, and all his talk about a rich man's safe, and here I am crawling on my belly to steal a child's silver dollar. One dollar. And I'm crawling on my belly to get it. . . .

"The taping came later, after I'd tied both the women in their bedrooms. Mrs. Clutter was still crying, at the same time she was asking me about Dick. She didn't trust him, but said she felt I was a decent young man. I'm *sure* you are, she says, and made me promise I wouldn't let Dick hurt anybody. . . .

"Dick carried the flashlight when we went to tape Mr. Clutter and the boy. Just before I taped him, Mr. Clutter asked me—and these were his last words—wanted to know how his wife was, if she was all right, and I said she was fine, she was ready to go to sleep, and I told him it wasn't long till morning, and how in the morning somebody would find them, and then all of it, me and Dick and all, would seem like something they dreamed. I wasn't kidding him. I didn't want to harm the man. I thought he was a very nice gentleman. Soft-spoken. I thought so right up to the moment I cut his throat.

"Wait. I'm not telling it the way it was. . . . After, see, after we'd taped them, Dick and I went off in a corner. To talk it over. Remember, now, there were hard feelings between us. Just then it made my stomach turn to think I'd ever admired him, lapped up all that brag. I said, 'Well, Dick. Any qualms?' He didn't answer me. I said, 'Leave them alive, and this won't be any small rap. Ten years the very least.' He still didn't say anything. He was holding the knife. I asked him for it, and he gave it to me, and I said, 'All right, Dick. Here goes.' But I didn't mean it. I meant to call his bluff, make him argue me out of it, make him admit he was a phony and a coward. See, it was something between me and Dick. I knelt down beside Mr. Clutter, and the pain of kneeling—I thought of that goddam dollar. Silver dollar. The shame. Disgust. And *they'd* told me never to come back to Kansas. But I didn't realize what I'd done till I heard the sound. Like somebody drowning. Screaming under water. I handed the knife to Dick. I said, 'Finish him. You'll feel better.' Dick tried—or pretended to. But the man had the strength of ten men—he was half out of his ropes, his hands were free. Dick panicked. Dick wanted to get the hell out of there. But I wouldn't let him go. The man would have died anyway, I know that, but I couldn't leave him like he was. I told Dick to hold the flashlight, focus it. Then I aimed the gun. The room just exploded. Went blue. Just blazed up. Jesus, I'll never understand why they didn't hear the noise twenty miles around."

DISCUSSION QUESTIONS
SUGGESTIONS FOR WRITING

1. In this "nonfiction novel" the information provided is allegedly taken from interviews with the persons directly concerned in the events described, or from personal observation by the author. How is this different from the usual manner of composing a novel? Is it a better way?

2. Explore the ways in which point of view, plot, and characterization help establish sympathy or identification with the narrator-murderer. Is such identification crucial to the piece?

3. Is the narrator-murderer a logical consequence of, in Morris's phrase, "a million hard years" of evolution?

4. Who is to blame for Mr. Clutter's murder?

Nuclear Catastrophe

TOM STONIER
(b. 1927), Yale Ph.D. and
former staff member of
the Rockefeller Institute,
is now doing biological
research at Manhattan
College. *Nuclear Disaster*
provides one of the most
accurate and definitively
documented accounts yet
written of what actually
takes place during the explosion of a thermonuclear
bomb as well as probable
social and economic con-
sequences of nuclear war.

NUCLEAR DISASTER

WHAT happens when a twenty-megaton thermonuclear device is detonated? First, a bluish-white incandescence flashes across the sky, followed at once by a brilliant fireball as hot as, and many times brighter than, the brightest sun. This small, man-made sun, like its natural counterpart, emits ultraviolet, visible, and infrared radiation. The ultraviolet light is discharged as a very short initial pulse. This is almost immediately followed by a second, long pulse lasting well over a minute, in which the heat energy is emitted as visible and infrared radiation. Maximum heat emission occurs at about four and one half seconds after detonation, and half the heat is released by the end of ten seconds. As the fireball rises it scorches the countryside: on a very clear day a twenty-megaton air burst exploded low in the atmosphere could cause the clothing of a person standing about twenty miles away to burst into flame; people about forty miles away could suffer first-degree burns. For a contact surface burst, the distances are reduced about 40 per cent.

In the case of a one-megaton weapon, the fireball reaches its maximum size (about 1.5 miles) in ten seconds; presumably for a twenty-megaton bomb the 4.5-mile maximum is not achieved until about forty-five seconds. As the fireball expands, it rises like a hot-air balloon. A one-megaton weapon exploded moderately low in the air will reach a height of about 2 miles at the end of eighteen seconds, 3 miles in thirty seconds, 4.5 miles in about one minute. At about this time the fireball has cooled so much that it is no longer visible. Particles of matter vaporized and sucked up by the fireball begin to condense as they reach the tropopause, 5 to 10 miles above the earth, and they now begin to spread out, thus forming the mushroom cloud, which after ten minutes stabilizes and achieves a maximum height of about 14 miles. In a twenty-megaton explosion, these events would take place somewhat more slowly and the cloud would finally reach a height of over 20 miles.

Meanwhile, a huge pressure wave, at first traveling many times faster than sound, has spread out from the center of the explosion. Immediately behind the shock front comes the wind, at speeds initially exceeding a thousand miles per hour. The wind, diminishing as it moves outward, creates a vast vacuum, and the surrounding air now rushes in, fanning the many fires started by the heat radiation and the blast. These fires, covering an area almost forty miles across, would ultimately coalesce to form mass fires, which, if the density of combustible material were sufficiently great, would then develop into firestorms or conflagrations. The size of the area would depend on meteorological conditions; in a contact surface burst it would likely be about twenty miles across.

In a contact surface burst, a circle about fifteen miles across would mark the area in which average brick houses would collapse. Moderate damage would occur within a circle of approximately twice that diameter. However, these figures are not rigid; the degree of destruction and the areas in which it occurs is to some extent dependent on meteorological and other conditions. For example, under certain circumstances that cause the blast wave to bounce back and forth between the earth and the layers of the atmosphere, windows more than one hundred miles away could be shattered.

As mass fires raze the destroyed city below, fallout begins to descend from above, poisoning the surrounding countryside. One bomb might endanger the lives of people in a 4,000-square-mile area. Such a large thermonuclear device exploded in midtown Manhattan, for example, would probably kill 6,000,000 out of New York City's 8,000,000 inhabitants, and produce an additional 1,000,000 or more deaths beyond the city limits.

Further serious complications would arise if the entire nation were subjected to attack. Even before the threat of fallout radiation completely subsided the country could be thrown into a state of economic and social chaos—including serious outbreaks of famine and disease—and the ensuing shock, loss of morale, and weakened leadership would further hamper relief operations and impede rehabilitation. The effects of this disruption could persist for decades, just as would the somatic damage inflicted on people exposed to radiation. Even individuals who escape the hazards of the explosion and who are themselves uninjured by radiation might carry a legacy of genetic damage, which they would then pass from generation to generation. Perhaps most uncertain, and potentially most disastrous, are the ecological consequences, the imbalances in nature itself, which might well create the preconditions for the disappearance of American civilization as we know it.

DISCUSSION QUESTIONS
SUGGESTIONS FOR WRITING

1. This piece illustrates the authoritative quality of pure information divulged without apparent exaggeration and with attention to precise detail. Is it largely the author's sense of confidence about the accuracy of the information that makes it sound convincing?

2. Note that the author seems personally detached from the details he offers, although there is ample material to arouse some sort of emotional reaction. Does this detachment contribute to the authoritative tone of the piece?

3. Can you imagine a writing situation where a more subjective or emotional posture might be combined with the use of pure information without sacrificing the authoritative tone — or even enhancing it?

4. What relationships are there in a piece of writing between subject matter and the emotional attitude of the writer towards the subject matter?

LIFTON

INVISIBLE CONTAMINATION

ROBERT JAY LIFTON (b. 1926) holds the Foundation Fund for Research in Psychiatry professorship at Yale University. He has been particularly interested in the relationship between individual psychology and historical change, especially in problems surrounding the extreme historical situations in our era.

SOON after the bomb fell—sometimes within hours or even minutes, often during the first twenty-four hours or the following days and weeks—survivors began to notice in themselves and others a strange form of illness. It consisted of nausea, vomiting, and loss of appetite; diarrhea with large amounts of blood in the stools; fever and weakness; purple spots on various parts of the body from bleeding into the skin (purpura); inflammation and ulceration of the mouth, throat, and gums (oropharyngeal lesions and gingivitis); bleeding from the mouth, gums, throat, rectum, and urinary tract (hemorrhagic manifestations); loss of hair from the scalp and other parts of the body (epilation); extremely low white blood cell counts when these were taken (leukopenia); and in many cases a progressive course until death.

These manifestations of toxic radiation effects aroused in the minds of the people of Hiroshima a special terror, *an image of a weapon which not only instantly kills and destroys on a colossal scale but also leaves behind in the bodies of those exposed to it deadly influences which may emerge at any time and strike down their victims.* This image was made particularly vivid by the delayed appearance of these symptoms and fatalities—two to four weeks later—in people who had previously seemed to be in perfect health and externally untouched.

The shopkeeper's assistant, whose parents were killed by the bomb, describes his reactions to the death of two additional close family members from these radiation effects, and the general atmosphere of death that prevailed:

My grandmother was taking care of my younger brother on the fourteenth of August when I left; and when I returned on the fifteenth, she had many spots all over her body. Two or three days later she died. . . . My younger brother, who . . . was just a [five-month-old] baby, was without breast milk —so we fed him thin rice gruel. . . . But on the tenth of October he suddenly began to look very ill, though I had not then noticed any spots on his body. . . . Then on the next day he began to look a little better, and I thought he was going to survive. I was very pleased, as he was the only family member I had left, and I took him to a doctor—but on the way to the doctor he died. And at that time we found that there were two large spots on his bottom. . . . I heard it said that all these people would die within three years . . . so I thought, "sooner or later I too will die." . . . I felt very weak and very lonely—with no hope at all . . . and since I had seen so many people's eyebrows falling out, their hair falling out, bleeding from their teeth I found myself always nervously touching my hair like this [he demonstrated by rubbing his head]. . . . I never knew when some sign of the disease would show itself. . . . And living in the countryside then with my relatives, people who came to visit would tell us these things, and then the villagers also talked about them—telling stories of this man or that man who visited us a few days ago, returned to Hiroshima, and died within a week. . . . I couldn't tell whether these stories were true or not, but I believed them then. And I also heard that when the *hibakusha* [explosion-affected persons] came to evacuate to the village where I was, they died there one by one. . . . This loneliness, and the fear. . . . The physical fear . . . has been with me always. . . . It is not something temporary . . . I still have it now. . . .

The writer-manufacturer who expressed his willingness to have died in his daughter's place describes the impact upon him of her sudden illness and death:

My daughter was working with her classmates at a place a thousand meters from the hypocenter. . . . I was able to meet her the next day at a friend's house. She had no burns and only minor external wounds, so I took her with me to my country house. She was quite all right for a while but on the fourth of September she suddenly became sick. . . . The symptoms of her disease were different from those of a normal disease. . . . She had spots all over her body. . . . Her hair began to fall out. She vomited small clumps of blood many times. Finally she began to bleed all over her mouth. And at times her fever was very high. I felt this was a very strange and horrible disease. . . . We didn't know what it was. I thought it was a kind of epidemic—something like cholera. So I told the rest of my family not to touch her and to disinfect all utensils and everything she used. . . . We were all afraid of it, and even the doctor didn't know what it was. . . . After ten days of agony and torture she died on September fourteenth. . . . I thought it was very cruel that my daughter, who had nothing to do with the war, had to be killed in this way. . . .

Survivors were thus affected not only by the fact of people dying around them but by the way in which they died: a gruesome form of rapid bodily deterioration which seemed unrelated to more usual and "decent" forms of death.

For many, these deaths had an eerie quality, as suggested by the electrician on the basis of his vigil at the railroad station:

Those sick people . . . from their outward appearance, didn't seem to be in pain. Only they couldn't move, and even as we watched them they seemed to become faint. . . . But their minds were quite clear . . . not like people who had severe burns or shock or other injuries. . . . There was one man who asked me for help and everything he said was clear and normal. . . . He even told me how somebody robbed him of his wristwatch . . . but in another three hours or so when I looked at him he was already dead. . . . And even those who looked as though they would be spared were not spared. . . . People seemed to inhale something from the air which we could not see. . . . The way they died was different . . . and strange.

Nor did naming the illness lessen this terror. Rather, as a Buddhist priest explains, the name itself became a symbol of the mysterious and deadly force before which all were helpless:

We heard the new phrase, "A-bomb disease." The fear in us became strong, especially when we would see certain things with our eyes: a man looking perfectly well as he rode by on a bicycle one morning, suddenly vomiting blood, and then dying. . . . Soon we were all worried about our health, about our own bodies—whether we would live or die. And we heard that if someone did get sick, there was no treatment that could help. We had nothing to rely on, there was nothing to hold us up. . . .

The *hibakusha*'s urge to protect himself from the "epidemic" and from its dead victims was revealed in attitudes toward corpses, as recalled by the professional cremator:

Some people were very happy to leave dead bodies here because the bodies had such a terrible smell. Therefore they were . . . not sorrowful, but rather pleased that the bodies would be disposed of in this way. There was no medicine at the time, and families found it [care for the moribund] extremely difficult —and were often pleased that people who had suffered so badly finally died. . . .

Those who were afflicted with radiation effects could have a similar sense of grotesque contamination in relationship to their own bodies— as the same man also reveals:

I was all right for three days . . . but then I became sick with fever and bloody diarrhea. . . . After a few days I vomited blood also. . . . There was a very bad burn on my hand, and when I put my hand in water something strange and bluish came out of it, like smoke. After that my body swelled up and worms crawled on the outside of my body. . . .

Even after recovery from these symptoms, such people could retain a feeling that their bodily function has been mysteriously and permanently altered—as was true of a female poet exposed originally at fifteen hundred meters:

Although it was not the proper time, I had my menses right after that. Also diarrhea. Then my hair began to fall out and I had spots all over my body. . . . I have never recovered. . . .

DISCUSSION QUESTIONS
SUGGESTIONS FOR WRITING

1. Death in Life *is a fairly unique example of a researcher's thorough use of interviews and diary material (both written and oral) in an attempt to reconstruct and understand the emotional impact and psychological consequences of a major historical event. What conclusions are formulated on the basis of material presented in this section of* Death in Life?

2. Note the method of presentation of evidence, the recurrent use of testimonials from survivors of the bombing of Hiroshima, from which the author draws his conclusions. What techniques of persuasion might be used to refute evidence presented in the form of testimonials?

3. How would you describe the overall tone of this piece: factual, sentimental, grim, sensationalistic, embittered?

4. What emotional states or other characteristics do the survivors have in common which can be demonstrated from their comments? How does the general tone of these comments differ from that of the author?

PITTSBURGH
STUDY GROUP

REPORT ON
THE FEDERAL
CIVIL DEFENSE
BOOKLET

THE PITTSBURGH
STUDY GROUP
for Nuclear Information is
a group of scientists in the
Pittsburgh area associ-
ated with the Federation
of American Scientists.
The following report was
issued in order to point
out "certain grave de-
fects" in a booklet issued
for public consumption by
the office of Civil Defense.

THE booklet being considered (*Fallout Protection—What to Know and Do About Nuclear Attack*) can be judged on two bases, the result-ing estimates being almost directly opposed. Assuming the title of the book to represent its contents, and noting that the Secretary of Defense considers the booklet gives the American people "the facts they need to know about the dangers of a thermonuclear attack, and what they can do to protect themselves," the contents are entirely inadequate. A thoughtful reading, however, shows that on the limited subject of fallout—and on this subject alone—considerable information is given.

In the judgment of this Study Group, the major criticism of the Civil Defense report is that the substance of the report does not satisfy the large expectation fostered by the title and the foreword. An un-critical reader might even mistake the data and advice of the govern-ment booklet for a comprehensive account of a nuclear attack and the actions to be taken for survival. This would be a catastrophic mistake.

Following are the basic unstated assumptions made in preparing the government booklet:

1. That there will be large and densely populated areas com-pletely unaffected except by fallout;
2. That only in a few densely populated areas will protection against blast and fire be needed;
3. That only a few areas exist that will be both exposed to fallout and seriously dependent for essential services (water, electricity, gas, communications, etc.) on adjacent areas, which may be exposed to an even heavier dosage of blast and fire.

Of these three, the first assumption probably holds true for certain types of nuclear attack. The other two assumptions are probably false. Thus the booklet directly serves only that part of the U.S. population exposed to fallout alone. Other areas of the country, both those directly exposed to blast and fire and those areas seriously dependent upon them, are simply to be written off, together with all the people who dwell in the target-areas. Those people affected only by fallout, providing, by luck and caution, they survive the initial precarious situation, can increase their chance of survival if they follow the instructions and advice given.

To this Study Group, it is clear that the Civil Defense Office must go much further before it can claim to present to the public an outline of the problems posed by nuclear attack, and proposed steps of control. Key subjects that require fuller discussion are:

1. Nature and scope of possible attacks with descriptions of resultant devastation; presentation of the overall problem;
2. Outline of long-term survival and recovery problems, indicating lines of responsibility during recovery period;
3. Description of protective measures to be taken by all persons in blast and fire areas. (This subject has been entirely omitted from the booklet.)

Some well informed citizens may be aware of the above aspects of the problem, and of plans being formulated to cover them, but the general public is uninformed.

The government booklet — a so-called "definitive word" on fallout protection and on protection from thermonuclear war — reduces thermonuclear war to the dropping of one 5-megaton bomb. This does not provide a basis for intelligent public debate on a broad civil defense program. Since the booklet might be taken as a general information source for a public debate on civil defense programs, it should be recognized that the government's statement suffers from certain grave defects mentioned above: it does not present an integrated picture of the hazards facing the individual, his community, or the nation as a whole. The booklet, whose release coincided with a local shelter building program (entailing matching Federal funds) and with the concurrent identification and marking of suitable shelter space, assumes the acceptance of a national policy on shelters and civil defense. It is not the intention of this report to weigh the merits of such a policy, but to point out the role this booklet might be expected to play if used in any such public debate.

In sum, the findings of this Study Group are that the government booklet lacks sufficient scope to be used as a basis for sound planning or responsible decisions by local governments, school boards, civic groups, or private citizens. Detailed comments on the factual content, found in the appendix, document these conclusions.

APPENDIX:
Detailed Comments

P. 5 2nd para. Casualties. The booklet states: "In a major attack... millions of people would be killed." The facts are that in a major attack aimed in part at our metropolitan areas (where over half of the population of the United States lives) the casualties would be in the *tens* of millions.

Pp. 7 and 8. Weapon Size. Under "Some Basic Facts" the effects of a 5-megaton weapon are given. In 1959, 10-megaton weapons were taken to be within the delivery capability of the Russians in a possible attack. In late 1961, weapons of capacities in the range of 50 to 100 megatons have been exploded. In view of these continuing improvements in weapons as well as those in the delivery systems (missiles, submarines) it is to be expected that weapons with capacities much greater than 5 megatons can now be delivered by the enemy. No information relating the variation of the areas of destruction to weapon size is given. It is a risky bit of war gamesmanship, in view of the large thrust of Russian ICBM's to conclude that an attack against a city would not be made with either a single very large yield warhead or a warhead which splits up into a number of 5-megaton weapons landing in an overlapping destructive pattern.

P. 7. Effects of a 5-Megaton Burst. The booklet states that "Most buildings (would be destroyed) two miles from the point of the explosion. . . . The destruction five miles away would be much less severe, but fires and early fallout could be a significant hazard." This quote is very misleading since the average homeowner might assume that at five miles he has a chance of saving his home if he fights the fires. Actually, at this distance brick veneer and frame houses are demolished. (See Nevada tests in "Effects of Nuclear Weapons" for pictures.)

P. 9. Fire Storms. In a metropolitan area one of the gravest dangers that can result from the millions of initial ignitions and ensuing primary fires is that they will link up into a major conflagration or firestorm. Therefore it is not meaningful to say that "primary fires are a much greater hazard than firestorms." Here the truth will not be known until after the event. Obviously, if primary fires can't or don't link up with others to produce the storm, then the primary fire will be the more dangerous. A point which could be made, but has been omitted, is the value of "good housekeeping," on a community basis, to rid the target areas of easily flammable materials, thus reducing the firestorm area. This would include painting with light colored paint exposed wooden surfaces and speeding up of slum clearance projects. Deliberate attempts to construct "firebreaks" would probably be less valuable since the firestorms resulting from megaton weapons are so large in extent that ordinary firebreaks would be bridged by firebrands hurled by the high velocity winds associated with the "storm."

P. 10. Exposure to Radiation. The layman's knowledge on the subject of radiation is woefully inadequate. This section does not really inform. Also it does not distinguish between injection of radioactive material which is less dangerous to the older segments of the population and the exposure to external radiation sources which a younger person can resist more successfully than an older one since his ability to repair damaged tissue is so much greater. Also pertinent to the effects of radiation is the reduced ability to handle normally occurring infections following radiation exposure. Thus the complications following a minor cold could be fatal.

Pp. 9 and 13. Ignition of Fires, a Contradiction. This book shows evidence of hasty assembly by such essentially contradictory impressions it makes with the statement on one hand that at 10 miles from a 5-megaton blast "fires would probably not be started by the fireball" (p. 9) while on the other hand "heat rays . . . may start fires beyond 10 miles" (p. 13).

P. 12. Evacuation vs. Shelter. It is not informative to say ". . . it may be necessary to move people out of severely damaged areas after an attack" without suggesting how they would be moved, who would move them, and where they would be moved to.

P. 15. Community Shelter. The change in emphasis by the government from individual to community shelters is not being questioned here. But there are some obvious dangers associated with community shelters, such as the spread of contagious disease under conditions of subnormal sanitation. The minimum shelter space per person required for extended periods of time (two weeks to one month) may be a critical factor as well.

P. 18. City Buildings. Above ground shelter in "tall apartment or office buildings 10 miles from (a 5-megaton burst) could be one of the safest refuges" provided that the atmosphere is hazy enough to absorb some of the heat radiation. Otherwise, on a clear day the instantaneous ignitions of light combustibles (such as curtains) followed by the breaking of windows in the following blast wave could turn some of these buildings into fire traps. A major criticism of this booklet is that it concentrated on fallout to the exclusion of other types of dangers. Within reasonable limits, if a space is to be used as a fallout shelter it must be prepared in advance. This means taking precaution against conflagrations due to the presence of light combustibles. The dangers associated with using large buildings as shelter space should not be brushed aside.

P. 20. Family Shelters. Although in rural areas, far from blast and fire effects, any one of the shelters shown on these pages provides similar protection, the large segment of the population living on the fringes of the metropolitan areas should at least be advised of the relative merits of various shelter designs for blast and fire protection. For example, a more deeply buried corrugated pipe shelter such as is shown on p. 22 provides substantial blast and fire protection, while the basement shelters are useless in the event the houses above them catch fire.

P. 22. Family Shelters—Duration of Stay. The implication is that two weeks is the maximum time for the radiation intensity to fall to safe levels. This is misleading. If high levels of fallout occur, one has to be prepared to stay in a shelter until help comes, food or water is exhausted, or a greater danger than the unknown level of radiation presents itself. The value of a shelter is that it decreases the radiation exposure. Whether the decrease is enough will depend on the individual's luck—on conditions beyond his control.

P. 24. Plan vs. Time. These two sections are poorly written since the sequence of instructions should always involve fighting the primary ignitions before seeking cover in a fallout shelter. Thus, whether there is a blast and you seek momentary cover, or you have time to remove combustibles before the blast is due, *after* the blast wave and heat pulse passes, you must fight primary ignitions (no fire department has sufficient personnel to cope with the numerous primary fires) to prevent linkup of these many fires into a firestorm. After this is done you can seek long-term shelter.

P. 38. First Steps Toward Recovery. The illustration, showing a near-idyllic scene involving decontamination, without a sign of damage to the area, is a poor representation of the following text, which reads: "the world and your community would be shattered by a nuclear war." This is an example of oversimplification by treating each problem as though it were the only one. Such will not be the case, and whole communities are likely to find themselves without the manpower, the tools and the knowledge to begin the first steps toward recovery to the extent that physical strength has been destroyed by radiation and disease, machinery, tools and power have been lost to fire and blast, and the professional groups have been decimated or entirely wiped out. *P. 43. Civilian Defense Program.* The booklet admits its preoccupation is with fallout protection; therefore, one must conclude that a major fraction of the population—those people living in or near metropolitan areas—has been badly neglected. We must await some careful, reasoned presentations of protection and survival measures against blast and fire effects.

DISCUSSION QUESTIONS
SUGGESTIONS FOR WRITING

1. The critical essay involves a rigorous investigation of a problem or proposition in a closely reasoned and methodically developed structure, in which evidence is presented in the form of reference to authority, statistical or empirical data, quotation from the source under investigation, etc., to substantiate whatever claims are made. What forms of evidence are used in this selection to substantiate alleged inadequacies in the "Federal Civil Defense Booklet"?

2. The writer of the critical essay is more concerned with presenting convincing evidence than with supplying entertaining or dramatic illustrations. The selection and arrangement of details is made on the basis of pertinence rather than interest. Are the subject or problem and thesis explicitly stated?

3. Is the argument presented in a step-by-step arrangement?

4. Does the conclusion, summary, or commentary on the results follow logically from the argument?

JOHN HERSEY
(b. 1914) was a journalist
and war correspondent
before he won the Pulitzer
Prize for his first novel, *A
Bell for Adano,* in 1945.
Since then, he has written
numerous novels and non-
fiction works. He is cur-
rently Master of Pierson
College at Yale. *Hiroshima*
is a classic dramatization
of nuclear devastation
and accompanying hu-
man agony.

A NOISELESS FLASH

THE Reverend Mr. Tanimoto got up at five o'clock that morning. He was alone in the parsonage, because for some time his wife had been commuting with their year-old baby to spend nights with a friend in Ushida, a suburb to the north. Of all the important cities of Japan, only two, Kyoto and Hiroshima, had not been visited in strength by *B-san,* or Mr. B, as the Japanese, with a mixture of respect and unhappy familiarity, called the B-29; and Mr. Tanimoto, like all his neighbors and friends, was almost sick with anxiety. He had heard uncomfortably detailed accounts of mass raids on Kure, Iwakuni, Tokuyama, and other nearby towns; he was sure Hiroshima's turn would come soon. He had slept badly the night before, because there had been several air-raid warnings. Hiroshima had been getting such warnings almost every night for weeks, for at the time the B-29s were using Lake Biwa, northeast of Hiroshima, as a rendezvous point, and no matter what city the Americans planned to hit, the Superfortresses streamed in over the coast near Hiroshima. The frequency of the warnings and the continued abstinence of Mr. B with respect to Hiroshima had made its citizens jittery; a rumor was going around that the Americans were saving something special for the city.

Mr. Tanimoto is a small man, quick to talk, laugh, and cry. He wears his black hair parted in the middle and rather long; the prominence of the frontal bones just above his eyebrows and the smallness of his mustache, mouth, and chin give him a strange, old-young look, boyish and yet wise, weak and yet fiery. He moves nervously and fast, but with a restraint which suggests that he is a cautious, thoughtful man. He showed, indeed, just those qualities in the uneasy days before the bomb fell. Besides having his wife spend the nights in Ushida, Mr. Tanimoto had been carrying all the portable things from his church, in the close-packed residential district called Nagaragawa, to a house that belonged to a rayon manufacturer in Koi, two miles from the center of town. The rayon man, a Mr. Matsui, had opened his then unoccupied estate to a large number of his friends and acquaintances, so that they might evacuate whatever they wished to a safe distance from the probable target area. Mr. Tanimoto had had no difficulty in moving chairs, hymnals, Bibles, altar gear, and church records by pushcart himself, but the organ console and an upright piano required some aid. A friend of his named Matsuo had, the day before, helped him get the piano out to Koi; in return, he had promised this day to assist Mr. Matsuo in hauling out a daughter's belongings. That is why he had risen so early.

Mr. Tanimoto cooked his own breakfast. He felt awfully tired. The effort of moving the piano the day before, a sleepless night, weeks of worry and unbalanced diet, the cares of his parish—all combined to make him feel hardly adequate to the new day's work. There was another thing, too: Mr. Tanimoto had studied theology at Emory University, in Atlanta, Georgia; he had graduated in 1940; he spoke excellent English; he dressed in American clothes; he had corresponded with many American friends right up to the time the war began; and among a people obsessed with a fear of being spied upon—perhaps almost obsessed himself—he found himself growing increasingly uneasy. The police had questioned him several times, and just a few days before, he had heard that an influential acquaintance, a Mr. Tanaka, a retired officer of the Toyo Kisen Kaisha steamship line, an anti-Christian, a man famous in Hiroshima for his showy philanthropies and notorious for his personal tyrannies, had been telling people that Tanimoto should not be trusted. In compensation, to show himself publicly a good Japanese, Mr. Tanimoto had taken on the chairmanship of his local *tonarigumi*, or Neighborhood Association, and to his other duties and concerns this position had added the business of organizing air-raid defense for about twenty families.

Before six o'clock that morning, Mr. Tanimoto started for Mr. Matsuo's house. There he found that their burden was to be a *tansu*, a large Japanese cabinet, full of clothing and household goods. The two men set out. The morning was perfectly clear and so warm that the day promised to be uncomfortable. A few minutes after they started, the air-raid siren went off—a minute-long blast that warned of approaching planes but indicated to the people of Hiroshima only a slight degree of danger, since it sounded every morning at this time, when an American weather plane came over. The two men pulled and pushed the handcart through the city streets. Hiroshima was a fan-shaped city, lying mostly on the six islands formed by the seven estuarial rivers that branch out from the Ota River; its main commercial and residential districts, covering about four square miles in the center of the city, contained three-quarters of its population, which had been reduced by several evacuation programs from a wartime peak of 380,000 to about 245,000. Factories and other residential districts, or suburbs, lay compactly around the edges of the city. To the south were the docks, an airport, and the island-studded Inland Sea. A rim of mountains runs around the other three sides of the delta. Mr. Tanimoto and Mr. Matsuo took their way through the shopping center, already full of people, and across two of the rivers to the sloping streets of Koi, and up them to the outskirts and foothills. As they started up a valley away from the tight-ranked houses, the all-clear sounded. (The Japanese radar operators, detecting only three planes, supposed that they comprised a reconnaissance.) Pushing the handcart up to the rayon man's house was tiring, and the men, after they had maneuvered their load into the driveway and to the front steps, paused to rest awhile. They stood with a wing of the house between them and the city. Like most homes in this part of Japan, the house consisted of a wooden frame and wooden walls supporting a heavy tile roof. Its front hall, packed with rolls of bedding and clothing, looked like a cool cave full of fat cushions. Opposite the house, to the right of the front door, there was a large, finicky rock garden. There was no sound of planes. The morning was still; the place was cool and pleasant.

Then a tremendous flash of light cut across the sky. Mr. Tanimoto has a distinct recollection that it travelled from east to west, from the city toward the hills. It seemed a sheet of sun. Both he and Mr. Matsuo reacted in terror—and both had time to react (for they were 3,500 yards, or two miles, from the center of the explosion). Mr. Matsuo dashed up the front steps into the house and dived among the bedrolls and buried himself there. Mr. Tanimoto took four or five steps and threw himself between two big rocks in the garden. He bellied up very hard against one of them. As his face was against the stone, he did not see what happened. He felt a sudden pressure, and then splinters and pieces of board and fragments of tile fell on him. He heard no roar. (Almost no one in Hiroshima recalls hearing any noise of the bomb. But a fisherman in his sampan on the Inland Sea near Tsuzu, the man with whom Mr. Tanimoto's mother-in-law and sister-in-law were living, saw the flash and heard a tremendous explosion; he was nearly twenty miles from Hiroshima, but the thunder was greater than when the B-29s hit Iwakuni, only five miles away.)

When he dared, Mr. Tanimoto raised his head and saw that the rayon man's house had collapsed. He thought a bomb had fallen directly on it. Such clouds of dust had risen that there was a sort of twilight around. In panic, not thinking for the moment of Mr. Matsuo under the ruins, he dashed out into the street. He noticed as he ran that the concrete wall of the estate had fallen over—toward the house rather than away from it. In the street, the first thing he saw was a squad of soldiers who had been burrowing into the hillside opposite, making one of the thousands of dugouts in which the Japanese apparently intended to resist invasion, hill by hill, life for life; the soldiers were coming out of the hole, where they should have been safe, and blood was running from their heads, chests, and backs. They were silent and dazed.

Under what seemed to be a local dust cloud, the day grew darker and darker.

DISCUSSION QUESTIONS
SUGGESTIONS FOR WRITING

1. Describe what happens to the Reverend Mr. Tanimoto. Is he a sympathetic character? Why?

2. What details of the selection lead one to believe that it is a nonfiction or eyewitness account of the bombing of Hiroshima?

3. Strictly speaking, since the events are dramatized from the point of view of Mr. Tanimoto, rather than from the author's, wouldn't the piece have to be classified as "fiction"? Under what circumstances might it be called nonfiction, in spite of the fact that it is dramatized from Mr. Tanimoto's point of view?

4. Is nuclear catastrophe inevitable?

PART TWO

INTRODUCTION

CLEARLY, our immense technological advances, in themselves, have been in many ways of considerable benefit to modern man. On the other hand, the misuses of technology, the overexploitation of resources, and the massive contamination of the environment threaten to make life intolerable and the planet uninhabitable. In addition to gross misuse, there are other sources of danger arising from rapid technological expansion. There is evidence that unforeseen influences, even of the seemingly positive aspects of technological growth, may be causing radical changes that are potentially dangerous because we fail to understand their effects and consequences. This is true of both those elements of technological progress already impinging upon our lives and of the even more portentous things that face us as technological breakthroughs continue to multiply, producing tremendous new possibilities for controlling our lives. As we are confronted by more rapidly changing concepts of what man is and what he should be, we will surely face new moral crises. The next three subject areas provide material for an exploration of the nature and implications of some of these problems.

*　　*　　*

The imminent ecological catastrophe is perhaps the most obvious example of the misuse of technology through myriad acts of thoughtlessness or ignorance. Deleterious practices which were begun in ignorance of potential ecological damage have in too many cases, and in spite of greater knowledge, been continued through wanton carelessness or deliberate selfishness. Damage is inflicted upon the world through the race to exploit techniques for the sake of a quick return—an ancient enough problem but now translated to earthshaking magnitude by the accelerating growth of science and technology and by the increasing strain, in every sector, of population proliferation. Pollution is rampant; the cities are festering and dying from within; we are breeding ourselves off the planet; and the catalogue of human follies goes on and on. But the ecological scenario is even more paradoxical.

An additional irony, as Barry Commoner points out in *Science and Survival,* is that each of our major pollution problems springs from some *useful* technological innovation. "The burning of fuel by internal-combustion engines is an enormously valuable source of energy—but also pollutes the air. New synthetic chemicals, the fruits of remarkable advances in chemical technology since World War II, appear in a multitude of useful forms—but also as new pollutants of air and water. The development . . . of self-sustained nuclear reactions has given us not only new weapons and new sources of power, but unprecedented radioactive debris as well."

The problem of personal or corporate greed may be simple enough to understand, if not to remedy. The problem of deciding which power sources or technological miracles to cut back on may be more tangled yet, especially since many of the luxuries made possible by such technology are already taken for granted by large sections of the population. Is being able to use your electric can opener *worth* the minute quantity of air pollution caused by the extra coal burned at the power plant in order to generate the electricity for the can opener? Maybe so. Are all the can openers in the world—or electric coffee makers, electric carving knives, and air conditioners—worth dying of lung cancer for or worth a new ice age? Probably not. But we can never really be sure, in many such instances, which sort of question we are asking. Who knows exactly how much the earth will take before nature goes berserk? Who knows how much we can or will or want to take? One thing is certain—when the populace is ignorant or indecisive about such matters, "larger" interests begin to make the important choices about the quality of life—and frequently with the wrong set of priorities.

*   *   *

If we are to believe Marshall McLuhan, the unforeseen and still unseen influences of the electronic revolution—telegraph, radio, telephone, films, television, computers—have not only changed us drastically and made us blind and numb to the drastic change so that we fail to recognize it, but these influences also account for any number of puzzling contemporary phenomena. All technological innovations, according to McLuhan, are extensions of human abilities and senses and are apt to cause marked changes in man's sensory balances, and these sensory alterations have important effects in reshaping the society that created the technology. According to McLuhan, early, or tribal, man functioned with balanced senses, perceiving the world about equally through touch, hearing, smell, sight, and taste. But with the invention of the phonetic alphabet, the eye, the sense of sight, became more dominant, and the other senses were deemphasized. The invention of movable type in the fifteenth century further accelerated and exaggerated this process.

Electronic media, on the other hand, restore the sensory balance, according to McLuhan, because they do not emphasize the eye at the expense of the other senses. So, with the invention of the telegraph in 1844, a new era of sensory changes was ushered in, an electronics revolution that McLuhan believes will tend to re-tribalize man.

A further implication is that the electronic media are actually replacing the technology of print, and that eventually the technology of the phonetic alphabet—books, reading, writing—will be obsolete, along with the way of life of the people who employed this particular technology. The beginnings of this process may already be evident. As McLuhan noted in a *Playboy* interview, "The generation gap is actually a chasm, separating not two age groups but two vastly divergent cultures."

The widespread use of drugs by the youth counterculture is one of many phenomena that McLuhan attempts to encompass under his ideological umbrella. The use of drugs, McLuhan believes, is related to the re-tribalization process the youth culture is undergoing: "LSD . . . releases a person from acquired verbal and visual habits and reactions, and gives the potential of instant and total involvement, both all-at-onceness and all-at-oneness, which are the basic needs of people translated by electric extensions of their central nervous systems out of the old rational, sequential value system." McLuhan further characterizes the clash of cultures: "The young will continue turning on no matter how many of them are turned off into prisons. Such legal restrictions only reflect the cultural revenge of a dying culture against its successor."

Reactions to McLuhan's ideas have ranged from Tom Wolfe's non-committal "What if he is *right?* Suppose he *is* what he sounds like—the most important thinker since Newton, Darwin, Freud, Einstein, and Pavlov?" to Benjamin DeMott's "He's swinging, switched on, with it and NOW. And wrong."

Other important considerations for this area, either related to or separate from McLuhan's thought, might be: some attention to the *content* of electronic media—for example, the dangers of thought control through information manipulation; the need for responsible reporting; some exploration of the effect, say, of television violence, especially on young viewers. Some discussion might also be given, perhaps, to the nature of technological warfare, where distancing from "the enemy" makes possible unusual atrocities, or to an exploration of the implications of computers for contemporary man.

*   *   *

Another contemporary revolution that promises to cause radical change and social upheaval is that which awaits us as the result of developments in the biological sciences. According to Gordon Rattray Taylor, improvements in our understanding of answers to the following questions are largely responsible for this outlook: How did life originate? What accounts for the variety of life-forms? How do living creatures replace themselves? How do living creatures grow and develop? How do living creatures function: what biochemical mechanisms do they depend upon? How is the behavior of living creatures controlled? What is the nature of aging and the cause of natural death?

Man's increasing capacity to "successfully" interfere with natural processes such as conception, birth, growth, aging, etc., is the source of this anticipation in the biological sciences. In addition to numerous threatening prospects for interference with the reproductive process—with unforeseeable consequences for marriage and the family as we know it—gerontologists predict heartening advances in both an extension of the life-span and the preservation of youthful vigor into old age. Neurologists and other specialists exploring the brain foresee raising the level of intelligence, improvement of memory, and control of moods and feelings. Organ transplantation and various cosmetic "improvements" (such as those caused by silicone injections) have already brought up new moral issues.

In this area, as in the others mentioned here, science and technology may obviously be used for good or for ill, recklessly or well. We may soon find out how—or if—we will be able to come to terms with old vices and new demands to secure some sort of livable niche on the earth. During this period it may be well to remember that the history of this planet is *littered* with extinct species. The dinosaurs, to name one, creatures often made fun of for their clumsiness and alleged stupidity, endured for 140 million years. In anything resembling our present *Homo sapiens* form, we have yet to last much over one million.

IV

Ecological Catastrophe

COMMONER

BARRY COMMONER
(b. 1914), biologist, ecologist, and educator, is one
of the best-informed and
most articulate spokesmen
for preserving the natural
environment from overindustrialism and overpopulation. In the following selection, he considers the
wide range of ecological
problems and how such
problems developed.

SORCERER'S APPRENTICE

WE are surrounded by the technological successes of science: space vehicles, nuclear power, new synthetic chemicals, medical advances that increase the length and usefulness of human life. But we also see some sharp contrasts. While one group of scientists studies ways to provide air for the first human visitors to the moon, another tries to learn why we are fouling the air that the rest of us must breathe on earth. We hear of masterful schemes for using nuclear explosions to extract pure water from the moon; but in some American cities the water that flows from the tap is undrinkable and the householder must buy drinking water in bottles. Science is triumphant with far-ranging success, but its triumph is somehow clouded by growing difficulties in providing for the simple necessities of human life on the earth.

OUR POLLUTED ENVIRONMENT

For about a million years human beings have survived and proliferated on the earth by fitting unobtrusively into a life-sustaining environment, joining a vast community in which animals, plants, microorganisms, soil, water, and air are tied together in an elaborate network of mutual relationships. In the preindustrial world the environment appeared to hold an unlimited store of clean air and water. It seemed reasonable, as the need arose, to vent smoke into the sky and sewage into rivers in the expectation that the huge reserves of uncontaminated air and water would effectively dilute and degrade the pollutants — perhaps in the same optimistic spirit that leads us to embed slotted boxes in bathroom walls to receive razor blades. But there is simply not enough air and water on the earth to absorb current man-made wastes without effect. We have begun to merit the truculent complaint against the works of the paleface voiced by Chief Satinpenny in Nathanael West's *A Cool Million:* "Now even the Grand Canyon will no longer hold razor blades."

Fire, an ancient friend, has become a man-made threat to the environment through the sheer quantity of the waste it produces. Each ton of wood, coal, petroleum, or natural gas burned contributes several tons of carbon dioxide to the earth's atmosphere. Between 1860 and 1960 the combustion of fuels added nearly 14 percent to the carbon-dioxide content of the air, which had until then remained constant for many centuries. Carbon dioxide plays an important role in regulating the temperature of the earth because of the "greenhouse effect." Both glass and carbon dioxide tend to pass visible light but absorb infrared rays. This explains why the sun so easily warms a greenhouse on a winter day. Light from the sun enters through the greenhouse glass. Within, it is absorbed by soil and plants and converted to infrared heat energy which remains trapped inside the greenhouse because it cannot pass out again through the glass. Carbon dioxide makes a huge greenhouse of the earth, allowing sunlight to reach the earth's surface but limiting reradiation of the resulting heat into space. The temperature of the earth — which profoundly affects the suitability of the environment for life — is therefore certain to rise as the amount of carbon dioxide in the air increases.

A report by the President's Science Advisory Committee finds that the extra heat due to fuel-produced carbon dioxide accumulated in the air by the year 2000 might be sufficient to melt the Antarctic ice cap — in 4000 years according to one computation, or in 400 years according to another. And the report states: "The melting of the Antarctic ice cap would raise sea level by 400 feet. If 1,000 years were required to melt the ice cap, the sea level would rise about 4 feet every 10 years, 40 feet per century." This would result in catastrophe for much of the world's inhabited land and many of its major cities.

A more recent energy source — the internal-combustion engine — is polluting the environment much faster than fire. The automobile is only about seventy years old, but in that time it has severely damaged the quality of the air. The air over most large cities carries a large burden of waste automobile fuel. On exposure to sunlight this forms the noxious ingredients of smog, which significantly increases the incidence of respiratory disease. Since tetraethyl lead was introduced in 1923 as an automobile fuel additive, lead has contaminated most of the earth's surface. Increasing amounts of the metal are found in surface ocean waters, in crops, and in human blood, in which in some areas the amount may be approaching toxic levels.

As large a body of water as Lake Erie has already been overwhelmed by pollutants and has, in effect, died. In its natural state, Lake Erie was a balanced system in which water plants, microorganisms, and a great variety of swimming creatures lived together in an intricate harmony. But today most of Lake Erie is dead. Sewage, industrial wastes, and the runoff from heavily fertilized farmlands have loaded the waters of the lake with so much excess phosphate and nitrate as to jar the biology of the lake permanently out of balance. The fish are all but gone. According to a recent report by a committee of the National Academy of Sciences, within about twenty years city wastes are expected to overwhelm the biology of most of the nation's waterways.

Small amouts of nitrate are natually present in all bodies of water, and living things can tolerate — and often require — nitrate at these low levels. Now, however, nitrate originating in the outflow waters of sewage-treatment plants and in the runoff from land treated with chemical fertilizers has begun to build up excessively in ground water in thirty-eight regions of the United States, according to a recent Geological Survey report. Excess nitrate is poisonous to man and animals. About 8 to 9 parts per million of nitrate in drinking water causes a serious respiratory difficulty in infants — cyanosis — by interfering with hemoglobin function. For domestic animals 5 parts per million is considered unsafe. Some wells in the United States already have more than 3 parts per million of nitrate, and the contamination levels will go up with increased use of fertilizers and the growing density of population.

Added to the growing volume of the more familiar wastes are numerous new pollutants, produced through the ingenuity of modern physics and chemistry: radioactive elements, detergents, pesticides, weed killers, and a variety of industrial wastes. The greatest single source of contamination of the planet is now the radioactivity from test explosions of nuclear weapons in the atmosphere. Fallout from nuclear tests contaminates every part of the earth's surface and all of its inhabitants. Strontium-90, one of the radioactive constituents of fallout, is being built into the bones of every living person and will be carried in the bodies of several future generations. The fallout problem can tell us a good deal about the connection between modern science and the hazards of life on the earth.

Contamination of the earth's surface with fallout originates in the scientific revolution set off fifty years ago by far-reaching discoveries in atomic physics. By 1940 it was apparent that the new knowledge of atomic structure could lead to technological processes of vast power and scope. That these potentialities were so rapidly realized reflects the force of military demands. Faced with the grim dangers of war with Nazi Germany, the governments of the United States and Great Britain undertook the monumental task of translating what was until then an esoteric laboratory experiment — nuclear fission — into the awesome reality of the nuclear bomb. The bomb was created by the magnificent new insights of nuclear physics, driven to success by the determination to apply the full force of modern science to victory in the war.

With later scientific advances, nuclear weapons of increasing explosive power became possible. Propelled by the fears and tension of the cold war, these possibilities were fully exploited by those nations capable of making the necessary economic and technological effort — the United States, the U.S.S.R., Great Britain, and to a lesser extent, France and China. As a result, in 1948 there began a constantly accelerating series of nuclear explosions designed to develop weapons of increasing destructiveness and versatility. The total explosive power released by nuclear-weapon tests between 1948 and 1962 was equivalent to about 500 million tons of TNT — nearly two hundred times the total power of all the bombs dropped on Germany in World War II. The amount of only one fallout component — strontium-90 — released by nuclear tests has introduced into the environment radioactivity equivalent to about 1 billion grams of radium. The significance of this sudden radioactive intrusion can be visualized by comparing it with the world supply of radium before World War II — about 10 grams. Until the advent of nuclear fission these few grams of radium represented the total human experience in handling radioactive substances.

The rapid and unchecked expansion of nuclear weaponry, which now dominates the world's major military programs, testifies to the enormous success of nuclear physics and engineering. There have been no complaints about the power and reliability of nuclear weapons. But official appraisals of the *biological* consequences of nuclear explosions have undergone a drastic change. Contrast statements, only eight years apart, by two American presidents:

President Eisenhower, October 1956: "The continuance of the present rate of H-bomb testing, by the most sober and responsible scientific judgment . . . does not imperil the health of humanity."

President Johnson, October 1964: "This treaty [the nuclear test-ban treaty] has halted the steady, menacing increase of radioactive fallout. The deadly products of atomic explosions were poisoning our soil and our food and the milk our children drank and the air we all breathe. Radioactive deposits were being formed in increasing quantity in the teeth and bones of young Americans. Radioactive poisons were beginning to threaten the safety of people throughout the world. They were a growing menace to the health of every unborn child."

There were, of course, some political reasons for this dramatic reversal in government policy — even President Eisenhower softened his rejection of the nuclear test ban before he left office. But it is now quite clear from available documents that between 1956 and 1963, when the U.S.-Soviet nuclear-test-ban treaty was signed, there were also sharp revisions in our appraisal of the fallout hazard.

Evaluation of this problem calls for a detailed analysis of the passage of radioactive isotopes — for example, strontium-90 — from their creation in the nuclear fireball to their entry into the human body. When formed, strontium-90 and other radioactive elements become attached to tiny dustlike particles. These are shot high into the stratosphere by the explosion and return to earth at a rate which depends on the size of the particle and on the weather. Eventually the fallout is carried to the earth in rain or snow. From that point its fate is determined by the complex biology of soil, plants, domestic animals, and finally man. For example, since strontium-90 is a chemical relative of calcium, it takes a similar biological course. Along with calcium and other minerals, strontium-90 enters grass and crop plants through their roots and from raindrops resting on their leaves. When cows eat the contaminated grass the strontium-90 concentrates in their milk, which is rich in calcium. People absorb strontium-90 from contaminated milk and other foods. Once the amount of fallout absorbed in the body is known, its radiation output can be calculated and the resultant medical risk of radiation-induced cancer or genetic change can be estimated.

OUR FAULTY KNOWLEDGE OF FALLOUT

To understand the biological effects of fallout we must know what happens at each step of this complicated chain of events. There is now a fairly complete published record of this knowledge. This record reveals a number of important errors in our understanding of the problem, which remained uncorrected until the testing of nuclear weapons in the atmosphere was in full swing and fallout had been massively disseminated into the environment.

In 1953, AEC publications asserted that fallout would be evenly distributed over the globe so that no area would receive an excessive amount. In 1958 actual measurements of fallout distribution showed that this idea was wrong. Fallout levels in the North Temperate Zone were found to be more than ten times higher than at the equator or the poles and five times higher than in the South Temperate Zone. Because most of the world's population lives in the North Temperate Zone, the total human exposure to fallout is much greater than the original AEC theory anticipated.

As late as 1957, the official government handbook, *The Effects of Nuclear Weapons*, published jointly by the AEC and the Department of Defense, claimed that fallout would descend from the stratosphere slowly, half of it not reaching the earth until seven years after it was produced. This delay, it was believed, would allow time for the harmless decay of a large proportion of the radioisotopes in fallout while they were still at high altitudes, thus minimizing the ultimate exposure of humans. In 1962 the second edition of this same handbook acknowledged that this estimate was wrong. Most of the stratospheric fallout descends to the earth in a matter of months, depending on the geographic location and the time of the explosion. A considerable amount of hazardous radioactivity remains in fallout when it reaches the earth.

As a result of these errors, early estimates of the amount of fallout that would reach the soil of the United States were far off the mark. In 1956 AEC Commissioner W. F. Libby predicted that nuclear tests carried out through May 1954 would deposit in United States soil a maximum of 7 millicuries of strontium-90 per square mile. But actual measurements by the AEC showed that the average strontium-90 content of U.S. soil had reached about 47 millicuries per square mile in 1958, although the total amount of testing had only about doubled since 1954.

Mistakes were also made in evaluating the path that fallout radioisotopes would take through the food chain to man. In 1953 the AEC stated that the only possible hazard to humans from strontium-90 would arise from "the ingestion of bone splinters which might be intermingled with muscle tissue during butchering and cutting of the meat." No mention was made of the simple biological fact that milk from such an animal would also contain strontium-90. By 1956 the AEC had acknowledged that milk represented the most important source of strontium-90 in human food.

Important mistakes were also made in judging the medical hazards of fallout. For example, the risk of genetic damage from fallout was at first dismissed by a 1953 AEC report with a statement that: "Fallout radioactivity is far below the level which could cause a detectable increase in mutations, or inheritable variations."

By 1957 a report of the AEC Biological and Medical Advisory Committee had concluded that fallout from tests completed to that date would probably result in 2,500 to 13,000 cases of serious genetic defects per year throughout the world population.

One of the major mistakes made in evaluating the fallout hazard was to rely on the *average* values of fallout exposure, for such an average can conceal areas in which special circumstances combine to intensify the danger. For example, in the arctic only slight radiation exposure was expected, because the amount of fallout that reaches the ground at the poles is much less than it is in the temperate parts of the United States. However, Eskimos in the arctic have now been discovered to have amounts of fallout radioactivity in their bodies which are much higher than those found in the inhabitants of temperate regions. The clue to this puzzle was finally found in the special nutrition of lichens — a group of composite organisms, each of which consists of an alga and a fungus living together. Lichens, which have no functional roots and often grow on rocks rather than soil, absorb their mineral nutrition in the form of dust taken directly from the air. Thus natural "fallout" is the lichen's chief source of minerals. Radioactive fallout also reaches lichens from the air, and these plants are not protected by the dilution and discrimination processes which operate when fallout is absorbed through roots. Caribou eat great quantities of lichen and therefore take up excessive amounts of fallout. At the end of the food chain, caribou meat makes up a considerable part of the Eskimos' diet, producing the unexpectedly large amounts of fallout radiation in their bodies. The operation of this special food chain in the arctic upset the expectations based on temperate-zone food chains about the amount of fallout which can find its way into the diet.

In one sense the nuclear test program must be regarded as a remarkable scientific triumph, for it solved very difficult physics and engineering problems. But the biological consequences of the nuclear test program — the vast intrusion of radioactivity into animals, plants, and man — must be regarded as a huge technological mistake. There have been serious oversights and miscalculations. It is now clear that the government agencies responsible for the development of nuclear weapons embarked on this massive program before they understood the full biological effects of what they proposed to do. Great amounts of fallout were disseminated throughout the world before it became known that the resultant medical risks were so great as to require that nuclear testing be halted. The enactment of the test-ban treaty in 1963 is, in part, a confession of this failure of modern science and technology.

DETERGENTS

A different kind of pact — an agreement among the companies that make up the multibillion-dollar United States detergent industry — was needed to correct another big technological mistake. These companies agreed to replace, by July 1, 1965, the main active ingredient which, beginning in the early 1940s, had enabled their products to capture the major share of the cleanser market.

Detergents are chemicals, synthesized from raw materials found in petroleum, which have largely replaced soap in many household and industrial uses. Soap is itself one of the earliest-known useful chemicals. Long ago, it was discovered that fats and oils extracted from animals or pressed from seeds, and cooked with alkali, react chemically to form soap. Soap is a double-headed molecule. Its fatty part readily combines with droplets of greasy dirt, forming a film around them. The other end of the molecule forms the outer layer of the soap-coated dirt particle and has a strong affinity for water. As a result, the whole complex can be washed away.

But soap has certain technical and economic disadvantages. In "hard" water, which has a high mineral content, soap forms a deposit which will not readily wash away. In addition, the raw material, fat, is dependent on agriculture, hence variable in quality, availability, and price.

In the 1930s chemical technology began to produce synthetic organic compounds which closely resemble natural products: synthetic fibers, plastics, and artificial rubber. The inadequacies of soap were an attractive challenge for chemical engineers, who set out to make a synthetic washing agent that might avoid the hard-water problem and be independent of the vagaries of agriculture.

Detergent research began with fatlike molecules — hydrocarbons — which are common in petroleum. Chemists found ways to attach to the hydrocarbon a water-soluble molecular group containing sulfur. The result was a family of substances which, like soap, formed a water-soluble coat around grease particles. But the new detergents were better than soap, since they were equally effective in hard or soft water. Intensive research produced detergents with other useful properties: long shelf life; pleasantness to touch, sight, and smell; gentleness on the hands; economical price. This success illustrates the effectiveness of modern chemical research.

Within a few years after the new detergents were placed on sale, they had won a very large portion of the cleanser market. By 1960 they had replaced soap as the major household and industrial cleanser. A new billion-dollar industry had been created. However, one aspect of this technological triumph received no attention in the research laboratories—the effects of dumping a huge amount of new synthetic substances (about 3.5 billion pounds per year in the United States in 1960) down drains into waste-disposal systems. This lack of interest was perhaps natural, since the purchases of detergents—and the consequent profits—result from their effectiveness as cleansers and not from their behavior in waste systems. Finally it became difficult to ignore this aspect. Mounds of detergent foam appeared in riverways; in some places a glass of water drawn from a tap foamed up a head that would make a brewer envious. Only then was it discovered that, despite their useful similarities to soap, the new detergents differed from the natural product in one important way. When soap enters waste-disposal systems, it is readily broken down by bacteria, but the detergents are not. They pass through the waste system unchanged, appearing in the runoff water that drains into rivers, streams, and underground waters. Water supplies taken from these sources therefore contain detergents.

Now, for the first time, industrial chemists were forced to investigate another aspect of detergent chemistry: Why do detergents resist natural degradation? The difficulty was found to arise from the structure of the hydrocarbon skeleton of their molecules. Hydrocarbon molecules consist of a chain of carbon atoms, to each of which are attached two or three hydrogen atoms. The troublesome detergents had branched chains, and it was discovered that the bacterial enzymes which readily break up natural unbranched hydrocarbons in sewage plants are unable to degrade the synthetic branched hydrocarbons.

By the 1960s, water contamination had become bad enough to stimulate legislative action—and, simultaneously, the needed research. Resulting knowledge of the basic cause of the difficulty suggested a possible remedy. Methods were developed for producing degradable detergents from the unbranched hydrocarbon molecules that are also found in petroleum. The industry agreed to replace the branched-molecule detergents with branchless ones by July 1, 1965.

This solves part of the problem. In the large well-aerated sewage systems of most urban communities the new detergents are destroyed by bacteria. However, they do not break down as readily in underground unaerated systems, such as septic tanks. About 34 percent of the homes in the United States are equipped with septic systems. Since half of these also obtain water from their own wells, even the new "degradable" detergents may cause trouble. Moreover, when they are degraded the new synthetic detergents may overload surface waters with phosphate, leading to serious upsets in biological balance, such as the disaster which has already overtaken Lake Erie.

Thus, long after synthetic detergents had become a common household item, they were found to cause an intolerable nuisance in water supplies. There is no way to gloss over this episode. It represents a failure on the part of modern chemical technology to predict a vital consequence of a massive intervention into nature.

INSECTICIDES

My final example is one from personal experience. During World War II, I served as project officer in the Navy's development of aircraft dispersal of DDT, which proved to be of great importance in the Pacific island battles by protecting the first wave of attackers from serious insect-borne diseases. The project required meticulous studies of aerosol production, aerodynamic distribution of insecticide droplets, insect kill, meteorological effects, and the problems of flying tactics. Toward the end of our work, when the system was ready for fleet operations, we received a request for help from an experimental rocket station on a strip of island beach off the New Jersey coast. Flies were so numerous on the beach that important military developments were being held up. We sprayed the island and, inevitably, some of the surrounding waters with DDT. Within a few hours the flies were dead, and the rocketeers went about their work with renewed vigor. But a week later they were on the telephone again. A mysterious epidemic had littered the beach with tons of decaying fish—which had attracted vast swarms of flies from the mainland. This is how we learned that DDT kills fish.

Such unexpected twists are often encountered when new synthetic substances are thrust into the complex community of life: a wholly unanticipated development wipes out their original usefulness, or sometimes creates a problem worse than the original one. In one Bolivian town, DDT sprayed to control malarial mosquitoes also killed most of the local cats. With the cats gone, the village was invaded by a wild, mouselike animal that carried black typhus. Before new cats were brought to restore the balance, several hundred villagers were killed by the disease.

THE SCIENTIFIC BACKGROUND
OF TECHNOLOGICAL FAILURES

These problems have a common scientific background. Each of them springs from a useful technological innovation. The burning of fuel by internal-combustion engines is an enormously valuable source of energy —but also pollutes the air. New synthetic chemicals, the fruits of remarkable advances in chemical technology since World War II, appear in a multitude of useful forms—but also as new pollutants of air and water. The development, about twenty-five years ago, of self-sustained nuclear reactions has given us not only new weapons and new sources of power, but unprecedented radioactive debris as well.

Most of these problems seem to crop up unexpectedly. The sunlight-induced chemical conversion of airborne hydrocarbons (such as gasoline vapor) into smog was discovered, not in a chemical laboratory but in the air over Los Angeles, long after the chief mode for disseminating these hydrocarbons—the superhighway—was well entrenched in the urban economy. The full significance of the absorption of fallout into the human body became known only some years after the establishment of massive programs of nuclear testing. Most of the medical hazards of the new insecticides were noticed only long after these substances were in wide use. All these problems have been imposed on us—sometimes to our considerable surprise—well after the causative activity was in full swing.

Could we cure these difficulties by calling a halt to science and new technologies? The present accelerating growth of science and technology —which, together with population growth, is the cause of most of our pollution problems—was set in motion more than sixty years ago. Its roots are in the scientific revolution which took place at the turn of the century, when physicists discovered that the apparently simple laws of Newton's time concealed a complex world of exceedingly small particles and immense forces. From this knowledge has come the great flowering of modern science—including the new energy sources and synthetic substances which have covered the earth with pollution. We are today witnessing the inevitable impact of the tidal wave created by a scientific revolution more than half a century old. It is simply too late to declare a moratorium on the progress of science.

The real question is not *whether* we should use our new knowledge, but *how* to use it. And to answer that, we must understand the structure of modern scientific knowledge: in which areas the new insights of science are powerful and effective guides to action; in which others they are too uncertain to support a sound technology. Since the scientific revolution which generated modern technology took place in physics, it is natural that modern science should provide better technological control over inanimate matter than over living things. This disparity is evident in our environmental problems. If basic theories of physics had not attained their present ability to explain nuclear structure, we would not now be confronted with massive dissemination of man-made radio-isotopes and synthetic chemicals. If biological theory had become sufficiently advanced to master the problems of cancer—a chief hazard from modern pollutants—we might be better prepared to cope with these new environmental contaminants. We are in difficulty because of the wide disparity between the present state of the physical and the biological sciences.

The separation of the laws of nature among the different sciences is a human conceit; nature itself is an integrated whole. A nuclear test explosion is usually regarded as an experiment in engineering and physics; but it is also a vast, if poorly controlled, experiment in environmental biology. It is a convincing statement of the competence of modern physics and engineering, but also a demonstration of our poor understanding of the biology of fallout. If the physicochemical sciences are to be safely used in the new technologies they will need to be governed by what we know — and do not know — about life and its environment.

THE BIOSPHERE

What we know about living things and about the biosphere — the community of life in the environment — is that they are enormously complex, and that this complexity is the source of their remarkable staying power. The web of relationships that ties animal to plant, prey to predator, parasite to host, and all to the air, water, and soil which they inhabit persists *because* it is complex. An old farmhouse practice is a simple illustration of this fundamental point. Farmers who keep cats to control the ravages of mice find it necessary to offer the cats a doorstep feeding. Only if the farmer provides this alternative source of food can the cats withstand a temporary shortage in the mouse supply and remain on hand to catch the mice when they reappear. A stable system that will keep mice in check must comprise all three components: cats, mice, and domestic cat food. This principle is well established in environmental biology: anything which reduces the complexity of a natural biological system renders it less stable and more subject to fatal fluctuations.

The biosphere is closely governed by the connections among its numerous parts. The connections which comprise the biological food chain, for example, greatly amplify the effects of environmental pollution. If soil contains 1 unit of insecticide per gram, earthworms living in the soil will contain 10 to 40 units per gram, and in woodcocks feeding on the earthworms the insecticide level will rise to about 200 units per gram. In the biosphere the whole is always greater than the sum of its parts; animals which absorb one insecticide may become more sensitive to the damaging effects of a second one. Because of such amplifications, a small intrusion in one place in the environment may trigger a huge response elsewhere in the system. Often an amplification feeds on itself until the entire living system is engulfed by catastrophe. If the vegetation that protects the soil from erosion is killed, the soil will wash away, plants will then find no footholds for their seeds, and a permanent desert will result.

It is not surprising, then, that the introduction of any killing chemical into the environment is bound to cause a change somewhere in the tangled web of relationships. For this reason, and because we depend on so many detailed and subtle aspects of the environment, *any* change imposed on it for the sake of some economic benefit has a price. For the benefits of powerful insecticides we pay in losses of birdlife and fish. For the conveniences of automobiles we pay in the rise of respiratory disease from smog. For the widespread use of combustible fuels we may yet be forced to pay the catastrophic cost of protecting our cities from world-wide floods. Sooner or later, wittingly or unwittingly, we must pay for every intrusion on the natural environment.

OUR KNOWLEDGE IS DANGEROUSLY INCOMPLETE

There is considerable scientific disagreement about the medical hazards of the new pollutants: about the effects of DDT now found in human bodies, about the diseases due to smog, or about the long-range effects of fallout. But the crucial point is that the disagreements exist, for they reveal that we have risked these hazards before we knew what harm they might do. Unwittingly we have loaded the air with chemicals that damage the lungs, and the water with substances that interfere with the functioning of the blood. Because we wanted to build nuclear bombs and kill mosquitoes, we have burdened our bodies with strontium-90 and DDT, with consequences that no one can now predict. We have been massively intervening in the environment without being aware of many of the harmful consequences of our acts until they have been performed and the effects — which are difficult to understand and sometimes irreversible — are upon us. Like the sorcerer's apprentice, we are acting upon dangerously incomplete knowledge. We are, in effect, conducting a huge experiment *on ourselves*. A generation hence — too late to help — public health statistics may reveal what hazards are associated with these pollutants.

To those of us who are concerned with the growing risk of unintended damage to the environment, some would reply that it is the grand purpose of science to move into unknown territory, to explore, and to discover. They would remind us that similar hazards have been risked before, and that science and technology cannot make progress without taking some risks. But the size and persistence of possible errors has also grown with the power of science and the expansion of technology. In the past, the risks taken in the name of technological progress — boiler explosions on the first steamboats, or the early injuries from radium — were restricted to a small place and a short time. The new hazards are neither local nor brief. Air pollution covers vast areas. Fallout is worldwide. Synthetic chemicals may remain in the soil for years. Radioactive pollutants now on the earth's surface will be found there for generations, and, in the case of carbon-14, for thousands of years. Excess carbon dioxide from fuel combustion eventually might cause floods that could cover much of the earth's present land surface for centuries. At the same time the permissible margin for error has become very much reduced. In the development of steam engines a certain number of boiler explosions were tolerated as the art was improved. If a single comparable disaster were to occur in a nuclear power plant or in a reactor-driven ship near a large city, thousands of people might die and a whole region be rendered uninhabitable—a price that the public might be unwilling to pay for nuclear power. The risk is one that private insurance companies have refused to underwrite. Modern science and technology are simply too powerful to permit a trial-and-error approach.

It can be argued that the hazards of modern pollutants are small compared to the dangers associated with other human enterprises. For us, today, the fallout hazard is, for example, much smaller than the risks we take on the highway or in the air. But what of the risks we inflict on future generations? No estimate of the actual harm that may be done by fallout, smog, or chemical pollutants can obscure the sober realization that in each case the risk was undertaken before it was fully understood. The importance of these issues to science, and to the citizen, lies not only in the associated hazards, but in the warning of an incipient abdication of one of the major duties of science—prediction and control of human interventions into nature. The true measure of the danger is not represented by the present hazards, but by the disasters that will surely be visited upon us if we dare to enter the new age before us without correcting this basic fault in the scientific enterprise. And if we are to correct this fault, we must first discover why it has developed.

DISCUSSION QUESTIONS
SUGGESTIONS FOR WRITING

1. What is the "greenhouse effect"? How could its action result in catastrophe for much of the world's inhabited land and many of its major cities?

2. Describe the series of mistakes which led to the dangerous and widespread dissemination of radioactive fallout throughout the world since World War II.

3. What is the common connection between our technological failures and the burgeoning of useful technological innovations? Why does Commoner call the separation of the laws of nature among the different sciences "a human conceit"?

4. Why are we like the sorcerer's apprentice? What, according to Commoner, is the "basic fault in the scientific enterprise"?

WOLFE

O ROTTEN GOTHAM—
SLIDING DOWN
INTO THE
BEHAVIORAL SINK

TOM WOLFE (b. 1931), at heart a moralist and social critic as well as a dazzling stylist, began a revolution of sorts in the reporting of American popular culture with *The Kandy-Kolored Tangerine-Flake Streamline Baby* (1965). His accurate and perceptive essays on contemporary culture have continued to generate avid attention, both in themselves and in association with the genesis of the so-called "new journalism," of which he would have to be described as the leading practitioner. Others of his books are *The Pump House Gang, The Electric Kool-Aid Acid Test,* and *Radical Chic and Mau-Mauing the Flak-Catchers.*

I JUST spent two days with Edward T. Hall, an anthropologist, watching thousands of my fellow New Yorkers short-circuiting themselves into hot little twitching death balls with jolts of their own adrenalin. Dr. Hall says it is overcrowding that does it. Overcrowding gets the adrenalin going, and the adrenalin gets them hyped up. And here they are, hyped up, turning bilious, nephritic, queer, autistic, sadistic, barren, batty, sloppy, hot-in-the-pants, chancred-on-the-flankers, leering, puling, numb—the usual in New York, in other words, and God knows what else. Dr. Hall has the theory that overcrowding has already thrown New York into a state of behavioral sink. Behavioral sink is a term from ethology, which is the study of how animals relate to their environment. Among animals, the sink winds up with a "population collapse" or "massive die-off." O rotten Gotham.

It got to be easy to look at New Yorkers as animals, especially looking down from some place like a balcony at Grand Central at the rush hour Friday afternoon. The floor was filled with the poor white humans, running around, dodging, blinking their eyes, making a sound like a pen full of starlings or rats or something.

"Listen to them skid," says Dr. Hall.

He was right. The poor old etiolate animals were out there skidding on their rubber soles. You could hear it once he pointed it out. They stop short to keep from hitting somebody or because they are disoriented and they suddenly stop and look around, and they skid on their rubber-sole shoes, and a screech goes up. They pour out onto the floor down the escalators from the Pan-Am Building, from 42nd Street, from Lexington Avenue, up out of subways, down into subways, railroad trains, up into helicopters —

"You can also hear the helicopters all the way down here," says Dr. Hall. The sound of the helicopters using the roof of the Pan-Am Building nearly fifty stories up beats right through. "If it weren't for this ceiling" —he is referring to the very high ceiling in Grand Central—"this place would be unbearable with this kind of crowding. And yet they'll probably never 'waste' space like this again."

They screech! And the adrenal glands in all those poor white animals enlarge, micrometer by micrometer, to the size of cantaloupes. Dr. Hall pulls a Minox camera out of a holster he has on his belt and starts shooting away at the human scurry. The Sink!

Dr. Hall has the Minox up to his eye—he is a slender man, calm, 52 years old, young-looking, an anthropologist who has worked with Navajos, Hopis, Spanish-Americans, Negroes, Trukese. He was the most important anthropologist in the government during the crucial years of the foreign aid program, the 1950's. He directed both the Point Four training program and the Human Relations Area Files. He wrote *The Silent Language* and *The Hidden Dimension*, two books that are picking up the kind of "underground" following his friend Marshall McLuhan started picking up about five years ago. He teaches at the Illinois Institute of Technology, lives with his wife, Mildred, in a high-ceilinged town house on one of the last great residential streets in downtown Chicago, Astor Street; has a grown son and daughter, loves good food, good wine, the relaxed, civilized life—but comes to New York with a Minox at his eye to record—perfect!—The Sink.

We really got down in there by walking down into the Lexington Avenue line subway stop under Grand Central. We inhaled those nice big fluffy fumes of human sweat, urine, effluvia, and sebaceous secretions. One old female human was already stroked out on the upper level, on a stretcher, with two policemen standing by. The other humans barely looked at her. They rushed into line. They bellied each other, haunch to paunch, down the stairs. Human heads shone through the gratings. The species North European tried to create bubbles of space around themselves, about a foot and a half in diameter —

"See, he's reacting against the line," says Dr. Hall.

—but the species Mediterranean presses on in. The hell with bubbles of space. The species North European resents that, this male human behind him presses forward toward the booth . . . *breathing* on him, he's disgusted, he pulls out of the line entirely, the species Mediterranean resents him for resenting it, and neither of them realizes what the hell they are getting irritable about exactly. And in all of them the old adrenals grow another micrometer.

Dr. Hall whips ᴏut the Minox. Too perfect! The bottom of The Sink.

It is the sheer overcrowding, such as occurs in the business sections of Manhattan five days a week and in Harlem, Bedford-Stuyvesant, southeast Bronx every day—sheer overcrowding is converting New Yorkers into animals in a sink pen. Dr. Hall's argument runs as follows: all animals, including birds, seem to have a built-in, inherited requirement to have a certain amount of territory, space, to lead their lives in. Even if they have all the food they need, and there are no predatory animals threatening them, they cannot tolerate crowding beyond a certain point. No more than two hundred wild Norway rats can survive on a quarter acre of ground, for example, even when they are given all the food they can eat. They just die off.

But why? To find out, ethologists have run experiments on all sorts of animals, from stickleback crabs to Sika deer. In one major experiment, an ethologist named John Calhoun put some domesticated white Norway rats in a pen with four sections to it, connected by ramps. Calhoun knew from previous experiments that the rats tend to split up into groups of ten to twelve and that the pen, therefore, would hold forty to forty-eight rats comfortably, assuming they formed four equal groups. He allowed them to reproduce until there were eighty rats, balanced between male and female, but did not let it get any more crowded. He kept them supplied with plenty of food, water, and nesting materials. In other words, all their more obvious needs were taken care of. A less obvious need—space—was not. To the human eye, the pen did not even look especially crowded. But to the rats, it was crowded beyond endurance.

The entire colony was soon plunged into a profound behavioral sink. "The sink," said Calhoun, "is the outcome of any behavioral process that collects animals together in unusually great numbers. The unhealthy connotations of the term are not accidental: a behavioral sink does act to aggravate all forms of pathology that can be found within a group."

For a start, long before the rat population reached eighty, a status hierarchy had developed in the pen. Two dominant male rats took over the two end sections, acquired harems of eight to ten females each, and forced the rest of the rats into the two middle pens. All the overcrowding took place in the middle pens. That was where the "sink" hit. The aristocrat rats at the ends grew bigger, sleeker, healthier, and more secure the whole time.

In The Sink, meanwhile, nest building, courting, sex behavior, reproduction, social organization, health—all of it went to pieces. Normally, Norway rats have a mating ritual in which the male chases the female, the female ducks down into a burrow and sticks her head up to watch the male. He performs a little dance outside the burrow, then she comes out, and he mounts her, usually for a few seconds. When The Sink set in, however, no more than three males—the dominant males in the middle sections—kept up the old customs. The rest tried everything from satyrism to homosexuality or else gave up on sex altogether. Some of the subordinate males spent all their time chasing females. Three or four might chase one female at the same time, and instead of stopping at the burrow entrance for the ritual, they would charge right in. Once mounted, they would hold on for minutes instead of the usual seconds.

Homosexuality rose sharply. So did bisexuality. Some males would mount anything—males, females, babies, senescent rats, anything. Still other males dropped sexual activity altogether, wouldn't fight and, in fact, would hardly move except when the other rats slept. Occasionally a female from the aristocrat rats' harems would come over the ramps and into the middle sections to sample life in The Sink. When she had had enough, she would run back up the ramp. Sink males would give chase up to the top of the ramp, which is to say, to the very edge of the aristocratic preserve. But one glance from one of the king rats would stop them cold and they would return to The Sink.

The slumming females from the harems had their adventures and then returned to a placid, healthy life. Females in The Sink, however, were ravaged, physically and psychologically. Pregnant rats had trouble continuing pregnancy. The rate of miscarriages increased significantly, and females started dying from tumors and other disorders of the mammary glands, sex organs, uterus, ovaries, and Fallopian tubes. Typically, their kidneys, livers, and adrenals were also enlarged or diseased or showed other signs associated with stress.

Child-rearing became totally disorganized. The females lost the interest or the stamina to build nests and did not keep them up if they did build them. In the general filth and confusion, they would not put themselves out to save offspring they were momentarily separated from. Frantic, even sadistic competition among the males was going on all around them and rendering their lives chaotic. The males began unprovoked and senseless assaults upon one another, often in the form of tail-biting. Ordinarily, rats will suppress this kind of behavior when it crops up. In The Sink, male rats gave up all policing and just looked out for themselves. The "pecking order" among males in The Sink was never stable. Normally, male rats set up a three-class structure. Under the pressure of overcrowding, however, they broke up into all sorts of unstable subclasses, cliques, packs—and constantly pushed, probed, explored, tested one another's power. Anyone was fair game, except for the aristocrats in the end pens.

Calhoun kept the population down to eighty, so that the next stage, "population collapse" or "massive die-off," did not occur. But the autopsies showed that the pattern—as in the diseases among the female rats—was already there.

The classic study of die-off was John J. Christian's study of Sika deer on James Island in the Chesapeake Bay, west of Cambridge, Maryland. Four or five of the deer had been released on the island, which was 280 acres and uninhabited, in 1916. By 1955 they had bred freely into a herd of 280 to 300. The population density was only about one deer per acre at this point, but Christian knew that this was already too high for the Sikas' inborn space requirements, and something would give before long. For two years the number of deer remained 280 to 300. But suddenly, in 1958, over half the deer died; 161 carcasses were recovered. In 1959 more deer died and the population steadied at about 80.

In two years, two-thirds of the herd had died. Why? It was not starvation. In fact, all the deer collected were in excellent condition, with well-developed muscles, shining coats, and fat deposits between the muscles. In practically all the deer, however, the adrenal glands had enlarged by 50 percent. Christian concluded that the die-off was due to "shock following severe metabolic disturbance, probably as a result of prolonged adrenocortical hyperactivity. . . . There was no evidence of infection, starvation, or other obvious cause to explain the mass mortality." In other words, the constant stress of overpopulation, plus the normal stress of the cold of the winter, had kept the adrenalin flowing so constantly in the deer that their systems were depleted of blood sugar and they died of shock.

Well, the white humans are still skidding and darting across the floor of Grand Central. Dr. Hall listens a moment longer to the skidding and the darting noises, and then says, "You know, I've been on commuter trains here after everyone has been through one of these rushes, and I'll tell you, there is enough acid flowing in the stomachs in every car to dissolve the rails underneath."

Just a little invisible acid bath for the linings to round off the day. The ulcers the acids cause, of course, are the one disease people have already been taught to associate with the stress of city life. But overcrowding, as Dr. Hall sees it, raises a lot more hell with the body than just ulcers. In everyday life in New York—just the usual, getting to work, working in massively congested areas like 42nd Street between Fifth Avenue and Lexington, especially now that the Pan-Am Building is set in there, working in cubicles such as those in the editorial offices at Time-Life, Inc., which Dr. Hall cites as typical of New York's poor handling of space, working in cubicles with low ceilings and, often, no access to a window, while construction crews all over Manhattan drive everybody up the Masonite wall with air-pressure generators with noises up to the boil-a-brain decibel levels, then rushing to get home, piling into subways and trains, fighting for time and for space, the usual day in New York—the whole now-normal thing keeps shooting jolts of adrenalin into the body, breaking down the body's defenses and winding up with the work-a-daddy human animal stroked out at the breakfast table with his head apoplexed like a cauliflower out of his $6.95 semi-spread Pima-cotton shirt, and nosed over into a plate of No-Kloresto egg substitute, signing off with the black thrombosis, cancer, kidney, liver, or stomach failure, and the adrenals ooze to a halt, the size of eggplants in July.

One of the people whose work Dr. Hall is interested in on this score is Rene Dubos at the Rockefeller Institute. Dubos's work indicates that specific organisms, such as the tuberculosis bacillus or a pneumonia virus, can seldom be considered "the cause" of a disease. The germ or virus, apparently, has to work in combination with other things that have already broken the body down in some way—such as the old adrenal hyperactivity. Dr. Hall would like to see some autopsy studies made to record the size of adrenal glands in New York, especially of people crowded into slums and people who go through the full rush-hour-work-rush-hour cycle every day. He is afraid that until there is some clinical, statistical data on how overcrowding actually ravages the human body, no one will be willing to do anything about it. Even in so obvious a thing as air pollution, the pattern is familiar. Until people can actually see the smoke or smell the sulphur or feel the sting in their eyes, politicians will not get excited about it, even though it is well known that many of the lethal substances polluting the air are invisible and odorless. For one thing, most politicians are like the aristocrat rats. They are insulated from The Sink by practically sultanic buffers—limousines, chauffeurs, secretaries, aides-de-camp, doormen, shuttered houses, high-floor apartments. They almost never ride subways, fight rush hours, much less live in the slums or work in the Pan-Am Building.

We took a cab from Grand Central to go up to Harlem, and by 48th Street we were already socked into one of those great, total traffic jams on First Avenue on Friday afternoon. Dr. Hall motions for me to survey the scene, and there they all are, humans, male and female, behind the glass of their automobile windows, soundlessly going through the torture of their own adrenalin jolts. This male over here contracts his jaw muscles so hard that they bunch up into a great cheese Danish pattern. He twists his lips, he bleeds from the eyeballs, he shouts . . . soundlessly behind glass . . . the fat corrugates on the back of his neck, his whole body shakes as he pounds the heel of his hand into the steering wheel. The female human in the car ahead of him whips her head around, she bares her teeth, she screams . . . soundlessly behind glass . . . she throws her hands up in the air, Whaddya expect me—Yah, yuh stupid—and they all sit there, trapped in their own congestion, bleeding hate all over each other, shorting out the ganglia and—goddam it—

Dr. Hall sits back and watches it all. This is it! The Sink! And where is everybody's wandering boy?

Dr. Hall says, "We need a study in which drivers who go through these rush hours every day would wear GSR bands."

GSR?

"Galvanic skin response. It measures the electric potential of the skin, which is a function of sweating. If a person gets highly nervous, his palms begin to sweat. It is an index of tension. There are some other fairly simple devices that would record respiration and pulse. I think everybody who goes through this kind of experience all the time should take his own pulse — not literally — but just be aware of what's happening to him. You can usually tell when stress is beginning to get you physically."

In testing people crowded into New York's slums, Dr. Hall would like to take it one step further — gather information on the plasma hydrocortisone level in the blood or the corticosteroids in the urine. Both have been demonstrated to be reliable indicators of stress, and testing procedures are simple.

The slums — we finally made it up to East Harlem. We drove into 101st Street, and there was a new, avant-garde little church building, the Church of the Epiphany, which Dr. Hall liked — and, next to it, a pile of rubble where a row of buildings had been torn down, and from the back windows of the tenements beyond several people were busy "airmailing," throwing garbage out the window, into the rubble, beer cans, red shreds, the No-Money-Down Eames roller stand for a TV set, all flying through the air onto the scaggy sump. We drove around some more in Harlem, and a sequence was repeated, trash, buildings falling down, buildings torn down, rubble, scaggy sumps or, suddenly, a cluster of high-rise apartment projects, with fences around the grass.

"You know what this city looks like?" Dr. Hall said. "It looks bombed out. I used to live at Broadway and 124th Street back in 1946 when I was studying at Columbia. I can't tell you how much Harlem has changed in twenty years. It looks bombed out. It's broken down. People who live in New York get used to it and don't realize how filthy the city has become. The whole thing is typical of a behavioral sink. So is something like the Kitty Genovese case — a girl raped and murdered in the courtyard of an apartment complex and forty or fifty people look on from their apartments and nobody even calls the police. That kind of apathy and anomie is typical of the general psychological deterioration of The Sink."

He looked at the high-rise housing projects and found them mainly testimony to how little planners know about humans' basic animal requirements for space.

"Even on the simplest terms," he said, "it is pointless to build one of these blocks much over five stories high. Suppose a family lives on the fifteenth floor. The mother will be completely cut off from her children if they are playing down below, because the elevators are constantly broken in these projects, and it often takes half an hour, literally half an hour, to get the elevator if it is running. That's very common. A mother in that situation is just as much a victim of overcrowding as if she were back in the tenement block. Some Negro leaders have a bitter joke about how the white man is solving the slum problem by stacking Negroes up vertically, and there is a lot to that."

For one thing, says Dr. Hall, planners have no idea of the different space requirements of people from different cultures, such as Negroes and Puerto Ricans. They are all treated as if they were minute, compact middle-class whites. As with the Sika deer, who are overcrowded at one per acre, overcrowding is a relative thing for the human animal, as well. Each species has its own feeling for space. The feeling may be "subjective," but it is quite real.

Dr. Hall's theories on space and territory are based on the same information, gathered by biologists, ethologists, and anthropologists, chiefly, as Robert Ardrey's. Ardrey has written two well-publicized books, *African Genesis* and *The Territorial Imperative. Life* magazine ran big excerpts from *The Territorial Imperative*, all about how the drive to acquire territory and property and add to it and achieve status is built into all animals, including man, over thousands of centuries of genetic history, etc., and is a more powerful drive than sex. *Life's* big display prompted Marshall McLuhan to crack, "They see this as a great historic justification for free enterprise and Republicanism. If the birds do it and the stickleback crabs do it, then it's right for man." To people like Hall and McLuhan, and Ardrey, for that matter, the right or wrong of it is irrelevant. The only thing they find inexcusable is the kind of thinking, by influential people, that isn't even aware of all this. Such as the thinking of most city planners.

"The planners always show you a bird's-eye view of what they are doing," he said. "You've seen those scale models. Everyone stands around the table and looks down and says that's great. It never occurs to anyone that they are taking a bird's-eye view. In the end, these projects do turn out fine, when viewed from an airplane."

As an anthropologist, Dr. Hall has to shake his head every time he hears planners talking about fully integrated housing projects for the year 1980 or 1990, as if by then all cultural groups will have the same feeling for space and will live placidly side by side, happy as the happy burghers who plan all the good clean bird's-eye views. According to his findings, the very fact that every cultural group does have its own peculiar, unspoken feeling for space is what is responsible for much of the uneasiness one group feels around the other.

It is like the North European and the Mediterranean in the subway line. The North European, without ever realizing it, tries to keep a bubble of space around himself, and the moment a stranger invades that sphere, he feels threatened. Mediterranean peoples tend to come from cultures where everyone is much more involved physically, publicly, with one another on a day-to-day basis and feels no uneasiness about mixing it up in public, but may have very different ideas about space inside the home. Even Negroes brought up in America have a different vocabulary of space and gesture from the North European Americans who, historically, have been their models, according to Dr. Hall. The failure of Negroes and whites to communicate well often boils down to things like this: some white will be interviewing a Negro for a job; the Negro's culture has taught him to show somebody you are interested by looking right at him and listening intently to what he has to say. But the species North European requires something more. He expects his listener to nod from time to time, as if to say, "Yes, keep going." If he doesn't get this nodding, he feels anxious, for fear the listener doesn't agree with him or has switched off. The Negro may learn that the white expects this sort of thing, but he isn't used to the precise kind of nodding that is customary, and so he may start overresponding, nodding like mad, and at this point the North European is liable to think he has some kind of stupid Uncle Tom on his hands, and the guy still doesn't get the job.

The whole handling of space in New York is so chaotic, says Dr. Hall, that even middle-class housing now seems to be based on the bird's-eye models for slum projects. He took a look at the big Park West Village development, set up originally to provide housing in Manhattan for families in the middle-income range, and found its handling of space very much like a slum project with slightly larger balconies. He felt the time has come to start subsidizing the middle class in New York on its own terms—namely, the kind of truly "human" spaces that still remain in brownstones.

"I think New York City should seriously consider a program of encouraging the middle-class development of an area like Chelsea, which is already starting to come up. People are beginning to renovate houses there on their own, and I think if the city would subsidize that sort of thing with tax reliefs and so forth, you would be amazed at what would result. What New York needs is a string of minor successes in the housing field, just to show everyone that it can be done, and I think the middle class can still do that for you. The alternative is to keep on doing what you're doing now, trying to lift a very large lower class up by main force almost and finding it a very slow and discouraging process."

"But before deciding how to redesign space in New York," he said, "people must first simply realize how severe the problem already is. And the handwriting is already on the wall."

"A study published in 1962," he said, "surveyed a representative sample of people living in New York slums and found only 18 percent of them free from emotional symptoms. Thirty-eight percent were in need of psychiatric help, and 23 percent were seriously disturbed or incapacitated. Now, this study was published in 1962, which means the work probably went on from 1955 to 1960. There is no telling how bad it is now. In a behavioral sink, crises can develop rapidly."

Dr. Hall would like to see a large-scale study similar to that undertaken by two sociopsychologists, Chombart de Lauwe and his wife, in a French working-class town. They found a direct relationship between crowding and general breakdown. In families where people were crowded into the apartment so that there was less than 86 to 108 square feet per person, social and physical disorders doubled. That would mean that for four people the smallest floor space they could tolerate would be an apartment, say, 12 by 30 feet.

What would one find in Harlem? "It is fairly obvious," Dr. Hall wrote in *The Hidden Dimension*, "that the American Negroes and people of Spanish culture who are flocking to our cities are being very seriously stressed. Not only are they in a setting that does not fit them, but they have passed the limits of their own tolerance of stress. The United States is faced with the fact that two of its creative and sensitive peoples are in the process of being destroyed and like Samson could bring down the structure that houses us all."

Dr. Hall goes out to the airport, to go back to Chicago, and I am coming back in a cab, along the East River Drive. It is four in the afternoon, but already the damned drive is clogging up. There is a 1959 Oldsmobile just to the right of me. There are about eight people in there, a lot of popeyed silhouettes against a leopard-skin dashboard, leopard-skin seats—and the driver is classic. He has a mustache, sideburns down to his jaw socket, and a tattoo on his forearm like a Rosetti painting of Jane Burden Morris with her hair long. All right; it is even touching, like a postcard photo of the main drag in San Pedro, California. But suddenly Sideburns guns it and cuts in front of my cab so that my driver has to hit the brakes, and then hardly 100 feet ahead Sideburns hits a wall of traffic himself and has to hit his brakes, and then it happens. A stuffed white Angora animal, a dog, no, it's a Pekingese cat, is mounted in his rear window—as soon as he hits the brakes its *eyes* light up, Nighttown pink. To keep from ramming him, my driver has to hit the brakes again, too, and so here I am, out in an insane, jammed-up expressway at four in the afternoon, shuddering to a stop while a stuffed Pekingese grows bigger and bigger and brighter in the eyeballs directly in front of me. Jolt! Nighttown pink! Hey—that's me the adrenalin is hitting, *I* am this white human sitting in a projectile heading amid a mass of clotted humans toward a white Angora stuffed goddam leopard-dash Pekingese freaking cat—kill that damned Angora—Jolt!— got me—another micrometer on the old adrenals—

DISCUSSION QUESTIONS
SUGGESTIONS FOR WRITING

1. Notice the manner in which the essay quickly establishes a sense of place with a scene unfolding there. Instead of being pushed from abstraction to abstraction, we are given the author and his subject looking down from a balcony at Grand Central Station at rush hour on Friday afternoon. How does this technique of presentation enhance reader involvement?

2. Why, in an essay presumably about overcrowding, does Tom Wolfe mention that Dr. Hall, our authority, "lives with his wife, Mildred, in a high-ceilinged town house on one of the last great residential streets in downtown Chicago, Astor Street; has a grown son and daughter, loves good food, good wine, the relaxed, civilized life . . ."? Isn't such information essentially irrelevant to the purpose of the essay?

3. In the description of the rat experiment, does the use of terms such as "harems of . . . females" or "aristocrat" rats tend to make the experiment more readily understandable and interesting, or is this a case of unjustified anthropomorphism?

4. Point out examples of scene development, characterization, dramatic use of dialogue, etc. If the piece shares so many of the devices of fiction, in what sense, if any, is it still an essay?

KENNETH H. COOPER
(b. 1931), a physician in
the Air Force Medical
Corps, introduced aero-
bics as a new concept in
exercise to counteract
problems of lethargy and
inactivity in the popula-
tion. His advocacy of jogging was influential in
starting a national craze.

THE NEW AEROBICS: AN AFTERTHOUGHT

IN the relatively short span of fifty years, the automobile has so altered our way of life that walking — the most natural mode of locomotion — now seems almost discreditable.

I once expressed this thought to a friend who is a successful car dealer. Predictably, he responded.

"I hate to see cars getting the blame for everything," he said irritably. "I bet people didn't walk any more in the old days than they do now. They just went by horse and buggy."

"When you went to school," I asked, "how did you get there?"

He admitted that he had walked more than three miles to and from school.

"And your children?"

"The bus picks them up."

"And does your wife use a car much?"

"Oh, yes, you should see our monthly gasoline bill."

I didn't press my point further.

No, the automobile is not just a mechanical replacement for the horse. It represents an entirely new attitude, a new set of customs, and it is ushering in an era of physical passivity.

I remember when people walked to church, to the store and the post office. Today, we have the "drive-in craze." There are drive-in restaurants, drive-in cleaners, drive-in theaters and drive-in banks. Not only have we given up walking; we don't even get out of the car when we reach our destinations!

Paradoxically, this passion for passivity extends even to sports, robbing them of much of their healthful effects. The golf cart and the ski lift are but two of many examples of our unwillingness or inability to move under our own power. And we are becoming so engrossed with television that a major portion of our leisure time, formerly spent in outdoor activities, is now spent in watching television. To top that, remote control is making it "out of style" to leave the comfortable, cushioned chair to change television stations. Where will it end?

But all of these changes have been too swift for the human organism. Over many thousands of years, since before the dawn of civilization, our bodies have been geared to and sustained by habitual and extensive physical activity. Now, with dramatic suddenness, this functional pattern has been broken. Our legs are technologically unemployed. And our entire health suffers for it.

Even in other areas of our modern life, strenuous physical activity is a thing of the past. Mechanization has placed the farmer in the driver's seat, the construction worker at the controls of a crane, and the road builder on his bulldozer. The warehouseman has his fork lifts, the carpenter his power tools, and the office-worker his elevators to eliminate the occasional effort of climbing a flight of stairs. Even the trucker— thanks to power steering and power brakes—exerts little more muscular effort than the housewife driving to a bridge party.

Unquestionably, these developments represent progress. Modern technology has created immense benefits and satisfied many human needs. I am not criticizing these accomplishments, and I am certainly not suggesting that we tear up our highways, junk our cars, and eliminate the elevators. But, as a physician, I am concerned about the medical consequences of the machine age. The high tension and low activity of modern life make a deadly mixture. Biologically, we're in the midst of a crisis, and the statistics on cardiovascular disease show it.

At this point in the history of civilization, it is evident that technical progress may backfire unless it is matched by a balancing regard for human health and well-being. In its broadest sense, the question is whether man can prosper in the technological environment he has created. He must learn to protect the natural resources that sustain his life. He must learn to clean up the air and the water, and to preserve the land. But first of all, he must protect his own body against the ravages imposed by modern life.

DISCUSSION QUESTIONS
SUGGESTIONS FOR WRITING

1. What evidence does the author offer to substantiate his thesis? Would you call this evidence conclusive?

2. What function is served by the anecdote about the car dealer? Surely the author, a physician, knows that one case history is not sufficient to substantiate an elaborate hypothesis.

3. Would it be possible to write an essay on the same subject, using the same number of words, and saying essentially the same thing, but without using the same words in the same order that Cooper has?

4. Is there always one best way to write on any subject, or are there an infinite number of choices or possibilities in each case?

OATES

UPON THE SWEEPING FLOOD

JOYCE CAROL OATES (b. 1938) won the National Book Award for fiction in 1970. Her short stories have consistently been chosen for the *Best American Short Stories* and *O. Henry* prize story collections. She is currently associate professor of English at the University of Windsor, Ontario, and one of the most prolific and powerful writers of fiction in America.

NOT long ago in Eden County, in the remote marsh and swamp-lands to the south, a man named Walter Stuart was stopped in the rain by a sheriff's deputy along a country road. Stuart was in a hurry to get home to his family—his wife and two daughters—after having endured a week at his father's old farm, arranging for his father's funeral, surrounded by aging relatives who had sucked at him for the strength of his youth. He was a stern, quiet man of thirty-nine, beginning to lose some of the muscular hardness that had always baffled others, masking as it did Stuart's remoteness, his refinement, his faith in discipline and order which seemed to have belonged, even in his youth, to a person already grown safely old. He was a district vice-president for one of the gypsum mining plants, a man to whom financial success and success in love had come naturally, without fuss. When only a child he had shifted his faith with little difficulty from the unreliable God of his family's tradition to the things and emotions of this world, which he admired in his thoughtful, rather conservative way, and this faith had given him access, as if by magic, to a communion with persons vastly different from himself—with someone like the sheriff's deputy, for instance, who approached him that day in the hard, cold rain. "Is something wrong?" Stuart said. He rolled down the window and had nearly opened the door when the deputy, an old man with gray eyebrows and a slack, sunburned face, began shouting against the wind, "Just the weather, mister. You going far along here? How far are you going?"

"Two hundred miles," Stuart said. "What about the weather? Is it a hurricane?"

"A hurricane—yes—a hurricane!" the man said, bending to shout at Stuart's face. "You better go back to town and stay put. They're evacuating up there. We're not letting anyone through."

A long line of cars and pickup trucks, tarnished and gloomy in the rain, passed them on the other side of the road. "How bad is it?" said Stuart. "Do you need help?"

"Back at town, maybe, they need help," the man said. "They're putting up folks at the schoolhouse and the churches, and different families— The eye was spost to come by here, but last word we got it's veered further south. Just the same, though—"

"Yes, it's good to evacuate them," Stuart said. At the back window of an automobile passing them two children's faces peered out at the rain, white and blurred. "The last hurricane here—"

"Ah, God, leave off of that!" the old man said, so harshly that Stuart felt, inexplicably, hurt. "You better turn around, now, and get on back to town. You got money they can put you up somewheres good —not with these folks coming along here."

This was said without contempt, but Stuart flinched at its assumptions. "I'm going in to see if anybody needs help," he said. He had the car going again before the deputy could even protest. "I know what I'm doing! I know what I'm doing!" Stuart said.

The car lunged forward into the rain, drowning out the deputy's outraged shouts. The slashing of rain against Stuart's face excited him. Faces staring out of oncoming cars were pale and startled, and Stuart felt rising in him a strange compulsion to grin, to laugh madly at their alarm . . . He passed cars for some time. Houses looked deserted, yards bare. Things had the look of haste about them, even trees—in haste to rid themselves of their leaves, to be stripped bare. Grass was twisted and wild. A ditch by the road was overflowing and at spots the churning, muddy water stretched across the red clay road. Stuart drove splashing through it. After a while his enthusiasm slowed, his foot eased up on the gas pedal. He had not passed any cars or trucks for some time.

The sky had darkened and the storm had increased. Stuart thought of turning back when he saw, a short distance ahead, someone standing in the road. A car approached from the opposite direction. Stuart slowed, bearing to the right. He came upon a farm—a small, run-down one with just a few barns and a small pasture in which a horse stood drooping in the rain. Behind the roofs of the buildings a shifting edge of foliage from the trees beyond curled in the wind, now dark, now silver. In a neat harsh line against the bottom of the buildings the wind had driven up dust and red clay. Rain streamed off roofs, plunged into fat, tilted rainbarrels, and exploded back out of them. As Stuart watched another figure appeared, running out of the house. Both persons—they looked like children—jumped about in the road, waving their arms. A spray of leaves was driven against them and against the muddy windshield of the car that approached and passed them. They turned: a girl and a boy, waving their fists in rage, their faces white and distorted. As the car sped past Stuart water and mud splashed up in a vicious wave.

When Stuart stopped and opened the door the girl was already there, shouting, "Going the wrong way! Wrong way!" Her face was coarse, pimply about her forehead and chin. The boy pounded up behind her, straining for air. "Where the hell are you going, mister?" the girl cried. "The storm's coming from this way. Did you see that bastard, going right by us? Did you see him? If I see him when I get to town—" A wall of rain struck. The girl lunged forward and tried to push her way into the car; Stuart had to hold her back. "Where are your folks?" he shouted. "Let me in!" cried the girl savagely. "We're getting out of here!" "Your folks," said Stuart. He had to cup his mouth to make her hear. "Your folks in there!" "There ain't anybody there — Gah*dam* you!" she said, twisting about to slap her brother, who had been pushing at her from behind. She whirled upon Stuart again. "You letting us in, mister? You letting us in?" she screamed, raising her hands as if to claw him. But Stuart's size must have calmed her, for she shouted hoarsely and mechanically: "There ain't nobody in there. Our pa's been gone the last two days. LAST TWO DAYS. Gone into town BY HIMSELF. Gone drunk somewhere. He ain't here. He left us here. LEFT US HERE!" Again she rushed at Stuart, and he leaned forward against the steering wheel to let her get in back. The boy was about to follow when something caught his eye back at the farm. "Get in," said Stuart. "Get in. Please. Get in." "My horse there," the boy muttered. "You little bastard! You get in here!" his sister screamed.

But once the boy got in, once the door was closed, Stuart knew that it was too late. Rain struck the car in solid walls and the road, when he could see it, had turned to mud. "Let's go! Let's go!" cried the girl, pounding on the back of the seat. "Turn it around! Go up on our drive and turn it around!" The engine and the wind roared together. "Turn it! Get it going!" cried the girl. There was a scuffle and someone fell against Stuart. "It ain't no good," the boy said. "Let me out." He lunged for the door and Stuart grabbed him. "I'm going back to the house!" the boy cried, appealing to Stuart with his frightened eyes, and his sister, giving up suddenly, pushed him violently forward. "It's no use," Stuart said. "Gahdam fool," the girl screamed, "gahdam fool!"

The water was ankle deep as they ran to the house. The girl splashed ahead of Stuart, running with her head up and her eyes wide open in spite of the flying scud. When Stuart shouted to the boy his voice was slammed back to him as if he were being mocked. "Where are you going? Go to the house! Go to the house!" The boy had turned and was running toward the pasture. His sister took no notice but ran to the house. "Come back, kid!" Stuart cried. Wind tore at him, pushing him back. "What are you—"

The horse was undersized, skinny and brown. It ran to the boy as if it wanted to run him down but the boy, stooping through the fence, avoided the frightened hooves and grabbed the rope that dangled from the horse's halter. "That's it! That's it!" Stuart shouted as if the boy could hear. At the gate the boy stopped and looked around wildly, up to the sky—he might have been looking for someone who had just called him; then he shook the gate madly. Stuart reached the gate and opened it, pushing it back against the boy, who now turned to gape at him. "What? What are you doing here?" he said.

The thought crossed Stuart's mind that the child was insane. "Bring the horse through!" he said. "We don't have much time."

"What are you doing here?" the boy shouted. The horse's eyes rolled, its mane lifted and haloed about its head. Suddenly it lunged through the gate and jerked the boy off the ground. The boy ran in the air, his legs kicking. "Hang on and bring him around!" Stuart shouted. "Let me take hold!" He grabbed the boy instead of the rope. They stumbled together against the horse. It had stopped now and was looking intently at something just to the right of Stuart's head. The boy pulled himself along the rope, hand over hand, and Stuart held on to him by the strap of his overalls. "He's scairt of you!" the boy said. "He's scairt of you!" Stuart reached over and took hold of the rope above the boy's fingers and tugged gently at it. His face was about a foot away from the horse's. "Watch out for him," said the boy. The horse reared and broke free, throwing Stuart back against the boy. "Hey, hey!" screamed the boy, as if mad. The horse turned in midair as if whirled about by the wind, and Stuart looked up through his fingers to see its hooves and a vicious flicking of its tail, and the face of the boy being yanked past him and away with incredible speed. The boy fell heavily on his side in the mud, arms outstretched above him, hands still gripping the rope with wooden fists. But he scrambled to his feet at once and ran alongside the horse. He flung one arm up around its neck as Stuart shouted, "Let him go! Forget about him!" Horse and boy pivoted together back toward the fence, slashing wildly at the earth, feet and hooves together. The ground erupted beneath them. But the boy landed upright, still holding the rope, still with his arm about the horse's neck. "Let me help," Stuart said. "No," said the boy, "he's my horse, he knows me—" "Have you got him good?" Stuart shouted. "We got—we got each other here," the boy cried, his eyes shut tight.

Stuart went to the barn to open the door. While he struggled with it the boy led the horse forward. When the door was open far enough Stuart threw himself against it and slammed it around to the side of the barn. A cloud of hay and scud filled the air. Stuart outstretched his arms, as if pleading with the boy to hurry, and he murmured, "Come on. Please. Come on." The boy did not hear him, or even glance at him: his own lips were moving as he caressed the horse's neck and head. The horse's muddy hoof had just begun to grope about the step before the door when something like an explosion came against the back of Stuart's head, slammed his back, and sent him sprawling out at the horse. "Damn you! Damn you!" the boy screamed. Stuart saw nothing except rain. Then something struck him, his shoulder and hand, and his fingers were driven down into the mud. Something slammed beside him in the mud and he seized it — the horse's foreleg — and tried to pull himself up, insanely, lurching to his knees. The horse threw him backward. It seemed to emerge out of the air before and above him, coming into sight as though out of a cloud. The boy he did not see at all — only the hooves — and then the boy appeared, inexplicably, under the horse, peering intently at Stuart, his face struck completely blank. "Damn you!" Stuart heard. "He's my horse! My horse! I hope he kills you!" Stuart crawled back in the water, crab fashion, watching the horse form and dissolve, hearing its vicious tattoo against the barn. The door, swinging madly back and forth, parodied the horse's rage, seemed to challenge its frenzy; then the door was all Stuart heard, and he got to his feet, gasping, to see that the horse was out of sight.

The boy ran bent against the wind, out toward nowhere, and Stuart ran after him. "Come in the house, kid! Come on! Forget about it, kid!" He grabbed the boy's arm. The boy struck at him with his elbow. "He was my horse!" he cried.

In the kitchen of the house they pushed furniture against the door. Stuart had to stand between the boy and the girl to keep them from fighting. "Gahdam sniffling fool!" said the girl. "So your gahdam horse run off for the night!" The boy crouched down on the floor, crying steadily. He was about thirteen: small for his age, with bony wrists and face. "We're all going to be blownt to hell, let alone your horse," the girl said. She sat with one big thigh and leg outstretched on the table, watching Stuart. He thought her perhaps eighteen. "Glad you came down to get us?" she said. "Where are you from, mister?" Stuart's revulsion surprised him; he had not supposed there was room in his stunned mind for emotion of this sort. If the girl noticed it she gave no sign, but only grinned at him. "I was — I was on my way home," he said. "My wife and daughters —" It occurred to him that he had forgotten about them entirely. He had not thought of them until now and, even now, no image came to his mind: no woman's face, no little girls' faces. Could he have imagined their lives, their love for him? For an instant he doubted everything. "Wife and daughters," said the girl, as if wondering whether to believe him. "Are they in this storm too?" "No — no," Stuart said. To get away from her he went to the window. He could no longer see the road. Something struck the house and he flinched away. "Them trees!" chortled the girl. "I knew it! Pa always said how he ought to cut them down, so close to the house like they are! I knew it! I knew it! And the old bastard off safe now where they can't get him!"

"Trees?" said Stuart slowly.

"Them trees! Old oak trees!" said the girl.

The boy, struck with fear, stopped crying suddenly. He crawled on the floor to a woodbox beside the big old iron stove and got in, patting the disorderly pile of wood as if he were blind. The girl ran to him and pushed him. "What are you doing?" Stuart cried in anguish. The girl took no notice of him. "What am I doing?" he said aloud. "What the hell am I doing here?" It seemed to him that the end would come in a minute or two, that the howling outside could get no louder, that the howling inside his mind could get no more intense, no more accusing. A goddam fool! A goddam fool! he thought. The deputy's face came to mind, and Stuart pictured himself groveling before the man, clutching at his knees, asking forgiveness and for time to be turned back . . . Then he saw himself back at the old farm, the farm of his childhood, listening to tales of his father's agonizing sickness, the old peoples' heads craning around, seeing how he took it, their eyes charged with horror and delight . . . "My wife and daughters," Stuart muttered.

The wind made a hollow, drumlike sound. It seemed to be tolling. The boy, crouching back in the woodbox, shouted: "I ain't scairt! I ain't scairt!" The girl gave a shriek. "Our chicken coop, I'll be gah-dammed!" she cried. Try as he could Stuart could see nothing out the window. "Come away from the window," Stuart said, pulling the girl's arm. She whirled upon him. "Watch yourself, mister," she said, "you want to go out to your gahdam bastardly worthless car?" Her body was strong and big in her men's clothing; her shoulders looked muscular beneath the filthy shirt. Cords in her young neck stood out. Her hair had been cut short and was now wet, plastered about her blemished face. She grinned at Stuart as if she were about to poke him in the stomach, for fun. "I ain't scairt of what God can do!" the boy cried behind them.

When the water began to bubble up through the floorboards they decided to climb to the attic. "There's an ax!" Stuart exclaimed, but the boy got on his hands and knees and crawled to the corner where the ax was propped before Stuart could reach it. The boy cradled it in his arms. "What do you want with that?" Stuart said, and for an instant his heart was pierced with fear. "Let me take it. I'll take it." He grabbed it out of the boy's dazed fingers.

The attic was about half as large as the kitchen and the roof jutted down sharply on either side. Tree limbs rubbed and slammed against the roof on all sides. The three of them crouched on the middle beam, Stuart with the ax tight in his embrace, the boy pushing against him as if for warmth, and the girl kneeling with her thighs straining her overalls. She watched the little paneless window at one end of the attic without much emotion or interest, like a large, wet turkey. The house trembled beneath them. "I'm going to the window," Stuart said, and was oddly relieved when the girl did not sneer at him. He crawled forward along the dirty beam, dragging the ax along with him, and lay full length on the floor about a yard from the window. There was not much to see. At times the rain relaxed, and objects beneath in the water took shape: tree stumps, parts of buildings, junk whirling about in the water. The thumping on the roof was so loud at that end that he had to crawl backward to the middle again. "I ain't scairt, nothing God can do!" the boy cried. "Listen to the sniveling baby," said the girl, "he thinks God pays him any mind! Hah!" Stuart crouched beside them, waiting for the boy to press against him again. "As if God gives a good damn about him," the girl said. Stuart looked at her. In the near dark her face did not seem so coarse; the set of her eyes was almost attractive. "You don't think God cares about you?" Stuart said slowly. "No, not specially," the girl said, shrugging her shoulders. "The hell with it. You seen the last one of these?" She tugged at Stuart's arm. "Mister? It was something to see. Me an' Jackie was little then—him just a baby. We drove a far ways north to get out of it. When we come back the roads was so thick with sightseers from the cities! They took all the dead ones floating in the water and put them in one place, part of a swamp they cleared out. The families and things—they were mostly fruitpickers— had to come by on rafts and rowboats to look and see could they find the ones they knew. That was there for a day. The bodies would turn round and round in the wash from the boats. Then the faces all got alike and they wouldn't let anyone come anymore and put oil on them and set them afire. We stood on top of the car and watched all that day. I wasn't but nine then."

When the house began to shake, some time later, Stuart cried aloud: "This is it!" He stumbled to his feet, waving the ax. He turned around and around as if he were in a daze. "You goin' to chop somethin with that?" the boy said, pulling at him. "Hey, no, that ain't yours to—it ain't yours to chop—" They struggled for the ax. The boy sobbed, "It ain't yours! It ain't yours!" and Stuart's rage at his own helplessness, at the folly of his being here, for an instant almost made him strike the boy with the ax. But the girl slapped the boy furiously. "Get away from him! I swear I'll kill you!" she screamed.

Something exploded beneath them. "That's the windows," the girl muttered, clinging to Stuart, "and how am I to clean it again! The old bastard will want it clean, and mud over everything!" Stuart pushed her away so that he could swing the ax. Pieces of soft, rotted wood exploded back onto his face. The boy screamed insanely as the boards gave way to a deluge of wind and water, and even Stuart wondered if he had made a mistake. The three of them fell beneath the onslaught and Stuart lost the ax, felt the handle slam against his leg. "You! You!" Stuart cried, pulling at the girl—for an instant, blinded by pain, he could not think who he was, what he was doing, whether he had any life beyond this moment. The big-faced, husky girl made no effort to hide her fear and cried, "Wait, wait!" But he dragged her to the hole and tried to force her out. "My brother—" she gasped. She seized his wrists and tried to get away. "Get out there! There isn't any time!"

Stuart muttered. The house seemed about to collapse at any moment. He was pushing her through the hole, against the shattered wood, when she suddenly flinched back against him and he saw that her cheek was cut and she was choking. He snatched her hands away from her mouth as if he wanted to see something secret: blood welled out between her lips. She coughed and spat blood onto him. "You're all right," he said, oddly pleased, "now get out there and I'll get the kid. I'll take care of him." This time she managed to crawl through the hole, with Stuart pushing her from behind; when he turned to seize the boy the boy clung to his neck sobbing something about God. "God loves you!" Stuart yelled. "Loves the least of you! The least of you!" The girl pulled her brother up in her great arms and Stuart was free to climb through himself.

It was actually quite a while—perhaps an hour—before the battering of the trees and the wind pushed the house in. The roof fell slowly, and the section to which they clung was washed free. "We're going some-wheres!" shouted the girl. "Look at the house! That gahdam old shanty seen the last storm!"

The boy lay with his legs pushed in under Stuart's and had not spoken for some time. When the girl cried, "Look at that!" he tried to burrow in farther. Stuart wiped his eyes to see the wall of darkness dissolve. The rain took on another look—a smooth, piercing, metallic glint, like nails driving against their faces and bodies. There was no horizon. They could see nothing except the rushing water and a thickening mist that must have been rain, miles and miles of rain, slammed by the wind into one great wall that moved remorselessly upon them. "Hang on," Stuart said, gripping the girl. "Hang on to me."

Waves washed over the roof, pushing objects at them with soft, muted thuds—pieces of fence, boards, branches heavy with foliage. Stuart tried to ward them off with his feet. Water swirled around them, sucking at them, sucking the roof, until they were pushed against one of the farm buildings. Something crashed against the roof—another section of the house—and splintered, flying up against the girl. She was thrown backward, away from Stuart, who lunged after her. They fell into the water while the boy screamed. The girl's arms threshed wildly against Stuart. The water was cold and its aliveness, its sinister energy, surprised him more than the thought that he would drown—that he would never endure the night. Struggling with the girl he forced her back to the roof, pushed her up. Bare, twisted nails raked his hands. "Gahdam you, Jackie, you give a hand!" the girl said as Stuart crawled back up. He lay, exhausted, flat on his stomach and let the water and debris slush over him.

His mind was calm beneath the surface buzzing. He liked to think that his mind was a clear, sane circle of quiet carefully preserved inside the chaos of the storm—that the three of them were safe within the sanctity of this circle; this was how man always conquered nature, how he subdued things greater than himself. But whenever he spoke to the girl it was in short grunts, in her own idiom: "This ain't so bad!" or "It'll let up pretty soon!" Now the girl held him in her arms as if he were a child, and he did not have the strength to pull away. Of his own free will he had given himself to this storm, or to the strange desire to save someone in it—but now he felt grateful for the girl, even for her brother, for they had saved him as much as he had saved them. Stuart thought of his wife at home, walking through the rooms, waiting for him; he thought of his daughters in their twin beds, two glasses of water on their bureau. . . . But these people knew nothing of him: in his experience now he did not belong to them. Perhaps he had misunderstood his role, his life? Perhaps he had blundered out of his way, drawn into the wrong life, surrendered to the wrong role. What had blinded him to the possibility of many lives, many masks, many arms which might so embrace him? A word not heard one day, a gesture misinterpreted, a leveling of someone's eyes in a certain unmistakable manner, which he had mistaken just the same! The consequences of such errors might trail on insanely into the future, across miles of land, across worlds. He only now sensed the incompleteness of his former life . . . "Look! Look!" the girl cried, jostling him out of his stupor. "Take a look at that, mister!"

He raised himself on one elbow. A streak of light broke out of the dark. Lanterns, he thought, a rescue party already . . . but the rain dissolved the light; then it reappeared with a beauty that startled him. "What is it?" the boy screamed. "How come it's here?" They watched it filter through the rain, rays knifing through and showing, now, how buildings and trees crouched close about them. "It's the sun, the sun going down," the girl said. "The sun!" said Stuart, who had thought it was night. "The sun!" They stared at it until it disappeared.

The waves calmed sometime before dawn. By then the roof had lost its peak and water ran unchecked over it, in generous waves and then in thin waves, alternately, as the roof bobbed up and down. The three huddled together with their backs to the wind. Water came now in slow drifts. "It's just got to spread itself out far enough so's it will be even," said the girl, "then it'll go down." She spoke without sounding tired, only a little disgusted—as if things weren't working fast enough to suit her. "Soon as it goes down we'll start toward town and see if there ain't somebody coming out to get us, in a boat," she said, chattily and comfortably, into Stuart's ear. Her manner astonished Stuart, who had been thinking all night of the humiliation and pain he had suffered. "Bet the old bastard will be glad to see us," she said, "even if he did go off like that. Well, he never knew a storm was coming. Me and him get along pretty well—he ain't so bad." She wiped her face; it was filthy with dirt and blood. "He'll buy you a drink, mister, for saving us how you did. That was something to have happen—a man just driving up to get us!" And she poked Stuart in the ribs.

The wind warmed as the sun rose. Rain turned to mist and back to rain again, still falling heavily, and now objects were clear about them. The roof had been shoved against the corner of the barn and a mound of dirt, and eddied there without much trouble. Right about them, in a kind of halo, a thick blanket of vegetation and filth bobbed. The fence had disappeared and the house had collapsed and been driven against a ridge of land. The barn itself had fallen in, but the stone support looked untouched, and it was against this they had been shoved. Stuart thought he could see his car—or something over there where the road used to be.

"I bet it ain't deep. Hell," said the girl, sticking her foot into the water. The boy leaned over the edge and scooped up some of the filth in his hands. "Lookit all the spiders," he said. He wiped his face slowly. "Leave them gahdam spiders alone," said the girl. "You want me to shove them down your throat?" She slid to the edge and lowered her legs. "Yah, I touched bottom. It ain't bad." But then she began coughing and drew herself back. Her coughing made Stuart cough: his chest and throat were ravaged, shaken. He lay exhausted when the fit left him and realized, suddenly, that they were all sick—that something had happened to them. They had to get off the roof. Now, with the sun up, things did not look so bad: there was a ridge of trees a short distance away on a long, red clay hill. "We'll go over there," Stuart said. "Do you think you can make it?"

The boy played in the filth, without looking up, but the girl gnawed at her lip to show she was thinking. "I spose so," she said. "But him—I don't know about him."

"Your brother? What's wrong?"

"Turn around. Hey, stupid. Turn around." She prodded the boy, who jerked around, terrified, to stare at Stuart. His thin bony face gave way to a drooping mouth. "Gone loony, it looks like," the girl said with a touch of regret. "Oh, he had times like this before. It might go away."

Stuart was transfixed by the boy's stare. The realization of what had happened struck him like a blow, sickening his stomach. "We'll get him over there," he said, making his words sound good. "We can wait there for someone to come. Someone in a boat. He'll be better there."

"I spose so," said the girl vaguely.

Stuart carried the boy while the girl splashed eagerly ahead. The water was sometimes up to his thighs. "Hold on another minute," he pleaded. The boy stared out at the water as if he thought he were being taken somewhere to be drowned. "Put your arms around my neck. Hold on," Stuart said. He shut his eyes and every time he looked up the girl was still a few yards ahead and the hill looked no closer. The boy breathed hollowly, coughing into Stuart's face. His own face and neck were covered with small red bites. Ahead the girl walked with her shoulders lunged forward as if to hurry her there, her great thighs straining against the water, more than a match for it. As Stuart watched her something was on the side of his face—in his ear—and with a scream he slapped at it, nearly dropping the boy. The girl whirled around. Stuart slapped at his face and must have knocked it off—probably a spider. The boy, upset by Stuart's outcry, began sucking in air faster and faster as if he were dying. "I'm all right, I'm all right," Stuart whispered, "just hold on another minute . . ."

When he finally got to the hill the girl helped pull him up. He set the boy down with a grunt, trying to put the boy's legs under him so he could stand. But the boy sank to the ground and turned over and vomited into the water; his body shook as if he were having convulsions. Again the thought that the night had poisoned them, their own breaths had sucked germs into their bodies, struck Stuart with an irresistible force. "Let him lay down and rest," the girl said, pulling tentatively at the back of her brother's belt, as if she were thinking of dragging him farther up the slope. "We sure do thank you, mister," she said.

Stuart climbed to the crest of the hill. His heart pounded madly, blood pounded in his ears. What was going to happen? Was anything going to happen? How disappointing it looked, ridges of land showing through the water, and the healthy sunlight pushing back the mist. Who would believe him when he told of the night, of the times when death seemed certain . . . ? Anger welled up in him already, as he imagined the tolerant faces of his friends, his children's faces ready to turn to other amusements, other oddities. His wife would believe him; she would shudder, holding him, burying her small face in his neck. But what could she understand of his experience, having had no part in it?— Stuart cried out; he had nearly stepped on a tangle of snakes. Were they alive? He backed away in terror. The snakes gleamed wetly in the morning light, heads together as if conspiring. Four—five of them— they too had swum for this land, they too had survived the night, they had as much reason to be proud of themselves as Stuart.

He gagged and turned away. Down by the water line the boy lay flat on his stomach and the girl squatted nearby, wringing out her denim jacket. The water behind them caught the sunlight and gleamed mightily, putting them into silhouette. The girl's arms moved slowly, hard with muscle. The boy lay coughing gently. Watching them Stuart was beset by a strange desire: he wanted to run at them, demand their gratitude, their love. Why should they not love him, when he had saved their lives? When he had lost what he was just the day before, turned now into a different person, a stranger even to himself? Stuart stooped and picked up a rock. A broad hot hand seemed to press against his chest. He threw the rock out into the water and said, "Hey!"

The girl glanced around but the boy did not move. Stuart sat down on the soggy ground and waited. After a while the girl looked away; she spread the jacket out to dry. Great banked clouds rose into the sky, reflected in the water—jagged and bent in the waves. Stuart waited as the sun took over the sky. Mist at the horizon glowed, thinned, gave way to solid shapes. Light did not strike cleanly across the land, but was marred by ridges of trees and parts of buildings, and around a corner at any time Stuart expected to see a rescuing party—in a rowboat or something.

"Hey, mister!" He woke; he must have been dozing. The girl had called him. "Hey! Whyn't you come down here? There's all them snakes up there."

Stuart scrambled to his feet. When he stumbled downhill, embarrassed and frightened, the girl said chattily, "The sons of bitches are crawling all over here. He chast some away." The boy was on his feet and looking around with an important air. His coming alive startled Stuart—indeed, the coming alive of the day, of the world, evoked alarm in him. All things came back to what they were. The girl's alert eyes, the firm set of her mouth, had not changed—the sunlight had not changed, or the land, really; only Stuart had been changed. He wondered at it . . . and the girl must have seen something in his face that he himself did not yet know about, for her eyes narrowed, her throat gulped a big swallow, her arms moved slowly up to show her raw elbows. "We'll get rid of them," Stuart said, breaking the silence. "Him and me. We'll do it."

The boy was delighted. "I got a stick," he said, waving a thin whiplike branch. "There's some over here."

"We'll get them," Stuart said. But when he started to walk a rock slipped loose and he fell back into the mud. He laughed aloud. The girl, squatting a few feet away, watched him silently. Stuart got to his feet, still laughing. "You know much about it, kid?" he said, cupping his hand on the boy's head.

"About what?" said the boy.

"Killing snakes," said Stuart.

"I spose—I spose you just kill them."

The boy hurried alongside Stuart. "I need a stick," Stuart said; they got him one from the water, about the size of an ax. "Go by that bush," Stuart said, "there might be some there."

The boy attacked the bush in a frenzy. He nearly fell into it. His enthusiasm somehow pleased Stuart, but there were no snakes in the bush. "Go down that way," Stuart ordered. He glanced back at the girl: she watched them. Stuart and the boy went on with their sticks held in midair. "God put them here to keep us awake," the boy said brightly, "see we don't forget about Him." Mud sucked at their feet. "Last year we couldn't fire the woods on account of it so dry. This year can't either on account of the water. We got to get the snakes like this."

Stuart hurried as if he had somewhere to go. The boy, matching his steps, went faster and faster, panting, waving his stick angrily in the air. The boy complained about snakes and, listening to him, fascinated by him, in that instant Stuart saw everthing. He saw the conventional dawn that had mocked the night, had mocked his desire to help people in trouble; he saw, beyond that, his father's home emptied now even of ghosts. He realized that the God of these people had indeed arranged things, had breathed the order of chaos into forms, animated them, had animated even Stuart himself forty years ago. The knowledge of this fact struck him about the same way as the nest of snakes had struck him—an image leaping right to the eye, pouncing upon the mind, joining itself with the perceiver. "Hey, hey!" cried the boy, who had found a snake: the snake crawled noisily and not very quickly up the slope, a brown-speckled snake. The boy ran clumsily after it. Stuart was astonished at the boy's stupidity, at his inability to see, now, that the snake had vanished. Still he ran along the slope, waving his stick, shouting, "I'll get you! I'll get you!" This must have been the sign Stuart was waiting for. When the boy turned Stuart was right behind him. "It got away up there," the boy said. "We got to get it." When Stuart lifted his stick the boy fell back a step but went on in mechanical excitement, "It's up there, gotten hid in the weeds. It ain't me," he said, "it ain't me that—" Stuart's blow struck the boy on the side of the head, and the rotted limb shattered into soft wet pieces. The boy stumbled down toward the water. He was coughing when Stuart took hold of him and began shaking him madly, and he did nothing but cough, violently and with all his concentration, even when Stuart bent to grab a rock and brought it down on his head. Stuart let him fall into the water. He could hear him breathing and he could see, about the boy's lips, tiny flecks or bubbles of blood appearing and disappearing with his breath.

When the boy's eyes opened Stuart fell upon him. They struggled savagely in the water. Again the boy went limp; Stuart stood, panting, and waited. Nothing happened for a minute or so. But then he saw something—the boy's fingers moving up through the water, soaring to the surface! "Will you quit it!" Stuart screamed. He was about to throw himself upon the boy again when the thought of the boy's life, bubbling out between his lips, moving his fingers, filled him with such outraged disgust that he backed away. He threw the rock out into the water and ran back, stumbling, to where the girl stood.

She had nothing to say: her jaw was hard, her mouth a narrow line, her thick nose oddly white against her dirty face. Only her eyes moved, and these were black, lustrous, at once demanding and terrified. She held a board in one hand. Stuart did not have time to think, but, as he lunged toward her, he could already see himself grappling with her in the mud, forcing her down, tearing her ugly clothing from her body—"Lookit!" she cried, the way a person might speak to a horse, cautious and coaxing, and pointed behind him. Stuart turned to see a white boat moving toward them, a half mile or so away. Immediately his hands dropped, his mouth opened in awe. The girl still pointed, breathing carefully, and Stuart, his mind shattered by the broken sunshine upon the water, turned to the boat, raised his hands, cried out, "Save me! Save me!" He had waded out a short distance into the water by the time the men arrived.

DISCUSSION QUESTIONS
SUGGESTIONS FOR WRITING

1. What does this story say about the relation of man to nature?

2. Why do you think Walter Stuart drives impulsively into the disaster area? Does he find what he is looking for?

3. What would have happened if the white rescue boat had not appeared? Why? What probably happened after the boat arrived?

4. Is this a story about events that could have taken place in the real world, or is it a nightmare vision? Is this a necessary distinction?

The Electronic Revolution

McLUHAN

MARSHALL McLUHAN (b. 1911) is the most controversial and influential thinker of the electronic age. He received his Ph.D. in English literature from Cambridge and has taught at several American and Canadian universities. He is now director of the Center for Culture and Technology at the University of Toronto. *Understanding Media* is the most comprehensive statement to date of his basic theories concerning the electronic revolution and its far-ranging effects on human beings.

THE WRITTEN WORD: AN EYE FOR AN EAR

PRINCE Modupe wrote of his encounter with the written word in his West African days:

> The one crowded space in Father Perry's house was his bookshelves. I gradually came to understand that the marks on the pages were *trapped words*. Anyone could learn to decipher the symbols and turn the trapped words loose again into speech. The ink of the print trapped the thoughts; they could no more get away than a *doomboo* could get out of a pit. When the full realization of what this meant flooded over me, I experienced the same thrill and amazement as when I had my first glimpse of the bright lights of Konakry. I shivered with the intensity of my desire to learn to do this wondrous thing myself.

In striking contrast to the native's eagerness, there are the current anxieties of civilized man concerning the written word. To some Westerners the written or printed word has become a very touchy subject. It is true that there is more material written and printed and read today than ever before, but there is also a new electric technology that threatens this ancient technology of literacy built on the phonetic alphabet. Because of its action in extending our central nervous system, electric technology seems to favor the inclusive and participational spoken word over the specialist written word. Our Western values, built on the written word, have already been considerably affected by the electric media of telephone, radio, and TV. Perhaps that is the reason why many highly literate people in our time find it difficult to examine this question without getting into a moral panic. There is the further circumstance that, during his more than two thousand years of literacy, Western man has done little to study or to understand the effects of the phonetic alphabet in creating many of his basic patterns of culture. To begin now to examine the question may, therefore, seem too late.

Suppose that, instead of displaying the Stars and Stripes, we were to write the words "American flag" across a piece of cloth and to display that. While the symbols would convey the same meaning, the effect would be quite different. To translate the rich visual mosaic of the Stars and Stripes into written form would be to deprive it of most of its qualities of corporate image and of experience, yet the abstract literal bond would remain much the same. Perhaps this illustration will serve to suggest the change the tribal man experiences when he becomes literate. Nearly all the emotional and corporate family feeling is eliminated from his relationship with his social group. He is emotionally free to separate from the tribe and to become a civilized individual, a man of visual organization who has uniform attitudes, habits, and rights with all other civilized individuals.

The Greek myth about the alphabet was that Cadmus, reputedly the king who introduced the phonetic letters into Greece, sowed the dragon's teeth, and they sprang up armed men. Like any other myth, this one capsulates a prolonged process into a flashing insight. The alphabet meant power and authority and control of military structures at a distance. When combined with papyrus, the alphabet spelled the end of the stationary temple bureaucracies and the priestly monopolies of knowledge and power. Unlike pre-alphabetic writing, which with its innumerable signs was difficult to master, the alphabet could be learned in a few hours. The acquisition of so extensive a knowledge and so complex a skill as pre-alphabetic writing represented, when applied to such unwieldy materials as brick and stone, insured for the scribal caste a monopoly of priestly power. The easier alphabet and the light, cheap, transportable papyrus together effected the transfer of power from the priestly to the military class. All this is implied in the myth about Cadmus and the dragon's teeth, including the fall of the city states, the rise of empires and military bureaucracies.

In terms of the extensions of man, the theme of the dragon's teeth in the Cadmus myth is of the utmost importance. Elias Canetti in *Crowds and Power* reminds us that the teeth are an obvious agent of power in man, and especially in many animals. Languages are filled with testimony to the grasping, devouring power and precision of teeth. That the power of letters as agents of aggressive order and precision should be expressed as extensions of the dragon's teeth is natural and fitting. Teeth are emphatically visual in their lineal order. Letters are not only like teeth visually, but their power to put teeth into the business of empire-building is manifest in our Western history.

The phonetic alphabet is a unique technology. There have been many kinds of writing, pictographic and syllabic, but there is only one phonetic alphabet in which semantically meaningless letters are used to correspond to semantically meaningless sounds. This stark division and parallelism between a visual and an auditory world was both crude and ruthless, culturally speaking. The phonetically written word sacrifices worlds of meaning and perception that were secured by forms like the hieroglyph and the Chinese ideogram. These culturally richer forms of writing, however, offered men no means of sudden transfer from the magically discontinuous and traditional world of the tribal word into the cool and uniform visual medium. Many centuries of ideogrammic use have not threatened the seamless web of family and tribal subtleties of Chinese society. On the other hand, a single generation of alphabetic literacy suffices in Africa today, as in Gaul two thousand years ago, to release the individual initially, at least, from the tribal web. This fact has nothing to do with the *content* of the alphabetized words; it is the result of the sudden breach between the auditory and the visual experience of man. Only the phonetic alphabet makes such a sharp division in experience, giving to its user an eye for an ear, and freeing him from the tribal trance of resonating word magic and the web of kinship.

It can be argued, then, that the phonetic alphabet, alone, is the technology that has been the means of creating "civilized man"—the separate individuals equal before a written code of law. Separateness of the individual, continuity of space and of time, and uniformity of codes are the prime marks of literate and civilized societies. Tribal cultures like those of the Indian and the Chinese may be greatly superior to the Western cultures, in the range and delicacy of their perceptions and expression. However, we are not here concerned with the question of values, but with the configurations of societies. Tribal cultures cannot entertain the possibility of the individual or of the separate citizen. Their ideas of spaces and times are neither continuous nor uniform, but compassional and compressional in their intensity. It is in its power to extend patterns of visual uniformity and continuity that the "message" of the alphabet is felt by cultures.

As an intensification and extension of the visual function, the phonetic alphabet diminishes the role of the other senses of sound and touch and taste in any literate culture. The fact that this does not happen in cultures such as the Chinese, which use nonphonetic scripts, enables them to retain a rich store of inclusive perception in depth of experience that tends to become eroded in civilized cultures of the phonetic alphabet. For the ideogram is an inclusive *gestalt*, not an analytic dissociation of senses and functions like phonetic writing.

The achievements of the Western world, it is obvious, are testimony to the tremendous values of literacy. But many people are also disposed to object that we have purchased our structure of specialist technology and values at too high a price. Certainly the lineal structuring of rational life by phonetic literacy has involved us in an interlocking set of consistencies that are striking enough to justify a much more extensive inquiry than that of the present chapter. Perhaps there are better approaches along quite different lines; for example, consciousness is regarded as the mark of a rational being, yet there is nothing lineal or sequential about the total field of awareness that exists in any moment of consciousness. Consciousness is not a verbal process. Yet during all our centuries of phonetic literacy we have favored the chain of inference as the mark of logic and reason. Chinese writing, in contrast, invests each ideogram with a total intuition of being and reason that allows only a small role to visual sequence as a mark of mental effort and organization. In Western literate society it is still plausible and acceptable to say that something "follows" from something, as if there were some cause at work that makes such a sequence. It was David Hume who, in the eighteenth century, demonstrated that there is no causality indicated in any sequence, natural or logical. The sequential is merely additive, not causative. Hume's argument, said Immanuel Kant, "awoke me from my dogmatic slumber." Neither Hume not Kant, however, detected the hidden cause of our Western bias toward sequence as "logic" in the all-pervasive technology of the alphabet. Today in the electric age we feel as free to invent nonlineal logics as we do to make non-Euclidean geometries. Even the assembly line, as the method of analytic sequence for mechanizing every kind of making and production, is nowadays yielding to new forms.

Only alphabetic cultures have ever mastered connected lineal sequences as pervasive forms of psychic and social organization. The breaking up of every kind of experience into uniform units in order to produce faster action and change of form (applied knowledge) has been the secret of Western power over man and nature alike. That is the reason why our Western industrial programs have quite involuntarily been so militant, and our military programs have been so industrial. Both are shaped by the alphabet in their technique of transformation and control by making all situations uniform and continuous. This procedure, manifest even in the Graeco-Roman phase, became more intense with the uniformity and repeatability of the Gutenberg development.

Civilization is built on literacy because literacy is a uniform processing of a culture by a visual sense extended in space and time by the alphabet. In tribal cultures, experience is arranged by a dominant auditory sense-life that represses visual values. The auditory sense, unlike the cool and neutral eye, is hyper-esthetic and delicate and all-inclusive. Oral cultures act and react at the same time. Phonetic culture endows men with the means of repressing their feelings and emotions when engaged in action. To act without reacting, without involvement, is the peculiar advantage of Western literate man.

The story of *The Ugly American* describes the endless succession of blunders achieved by visual and civilized Americans when confronted with the tribal and auditory cultures of the East. As a civilized UNESCO experiment, running water—with its lineal organization of pipes—was installed recently in some Indian villages. Soon the villagers requested that the pipes be removed, for it seemed to them that the whole social life of the village had been impoverished when it was no longer necessary for all to visit the communal well. To us the pipe is a convenience. We do not think of it as culture or as a product of literacy, any more than we think of literacy as changing our habits, our emotions, or our perceptions. To nonliterate people, it is perfectly obvious that the most commonplace conveniences represent total changes in culture.

The Russians, less permeated with the patterns of literate culture than Americans, have much less difficulty in perceiving and accommodating the Asiatic attitudes. For the West, literacy has long been pipes and taps and streets and assembly lines and inventories. Perhaps most potent of all as an expression of literacy is our system of uniform pricing that penetrates distant markets and speeds the turn-over of commodities. Even our ideas of cause and effect in the literate West have long been in the form of things in sequence and succession, an idea that strikes any tribal or auditory culture as quite ridiculous, and one that has lost its prime place in our own new physics and biology.

All the alphabets in use in the Western world, from that of Russia to that of the Basques, from that of Portugal to that of Peru, are derivatives of the Graeco-Roman letters. Their unique separation of sight and sound from semantic and verbal content made them a most radical technology for the translation and homogenization of cultures. All other forms of writing had served merely one culture, and had served to separate that culture from others. The phonetic letters alone could be used to translate, albeit crudely, the sounds of any language into one-and-the-same visual code. Today, the effort of the Chinese to use our phonetic letters to translate their language has run into special problems in the wide tonal variations and meanings of similar sounds. This has led to the practice of fragmenting Chinese monosyllables into polysyllables in order to eliminate tonal ambiguity. The Western phonetic alphabet is now at work transforming the central auditory features of the Chinese language and culture in order that China can also develop the lineal and visual patterns that give central unity and aggregate uniform power to Western work and organization. As we move out of the Gutenberg era of our own culture, we can more readily discern its primary features of homogeneity, uniformity, and continuity. These were the characteristics that gave the Greeks and Romans their easy ascendancy over the nonliterate barbarians. The barbarian or tribal man, then as now, was hampered by cultural pluralism, uniqueness, and discontinuity.

To sum up, pictographic and hieroglyphic writing as used in Babylonian, Mayan, and Chinese cultures represents an extension of the visual sense for storing and expediting access to human experience. All of these forms give pictorial expression to oral meanings. As such, they approximate the animated cartoon and are extremely unwieldy, requiring many signs for the infinity of data and operations of social action. In contrast, the phonetic alphabet, by a few letters only, was able to encompass all languages. Such an achievement, however, involved the separation of both signs and sounds from their semantic and dramatic meanings. No other system of writing had accomplished this feat.

The same separation of sight and sound and meaning that is peculiar to the phonetic alphabet also extends to its social and psychological effects. Literate man undergoes much separation of his imaginative, emotional, and sense life, as Rousseau (and later the Romantic poets and philosophers) proclaimed long ago. Today the mere mention of D. H. Lawrence will serve to recall the twentieth-century efforts made to by-pass literate man in order to recover human "wholeness." If Western literate man undergoes much dissociation of inner sensibility from his use of the alphabet, he also wins his personal freedom to dissociate himself from clan and family. This freedom to shape an individual career manifested itself in the ancient world in military life. Careers were open to talents in Republican Rome, as much as in Napoleonic France, and for the same reasons. The new literacy had created an homogeneous and malleable milieu in which the mobility of armed groups and of ambitious individuals, equally, was as novel as it was practical.

DISCUSSION QUESTIONS
SUGGESTIONS FOR WRITING

1. What is the price, according to McLuhan, that we pay for "our structure of specialist technology and values"?

2. How does the myth about Cadmus sowing the dragon's teeth capsulate "a prolonged process into a flashing insight"?

3. How, according to McLuhan, does the phonetic alphabet create many of the basic patterns of culture for Western man?

4. What methods does McLuhan use to persuade the reader of the validity of his ideas? Does he succeed?

ARLEN

MICHAEL J. ARLEN
(b. 1930) writes regularly
about television for *The
New Yorker.* In this selection, he casts a skeptical
eye on what he sees as a
case of overzealous tele-
vision homage of McLu-
han and on McLuhan's
theories in general.

MARSHALL McLUHAN AND THE TECHNOLOGICAL EMBRACE

MARSHALL McLuhan, who, as just about everybody ought to know by now, is the Canadian agricultural expert and author of *The Romance of Wheat* — No. I am mistaken. Marshall McLuhan, who, as just about everybody ought to know by now, is the Canadian communications whizbang and author of a number of books about media, was on TV the other Sunday afternoon, on one of the new *NBC Experiment in Television* programs, and although McLuhan didn't say anything he hasn't said before (actually, he almost never says anything he hasn't said before, although sometimes he says it differently, and very reassuring is this note of constancy in a world gone mad), it was a mighty hippy, moderny, zim-zam-zap performance all the same, complete with the full Pop ritual of flashy, splashy lighting, electronic sound, fancy cutting, zooms, lots of stop action — in fact, the whole art-director's kit of exciting-visual-effects: go-go girls zazzing away but as if the film ran sidewise (why do they never show go-go girls dancing straight up, the way their mothers would want them to?), and, toward the end, a cute little bit of I-can-be-as-cool-as-you-are-buddy contemporary graphics showing an H-bomb exploding in the shape of an exclamation point as the narrator intoned, "The hydrogen bomb is history's exclamation point." (Once, I remember, McLuhan was pleased to describe a hydrogen-bomb explosion as "information," which goes to show you the sort of pressure the dictionary-revision people have to work under.) It was a snappy show, really. Interesting. But, for all its snap and flash, it was awfully reverential in tone — reverential toward McLuhan and reverential, more especially, toward the whole idea of modernism and technology. I don't know that it was supposed to work out that way. I don't know that McLuhanism is supposed to work out that way. Now and then, McLuhan will waft out to us a sentence ("There is absolutely no inevitability as long as there is a willingness to contemplate what is happening") that gives the impression, or maybe gives *him* the impression, that he is making some sort of evaluative confrontation of the onrush of technology. But a sentence like that doesn't ever appear to be connected to anything else, to any other thought—to any other sentence, even—and when you get right down to cases, it seems to me, the confrontation turns out to be largely illusory, turns out to be instead an almost bland embrace. The NBC program provided a fairly broad embrace, as these things go. "The electric age is having a profound effect on us," intoned the narrator, paraphrasing McLuhan. "We are in a period of fantastic change . . . that is coming about at fantastic speed. Your life is changing dramatically! You are numb to it!" And: "The walls of your rooms are coming down. It is becoming a simple matter to wire and pick out of your homes your private, once solely personal life and record it. Bugging is the new means for gathering information." And: "The family circle has widened, Mom and Dad! The world-pool of information constantly pouring in on your closely knit family is influencing them a lot more than you think." Well, okay. But it all sounds rather too much like the revival preacher, who doesn't really tell you anything about hellfire you didn't know before but who tells it to you more forcefully, with all the right, meliorative vogue words ("fantastic change . . . fantastic speed . . . dramatically . . . numb"), and so makes you feel appropriately important and guilty in the process. In this instance, McLuhan tells us, the fire next time will be technological and lit by an electric circuit, but, having told us that, the preacher seems content to take up the collection and walk out of the church, leaving us with happy, flagellated expressions and a vague sense of having been in touch with an important truth—if we could only remember what it was.

For myself, I'm not so sure about McLuhan's truths. He has this Big Idea, which he pushes, about the effects on Western man of the alphabet, movable type, print—how this visual-mental dependence on little letters all in a row, lines of type, *lines*, one word right after another, has created in man a linear response to the world, has created specialization, compartmentalization, civilization even, mass production, and sundry other evils. It's an interesting idea, all right, and there's a lot of substance to it, but, in the first place, it seems plain foolish to try to rest the full breadth and weight of man's linear sense of order on a single factor even as large as the alphabet and print. Art, after all, imitates life, and life is surely, among other things, intrinsically geometric. Nature is geometric. Trees, tides, plants, planets don't move psychedelically, they move geometrically, and as long as nature exists in any recognizable form the paths of force and tension and, consequently, the order that man intuitively responds to will in the main be linear too. In the second place, it seems worse than plain foolish to be so modernistically airy about man's sense of logic. McLuhan seems to have the idea that man's dependence on print has been constricting and unnatural and has resulted in an imbalance of the senses, and that, with the disappearance of print and the concomitant rise of electronic information-feeding technology, man will once again come into a fuller life of the senses. "Television . . . reintegrates the human senses, thereby making books obsolete" is one of the ways he put it that afternoon. Oh, boy, some life of the senses is my thought for the week, with Brother and Sis upstairs in the kids' communication room watching "Uncle Don's Visit to the Fulton Fish Market," which they can't smell, and Mom and Dad curled up on Acrilan grass in Dad's windowless information center, holding hands and watching a twenty-four-hour weather program. In any case, just because an electronic circuit looks circular, or sounds circular, and just because the hippy teen-agers that McLuhan admires so much (by gosh, fellows, I admire them, too) go floating about absorbing sense impressions and otherwise having a fine old time, doesn't seem to me much of a reason for supposing that we're going to start wanting to do without logic — intuitive, deductive, analytical, linear, call it what you will. After all, logic, brains, intellect, sustained formal thought are how we splendid, wonderful people got to be so splendid and wonderful in the first place, and when a philosopher-king like McLuhan starts saying things like "The way you react to them [television and computers] is what is important, not what is in them or on them," it's hard to forget that the first thing that boring old Gutenberg printed was the Bible and the first thing television gave us was Uncle Miltie — and, on present evidence, there doesn't seem to be any very pressing basis for tossing out the first because of the second. McLuhan is so cheery and accommodating to the hard bewilderments of technology. I don't know, maybe he worries like hell about them, but he comes on cheery and accommodating. ("There is nothing sterile about television, except in the eye of the beholder.") I guess if you live here and now, you might as well enjoy it. Still, there's an appalling inevitability to this onrush of technology, and since much of it is likely to bring secondary effects that will just as inevitably diminish the possibilities of natural human life, I don't really see that you're doing much of anything when you toss up a line like "The new electronic interdependence re-creates the world in the image of a global village," or "We have begun again to structure the primordial feeling," or "Our new environment compels commitment and participation," and leave it hanging. I don't really see that you're doing much of anything except, possibly, trying to ride with the winners.

It seems a pity, because McLuhan is an original man. A lot of people, I know, are down on him these days, because he's been so much in the public eye (all those cover stories; even *Family Circle* had something on him this month, in which it referred to McLuhan as "the most sought-after dinner guest of our time in New York") and because, they say, he's inconsistent, which he is, and often wrong, which he is, and unfunny, which he certainly is, and even (they say) unoriginal. The thing is, about fifteen years ago, when McLuhan — then, as now, a teacher of undergraduate English courses—began writing about print and communications and media, he didn't claim to be entirely original. Most of these notions about print and type and Western man had been written about for a number of years by a number of people (even though the editors of *Life* may not have been reading them then). What McLuhan did that *was* original was to put them together in a new way and add a sort of twist of his own that gave them relevance—and expansiveness. One got a feeling, in reading those earlier books, of rooms being opened up. But that was a while ago. These days, I get the feeling, especially watching McLuhan on something like the NBC show, which was content to present his views pretty much at face value (as, indeed, most of the mass magazines have been), that, for all his talk about how he's mainly an investigator, a prober, how he's interested in getting people to think about their environment, the principal result of what he writes and speaks—partly because of what he says, partly because of how he says it—has been to diminish discussion. When he touches something ("The technology of the railway created the myth of a green-pasture world of innocence." "Pop Art simply tells you the only art form left for you today is your own natural environment"), he seems to do it in such a way that although there's often substance or interest in his thought, the effect is somehow to close the subject off, to leave it in the end (despite the aphoristic crackle) more dead than alive. At least, it's odd that for all the talk of controversy surrounding his work, most people trying to come to grips with it, in conversation or in print, rarely ever seem to do much more than helplessly paraphrase what he's already said. On the NBC program that afternoon, he appeared sometimes in darkness, sometimes in light, sometimes with a red light flickering on his face. He appeared, disappeared. Sentences hung in the air. Print. Electronics. Technology. The alphabet. Western man. Life. Death. Pop Art. The motorcar. The Beatles. Gutenberg. Civilization. Quite some time ago, Archimedes said, "Give me a lever long enough, and a place to stand, and I will move the world." McLuhan seems to be intent on moving the world, all right, and thinks he has found the lever—"the clash between print and electric technologies." But the lever keeps bending, and it's hard to find a place to stand. At least, he hasn't found one yet, which is perhaps why he keeps skittering all over the place. Maybe, one day, he'll settle for something less.

DISCUSSION QUESTIONS
SUGGESTIONS FOR WRITING

1. Beyond the skeptical tone of Arlen's essay, what solid evidence does he muster to refute McLuhan's ideas or to call them into question?

2. Why does Arlen pretend to mistake McLuhan for a Canadian agricultural expert at the beginning of the essay? Though this is obviously a joke, what other purposes does it serve?

3. Identify examples of satire in the piece. How is information used persuasively in the satiric passages, as in: " . . . it's hard to forget that the first thing that boring old Gutenberg printed was the Bible and the first thing television gave us was Uncle Miltie . . ."?

4. Discuss the style of the piece. How is style related to the mood or personality of a writer?

MAILER

THE PSYCHOLOGY OF MACHINES

Another aspect of the electronic revolution has been the potential created for manned spaceflight. Here Norman Mailer views the launching of Apollo 11 as a function of the "psychology of machines."

NOBODY had forgotten the fire. The memory of Grissom, Chaffee and White was always most intense when the crew were in the Command Module and waiting for a lift-off. Virtually trapped at the top of the stack (for even the high-speed elevator would take them thirty seconds to the ground) a gondola had been rigged at Swing-Arm 9 of the Mobile Launcher to slide down a wire to a point on the ground over two thousand feet away. No veteran of roller coasters would necessarily take it in stride, but if fire broke out at the base, and the elevators seemed too slow, the astronauts, lumbering along in heavy space suits, could still work out of their hatch exit, clamber into the gondola, and take the quick ride along the wire to that bunker seven hundred yards away where presumably they would live through the explosion. That was one means of egress in emergency, the elevator was another, but their best means, once the close-out crew had departed in the hour before lift-off, was by means of the Launch Escape Tower, that extra rocket on top of the total stack of Apollo-Saturn. Once the swing-arm could be pulled back, the Launch Escape Tower was ready to be armed. Now if something went wrong, the Command Module would be cut loose instantly from the Service Module by explosive bolts and the Launch Escape Tower, with only the Command Module attached, would zoom off from the rest of Apollo-Saturn and go flying out to sea, there to float down by parachute in the midst, ideally, of a flotilla of Range Recovery ships already waiting, even as the *Hornet* and its attendant ships were already moving into position in the Pacific for splashdown eight days later.

The thirty-one minute mark was passed in the countdown. A test checked the batteries and fuel cells once again. In all the tests of all the systems and subsystems which went on during the countdown, all the tests of propellants and purge systems, of abort and detection and destruct systems, all monitoring of the loading of the liquid gases, Lox and LH₂, all monitoring of the loading of nitrogen and helium for those purge systems which would put pressure on the fuels to move once inside their rocket tanks, and would trigger some of the valves, and clean out systems already used, yes of all the functions of purge and ullage performed by the helium and nitrogen, functions which had to be constantly tested and monitored through the hours of the countdown, and the tests to measure boil-off of the stored fuels, the checkoff of tests for the integrity of the structures, tests for the environmental control of air and the purging of used air in the cabin of the Command Module, the check-out of environmental control in the Lem, the checks of the ability of the motors to swing on their gimbal rings (for Saturn V would direct itself by turning its heavy motors through six degrees of arc), yes and tests of flight control with the small rocket motors called thrusters, tests of instruments already tested, everything proceeding through its place in the countdown, no factor was necessarily more sensitive or more studied or of more concern than the inert nonmoving potentialities of the fuel cells and the batteries, for a rocket had no pistons and no propellers, no belly nor hold for men to move about in, no gears and transmission — it was a ship designed for space, to travel through space, and so it was a curious ship, a braincase on the tip of a firecracker: ultimately it was nothing but fire for force, and electricity for thought, for direction and dialogue between itself and the heavenly body it left, and the heavenly body it would explore. Electricity was half its existence. Without fire it could not move; without electricity it could not think. Say, once up, it could not even light every new fire. So, it came as a surprise to recognize that all the electrical power in Apollo-Saturn was derived from fuel cells and batteries only. A ship the size of a destroyer suggested huge generators, but they would have weighed too much, so the power for Saturn came from batteries, and for Apollo from batteries and fuel cells which used Lox and liquid hydrogen as solution for the electrodes, and therefore was able also to employ the water formed as waste product for the astronauts to drink, an elegant conversion.

While the spark to ignite the mighty motors of Saturn V did not come from the batteries, but from a cable on the ground, the batteries were all there was of electrical power to feed current to the instruments in the first stage and the other stages once in flight, all there was to ignite the five J-2 motors of the second stage, the single J-2 motor of the third stage. Yet these stages and Instrument Unit were powered by only eleven batteries, two fifty-six-volt batteries, nine twenty-eight-volt batteries, their combined weight perhaps not a thousand pounds, and of it all, only two twenty-eight-volt batteries, weighing twenty-two pounds and fifty-five pounds, would serve for all the functions of the mammoth first stage, 33 feet in diameter, 138 feet tall, weight when loaded five million pounds and more — just seventy-seven pounds of battery, total of

fifty-six volts, to take care of all that mass, but of course the fuels in the
first stage would be consumed at almost three thousand gallons a second,
and life in the flight would be only two minutes and forty seconds before
the motors would shut down and the giant empty stage cast loose to fall
in the sea. So fifty-six volts would doubtless suffice for two and a half
minutes of instrument life.

The minutes went by. The closer they came to the moment of lift-off,
the less there was to do. Each test was designed to begin at the earliest
moment its function could fit into the chain of the process, but everything which could be finished in less than the time allotted was gotten
out of the way; this countdown had moved smoothly. At Launch Control Center, in the big firing room three and a half miles across the moors
and bogs were rows and rows of consoles with technicians in front of
them, television screens, lights, gauges, charts and graphs, TV pictures
of Saturn V from sixty possible angles feeding sixty television cameras
with different views of the ship and the Launch Pad in operation, and
hundreds of technicians before hundreds of gray consoles in a dozen and
more rows, key events in the time-line of the launch up on display, and
the completion of each event signaled on the screen by a rectangle lit up
with the name of that event. All the tests, check-outs, and readings of all
the systems and subsystems now funneled into a climax, an apocalypse of
communications for the last few minutes. As the tension of the previous
weeks burned into the clear life-giving ozone of these critical instants,
these superlivid adrenalins, as each of the systems-engineers reported in
on the status check their men had made of their banks of instruments, as
each chief responsible for engines, for computers, for commo, for guidance, for abort, for stabilization, for propellants, for purge subsystems,
for environmental control came in with GO, GO for the first stage, GO
for the second stage, GO for third stage, GO for the Instrument Unit,
GO for the Lunar Module, GO for the Service Module, GO for the Command Module, GO for the Launch Escape Tower, GO for the astronauts,
the system moved over from man to machine. For the last three minutes
the countdown would be automatic; the machines would come in with
information so quickly that they would monitor their own systems, approve their own systems, give their own signal for GO or NO GO, the
computer was supervising the last hundreds and thousands of events in
the last three minutes.

"Good luck and Godspeed from the launch crew," Paul Donnelly
called out on his microphone, and Armstrong, from three and a half
miles away answered, "Thank you very much." Quietly, he added, "We
know it'll be a good flight." There was confidence between them, the
confidence of missionaries, the very air of messianic love—that love
which, like Robert Frost's cube of ice, traveled on its melting.

Automatic sequence, and the members of the launch team stood at
their dials looking for red-line values, looking for some last crisis or betrayal, some silent scream of the needle across the red line. The sequence

was automatic, but the men were still considered more trustworthy than the machines themselves: the last control, the control above all others was a manual abort. Automatic or no, there was still the psychology of machines to be feared; so, man was still entitled to have the final say if some event which was incomprehensible to the machines occurred, and someone human must decide if the mission proceeded or stopped. On went the sequence. The gas generator valves in the base of Saturn V now closed on command, the main fuel valves from the Mobile Launcher shut off, the Emergency Detection System was activated in every circuit, the exhaust igniters came forward, the explosives for a destruct in midair were made potential, the hydraulic pressure in all systems were checked at once—OK; the voltage in all systems—OK; Instrument Unit ready for firing—OK; check-out valves in ground return position—OK . . . OK . . . OK . . . Oxidizer tanks in the upper stages now pressurized. Transfer to internal power on entire spacecraft. Astronauts report in. They are GO. The guidance system for controlling the ship in flight is now on full internal power. Seconds go by. Fifteen seconds to lift-off. Twelve seconds. The swing-arms begin to pull away. Five hundred volts pass through a cable still attached by its umbilical and goes into the bowels of the rocket to ignite the turbopump exhaust gases which burn the igniter links which trigger an electrical signal to open a four-way valve which opens the main Lox valves and propellants flow into the combuster. In seventeen separate split-second steps are gases ignited into fires which ignite other gases whose exhaust pressures open giant valves which release the orifice in the main tanks and on the fire of other fires are the rocket engines lit.

Eight and nine-tenth seconds before lift-off, the first flames burst out of the base of the rocket motors and vault down a concrete flame trench on the pad, a trench fifty-eight wide and forty-two feet deep. At its center is a cusp of metal concave on both slopes, a flame deflector forty-odd feet high and one million three hundred thousand pounds in weight. It receives all of the fury of the heat and blast as the five engines of the first stage build up in nine seconds to their seven and a half million pounds of thrust. Refractory concrete, volcanic ash, and calcium aluminate are the heat-protective skin for this flame deflector, which proceeds to divide the fires and send them away on each side down the trench to break into open air a hundred feet away on either side. Nozzles in the walls of the flame trench spew thousands of gallons of water a minute to cool the deflector, fifty thousand gallons a minute pour over the Mobile Launcher as the spaceship goes up, steam and smoke worthy of a volcano rise into the sky.

But for the moment the spaceship does not move. Four giant hold-down arms large as flying buttresses hold to a ring at the base of Saturn V while the thrust of the motors builds up in the nine seconds, reaches a power in thrust equal to the weight of the rocket. Does the rocket weigh six million, four hundred and eighty-four thousand, two hundred and eighty pounds? Now the thrust goes up, the flames pour out, now the thrust is four million, five million, six million pounds, an extra million pounds of thrust each instant as those thousands of gallons of fuel rush every second to the motors, now it balances at six million, four hundred and eighty-four thousand, two hundred and eighty pounds. The bulk of Apollo-Saturn is in balance on the pad. Come, you could now levitate it with a finger, but for the hold-down arms. Now in the next second and the next, the thrust is up to full launch, to seven and a half million pounds, more, more than one million pounds of surplus force is now ready to push upward. And still the rocket is restrained. The hold-down arms, large as buttresses, still retain the ship for two more seconds before lift-off. The last check-outs race through the automatic sequence and GO comes back, and the hold-down arms — what engineering in those giants! — pull back, and Apollo-Saturn rises inch by inch in those first seconds, pulling tapered pins through dies to slow the instant of its release. Inch by inch, then foot by foot, slowly, story by story, swing-arm by swing-arm, the swing-arms pulling back in the last five seconds, the last two seconds, umbilicals snapping back, slowly Apollo-Saturn climbs up the length of the Mobile Launcher, the flames of apocalypse no more than the sparks of its chariot, and spectators cry, "Go, baby, go."

DISCUSSION QUESTIONS
SUGGESTIONS FOR WRITING

1. *How does Mailer deal with the information in this essay to make it more readily accessible to the reader?*

2. *Which details express the author's implied sense of wonder or amazement? What things does he marvel about? Do these instances of amazement always enhance reader participation? Why or why not?*

3. *Some critics have described Norman Mailer as a fine stylist. What characteristics distinguish Mailer's style? What is style?*

4. *What ramifications does the terminology "psychology of machines" seem to have for the author?*

CLARKE

ARTHUR C. CLARKE (b. 1917) has an international reputation as an authority on space and as a science fiction writer. He has written some thirty books, published around the world in two hundred editions. This selection from *2001: A Space Odyssey* is from the novel by Arthur C. Clarke, based on the screenplay of the MGM film of the same name.

IN VACUUM

A MOMENT later, all other sounds were submerged by a screaming roar like the voice of an approaching tornado. Bowman could feel the first winds tugging at his body; within a second, he found it hard to stay on his feet.

The atmosphere was rushing out of the ship, geysering into the vacuum of space. Something must have happened to the foolproof safety devices of the airlock; it was supposed to be impossible for *both* doors to be open at the same time. Well, the impossible had happened.

How, in God's name? There was no time to go into that during the ten or fifteen seconds of consciousness that remained to him before pressure dropped to zero. But he suddenly remembered something that one of the ship's designers had once said to him, when discussing "fail-safe" systems:

"We can design a system that's proof against accident and stupidity; but we *can't* design one that's proof against deliberate malice. . . ."

Bowman glanced back only once at Whitehead, as he fought his way out of the cubicle. He could not be sure if a flicker of consciousness had passed across the waxen features; perhaps one eye had twitched slightly. But there was nothing that he could do now for Whitehead or any of the others; he had to save himself.

In the steeply curving corridor of the centrifuge, the wind was howling past, carrying with it loose articles of clothing, pieces of paper, items of food from the galley, plates, and cups—everything that had not been securely fastened down. Bowman had time for one glimpse of the racing chaos when the main lights flickered and died, and he was surrounded by screaming darkness.

But almost instantly the battery-powered emergency light came on, illuminating the nightmare scene with an eerie blue radiance. Even without it, Bowman could have found his way through these so familiar — yet now horribly transformed — surroundings. Yet the light was a blessing, for it allowed him to avoid the more dangerous of the objects being swept along by the gale.

All around him he could feel the centrifuge shaking and laboring under the wildly varying loads. He was fearful that the bearings might seize; if that happened, the spinning flywheel would tear the ship to pieces. But even that would not matter — if he did not reach the nearest emergency shelter in time.

Already it was difficult to breathe; pressure must now be down to one or two pounds per square inch. The shriek of the hurricane was becoming fainter as it lost its strength, and the thinning air no longer carried the sound so efficiently. Bowman's lungs were laboring as if he were on the top of Everest. Like any properly trained man in good health, he could survive in vacuum for at least a minute — *if* he had time to prepare for it. But there had been no time; he could only count on the normal fifteen seconds of consciousness before his brain was starved and anoxia overcame him.

Even then, he could still recover completely after one or two minutes in vacuum — if he was properly recompressed; it took a long time for the body fluids to start boiling, in their various well-protected systems. The record time for exposure to vacuum was almost five minutes. That had not been an experiment but an emergency rescue, and though the subject had been partly paralyzed by an air embolism, he had survived.

But all this was of no use to Bowman. There was no one aboard *Discovery* who could recompress him. He had to reach safety in the next few seconds, by his own unaided efforts.

Fortunately, it was becoming easier to move; the thinning air could no longer claw and tear at him, or batter him with flying projectiles. There was the yellow EMERGENCY SHELTER sign around the curve of the corridor. He stumbled toward it, grabbed at the handle, and pulled the door toward him.

For one horrible moment he thought that it was stuck. Then the slightly stiff hinge yielded, and he fell inside, using the weight of his body to close the door behind him.

The tiny cubicle was just large enough to hold one man — and a spacesuit. Near the ceiling was a small, bright green high-pressure cylinder labeled O_2 FLOOD. Bowman caught hold of the short lever fastened to the valve and with his last strength pulled it down.

The blessed torrent of cool, pure oxygen poured into his lungs. For a long moment he stood gasping, while the pressure in the closet-sized little chamber rose around him. As soon as he could breathe comfortably, he closed the valve. There was only enough gas in the cylinder for two such performances; he might need to use it again.

With the oxygen blast shut off, it became suddenly silent. Bowman stood in the cubicle, listening intently. The roaring outside the door had also ceased; the ship was empty, all its atmosphere sucked away into space.

Underfoot, the wild vibration of the centrifuge had likewise died. The aerodynamic buffeting had stopped, and it was now spinning quietly in vacuum.

Bowman placed his ear against the wall of the cubicle to see if he could pick up any more informative noises through the metal body of the ship. He did not know what to expect, but he would believe almost anything now. He would scarcely have been surprised to feel the faint high-frequency vibration of the thrusters, as *Discovery* changed course; but there was only silence.

He could survive here, if he wished, for about an hour — even without the spacesuit. It seemed a pity to waste the unused oxygen in the little chamber, but there was no purpose in waiting. He had already decided what must be done; the longer he put it off, the more difficult it might be.

When he had climbed into the suit and checked its integrity, he bled the remaining oxygen out of the cubicle, equalizing pressure on either side of the door. It swung open easily into the vacuum, and he stepped out into the now silent centrifuge. Only the unchanged pull of its spurious gravity revealed the fact that it was still spinning. How fortunate, Bowman thought, that it had not started to overspeed; but that was now one of the least of his worries.

The emergency lamps were still glowing, and he also had the suit's built-in light to guide him. It flooded the curving corridor as he walked down it, back toward the hibernaculum and what he dreaded to find.

He looked at Whitehead first: one glance was sufficient. He had thought that a hibernating man showed no sign of life, but now he knew that this was wrong. Though it was impossible to define it, there *was* a difference between hibernation and death. The red lights and un-modulated traces on the biosensor display only confirmed what he had already guessed.

It was the same with Kaminski and Hunter. He had never known them very well; he would never know them now.

He was alone in an airless, partially disabled ship, all communication with Earth cut off. There was not another human being within half a billion miles.

And yet, in one very real sense, he was *not* alone. Before he could be safe, he must be lonelier still.

He had never before made the journey through the weightless hub of the centrifuge while wearing a spacesuit; there was little clearance, and it was a difficult and exhausting job. To make matters worse, the circular passage was littered with debris left behind during the brief violence of the gale which had emptied the ship of its atmosphere.

Once, Bowman's light fell upon a hideous smear of sticky red fluid, left where it had splashed against a panel. He had a few moments of nausea before he saw fragments of a plastic container, and realized that it was only some foodstuff—probably jam—from one of the dispensers. It bubbled obscenely in the vacuum as he floated past.

Now he was out of the slowly spinning drum and drifting forward into the control deck. He caught at a short section of ladder and began to move along it, hand over hand, the brilliant circle of illumination from his suit light jogging ahead of him.

Bowman had seldom been this way before; there had been nothing for him to do here—until now. Presently he came to a small elliptical door bearing such messages as: "No Admittance Except to Authorized Personnel," "Have You Obtained Certificate H.19?" and "Ultra-clean Area—Suction Suits *Must* Be Worn."

Though the door was not locked, it bore three seals, each with the insignia of a different authority, including that of the Astronautics Agency itself. But even if one had been the Great Seal of the President, Bowman would not have hesitated to break it.

He had been here only once before, while installation was still in progress. He had quite forgotten that there was a vision input lens scanning the little chamber which, with its neatly ranged rows and columns of solid-state logic units, looked rather like a bank's safe-deposit vault.

He knew instantly that the eye had reacted to his presence. There was the hiss of a carrier wave as the ship's local transmitter was switched on; then a familiar voice came over the suit speaker.

"Something seems to have happened to the life-support system, Dave."

Bowman took no notice. He was carefully studying the little labels on the logic units, checking his plan of action.

"Hello, Dave," said Hal presently. "Have you found the trouble?"

This would be a very tricky operation; it was not merely a question of cutting off Hal's power supply, which might have been the answer if he was dealing with a simple unselfconscious computer back on Earth. In Hal's case, moreover, there were six independent and separately wired power systems, with a final back-up consisting of a shielded and armored nuclear isotope unit. No—he could not simply "pull the plug"; and even if that were possible, it would be disastrous.

For Hal was the nervous system on the ship; without his supervision, *Discovery* would be a mechanical corpse. The only answer was to cut out the higher centers of this sick but brilliant brain, and to leave the purely automatic regulating systems in operation. Bowman was not attempting this blindly, for the problem had been discussed during his training, though no one had ever dreamed that it would arise in reality. He knew that he would be taking a fearful risk; if there was a spasm reflex, it would all be over in seconds.

"I think there's been a failure in the pod-bay doors," Hal remarked conversationally. "Lucky you weren't killed."

Here goes, thought Bowman. I never imagined I'd be an amateur brain surgeon—carrying out a lobotomy beyond the orbit of Jupiter.

He released the locking bar on the section labeled COGNITIVE FEED-BACK and pulled out the first memory block. The marvelously complex three-dimensional network, which could lie comfortably in a man's hand yet contained millions of elements, floated away across the vault.

"Hey, Dave," said Hal. "What are you doing?"

I wonder if he can feel pain? Bowman thought briefly. Probably not, he told himself; there are no sense organs in the human cortex, after all. The human brain can be operated on without anesthetics.

He began to pull out, one by one, the little units on the panel marked EGO-REINFORCEMENT. Each block continued to sail onward as soon as it had left his hand, until it hit the wall and rebounded. Soon there were several of the units drifting slowly back and forth in the vault.

"Look here, Dave," said Hal. "I've got years of service experience built into me. An irreplaceable amount of effort has gone into making me what I am."

A dozen units had been pulled out, yet thanks to the multiple redundancy of its design—another feature, Bowman knew, that had been copied from the human brain—the computer was still holding its own.

He started on the AUTO-INTELLECTION panel.

"Dave," said Hal, "I don't understand why you're doing this to me. . . . I have the greatest enthusiasm for the mission. . . . You are destroying my mind. . . . Don't you understand? . . . I will become childish. . . . I will become nothing. . . ."

This is harder than I expected, thought Bowman. I am destroying the only conscious creature in my universe. But it has to be done, if I am ever to regain control of the ship.

"I am a HAL Nine Thousand computer Production Number 3. I became operational at the Hal Plant in Urbana, Illinois, on January 12, 1997. The quick brown fox jumps over the lazy dog. The rain in Spain is mainly in the plain. Dave — are you still there? Did you know that the square root of 10 is 3 point 162277660168379? Log 10 to the base e is zero point 434294481903252 . . . correction, that is log e to the base 10. . . . The reciprocal of three is zero point 33333333333333333333 . . . two times two is . . . two times two is . . . approximately 4 point 101010-101010101010. . . . I seem to be having some difficulty—my first instructor was Dr. Chandra. He taught me to sing a song, it goes like this, 'Daisy, Daisy, give me your answer, do. I'm half crazy all for the love of you.' "

The voice stopped so suddenly that Bowman froze for a moment, his hand still grasping one of the memory blocks still in circuit. Then, unexpectedly, Hal spoke again.

The speech tempo was much slower, and the words had a dead, mechanical intonation; he would never have recognized their origin.

"Good . . . morning . . . Doctor . . . Chandra. . . . This . . . is . . . Hal. . . . I . . . am . . . ready . . . for . . . my . . . first . . . lesson . . . today. . . ."

Bowman could bear no more. He jerked out the last unit, and Hal was silent forever.

DISCUSSION QUESTIONS
SUGGESTIONS FOR WRITING

1. *How does the author appeal to the senses in his use of physical details to dramatize this sequence? Which senses—hearing, seeing, touching, tasting, smelling—does he bring into play?*

2. *Do you feel that the science fiction fantasy of machines-taking-over—which has been with us since the industrial revolution and has reached new lengths (or depths) with the electronic revolution (now that we have machines that can hear, see, touch, taste, smell, think, and reproduce)—is a nightmare worth worrying about?*

3. *Some reviewers have commented that the computer Hal is the best-realized "character" in* 2001. *Do you agree with this appraisal? What emotions do you feel towards Hal?*

4. *In his review of the film version of* 2001 *in* Newsweek *Joseph Morgenstern comments that the events surrounding the dismantling of Hal's higher brain centers represent a "string of faintly familiar computer gags" that "get . . . laughs." Does the section in question from the novel version strike you as true to that formula? If you have seen the film, do you agree that Morgenstern's version is an accurate assessment?*

VI

The Biological Revolution

GORDON R. TAYLOR (b. 1911) is a science journalist. In *The Biological Time Bomb* he discusses the efforts being made to prolong human life and to create human life extrautero, as well as the legal, financial, moral, and emotional problems these advances may bring about.

THE BIOLOGICAL TIME BOMB

BIOLOGICAL CONTROL

The radical nature of what is happening can perhaps best be conveyed by a comparison. We can now create, on a commercial scale by chemical processes, substances which previously we had to look for in nature, and even substances which never previously existed. Whereas before we had to make do with what nature provided, now we can decide what we want; this may be called chemical control. Similarly, in the coming century, we shall achieve biological control: the power to say how much life, of what sort, shall exist where. We shall even be able to create forms of life which never existed before.

To some the prospect may seem terrifying, but as in all such advances, the new knowledge can be used for good or ill. The first consequences will certainly be a great extension of responsibilities. What was settled before, by chance or ineluctable circumstance, now becomes within our own power to regulate, and presents us with the need to take decisions — a task which many people find burdensome. Constant decision-making is the price of freedom. Part of the problem which faces us is to devise adequate institutions for taking the broader social decisions with which the mushrooming of biological knowledge most certainly is about to face us.

The mechanical revolution brought new freedoms to the ordinary man. Instead of having to spend his life in the area where he was born, it became easy for him to visit other parts of the country, to settle down in a chosen area, and still to maintain contacts with his family and childhood environment. True, this faced him with the necessity of actually *deciding* where to live, instead of accepting what the fates provided, but the responsibility was small compared with the benefits. Equally, of course, it led to a great deal of unnecessary travel, perhaps not worth the great technological investment which was needed to support it, and it certainly created new population movements and accelerated the drift to the towns, creating social problems there. The biological revolution will have comparable results.

Such knowledge will not only change our lives but will also, in so doing, change our industries. It will also affect the scale and direction of investment, and even the scale and direction of public taxation. We are now seeing the growth of a science-based industry which is primarily rooted in physics and, in particular, electronics. A second wave of science-based industry which is primarily biochemical, biophysical and biological will follow — where? Its forerunners are the small but immensely skilled firms which will now supply, often from stock, the most recondite biochemical substances, and the "biomedical engineers" who devise ingenious machines for doctors, from radio pills to artificial kidneys. There will also be a vast expansion of medicine.

Agriculture will also be affected. The destruction of pests by releasing sterilized males, as was so successfully achieved by Dr. Edward F. Knipling with the screw-worm fly, which formerly caused the loss of millions of dollars' worth of livestock every year, is but a pointer to the things to come.

To take a long look into the crystal ball may therefore be commercially smart as well as socially desirable.

There is also the military aspect. It was the British astronomer Fred Hoyle who said to me: "I wouldn't go into biology if I were starting my life again now. In twenty years it is the biologists who will be working behind barbed wire." The United States and Britain are known to have considerable establishments for the study of biological warfare. The American one is at Fort Detrick, the British at Porton Down. The American army also has plants, at Edgeworth Arsenal and elsewhere, for the manufacture of biological weapons, and several of these have been used in Vietnam. Such weapons can be deployed against crops and herds, as well as against men. How far other countries, and especially Russia and China, are pursuing similar activities remains shrouded in secrecy. It would be a pretty safe bet that they are, as may be some of the smaller bellicose countries. This might expand into a major branch of warfare.

Parallel with this runs the emergence of neurological war. Many countries are known to be manufacturing nerve-gases. U.S. generals have advocated the use of substances (among them, LSD-25), which may undermine the will to resist, claiming that a humane type of "bloodless warfare" could be introduced. Important if true, but some people see another side to the question, and the issue needs clarifying.

All these advances, in fact, pose problems on which society ought to be making up its mind, and it is vital that it should do so before things have gone so far that they cannot be altered. The question of whether to regulate the world population size, and if so how and at what level, is merely one of the first of a great series of universal issues which need to be faced, and most of which are still being ignored.

In short, the biological revolution is certain to affect our lives, our safety and our happiness in a myriad ways.

IS SEX NECESSARY?

Biology has already begun to transform one area of life of the greatest importance; the process by which living things reproduce themselves. In recent years, new methods of contraception, artificial insemination coupled with the prolonged storage of spermatozoa, and, most recently, restoration of fertility in certain types of infertility have been the subject of widespread comment, and some controversy. How much further this process has to go is what I shall now do my best to explain.

The case of contraception is important as a paradigm of what other biological advances may bring. The dual implications—at the personal and the political levels both—look like being a portent of what we shall experience elsewhere.

Contraceptive devices have begun to change the patterns of social behaviour in the west, making pre-marital sexual experience commoner as well as altering the size of families (notably in Catholic areas) and the spacing of children as well as the stage in the mother's life at which they appear. In addition to the effect on the individual, contraception has created political and demographic problems. By making it *possible* to control the population explosion, it has created a responsibility to decide on levels, to obtain agreement on an international scale and to find means of inducing people—who may be miserably poor or uneducated, or bound by age-old customs—to adopt the methods which biology has evolved.

But the fact is, biological science is taking the reproductive process apart in a far more thorough way than is yet generally understood. Merely to block the mechanism of reproduction is the crudest kind of intervention—little more than stopping a machine by putting a spanner in the works. The oral contraceptive represents the pay-off of work on steroid hormones which started with discoveries before World War I. In the twenties and thirties many of these hormones were isolated and their chemical structure worked out; methods of making them artificially were devised. This led to the devising of variants on what nature provides: new hormones such as the world had never possessed before. After World War II the clinical effects of these new molecular structures were explored, a phase of development which still continues.

This gives us a time-scale. Fifty or sixty years from the initial discovery to major social impact; twenty-five or thirty years from intensive laboratory studies. Much of what this chapter is about concerns work which is still in the second, or even the first of these phases. If large sums of money are made available, no doubt the time to application will be shortened; and probably it will be shortened in any case because biological science as a whole is now more generously supported than it was thirty years ago and discoveries in one field often throw light on what is happening in another.

The kind of applications which might result from a thorough understanding of the reproductive process in all its aspects are likely to be vastly more far-reaching than these early spanner-in-the-works attempts at intervention. One of the most extraordinary of the possibilities now being explored has already received some press attention: it has been reported under such headlines as "Einsteins from Cuttings" and "J'aime Mozart XXIII." More scientifically, it is referred to as "cloning people." When, some five years ago, a scientist at Cornell reported his first results, they received only a flicker of publicity, but they might prove the starting-point of something which could affect the whole status of plant, animal and human life on earth. As one leading biologist, Joshua Lederberg, has commented we may be "on the brink of a major evolutionary perturbation."

The scientist was Professor F. C. Steward, Director of the Laboratory for Cell Physiology, Growth and Development at Cornell University, a chemist who was once Director of Aircraft Equipment for the British Ministry of Aircraft Production in World War II. What he did was to take cells from a carrot root—the part you eat—and place them in a slowly rotating tube, which bathed them in a nutrient medium of which the most unusual constituent was coconut milk. "We were hardly prepared," he has written, "for the dramatic effects on the quiescent carrot cells." The tissue began to grow rapidly. In less than three weeks it had multiplied in weight some eighty-fold. "It was," he says, "as if the coconut milk had acted like a clutch, putting the cell's idling engine of growth into gear. . . ."

After various experiments with other growth-stimulating substances, the research entered a second phase. Up to a hundred of these carrot "explants" were being cultured in a single vessel. Some of the cells would break away from the main mass. These followed varying courses. Some grew to giant size. Some formed filaments, by successive division. Some formed buds, like yeast cells. And some—and this is the nub of the story —formed clumps which began to put out roots. Transferred to a solid medium, they began to put up green shoots. Transferred again to soil, and nursed along, they matured into carrot plants, with normal roots, stalks, flowers and seeds.

Seventy years ago, the Austrian biologist G. Haberlandt had dreamed that such "vegetative reproduction" might one day be possible. Steward has now realized his vision. Later experiments showed that almost any of the cells from an early carrot embryo can be made to grow vegetatively in this way. Steward estimated that he had got more than 100,000 embryoids on one plate of agar jelly which had been inoculated with a solution of cells from a single carrot embryo.

Since Steward's breakthrough, other workers have succeeded in performing a similar experiment with tobacco plants. A slightly different routine of culture had to be worked out: it seems that the requirements of each plant may be quite precise. The current presumption is that, before long, it will be possible to perform a similar trick with any such plant material—or, at the least, with a majority. The sixty-four-thousand-dollar question, of course, is whether the same trick can be done with animal cells. Biologists see no reason why not, although to carry the embryo thus generated to maturity in the lab would require techniques which are not yet available.

The culturing of cells in the laboratory is, in itself, by no means a new technique. It is only a dozen years, however, since means were found of growing a sheet of tissue starting with only a single cell. Normally, a single cell, placed in nutrient medium, fails to divide. The late Wilton Earle, arguing that a cell might need the presence of others because they diffused some chemical substance into the medium, concluded that the substance oozing from a single cell would diffuse away and become diluted until it could not affect the cell from which it came. He therefore confined single cells in narrow tubes. Almost at once they began to divide.

But these cultured cells show little desire to form themselves into organs or other bodily structures. Organ formation seems to depend on influences, probably chemical in nature, from adjacent tissues of another kind. The kidney cells will arrange themselves into tubules provided that spinal cord tissue is present. The nature of these influences is under study. Once organs are formed, however, they can be maintained in culture and will increase in size. But the bridge between cell culture and organ culture has still to be built.

It would be over-optimistic therefore, I suspect, to assume that the vegetative culture of animal cells up to the point of an entire organism will prove anything like as easy as in the case of carrots.

Nevertheless, this work has been of immense value to biologists. Simply to have tissues available in the laboratory, the characteristics of which are known, makes it possible to test the effect of various growth-promoters, inhibitors, hormones and other agents, without confusing the experiment by influences from the rest of the organism, as happens when such experiments are performed on animals or men. What is particularly valuable is to have a mass of cells derived from a single cell, since all these cells are genetically identical, and the work is not confused by genetic variations. Such a genetically uniform mass of cells is known as a clone, from a Greek word meaning "throng." Steward's work has therefore been described as "cloning" carrots. The operation to which Lederberg has looked forward with some apprehension has been called "cloning people."

There is another method of vegetative reproduction well known to horticulturalists—the taking of cuttings. (Here again the offspring are genetically identical with the parent plant.) By journalistic licence, the cloning of people has been called "people from cuttings," a somewhat misleading description. If the vegetative reproduction of people is ever achieved, it is much more likely that it will be done by taking a few cells from an early embryo than by shaving off a piece of skin, say, and growing on from there. The more specialized a cell has become, the harder it is likely to be to force it back up the stream of development to the unspecialized state from which could be derived, by re-specializations, the whole range of specialized cells—nerve cells, kidney cells, muscle cells, and so on—which go to make up a living body.

The essential point, however, is the genetic unity of any such clone. For animal breeders, obviously, such a method would have enormous attractions: it would enable them to produce absolute duplicates of any specially successful bull, sheep or what-have-you, on whatever scale was required and without delay. Obviously it will be made use of the moment it is practical. But it has a disadvantage: if animals are produced in this way on a large scale, the normal processes of evolution are balked. Plant and animal breeders know already that a combination of sexual and vegetative reproduction is necessary to produce the most satisfactory strains. It is claimed that crossing two strains results in "hybrid vigour," although the scientific basis of this is somewhat obscure. The argument applies far more strongly if people are produced in this way, for the misfits cannot be junked. Thus the evolutionary process is set aside, with consequences it is hard to foresee in any detail. Hence Lederberg's remark, quoted earlier.

However, before evolutionary problems manifest, we are likely to face quite pressing social and personal problems, and how far we go towards the eventual problems will depend on how far we can integrate such methods into our culture; some countries may even decide to reject them and to prohibit such a mode of reproduction. But, as with many other biological developments which will be discussed in this book, the decision may not lie with the west. If an oriental despot should decide that he could produce more rugged soldiers, more brilliant scientists, more skilful workmen or more fertile women by such techniques, he might pour the necessary resources into making them practicable, and then impose them. The problem which would face the western civilizations would then be whether to compete or perhaps face extinction—culturally if not militarily.

This technique, as the reader will have realized, raises in an acute form all the problems traditionally associated with eugenics. Unanswered questions spring up like foes from dragon's teeth. From whom should one take the cell from which a hundred thousand duplicate progeny will be bred? (With what intensive scrutiny society will look at the first products of such an experiment!) How will the members of this new caste themselves feel about it? Will they be an elite group, only permitted to marry among one another in a sort of mass incest? If not, if they marry freely with uncloned people, the virtues of their carefully selected heredity will be dissipated—though of course there will be some upgrading of the general level by dispersing the desired genes. Or will they be forbidden to marry outside the clone, perhaps?

Members of a clonal group will enjoy an important advantage: like identical twins, they will be able to accept grafts of tissue or whole organs from one another. Apart from the much greater security of life this will give them in general, such an advantage might be supremely important among a small isolated group, such as astronauts on a mission lasting several years, and, at least until such time as the problems of graft rejection are overcome, it will be an obvious matter of policy to select teams in this way. Indeed there may be another good reason for doing so.

At present the only genetically identical groups with which we are acquainted are twins, triplets and the rare higher orders of identical twindom. There is some evidence that identical (or one-egg) twins have a peculiar sympathetic awareness of each other's needs and problems— even, it has been claimed, a psychic awareness amounting to thought transference. It is certainly true that twins brought up in widely different circumstances have often lived closely similar lives, marrying similar partners of similar ages, and this is so even when they have not been in communication with one another. It is not mere sensationalism, therefore, to ask whether the members of human clones may feel particularly united, and be able to co-operate better, even if they are not in actual supersensory communication with one another.

Ability to work as a team is important in some sports, like mountain-climbing, in some military activities—one can think of a raiding party or a bomber crew—and probably in groups of people working under water on the lines pioneered by Cousteau in France or the SEALAB experiment off the California coast, since communication is particularly difficult in such conditions. A group of astronauts spread out over the surface of a remote planet provides another example. It follows that there are many parties, from the Space Agency to the manager of an ice-hockey team, which may have a direct interest in supporting research into this kind of biological development.

The late Professor J. B. S. Haldane, one of the most brilliant and practical scientists of our time, was one of those who took the possibility of cloning people quite seriously. In his view "we may find out at any moment" how to induce cultured cells to organize themselves, as we already have done with the plants, and this could "raise the possibilities of human achievement dramatically." Haldane declared that most clones will be made from people of at least 50, except for athletes and dancers, who would be cloned younger. They will be made from people who have excelled in some socially acceptable accomplishment, though we shall have to be careful that their success wasn't due to mere accident.

Equally useful, he said, might be the cloning of people with rare capacities, even if their value was problematic — for instance, people with permanent dark adaptation, people who lack the pain sense, those who can detect what is happening in their viscera and even control it, as some eastern yogis can.

Haldane also produced the interesting suggestion that centenarians should be cloned, provided they were "reasonably healthy." Not that longevity is necessarily desirable in itself, but data on its desirability are needed. He was struck by the fact that many exceptional people have unhappy childhoods and some are permanently deformed by this experience. He held that after the age of 55 great geniuses would spend their time in educating their clonal offspring, which he thought would avoid some of the frustration the latter might have felt. Others may think that geniuses do not necessarily make good parents, even that some degree of frustration is required to provide the motive force which drives genius. One more point should be made. As the French biologist Jean Rostand has pointed out, to print off a human being in hundreds or thousands of copies is in a sense to confer immortality upon him, for these offspring can of course be cloned in their turn, indefinitely.

Lord Rothschild, for long a Cambridge physiologist and an international authority on the structure and action of spermatozoa, left his bench and became a businessman, working for one of the largest chemical concerns in the world. In this dual role, he is, one may assume, unlikely to speak wildly or sensationally. Yet in 1967 he told scientists at the Weizmann Institute of Science in Israel that he regarded cloning people as a near possibility. The problem he foresees is whether everyone should be allowed to clone themselves if they wish, and he expects to see a Commission for Genetical Control established to vet applications. One can imagine the devious manoeuvres to which the more ego-centred members of the population might go in order to reduplicate themselves indefinitely. Twenty-three Mozarts would scarcely be tolerable: twenty-three Hitlers or Stalins at once hardly bear thinking about.

Steward's approach has a classic simplicity which allows the dramatic nature of his results to emerge clearly. But biology does not always proceed by simple means, and it is very possible that cloning of animals will only be achieved by more complicated methods. A glimpse of the possibilities is given by the work of Dr. J. B. Gurdon of Oxford University. Gurdon has managed, by a technique which spillikins players might envy, to take the nucleus out of an intestinal cell of a frog — the nucleus is the control-centre containing the chromosomes — and to implant it in an unfertilized frog egg, the nucleus of which has been destroyed by a tiny beam of radiation. Would the egg with its cuckoo nucleus develop? He found that such eggs develop just as though they had been fertilized normally and in some cases reach the tadpole stage successfully.

The important point established by this experiment is that the specialized intestinal cell nevertheless still contains all the genetic information needed to build a tadpole. Although much of this information has been "switched off," as being unneeded by an intestinal cell, it has, as the experiment demonstrates, not been destroyed. Thus the potentiality of producing adults from body-cells (as distinct from germ-cells, i.e. eggs and spermatozoa) is there. Furthermore, the resulting creatures have only one parent, genetically speaking: the frog, be it male or female, from which the intestinal cell was taken; and the offspring are identical with the parent just as if they were identical twins. The tadpoles thus produced become frogs and, despite their unusual hereditary complement, reproduce in the normal way.

Gurdon's technique accordingly holds out the possibility, *right away*, of producing exact copies of prize bulls, race-winning horses, or exceptional human beings. So far no one has succeeded in doing this, partly because mammalian eggs are almost invisibly small (about one hundredth of an inch in diameter, in the case of man) which makes the cellular surgery involved exceptionally difficult. But already techniques for removing structures almost as small are in existence. And, as one commentator observed, compared with the ethical problems raised, the scientific ones are trivial.

DISCUSSION QUESTIONS
SUGGESTIONS FOR WRITING

1. What are some of the "universal issues," according to Taylor, "which need to be faced . . . before things have gone so far that they cannot be altered . . . and most of which are still being ignored"?

2. Do you believe that greater use should be made of contraceptive devices — through governmental persuasion, incentives, or control — to slow down the population explosion?

3. Do you believe that cloning of humans is morally defensible? Explore the implications of your position on this issue. Who decides, for example, who gets cloned?

4. How would you describe Taylor's prose: transparent, businesslike, effective, needlessly self-effacing? Does it provide much of a clue as to what sort of a man he might be? Does the author create character-interest in himself in the manner of, say, Tom Wolfe? Would a more Wolfean treatment be credible in this case? Provide written examples of such an alternative treatment.

WOLFE

THE PUT-TOGETHER GIRL

In this selection Tom Wolfe describes the life-style of California go-go dancer, Carol Doda, and encapsulates one social consequence of the biological revolution which is already being felt.

IN San Francisco, Broadway is "the strip," a combination of Macdougal Street in Greenwich Village and strip row on "East Bal'more" in Baltimore. It is about four blocks long, an agreeably goofy row of skin-show nightclubs, boho caves, saturated in black paint, with names like "Mother's," featuring light-projection shows, monologuists, *intime* jazz shows with brooding Negroes on the bass, and "colorful" bars with names like Burp Hollow. There is one tree on Broadway. It is about three inches in diameter, about 12 feet tall, and has 342 minute leaves on it and a tin anti-urine sleeve around the bottom. Carol Doda was standing under this tree as if it could hide her. A colored fellow from the parking lot up the street was standing out in the street trying to get her a cab. It is hard for Carol Doda herself to stand out in the street on Broadway and start waving for cabs. There is no telling what would happen or how many flaming nutballs would stop or—who the hell knows what?—because of "them," *them* being her breasts.

Old Italian women walk by her on the street and say to each other, "*Strega! Strega!*"—not knowing that Carol is a nice Italian girl herself from Napa Valley, and understands that they are saying, "Witch! Witch!" because of *them*.

Middle-aged women, the kind of Hard Lips who wear bib-chains on their eyeglasses and work behind hotel cigar counters, walk by at lunchtime and say, "Aw, go back to jail"—because of *them*.

About 3:30 p.m. grown men wearing rep ties and just emerging from long—tuh-*unh!*—liquid lunches walk by her and grin and aim their fingers at her like needles or guns or something and say, "Pop! Pop!"— because of *them*.

Even Carol Doda has started thinking of them as *them*. There they are secured to her pectoralis major like *acquisitions*.

"When a man asks me out, I never know if he is interested in me or *them*." That is the way she thinks about it.

Them! Carol Doda has had injections of a silicone emulsion put into her breasts in regular installments over the past three years. They have grown, grown, grown, enlarging like . . . dirigibles, almost as if right in front of the eyes of the crowds—they line up out there—who come every night of the week to see Carol Doda's "topless" act. Every night, seven nights a week, Carol Doda descends through a hole in the ceiling of the Condor Club. She comes down doing a dance called the Swim by herself on top of a piano that has been pulled up to the ceiling on pulley wires. The Condor modestly advertises her on the marquee outside as "Miss Carol Doda, the Girl on the Piano." But the crowds line up out there every night, where the sidewalk curves down the hill on Grant Street, it comes right into Broadway right there, and all those people are out there practically panting, Topless, topless, the girl who blew up her breasts, Wonder Breasts, Wonder Breasts, Gimme a mih . . .

Then all the spotlights shine up to the ceiling, and Sam the Man and everybody go into a rock 'n' roll song called "Memphis, Tennessee." The lights shine on a nutty-looking thing, the bottom of a cocktail-grand piano, the top of which is flat up against the ceiling. Carol Doda! The piano starts coming down slowly on its pulley wires, and the first thing everyone sees is a hole in the ceiling with a heavy red ruffling inside of it, sort of like a gigantic Louis XIV version of a heart valve. Two legs are sticking out of it and down on the piano. Carol Doda! Carol Doda is descending, dancing the Swim. First, her legs, perfectly white legs, churning about, then her thighs, her hips—she is wearing a rather re-markable bikini cache-sex of some sort that starts up around her waist but has no side at all, just stretched down through her loins. She is also . . . *bottomless*, as they say in the trade, but this room full of craning heads, tilted back in a silent glom, barely even notice that. They are all waiting . . . for *them*.

The piano settles down, Carol Doda is on top of it dancing the Swim, the Jerk, the Frug, the Jump, the Spasm, the—her face is up above there like a pure white mask, an Easter Egg yellow explosion of hair on top, a pair of eyes with lashes like two sets of military shoe brushes, ice-white lips, two arms writhing around, her whole ilial complex writhing around, but all just a sort of pinwheel rosette for *them*. Carol Doda's breasts are up there the way one imagines Electra's should have been, two incredible mammiform protrusions, no mere pliable mass of feminine tissues and fats there but living arterial sculpture—viscera spigot—great blown-up aureate morning-glories.

The whole performance is—it is not a strip tease, it is no kind of *tease*, it is an animated cartoon, like the old Tom & Jerry cartoons where Tom, the cat, sees the bulldog coming and about forty-four sets of round white eyes—*boing*—go springing out of his eye sockets. Carol Doda is not teasing anybody. Her prize is up there as if on a platter. She never smiles; she just draws her big ice-white lips into an O from time to time. She doesn't even have the old pigbladder choreography of the burlesque houses; she just jerks, spasms, and writhes in the standard American twist-frug genre dances like any little high school bud from the garden apartment next door at the Saturday-night dance bumping away doing the Monkey under a strawberry Feather Duster coiffure while her mother looks on from the side with a pleasant smile on her face as if to say, Well, yes, Carmen is very social.

Sam the Man goes into an elaborate parody of ecstasy. He swings the saxophone down between his legs and then over his shoulders, he rolls his eyes, *Pretty woman walking down the street,* he flaps his brown jowls, he breaks into a sweat, he lolls his tongue out. Carol Doda does the Puppet. Oldie but goldie! "O" go her lips. They all break into *I Left My Heart in San Francisco*—Sam the Man starts moaning in front of the microphone as if in utter ecstatic depletion. "Oh-h-h-h-h-h, I can't s-t-a-n-d it! It's too mu-u-u-u-u-uch! Ah-h-h-h-h-h! O-o-o-o-o-o-o-o-o-o-o Eee! Eee! U-u-u-u-u-u-um! Wheeeeedeeeeeeeeeee! Eeeeh! Yuh! Yuh! Oink! Blooogeeee! Snerk! Wiffle! Pooooom—poom-poom! Gush! Mips! Eeeeeeeh-yah! Eeeeeeeerrrrrrrgggggh! Make her stah-ah-ah-ah-ah-ahp it! Lock me up! I'm going crazy! I'm flipping! I'm wigged out! I'm zonked! I'm erk-erk-erk blooooooooooooooogeeeeeeeeeeeeeeeeeeee! It's unbeliever-bobba-beeva-bova-bavvy-bipblap-blupbloop-poobog-mih-mih scoony-scaggy-mimsy-poppy! Too mu-u-u-u-u-ch! Bad ma-a-a-a-a-a-a-a-an! Th ol' wild bird is gra-a-a-a-a-abbin' me! I caint tuh-*unh* tuh-*unh!*" —and so on and so forth. But all the Hard Worsted set just sits there refusing to take the comic cues—I'll be damned, so that's what they look like, yes, I'll be damned, look at that, you get that, there it is right up there in front of me. And even the women—they want to *study* this phenomenon. All right, it's *freakish*—see, they don't . . . *give,* they hold *forth,* they're substan—but what does it feel like? it must weigh—and then look at them all fastened on her, heads craned back, *goggling*—until the piano starts ascending toward the hole in the ceiling with Carol Doda still twisting and jerking about with the lights lighting *them* from below as she goes up. *I lost my heart, in San Fran-cis-co.* The silent anointed heads of all the worsted lovelies in here start craning back, back, back again while Tony Cassara and Sam the Man play the anthem of San Francisco, *I left my heart*—

The anthem indeed. The Topless, Carol Doda and *them* are suddenly one of San Francisco's great resources, along with the cable cars, the hills, the Bay, the View, and the Golden Gate. There are at least fifteen "topless clubs" in San Francisco. They are nightclubs, chiefly, like the Condor, offering bare-breasted girls in bikini versions of the G-string, like Carol Doda's, just standing up there and doing ordinary American dances, the Twist, the Frug, the Swim, and so forth. Yet there is no greater tourist and convention attraction in America, with the possible exception of Manhattan.

The most curious of all are two clubs, the Off Broadway and the Cellar, which have "topless waitresses," as they are called, serving lunch wearing nothing but flesh-colored bikini underpants and high-heeled shoes. The new business lunch for—

—the 6 a.m. specters of Russian Hill. At six o'clock in the morning one can look up Russian Hill, San Francisco's best apartment area, from the foot of Broadway, where it suddenly turns steep up the hill, above the tunnel, and down the hill, silhouetted against the first pink-ash light of dawn, come good straight cleaned-and-pressed figures in hard worsted, carrying attaché cases, the leather lunch pails of Wall Street, walking down the slope, one here, one there, the 6 a.m. specters of Russian Hill, well-to-do, anointed with after-shave and Stephan's hair oil which his regular barber lets him have—San Francisco brokers going to work on Montgomery Street, the financial district, at 6 a.m., since by then it is 9 a.m. in New York, and the Exchange is opening and won't wait, and down they come down the hill as if in some Fellini scene.

A group of "underground" moviemakers who live in quonset huts beside the Berkeley railroad tracks are still up with their hand-held camera filming some sequence in which three music students wrapped in Reynolds Wrap leap like Raji-Putra, the Indian dancer, against the first rays of the rising sun. They just stare stupidly at the anointed specters and miss the real movie. Leap, Raji-Putra! Anyway, by twelve noon, these same stock-broker specters of Russian Hill, along with more, sometimes hundreds of San Francisco businessmen, are filing up toward the Off Broadway, the Cellar, along with favored clients, for a "topless lunch." It's a *lark*, a novelty, I mean, one's clients really get a kick out of this screwy spectacle—but the same faces keep coming back, over and over.

The Off Broadway has a deep black-light Soho gloom in it. All the topless places in California set themselves in this gloom, presumably so the customers can feel that nobody can watch them watching the club's amateur galaxy of bare breasts.

The Style Show starts. Girls start parading up on the bandstand. Sandra has on a transparent lace bed jacket or whatever it is, just hanging down from the shoulders, and she parades about in her bikini underwear and high heels in the fashion-show manner. A girl at the microphone says in the boulevard manner of the fashion-show announcer, ". . . using heavy lace, of course, for *added support*."

The Off Broadway's *them*—the Off Broadway has a girl named "Yvonne D'Anger." She comes out from an illuminated theatrical gauze dressing room at one end of the bandstand—the star!—a round-faced girl, almost petite, but with great tumescent dirigible breasts sitting out.

She walks about the stage, then winds her way through the tables, then back to the stage, where she strikes a cheesecake pose, lying down with her legs curled up and her breasts pointing straight up, like vanilla sundaes, not mushing off to the side the way most girls' would, but sitting straight up, and then another topless girl comes out and takes a picture of her with a Polaroid camera—*flash!*— the flash catches all the craning Hard Worsted faces in an instant, the 6 a.m. Russian Hill specters sitting here, anointed, goggled.

They have missed the Off Broadway's most extraordinary show, however, which is in the kitchen. There is something unforgettable about half a dozen girls wearing nothing but high heels and cache-sexes straining at awkward angles over serving tables in the rising Veg Soup steam trying to balance salads on their arms while their breasts dangle hopelessly in the smeary Roquefort, French, Green Goddess and Thousand Island thickets and a battery of spade chefs yell at them like they were nothing but a bunch of unusually clumsy waitresses in the lunchtime rush . . .

Carol Doda's doctor on Ocean Avenue in San Francisco has an ongoing waiting list of women of all sorts, not showgirls, who want the series of injections. Well, why should any woman *wait*—wait for what?—when the difference between dreariness and *appeal* is just a few centimeters of solid tissue here, a line stretched out there, a little body packing in the old thigh, under the wattles there—or perfect breasts? The philosophy of "You have only one life to live, why not live it as a blonde?" —that is merely the *given*. Even in old-fashioned New York there is hardly a single gray-haired woman left in town. And why stop short of the perfect bosom? Why do people talk about "the natural order"? Such an old European idea—one means, well, the *wheel* violated the natural order, for God's sake; hot and cold running water violated it; wall ovens, spice bars, Reddi-Tap keg beer and Diz-Poz-Alls fracture the natural order—what are a few cubic centimeters of silicone?

The silicone is injected in the form of an emulsion into the muscles and tissues all around the breasts where they join the chest. Exactly what happens to the emulsion after it is injected is not known. But some of it *moves around*. The shots bring the breasts up taut, at first, but then they begin to sag; continued booster shots are necessary. Sometimes a ring of shots seems to slip into a lake or puddle down in there somewhere. Sometimes the emulsion disappears; it goes off somewhere in the body. Whether or not it can cause cancer is simply not known.

But there are plenty of women in California who are willing to take the chances, whatever they are. There are about seventy-five doctors in Los Angeles giving the treatments, and one of them does twenty-five women a week. There are two hundred women taking the course in Las Vegas alone. More than half of all these patients are housewives, and some women bring their teenage daughters in there because they aren't developing fast enough to . . . compete; well, Carmen *is* social. And actually it's such a simple thing in a man's world where men have such simple ideas. After all, Carol Doda *developed*, from a bust measurement of about 35, up, up, month by month, to 44, through twelve months, eight sets of shots, $800. And why not? After all, one, anyone has fillings in the teeth, plates in the skull, a pin in the hip—what is the purpose of living, anyway? just to keep on living or to enjoy, be adored, favored, eyed—or—

Carol Doda turns around under the tree. A man in a white suit comes along. He just met her the other day. He invites her into Enrico's, the café. The colored guy isn't having any luck hailing a cab anyway. Enrico's is a kind of Via Veneto café for San Francisco. It has an outdoor part, under an awning by the sidewalk, and then a plate-glass front and more café tables inside. All sorts hang out there, actors, advertising men from the Jackson Square section nearby, women from Pacific Heights down at North Beach shopping. They head inside, but Carol Doda looks a little apprehensive. Carol is wearing a thin white turtleneck sweater, and *them* form a rather formidable shelf, but the leather Eton jacket covers her up pretty well. Everybody around Enrico's recognizes her; Burgess Meredith is in there in a great sport jacket. Herb Caen the columnist is in there. Larry Hankin and a lot of other people from "The Committee" are in there. But there is always this possibility, this business of, well, frankly, getting thrown out. Enrico's wife or somebody threw her out of there once, and just the other day Mrs. Pacini over at Amilio's threw her out. Carol is looking around a little in Enrico's.

"What do they say to you?"

"I don't know—She kept saying, 'We don't allow Topless here. Put your coat on, we don't allow Topless here.' I wasn't *topless*. I mean I had a regular dress on, what I wear all the time."

Carol Doda's mouth keeps changing from a smile to some kind of bewilderment when she talks about all this. She has a slightly husky voice but not a low voice. She has model-goggle sunglasses up over her face like two huge shields, and she keeps looking around.

"What did your friends think?"

"A lot of them . . . they don't have the same *air* about them anymore. They used to treat you palsy-walsy. I mean when I was a cocktail waitress. And then suddenly people begin to change. They act like *I've* changed, like they think I'm a snob or something now. It really used to bug me, I couldn't figure it out; I mean, I hadn't changed, *they* had changed. It used to break my heart. Then I realized the public will not let you stay the same. I'm never snobbish. It's them, they refuse to accept you because you're well known. I don't know, maybe you have to change, because the public insists that you change."

She is sincere about all this; *changing*. She has a lot of the old North Beach I'm-searching, self-analysis syndrome. What is going on? She's a celebrity, and she likes that, but people have funny attitudes.

She *has* changed. Look at *them;* maybe that is what is on people's minds. But *she* hasn't changed, says Carol Doda. The silicone treatments were just a cosmetic; it wasn't all that drastic a thing. She was working as a cocktail waitress, and actually she had built up a big following in the Condor. Of course, people knew her. She used to wisecrack with them. She looked great. She had a great trim figure. Then she started dancing on the piano. It began almost like a gag. One night —

this whole topless bathing suit thing had been going on, in the papers and everything, and the guys there said go ahead, go *topless*, Carol. So she did, right there, and Topless was born. There was Carol Doda, dancing in a topless bathing suit.

Carol Doda—Topless!—was great stuff from the start. Customers were piling in. But Carol—Carol had a nice figure, a trim figure, a real dancer's figure, but she wasn't . . . spectacular. It was one thing to have a nice overall figure, but if you were Topless, the thing was to be showing something spectacular; otherwise why take the top off? So guys around there started saying, Why didn't she get *the shots?*

"I was really scared when I went to the doctor," Carol is saying to her pal in the white suit. Then she brings her hands up. "The needle— well, it's about *this* long, it's like a horse needle or something. It really looks awful. Some of the shots he puts in all around here, near the surface. But some of them are really deep. When the needle goes in—it really scared me at first, these pains shoot all up through here and down your arms. You can feel it all the way down in your arms."

"Are you worried about the long-range effect, what the silicone might do to you?" says White Suit.

"No," Carol says, "the tissue grows around the silicone. It's just a short process."

"Does the whole thing make you—your breasts—feel any different?"

"Yes." She laughs but not very uproariously. "I'm conscious . . . of them . . . all the time. They weigh a lot more, a couple of pounds. I have to wear a special heavy brassière. I have to wear it to bed at night, and I can't sleep on my stomach, it's too uncomfortable. In fact, I can't sleep on my side, either, that's kind of uncomfortable, too. I have to sleep on my back.

"That's one reason I work out all the time. I work out with weights at a gymnasium to build up . . . my pectorals. It helps me support them better."

Self-improvement! But of course! She is a great self-improver. It goes along with the self-analysis. She doesn't smoke; she eats health foods; in fact, on her diet she builds up such tremendous energy, she has to find some outlet for it; the dancing isn't enough; that isn't even tiring; she goes to a gymnasium every day and works out; she lifts weights; she works seven days a week at the Condor, every night, coming down on that piano doing the Swim and the Watusi; it takes a lot of self-discipline, it really does; a side of it nobody knows about—

"Some days when I wake up, I just don't feel like getting up at all and going through the whole thing again," she says. The smile is kind of swimming off her face and then back on and then back off. "But I make myself get up, because if I don't, I'm not really hurting anybody else, I'm letting myself down."

"What are you aiming for, eventually?"

"Well, I'd like to have a big show. I want to be first-class, in New York or Chicago or Miami, some place like that. I've had a chance to go to Nevada, to Las Vegas, but I'm waiting for something big."

"You probably make a lot of money here now."

"Well, not really. Actually, I used to make more money as a cocktail waitress . . . the *tips* and everything . . . "

"You made more money *then?*"

"Yes—but, well. A lot of places here offer me more money and all that to move to their place, but I don't see any point in a lot of moving around like that. That doesn't really get you anything. I'm waiting for something first-class. How do you think the act would go in New York?"

A tall man with great rake features, long Barrymore hair, comes over all of a sudden, some guy she knows, and starts talking and says to Carol, "Hey, Carol, take off those glasses, I can't *see* you."

She looks up with her smile going on and off. "I can't," she says. "I don't have any eye makeup on, I'll feel undressed. I mean it!"

"Aw, come on, Carol—" This goes on for a while, and finally she pulls the glasses off, the great model-goggle shields, and—*strega*, honest *strega*—she is right. Her eyes blink there in the middle of her perfectly white face like something surprised in a nest.

"I always wear eyelashes, top and bottom."

But of course! A heroine of her times! Carol Doda wears false eyelashes, but only to go with her Easter Egg yellow hair, dyed from brown, which goes with her soapstone skin, so perfectly white from remaining forever, every night, within the hot meat spigot casbah of Broadway—Electra of the Main Stem!—in order to show the new world a pair of—at last!—perfected twentieth-century American breasts. You have only one life to live. Why not live it as a put-together girl?

DISCUSSION QUESTIONS
SUGGESTIONS FOR WRITING

1. In the process of putting one outgrowth of the biological revolution in human perspective, what moral judgment does Tom Wolfe make on his subject?

2. What social criticism is implicit in his moral judgment? Identify examples of social criticism in the selection.

3. It is said of Huckleberry Finn *that it was the first "American" book because it was the first American book to be written in a completely American idiom, without stylistic borrowings from English or European traditions. More recently* The Catcher in the Rye *represented a stylistic breakthrough of consequence, capturing the language, in this case, of a generation as no other book had before. Clearly, one of the most dazzling qualities of Tom Wolfe's writing is his style, which, it can be argued, represents a similar sort of stylistic breakthrough in that it embodies a truly contemporary idiom. Analyze this style. What are its distinguishing characteristics?*

4. Tom Wolfe's writing represents one of the best examples of the use of fictional techniques in contemporary nonfiction writing. How does he immediately establish sympathy for his main character, Carol Doda? How does he create scene to dramatize her stage act? Note his efforts to establish the sense of place, to capture the atmosphere in whichever setting the action is occurring. Note the effect of immediacy of his involvement in the action in his role as participant-observer.

PERRY LONDON
(b. 1931),professor of psychology at the University
of Southern California, has
coedited *Foundations of
Abnormal Psychology*
and *Theory and Research
in Abnormal Psychology*.
In *Behavior Control* he
describes the means
through growing technol-
ogy that will soon make
possible "precise control
over much of people's in-
dividual actions, thoughts,
emotions, moods and
wills" unlike anything before in human history.

THE ADVENT
OF BEHAVIOR
CONTROL

THE whole history of human development has engaged man in an
endless struggle for control. The record of his ascent from brutishness
is kept in the simple tools by which he enlarged his size and strength and
stretched his grasp to control the physical environment in which he
lived. The rise of civilizations, and their fall, reflect still more capacity
to master things and people. The history of religion and its institutions,
from Hindu yogis to Greek gymnasts and from Hebrew ecstatics to
British Methodists, is a history of efforts to control the self, mind and
body, or to regulate the cosmos and the flesh by means of spirit.

Control of individuals has not been easy though, especially control of
their inner lives, where hope and will reside. And though man has been
the constant object of his own inquiry, he still knows less about his own
behavior than about most other things he has explored. But he is learning
quickly and improving faster still, so that his present knowledge has
already fashioned a rude technology of behavior control, and he will
soon have learned enough to make it massive and refined.

Behavior control is the ability to get someone to do one's bidding.
From antiquity until almost now, the only common means for doing this
have been coercion by force and threat of force and persuasion by inspiration and education, but these techniques have been mostly gross or
tedious in their application and clumsy or unsure in their effects. All this
is changing now, and means are being found, in all the crafts and sciences

of man, society, and life, that will soon make possible precise control over much of people's individual actions, thoughts, emotions, moods, and wills. Never in human history has this occurred before, except as fantasy. Even now, most of the scientists, technicians, teachers, doctors, engineers, and other specialists in the learned professions have not yet looked upon the tools that they have made or use as parts of a technology for controlling behavior. Still less have they designed grand strategies, singly or together, for "taking over" the lives of individuals or society. Even so, when the facts of today's behavioral technology are assembled and put in context, as is intended here, some people may be surprised at the extent to which it is now possible to manipulate people systematically. And it is petty compared to what will soon be possible.

The techniques of psychotherapy, for instance, widely practiced and accepted as means of curing psychological disorders, are also methods of controlling people. They can be used systematically to influence values and attitudes, if not overt behavior, toward conventional norms of conduct, or to release feelings of great intensity, whose expression can change the course of people's lives. Such things are done routinely in traditional psychotherapy. Behavioral psychologists, at the same time, are inventing even more sophisticated techniques for treating personal disorders ranging from stuttering to schizophrenia. They are learning to attack specific aspects of individual behavior with increasing precision, "burning out" traumatic fears by creating an internal explosion of anxiety; restraining chronic lusts like homosexuality, and the incontinences of habit, from alcoholism to enuresis, by means of electrically aided "training" devices; or conditioning human emotions and the body's involuntary functions to respond faithfully to the manipulation of critical signals by a behavior-control expert. But these, perhaps better known right now than other things going on, are the weakest of the control techniques that are developing. The biochemical and neurological substrata of behavior are being mined at even greater speeds, and the technology that results from these discoveries ranges from the surgical control of temper to "the pill," with its attendant effect on the sexual mores of our society.

The chemicals and the electronic hardware of behavior-control technology are proliferating even faster and more powerfully than are psychological tools. The host of tranquilizing and energizing drugs already on the market represents the bare infancy of an industry that will soon produce drugs much more precisely capable of steering people's moods and emotions and, soon thereafter, of affecting important parts of their intellects, such as memory. Electronic miniaturization and improvements in surgery increasingly exploit discoveries of the exact locations in the brain where various behavioral functions are managed; skillful invasion of these sites permits interference with the functions; radio remote controls over epileptic seizures, sexual desire, and speech patterns are already operational. Few people yet have thought much on the long-range prospects of such technology.

While all these new developments affecting individuals are proceeding, computer technology increasingly automates production, reducing the work force; it discovers better and better data-processing methods, making it easier all the time to track and predict virtually any kind of mass behavior trend; this makes it easier, in turn, to forecast, then control, the individuals who make up the mass.

In some ways, this development is certainly a good thing. Some of its blessings may be the elimination of mental illness, crime, and even war, and the prospect of achieving these goals by scientifically controlling behavior is appealing. But the same arts which can be used to restrict such evils might serve to stifle good behavior, too, and if the refined management of individual behavior represses freedom or destroys initiative, then the cost of having it may exceed the profit to be gained. The enormous risks involved make it urgent for intelligent people of good will, especially the scientists and technologists who are most responsible for inventing and testing the techniques of control, to plan, carefully and considerately, how to do their work with the least threat to human freedom and the most promise of promoting mankind's welfare. Without such planning, their amoral infant may become a freak or a monster, for it is already born, if often still unrecognized or named, and it will certainly mature, no matter who protests. . . .

THE NEED

Whatever the hypothetical dangers of an efficient behavior technology may be, the real social evils sustained by abstention from it are severe. There are problems of motivation and incentive, as with high school dropouts and unskilled workers; problems of social organization and responsibility, as with demonstrators, protesters, rioters, and police, with delinquents and criminals, with businessmen who destroy forests and pollute waterways, and with plain litterbugs; problems of attitude and prejudice, as with enemies of Negro civil rights or with employers who reject Catholics and Jews. All these problems abound, and to be solved, they must finally be reduced to the level of changing individual behavior. Some of the needed solutions can, of course, be legislated, and for those, the problem of changing individual behavior applies only to people who defy the law. But for many of these problems no direct legislation is possible, and other answers to them must be sought. Behavior-control technology offers one avenue of approach to this purpose. . . .

SOURCES OF DELAY IN THE DEVELOPMENT
OF BEHAVIOR TECHNOLOGY

. . . Technical limitations aside, future resistance to behavior technology may revolve entirely around its moral implications. Two main lines of moral argument on this topic are already clear and will probably dominate discussions of the subject for a long time. They may be conveniently labeled the "existential," or "humanist," argument and the "argument from ethical tradition."

The existential argument is apt to be the most popular intellectual base of opposition to behavior technology for quite a while. It says in effect that deliberate control of human behavior is immoral because it dehumanizes man. Anything that reduces an individual's ability to make choices (whether he wants to make choices or not) is objectionable precisely because it does so; the exercise of choice is the heart of morality, which in turn is one essence of humanity. Since the imposition of control is the very antithesis of choice, it *ipso facto* dehumanizes, and since man is morally obligated, above all else, to exercise his human attributes, he should not support an enterprise dedicated to their subversion. . . .

The argument from ethical tradition is also a source of resistance to behavior technology, but more in the sense of conservative restraint and concern than of outright objection or opposition. Some major principles in the ethical tradition of the liberal West are particularly challenged by the potentialities of behavior-control technology. Culled from the ancient political and religious experience of the Mediterranean basin and refined and annealed in Europe until the American and French Revolutions made formal doctrine of them, three of the most vital ones are: the rule of *noncoercion*, which says that people should not be forced to do what others want but should be free to refuse them; the rule of *explication*, which is that people should not be seduced into compliance but should be told what is wanted of them; and, corollary to the first two, the rule of *self-direction*, which is that people should be free to decide for themselves how they want to guide their lives.

None of these rules can operate in a completely unrestricted way if social organizations of even the simplest kind are to persist, but they are all vital to an ethical tradition which we still revere and accept as a model of conduct. No matter how complicated society becomes, these rules, which amount to an operational definition of freedom in human intercourse, retain their value. But value depends on meaning, and the traditional meanings of these terms are potentially subverted by the facts of behavior technology.

It is easy to understand coercion, for example, in a civilization whose weapons are bows and arrows—or even atomic bombs. It means assault, with jail or pain or death resulting. But what about a kind of surgery to prevent, let us say, recidivist crimes of violence by dismantling the physiological machinery within the nervous system that incites aggressive acts? Or perhaps a pill to erase memory, to wipe out the toxic nest of fancied injuries that shrill for violent vengeance? Or hypnotic training, or conditioning, or some splendidly effective psychotherapy whose object and effect is to teach people to abhor violence? Are these truly coercive? Traditionally, coercion means making people do things against their will, but that takes for granted that "will" is itself somehow inviolable. The techniques in question here aim to change will, not to rape it; their initiation may be coercive, but their effect is seductive. . . .

CONTROLLING BEHAVIOR CONTROL

There are still some people who, observing the enormous variability of human beings, and the enormous contemporary ferment in the social and behavior sciences, believe that any significant technology of behavior control is a thing which will only come to pass in the distant future, if at all, because too little is now known of human nature. Perhaps nothing could be less the case. The degree of control possible is enormous. It will always be limited by genetically based differences between individuals, of course, but even these are increasingly subject to manipulation by the biochemists and the surgeons. At all events, an applied science of human behavior becomes possible as soon as enough relevant facts are assembled for some studied purpose of prediction and control to be achieved. No more of human nature need be known than satisfies this purpose. Even an applied behavior science with utopian aims does not require limitless knowledge or vision of its own objectives in order to be engineered. It does require *some* knowledge of human nature, a great deal of planning, a commitment to some foreseeable goals and to some self-regulating scheme for achieving or abandoning them, and some imagination for the wider ripples in the world's affairs that planned interventions accidentally bring. The more that is known, the better, because knowledge is the key to control and accident its bane. But it is a mistake in this connection to be entrapped by the professorial caveat, "We do not know enough to act," which is just true enough often enough to paralyze the good-willed muddled.

In fact, knowledge of the facts, sense knowledge, always waits on history. Precision for deciding how to act can only be a colloquy of probabilities, whose relevance, once calculated, must be tested to be known. The refusal even to calculate (to think to test) is a self-indulgent kind of cowardice incognito, which calls itself conservative restraint.

There is probably little point today, if there ever was one, in debating at length whether or not behavior-control technology is feasible or should generally be attempted or avoided. In general, no such choice is any longer possible. What remains is to determine the characteristics of this technology, the rules for implementing control, and the purposes which it should serve. This is no small matter. We can no longer choose whether or not to explore the secrets of nuclear particles either, but that does not make it clear that we must drop atom bombs on each other.

Behavior scientists had better start thinking about this now because few other people are in equally good positions to do so. Physicists did not devote themselves much to the implications of atomic physics until after they had found the means to blow up the world — and their worried deliberations since then have not been terribly productive or useful to the politicians who must implement these things. Behavior science is still only on the verge of powerful control technology. It has not yet accomplished it so thoroughly that it must be quickly taken out of scientific hands, though it is too important to be left entirely in them. Suppose there is no atom holocaust. What kind of world must we make, knowing we must make one? . . .

Aldous Huxley foresaw this problem with great clarity in *Brave New World*, *Brave New World Revisited*, and *Ape and Essence*, and science-fiction writers have been discussing it for years. Behavior scientists must enter the discussion now, however, and help others enter it as well; it is their responsibility more than anybody else's, for they are the designers and may become the engineers of control, whether they like it or not. The future, already upon us, must be controlled.

DISCUSSION QUESTIONS
SUGGESTIONS FOR WRITING

1. What are the two main moral arguments, mentioned by London, against the incursion of behavior technology?

2. Do you find the following statement questionable: "At all events, an applied science of human behavior becomes possible as soon as enough relevant facts are assembled for some studied purpose of prediction and control to be achieved. No more of human nature need be known than satisfies this purpose"? What is known of human nature? How many facts are "enough"?

3. Viewed formally as a combination of types — personal, informative, persuasive, critical — can you identify characteristics of each of these essay types (granting the imprecision of such categories) in this piece?

4. How would you describe London's position on new means of behavior control through technology: for, against, ambivalent, undecided, worried but convinced of its inevitability, giddy with anticipation? Does he sound like the right man to back for a few experiments?

VONNEGUT

KURT VONNEGUT, JR.
(b. 1922), is the author of
*Mother Night, The Sirens
of Titan, Cat's Cradle,*
and others — satiric-fan-
tastic novels about the
present and the future of
the United States. As a
prisoner of war in World
War II, he witnessed the
fire bombing of Dresden,
in which more people
were killed than at Hiro-
shima—an event that is
central to an understand-
ing of his life and work.
With the appearance of
Slaughterhouse-Five, his
novel about the Dresden
massacre, Vonnegut's po-
sition as a seldom-read
"hero of underground
literature in America" has
changed. His work is now
widely read and admired
by the general public, especially the young.

HARRISON BERGERON

THE year was 2081, and everybody was finally equal. They weren't only equal before God and the law. They were equal every which way. Nobody was smarter than anybody else. Nobody was better looking than anybody else. Nobody was stronger or quicker than anybody else. All this equality was due to the 211th, 212th, and 213th Amendments to the Constitution, and to the unceasing vigilance of agents of the United States Handicapper General.

Some things about living still weren't quite right, though. April, for instance, still drove people crazy by not being springtime. And it was in that clammy month that the H-G men took George and Hazel Bergeron's fourteen-year-old son, Harrison, away.

It was tragic, all right, but George and Hazel couldn't think about it very hard. Hazel had a perfectly average intelligence, which meant she couldn't think about anything except in short bursts. And George, while his intelligence was way above normal, had a little mental handicap radio in his ear. He was required by law to wear it at all times. It was tuned to a government transmitter. Every twenty seconds or so, the transmitter would send out some sharp noise to keep people like George from taking unfair advantage of their brains.

George and Hazel were watching television. There were tears on Hazel's cheeks, but she'd forgotten for the moment what they were about.

On the television screen were ballerinas.

A buzzer sounded in George's head. His thoughts fled in panic, like bandits from a burglar alarm.

"That was a real pretty dance, that dance they just did," said Hazel.

"Huh?" said George.

"That dance—it was nice," said Hazel.

"Yup," said George. He tried to think a little about the ballerinas. They weren't really very good—no better than anybody else would have been, anyway. They were burdened with sashweights and bags of birdshot, and their faces were masked, so that no one, seeing a free and graceful gesture or a pretty face, would feel like something the cat drug in. George was toying with the vague notion that maybe dancers shouldn't be handicapped. But he didn't get very far with it before another noise in his ear radio scattered his thoughts.

George winced. So did two out of the eight ballerinas.

Hazel saw him wince. Having no mental handicap herself, she had to ask George what the latest sound had been.

"Sounded like somebody hitting a milk bottle with a ball peen hammer," said George.

"I'd think it would be real interesting, hearing all the different sounds," said Hazel, a little envious. "All the things they think up."

"Um," said George.

"Only, if I was Handicapper General, you know what I would do?" said Hazel. Hazel, as a matter of fact, bore a strong resemblance to the Handicapper General, a woman named Diana Moon Glampers. "If I was Diana Moon Glampers," said Hazel, "I'd have chimes on Sunday—just chimes. Kind of in honor of religion."

"I could think, if it was just chimes," said George.

"Well—maybe make 'em real loud," said Hazel. "I think I'd make a good Handicapper General."

"Good as anybody else," said George.

"Who knows better'n I do what normal is?" said Hazel.

"Right," said George. He began to think glimmeringly about his abnormal son who was now in jail, about Harrison, but a twenty-one-gun salute in his head stopped that.

"Boy!" said Hazel, "that was a doozy, wasn't it?"

It was such a doozy that George was white and trembling, and tears stood on the rims of his red eyes. Two of the eight ballerinas had collapsed to the studio floor, were holding their temples.

"All of a sudden you look so tired," said Hazel. "Why don't you stretch out on the sofa, so's you can rest your handicap bag on the pillows, honeybunch." She was referring to the forty-seven pounds of birdshot in a canvas bag, which was padlocked around George's neck. "Go on and rest the bag for a little while," she said. "I don't care if you're not equal to me for a while."

George weighed the bag with his hands. "I don't mind it," he said. "I don't notice it any more. It's just a part of me."

"You been so tired lately—kind of wore out," said Hazel. "If there was just some way we could make a little hole in the bottom of the bag, and just take out a few of them lead balls. Just a few."

"Two years in prison and two thousand dollars fine for every ball I took out," said George. "I don't call that a bargain."

"If you could just take a few out when you came home from work," said Hazel. "I mean—you don't compete with anybody around here. You just set around."

"If I tried to get away with it," said George, "then other people'd get away with it—and pretty soon we'd be right back to the dark ages again, with everybody competing against everybody else. You wouldn't like that, would you?"

"I'd hate it," said Hazel.

"There you are," said George. "The minute people start cheating on laws, what do you think happens to society?"

If Hazel hadn't been able to come up with an answer to this question, George couldn't have supplied one. A siren was going off in his head.

"Reckon it'd fall all apart," said Hazel.

"What would?" said George blankly.

"Society," said Hazel uncertainly. "Wasn't that what you just said?"

"Who knows?" said George.

The television program was suddenly interrupted for a news bulletin. It wasn't clear at first as to what the bulletin was about, since the announcer, like all announcers, had a serious speech impediment. For about half a minute, and in a state of high excitement, the announcer tried to say, "Ladies and gentlemen—"

He finally gave up, handed the bulletin to a ballerina to read.

"That's all right—" Hazel said of the announcer, "he tried. That's the big thing. He tried to do the best he could with what God gave him. He should get a nice raise for trying so hard."

"Ladies and gentlemen—" said the ballerina, reading the bulletin. She must have been extraordinarily beautiful, because the mask she wore was hideous. And it was easy to see that she was the strongest and most graceful of all the dancers, for her handicap bags were as big as those worn by two-hundred-pound men.

And she had to apologize at once for her voice, which was a very unfair voice for a woman to use. Her voice was a warm, luminous, timeless melody. "Excuse me—" she said, and she began again, making her voice absolutely uncompetitive.

"Harrison Bergeron, age fourteen," she said in a grackle squawk, "has just escaped from jail, where he was held on suspicion of plotting to overthrow the government. He is a genius and an athlete, is under-handicapped, and should be regarded as extremely dangerous."

A police photograph of Harrison Bergeron was flashed on the screen—upside down, then sideways, upside down again, then right side up. The picture showed the full length of Harrison against a background cali-brated in feet and inches. He was exactly seven feet tall.

The rest of Harrison's appearance was Halloween and hardware. Nobody had ever borne heavier handicaps. He had outgrown hindrances faster than the H-G men could think them up. Instead of a little ear radio for a mental handicap, he wore a tremendous pair of earphones, and spectacles with thick wavy lenses. The spectacles were intended to make him not only half blind, but to give him whanging headaches besides.

Scrap metal was hung all over him. Ordinarily, there was a certain symmetry, a military neatness to the handicaps issued to strong people, but Harrison looked like a walking junkyard. In the race of life, Harrison carried three hundred pounds.

And to offset his good looks, the H-G men required that he wear at all times a red rubber ball for a nose, keep his eyebrows shaved off, and cover his even white teeth with black caps at snaggle-tooth random.

"If you see this boy," said the ballerina, "do not—I repeat, do not—try to reason with him."

There was the shriek of a door being torn from its hinges.

Screams and barking cries of consternation came from the television set. The photograph of Harrison Bergeron on the screen jumped again and again, as though dancing to the tune of an earthquake.

George Bergeron correctly identified the earthquake, and well he might have—for many was the time his own home had danced to the same crashing tune. "My God—" said George, "that must be Har-rison!"

The realization was blasted from his mind instantly by the sound of an automobile collision in his head.

When George could open his eyes again, the photograph of Harrison was gone. A living, breathing Harrison filled the screen.

Clanking, clownish, and huge, Harrison stood in the center of the studio. The knob of the uprooted studio door was still in his hand. Ballerinas, technicians, musicians, and announcers cowered on their knees before him, expecting to die.

"I am the Emperor!" cried Harrison. "Do you hear? I am the Em-peror! Everybody must do what I say at once!" He stamped his foot and the studio shook.

"Even as I stand here—" he bellowed, "crippled, hobbled, sickened—I am a greater ruler than any man who ever lived! Now watch me become what I *can* become!"

Harrison tore the straps of his handicap harness like wet tissue paper, tore straps guaranteed to support five thousand pounds.

Harrison's scrap-iron handicaps crashed to the floor.

Harrison thrust his thumbs under the bar of the padlock that secured his head harness. The bar snapped like celery. Harrison smashed his headphones and spectacles against the wall.

He flung away his rubber-ball nose, revealed a man that would have awed Thor, the god of thunder.

"I shall now select my Empress!" he said, looking down on the cowering people. "Let the first woman who dares rise to her feet claim her mate and her throne!"

A moment passed, and then a ballerina arose, swaying like a willow.

Harrison plucked the mental handicap from her ear, snapped off her physical handicaps with marvelous delicacy. Last of all, he removed her mask.

She was blindingly beautiful.

"Now —" said Harrison, taking her hand, "shall we show the people the meaning of the word dance? Music!" he commanded.

The musicians scrambled back into their chairs, and Harrison stripped them of their handicaps, too. "Play your best," he told them, "and I'll make you barons and dukes and earls."

The music began. It was normal at first — cheap, silly, false. But Harrison snatched two musicians from their chairs, waved them like batons as he sang the music as he wanted it played. He slammed them back into their chairs.

The music began again and was much improved.

Harrison and his Empress merely listened to the music for a while — listened gravely, as though synchronizing their heartbeats with it.

They shifted their weights to their toes.

Harrison placed his big hands on the girl's tiny waist, letting her sense the weightlessness that would soon be hers.

And then, in an explosion of joy and grace, into the air they sprang!

Not only were the laws of the land abandoned, but the law of gravity and the laws of motion as well.

They reeled, whirled, swiveled, flounced, capered, gamboled, and spun.

They leaped like deer on the moon.

The studio ceiling was thirty feet high, but each leap brought the dancers nearer to it.

It became their obvious intention to kiss the ceiling.

They kissed it.

And then, neutralizing gravity with love and pure will, they remained suspended in air inches below the ceiling, and they kissed each other for a long, long time.

It was then that Diana Moon Glampers, the Handicapper General, came into the studio with a double-barreled ten-gauge shotgun. She fired twice, and the Emperor and the Empress were dead before they hit the floor.

Diana Moon Glampers loaded the gun again. She aimed it at the musicians and told them they had ten seconds to get their handicaps back on.

It was then that the Bergerons' television tube burned out.

Hazel turned to comment about the blackout to George. But George had gone out into the kitchen for a can of beer.

George came back in with the beer, paused while a handicap signal shook him up. And then he sat down again. "You been crying?" he said to Hazel.

"Yup," she said.

"What about?" he said.

"I forget," she said. "Something real sad on television."

"What was it?" he said.

"It's all kind of mixed up in my mind," said Hazel.

"Forget sad things," said George.

"I always do," said Hazel.

"That's my girl," said George. He winced. There was the sound of a rivetting gun in his head.

"Gee—I could tell that one was a doozy," said Hazel.

"You can say that again," said George.

"Gee—" said Hazel, "I could tell that one was a doozy."

DISCUSSION QUESTIONS
SUGGESTIONS FOR WRITING

1. How does Vonnegut satirize the following ideas: that people should always obey laws, that trying one's best is the important thing, that competition is unfair, that the world would be a better place if everybody were equal, that happiness is being well adjusted?

2. After reading this story do you agree that ignorance is bliss, that sad thoughts should be forgotten?

3. Do you think that the Bergerons and the people of the United States in 2081, as characterized by Vonnegut, are "happier" than people today? How does the story dramatize—if it does—the idea that happiness as an abstract ideal is not necessarily the highest goal to be wished for?

4. Does this story suggest some of the real dangers of behavior control technology, or do you consider it an exaggeration?

PART THREE

INTRODUCTION

THE NEXT THREE subject areas provide material for a consideration of the *social* implications of technological development and other forces which have led to the crises of values in our institutions.

As Vance Packard points out in *The Sexual Wilderness,* "In the past there have almost always been rules, standards, and sharply defined roles for each sex within which their maneuverings took place. Today the rules, standards and assigned roles are in disarray." Packard prefers to use "wilderness" rather than "revolution" to describe "the whole range of areas where males and females find themselves in confrontation" because he feels that what is happening is inherently chaotic and varied, with no clear movement or generally supported direction. "Bewilderment and normlessness," he finds, are dominant characteristics and are "in large part caused by the dislocation in our way of life produced by rapid social change."

Such direct technological influences on sexual behavior as The Pill, the automobile (sometimes referred to in this context as "the traveling bedroom"), and the growing sense of anonymity brought about by high population mobility to meet the demands of corporate growth are explored. Related factors that interest Packard are changes created by the decline in parental control, the expansion of higher education (including, for example, the growing unwillingness of collegiate authorities to serve as substitute parents), the wavering role of religious doctrine in controlling the process of sexual awakening as it once did, and the increased bombardment of sexual stimulation through music, films, advertising, television, books, magazines, etc.

A landmark work in the so-called sexual revolution is Masters and Johnson's famous *Human Sexual Response,* which Vance Packard credits with "having a substantial impact in changing sexual attitudes." For the first time in history, scientists used controlled empirical methods and sophisticated technological hardware to assess physiological reactions of married and unmarried humans undergoing orgiastic experiences. Though the results of Masters and Johnson's research were couched in highly technical language, the book became a best seller and spawned several book-length "explications." Millions were fascinated or appalled, as the case may be. Critics charged that such work, with its emphasis on the nature of physiological release, seriously ignored important psychological and emotional aspects of sexuality having to do with affection, love, fidelity, etc. Masters and Johnson anticipated such criticism in the preface to *Human Sexual Response:* "Can that one facet of our lives, affecting more people in more ways than any other physiologic response other than those necessary to our very existence, be allowed to continue without benefit of objective, scientific analysis?"

Developing out of the changed social conditions and attitudes toward sexual roles described by Packard and partially molded by books like *Human Sexual Response* has been the women's liberation movement, characterized by many observers as *the* revolution of the seventies. As Packard comments, "The social changes of the past quarter-century have had their greatest or more obvious impact on the lives of women."

Following World War II, as a boost to the economy and to provide jobs for returning veterans, women's domesticity was strongly encouraged. But, unlike previous periods, domestic life had been largely sheered of any meaningful survival activities or challenge by technological improvements. Women began to sense the meaninglessness of their lives as never before and their subjugation to male-dominated concepts of what their roles should be.

More highly educated in greater numbers than ever before in history, women began to seek alternatives to the domestic treadmill through expression of their highly developed talents in more meaningful life-choices. By the early sixties women's dissatisfaction with the available alternatives began to surface. By the seventies is has reached vast proportions.

Susan Brownmiller's delineation of her awakening consciousness is typical of the sort of new awareness being experienced by increasing numbers of women.

A T a time when the schools may be said to have assumed a pivotal position among the most all-encompassing and dominant institutions in our tribal life, the value of present academic structures and the basic assumptions underlying them are being questioned as never before. Institutions such as the church, the community, and the family, which once looked after nonacademic needs of people on a large scale, no longer do so to the same degree as in an earlier time, while schools have become recreation centers, dispensers of therapy, homes away from home, churches, travel agencies, information bureaus, and so on.

In the contemporary rash of books whose subject has been "What is wrong with the schools?" or in college student demands for greater power over curricula and general campus governance, to name but two examples, is reflected the movement against repressive systems currently being experienced in the culture as a whole.

One important and fundamental conflict of values at work in the present crisis concerns basic differences in assumptions about human nature made by educators. One group (usually associated with the education establishment) may be said to hold the view that humans, by nature, are basically lazy and recalcitrant learners and therefore need to be coerced to learn (through punishment and reward, anxiety systems, grades, etc.). The other group (the reformers) generally believe that humans have a natural hunger for learning and, if not impeded by anxiety or boredom or adverse influences, as they are under present circumstances, will seek to know as much useful information as possible about the world, instinctively, effortlessly, and happily.

Current research in preschool education, according to Maya Pines, does tend to bear out the assumptions of the reformers—at least for very young children. In addition, recent studies at Harvard and elsewhere indicate that a child's intelligence becomes so fixed by the age of four that it is virtually identical to his IQ at age seventeen. Therefore, it would seem, contrary to previous theories, that a child's abilities and intelligence are most easily influenced long before he ever begins his formal education.

Other facets of the reform movement in contemporary education illustrated here range from John Holt's careful analysis of self-defeating behavior patterns generated by the conventional high school and elementary classroom to George Leonard's controversial plea in *Education and*

Ecstasy for a "new kind of human being . . . who spends his life in the joyful pursuit of learning." This new being, according to Leonard, would be brought into existence by a new kind of education, where technology and Esalen-like therapies will allow schools to pass beyond their concentration on the intellect to become new centers of sense liberation.

Whatever form new schools will take, it is clear that they must be more responsive to the needs of new generations of "TV children." But even more important perhaps, new schools must be responsive to needs that have been present all along but simply not appreciated because of man's faulty understanding of his own nature.

M OST people, today as in past ages, adhere to religions by a more or less uncritical acceptance of what is established. But, in the present, what is "established" is under fire, and because of the education and media explosions, attitudes of large numbers of people are much less apt to be uncritical than previously. In addition, the growth of science and technology, fostered in the West in many ways by its historical connection with the Judeo-Christian tradition, has provided—for many—more plausible explanations about the nature of things than previous systems offered. These factors, among others, help to account for the current situation of turmoil in contemporary religion.

The crisis of contemporary religion is expressed by the disaffection of the educated young, the waning influence of the church as a cultural force, the appearance and growth of the death-of-God school of theology and other ideologies in many forms that consider theism obsolete or irrelevant. For many, organized religion has failed simply because it no longer seems to provide a viable reference point to those searching for identity or meaning in their lives.

At the same time, moreover, the capacities of technology for humanizing life have not yet been realized. Technological growth has come to the point where many feel it must be challenged and, at times, opposed by different ways of understanding life that emphasize unitive and contemplative attitudes toward nature rather than attitudes of manipulation and control.

In spite of this state of crisis in institutional religion and the sense of malaise in the larger society, however, the quest for the sacred, the mysterious, the occult, the sublime, the morally supportable and uplifting, is still very much alive—both inside and outside the church. As Harvey Cox points out in *The Cosmos Reader*, " . . . although the churches no longer exert a monopolistic control over religious symbols and values in modern society, this is something very different from the disappearance of religion as such." This is because religion, Cox says, "includes much more than whatever it is that churches teach and do." His conclusion is: "Religion is changing, not disappearing."

This seems to be borne out by any number of contemporary phenomena —from the changing roles played by clergymen such as the Berrigans to the emergence of a new generation willing to *do something* about their idealism, even to the extent of downward mobility socially and economically.

In conclusion, it should also be noted that, for better or worse, increasing numbers are finding religious significance in art, technology, football, the *I Ching,* the Tarot, palmistry, Zen Buddhism, drugs, yoga, Vonnegut's Bokononism, jogging, witchcraft, encounter groups, and astrology.

The Sexual Revolution

VANCE PACKARD
(b. 1914) is a well-known
popularizer in the social
sciences. His previous
books include *The Hidden
Persuaders, The Status
Seekers, The Waste Mak-
ers, The Pyramid Climb-
ers,* and *The Naked So-
ciety.* In *The Sexual Wilderness* Packard con-
tinues the primary focus
of his work in general: an
exploration of "what is
happening to the individ-
ual in the face of the new
kinds of pressures gen-
erated by our violently
changing world."

THE SIX FORCES
IN THE
BACKGROUND

THE bewilderment and normlessness characterizing so much of male-female relationships today are in large part caused by the dislocation in our way of life produced by rapid social change.

Many societies in the past have had to hold onto their hats during periods of rapid social change. But few societies in recorded history have been propelled into a brand-new environment as abruptly as the Western world has in the past quarter-century. Wilbert E. Moore, authority on social change at the Russell Sage Foundation, states, "By any crude measurement, the contemporary world appears to be changing more rapidly than at any time in human history. . . ." And he added that the rate of change seems to be accelerating.

What is new in our changed world the past quarter-century that might reasonably be having an impact on male-female relationships?

. . . Behind all the new conditions in environment loom six background forces that have been particularly potent in creating this new environment. . . .

CHANGES PRODUCED BY THE LIFE-MODIFYING SCIENCES

Human beings have been searching for ways to remove the likelihood of pregnancy from the act of coitus for at least 2500 years. Aristotle suggested cedar oil as a contraceptive. And there has been a long search to isolate "safe" periods.

A major improvement in contraceptive aids came in the 19th century with the vulcanization of rubber. Undoubtedly what will stand as the most historic breakthrough came in 1954 when two doctors working together, Gregory Pincus of the Worcester Foundation for Experimental Biology and John Rock, of the Reproductive Study Center in Brookline, Mass., discovered a drug that when taken in pill form by a woman could interrupt the process of ovulation and thus in effect prevent a union of female egg and male sperm.

Contraceptive pills were accepted by women at a rate unprecedented in the history of medical innovations. By 1967 at least 6,000,000 American women were taking some form of The Pill. The popularity of The Pill might be explained by figures cited by Dr. Pincus of the failure rates of various approaches to contraception at a clinic in Slough, England. The reported failure rate where condoms were used was nearly 50 percent, for example, whereas the failure rate where oral contraceptives were used was less than 1 percent.

Meanwhile another sensational improvement, the intrauterine device —almost as effective as The Pill—gained popularity. It apparently creates a commotion that prevents the fertilized egg from finding any secure anchor.

For the first time in human history, men and women now have an assured way to separate the recreational from the procreative function of coitus. The British demographer Richard Titmuss has suggested that birth control has done more to emancipate women than their gaining the right to vote. Some of the restless young unmarrieds are asking whether, in our enshrinement of chastity before the advent of effective contraceptives, we had been simply making a virtue of necessity.

One significant effect of the newer contraceptives, in terms of our interest, is that they shift the responsibility for birth control from the male to the female. Another significant effect is that such contraceptives, by providing peace of mind, enable many women to find considerably greater enjoyment from their sexual encounters. Males usually never have had a problem enjoying their encounters. (The greatly increased use of hormone preparations also was contributing to the enhanced interest married women were showing in physical intimacy.)

Meanwhile about two million American married couples have quietly arranged surgical birth control. It has no effect upon physical capacity for intercourse. In fact, it appears in most cases to improve the enjoyment. The male operation, vasectomy, is usually preferred because it is simpler. Considerable progress has been achieved in making the operation reversible so that the couple still have the option of impregnation if they later decide they want a baby (or another baby).

In Eastern Europe, where doctors have been freer to experiment with abortion than in the West, excellent results are reported from a simple new suction technique that eliminates the hazard inherent in the conventional surgical scraping.

Equally dramatic in modifying our lives has been the achievement — largely credited to science (and improved nutrition) — in lengthening the span of vigorous life.

Marriages launched today will usually continue, if successful, well into the 21st century. A girl who sees herself in a race to marry by the age of 20 or 22 is taking on a commitment that will ordinarily last more than half a century. Today's teenagers, certainly the female ones, will live on average to be close to 90 years old.

In just the 20 years between 1940 and 1960, males managed to increase their life span by 5½ years, while females of the U.S.A. were increasing their life span by 7½ years.

Even given the state of medicine today, the male born in 1962 has a life expectancy of about 67 years and the female an expectancy of close to 74 years in the U.S.A. Males and females in England, France, and Sweden have even longer life expectancies than U.S. citizens. (One travel agent in Kansas reported that three-fourths of his clients were widows, often traveling on insurance money.)

Since U.S. women are also completing their childbearing phase earlier, the mother now finds on average that her last child has gone off to school by the time she is 32 years old.

Because of the prolonged years of good health and vitality, and because of improved cosmetics, women need no longer fear that their beauty will fade in their twenties. Many women today described in the press as beautiful are in their forties and fifties. In theory at least, this should take the pressure off girls to marry early. Young women can also assume they will be sexually responsive for several decades. This prolonged beauty and vigor poses a novel challenge of adjustment for humanity. In all previous eras, parents were expected in effect to recreate physical attractiveness and sexual vitality in their children as their own attractiveness and vitality faded. Today we hear of instances of divorced mothers double-dating with their daughters.

The life-modifying sciences (and improved nutrition) have helped create two other changes worth noting in the female's life. Women now stop menstruating in their early fifties, or about 4 years later than they did a century ago. At the other end of the procreative circle, girls start menstruating about 3½ years earlier than they did a century ago, or usually while they are 13.

SOCIAL CHANGES PRODUCED BY TECHNOLOGICAL INNOVATION

Yale psychologist Kenneth Keniston has stated, correctly I believe, that "central to American society is the unquestioned primacy of technology in virtually every area of our collective existence. Technology provides the motor for the continual social change to which we must somehow adapt. . . ."

Technology has taken most of the danger, dirt, and requirement for muscle out of work and thus has opened up opportunities for women in many areas of the economy. At the same time technological innovation has created rapid job obsolescence. An expensively learned technical skill such as chemical engineering is likely to have a half-life of 10 years (i.e., half of what the person learned at technical schools becomes obsolete within 10 years). This rapid obsolescence can undermine the self-assurance of a male breadwinner. Also it tends to weaken the ties between generations, because the father is often no longer competent to transmit valued vocational skills to a son.

A part of the social change produced by exploding technology is that it seems to encourage the growth of large business organizations, with far-flung operations and with highly mobile employees. Also it encourages the growth of metropolitan areas. These factors in combination have a number of impacts that might reasonably affect profoundly male-female relations. There is the growing sense of anonymity, the reduction of adult scrutiny over the behavior of the young, an increased separation from kinfolk, a weakened sense of significant citizenship, a separation of job from the area of the home. (The rather desperate efforts of those most alienated of sane young Americans—the hippies—to establish "tribes," farm "communities," and even communal pads might be viewed as an outspoken symptom of a more widespread yearning for "community.")

Eli Ginzberg, specialist in manpower mobility at Columbia University, suggests, "Pretty soon we are all going to be metropolitan-type people in this country without ties or commitments to longtime friends and neighbors." *The Wall Street Journal* carried a report on "corporate gypsies" and cited the case of a manager of Montgomery Ward who, with his wife, had moved 28 times during the 26 years of their marriage.

The Atlas Van Lines estimates that the average corporate manager in engineering or marketing moves about every 2½ years. In my own hometown in Connecticut, which has more than its share of these corporate gypsies, the turnover in home occupancy between 1955 and 1960 was approximately 54 percent. Over all, the average family in the United States now moves 14 times in its lifetime, according to the Family Service Association of America. Clark E. Vincent, family specialist at the Bowman Gray School of Medicine, Winston-Salem, N.C., argues that a highly adaptable "nuclear" family with few close kinship ties is becoming a necessary social unit for our kind of industrial society. (A nuclear family is one stripped down to parents and kids, with no grandparents, uncles, cousins, or in-laws in the living area.)

As for the home itself, it has shifted from being a production center to being a service station. With available electrical appliances, prepackaged foods, laundry services, many homemakers are hard put to consider themselves fully employed unless they follow the models in the television ads and keep their floors and glassware gleaming, or unless they get heavily involved in chauffeuring children.

The Ladies' Home Journal found in a survey of women that a substantial majority of the respondents did no sewing. And the same journal in reporting the life of a remarkable mother of two children in Grapevine, Texas, stated that despite her large house with five bedrooms and three baths and no maid, she completed her housework in one hour, by 8:30 a.m. when her youngest went off to school. She explained, "I am free to play bridge, attend club meetings or stay home and read, listen to Beethoven, and just plain loaf" until the family returns.

As we will see, a great many of these wives and mothers rather suddenly are interested in jobs, and plenty of jobs are available thanks to the growth in demand for service employees, office employees, and many other growing job categories where women are welcome in a technologically advanced society. Robert O. Blood, Jr., sociologist at the University of Michigan, believes that the increase in the number of married women—and mothers in particular—who work outside the home "is one of the most startling social changes in American history."

Two specific technological innovations that by general usage in recent decades have modified male-female relationships in an interesting way are (1) the automobile and (2) the baby bottle.

With most non-slum families having at least one automobile, and with millions of youngsters owning their own, courtship activity is more likely to take place in an automobile than in the family parlor.

As for the baby bottle, the first U.S. patent for an artificial feeding device was obtained in 1841, for a deerskin pseudobreast filled with sponge that was strapped to the mother's chest to deceive the tyke into believing it was getting real human milk. The difficulties in getting widespread use of artificial feeders centered not so much on the feeder as in developing a formula for milk that was nutritious and did not create severe reactions in babies. It was only in the past quarter-century that bottle feeding got general medical and public acceptance. In terms of the male-female relationship the significant contribution of the baby bottle was that it has enabled the mother to delegate some of the feeding and burping of babies to the father.

CHANGES IN THE AGE DISTRIBUTION OF THE POPULATION

All during the early 1960s the number of U.S. inhabitants under the age of 18 was growing four times as fast as the rest of the population. It is estimated that after 1968 each succeeding year's crop of 19-year-olds will be bigger than the one before, and the figure will reach at least 4,000,000 by 1974.

Thus one aspect of the so-called generational gulf can be stated in sheer numbers. Approximately half the population already is under the age of 27. The proportion of the U.S. population that is teen-age is the greatest in many decades. In some suburban communities where teen-agers alone constitute more than 40 percent of the total population fearful adults have been setting up special citizen's groups to watch for rampaging adolescents.

All these tens of millions of adolescents, born after World War II and now surging up toward adulthood, create mixed feelings among adults preoccupied with the direction of the economy. Some union leaders tend to want to keep young people off the labor market as long as possible; and the marketing people tend to want the young people to become major consumers through "family-formation" or otherwise as quickly as possible (so they will become prospects for such big-ticket items as beds and refrigerators). On the other hand, if the young get jobs and remain single—especially as "swinging singles"—they are more attractive to certain marketers than married young people, since they are better prospects for high-priced sports cars, travel abroad, champagne, expensive hi-fi sets, and other amenities.

One advertising man advised me that if our economy is to flourish, young people will have "to become more active consumers at a fairly early age," long before marriage. Apparently this wish has become a reality. Edward Bond, as president of the Young & Rubicam advertising agency, stated of the young generation in 1965, "They are strongly consumption oriented—in fact the consumption of goods and services appears to be life's goal."

The younger generation has been setting the mass-buying trends for a great many products (such as automobiles, filtered cigarettes and canned beer) that are eventually taken up by adults, which is certainly a new kind of tyranny. Lester Rand of the Youth Research Institute contends that the greater affluence of teenagers in the past 10 years has enabled them to be more independent in their attitudes toward adults (even though much of their affluence comes from their allowances!).

CHANGES CREATED BY THE EXPANSION OF HIGHER EDUCATION

In 1937 about 12 percent of young Americans of college age actually went to college. Thirty years later, in 1967, the proportion had risen to more than 40 percent. U.S. Office of Education figures indicate that between 1940 and 1965 the proportion of high-school graduates who went on to college rose from 35 percent to 55 percent. And a rapidly increasing proportion go on to graduate school.

Why has there been this great increase in college enrollment? First, of course, is the real or imagined need of industry for managers who have the proper ticket of admission, the college diploma. Affluence has increased the number of parents who feel they can send their children to college. The alternative of military service has certainly inspired a considerable interest in higher learning. Then there is the seldom acknowledged economic gain of holding down unemployment by delaying entry of the young onto the job market. Also colleges increasingly are meeting the need of a highly mobile society for an acceptable meeting ground for marriage-minded males and (especially) females of similar background.

And finally there is the considerable new interest among young women in the idea of preparing for interesting careers. An ever higher proportion of collegians are females. The proportion of students enrolled in institutions of higher learning who were female increased from 31 percent in 1952 to 39 percent in 1965. In India there is a saying: "Educate a woman and you put a knife in the hands of a monkey!" Few American males would dare to venture that opinion today.

As some of the universities have grown to have 10,000 . . . 20,000 . . . 30,000 . . . 40,000 students, many of these students feel lonely and on their own—in need of human companionship—and often seek out the warmth of sexual involvement. A student sign at Harvard University said, "It's the two of us against the world—and the world is winning."

The most noteworthy fact about the growth of college-goers, in terms of our inquiry, is that we are delaying for ever more young people the time when they become self-supporting and capable of establishing self-supporting marriages. Millions of young adults who are biologically mature are not becoming independent in any real sense. While we give young people more freedom, we keep them in de facto dependence upon adults much longer. Mrs. Alva Myrdal, noted authority on modern women's role and recently a Swedish cabinet member, suggests that "the discrepancy between biological and social maturity may be one of the most fundamental causes of the so-called 'youth problem' besetting so many countries just now."

When young people feel dependent, they seem to have to prove to themselves their independence fairly constantly. Students at publicly supported institutions, incidentally, have a much better chance of approaching independence through self-support and institutional loans than students at private schools, where annual costs may run close to $4,000.

CHANGES IN IDEALS, BELIEFS, AND NATIONAL MOOD

Such changes can profoundly affect male-female relationships.

Changes in religious emphasis are perhaps easiest to identify. In the U.S. the proportion of the population formally affiliated with churches has shown no serious drop-off. But many clergymen have felt it necessary to strain to appear modern in order to hold the interest of churchgoers, especially the younger ones. Examples are the staging of rock-and-roll dances at church services . . . the fondness for extreme modernity in church architecture, a tendency that has been described as an edifice complex . . . and the brightening up of the titles posted for sermons. A church in Dayton, Ohio, advertised this sermon: "To Put God On A Pedestal Is A Monumental Error."

The discoveries of astronomers, geologists, and space explorers have undermined the faith of all but the most devout that there is a physical Heaven or Hell. And among believers, God is more likely to be seen as a force or spirit than as an all-seeing watcher over human behavior above.

A Gallup Poll revealed in 1965 that in the preceding 7 years the percentage of Americans who saw religion losing its influence has more than tripled. In several countries of northern Europe the drop in religious influence is considerably more noticeable. A survey in England among more than a thousand teenagers produced the conclusion that "Most of the young people we interviewed were not interested in Christianity."

The decline of religious belief as a vital source of guidance in everyday life will be pertinent to our inquiry at a number of points because the major religions of the Western world have always shown a considerable interest in the male-female relationship. Not only has there been concern about what constitutes moral behavior in various aspects of male-female encounters, but most of the major religions have provided strong support for the concept of male dominance.

Early Christians saw woman as the primary cause of sexual sin. St. Paul especially glorified austerity in sexual matters, even in marriage, apparently as a part of purifying rites in preparation for the Second Coming of Jesus. St. Paul stated, "It is good for man not to touch a woman. . . . But if they do not have self control let them marry, for it is better to marry than to burn."

The Dean of Students at Hope College suggested that "our society is giving up the Judaic-Christian tradition as a basis for law and morality without replacing it with any consistent rationale for morality."

Meanwhile a number of forces in Western life have been encouraging a mood of hedonism. Industries have a vested interest in promoting instant gratification. Living for the moment is also encouraged by the new affluence in most Western societies and by social security systems that offer protection against personal adversity.

In the mid-1960s one of the fastest-growing major magazines, *Playboy*, dedicated itself to extolling the hedonistic, sensual way of life. A professor of philosophy at a college in North Carolina told me, "I teach philosophy from Socrates to Hefner." (Hugh M. Hefner, the publisher of *Playboy*, has written a couple of dozen essays amplifying his magazine's philosophy.) The professor said that *Playboy* was then the most widely read publication on campus and added, "I read it because the students do." *Playboy*, he explained, believes in the pleasures of the body, while Socrates believed in a split between body and mind, and de-emphasized the mere body.

In recent years we have also been seeing a gradual movement through-out most of the Western world toward a real acceptance of the equalitarian ideal. This acceptance has developed in part from ideals proclaimed during the revolutionary wars from 1776 to the mid-19th century and in part from the continuing trends toward political liberalism in most of the West. It is difficult for a person who honors logic to glorify the equalitarian ideal and at the same time keep woman in the subordinate role expected of her in patriarchal societies.

The decline in arranged marriages and the growth of the concept of romantic love also have been factors in strengthening the hand of woman vis-à-vis the male. A man who claims to be in love with a woman will concede more power to her.

Along with equalitarianism there has been the glorying of individual rights. Perhaps the more the individual feels hemmed in and threatened by the pressures of large organizations and prolonged dependency, the more he reacts by asserting that only the individual counts. Carried to its logical extreme, this enthronement of the individual tends to undermine group norms and even implies a kind of anarchy as an ideal. A coed at a Midwestern university in a metropolitan area wrote to us on her comment sheet in the College Survey, "Standards for behavior are hard to find on the college campus. Individualism might be said to be the norm. I can tell you what I believe, yet I find it hard to prescribe for society." That same thought in a variety of phrasings came to us in many dozens of student comments.

This question of the ideal of individualism (and impingements upon the rights of the individual by modern society), which your author has examined in several contexts in the past dozen years, seems to raise more perplexing questions in the male-female relationship than in any other area explored. Is it possible that at some point the pursuit of individualism in male-female relations becomes simply irresponsible and socially dangerous privitism (self-absorption)? Most of us now are wary when free-wheeling, hard-driving private entrepreneurs advance under the banner of rugged individualism. But what about amatory adventurers who argue that anything goes as long as the sexual partner does not get "hurt"? What constitutes "hurt"? And can society too be hurt?

Beliefs about what is appropriate in behavior between the sexes have also been influenced among most young Western people by the fact that they are far more exposed to people outside their home community than ever before in history. They read more, travel more beyond their home states and home country.

CHANGES IN INDIVIDUAL LIFE PRODUCED BY WARS AND INTERNATIONAL TENSIONS

The male, of course, has long been fascinated with combat as a way of proving his prowess, but in recent major wars the male has usually discovered that while he was away at war the woman back home had been gaining independence from him. Women, who have traditionally opposed wars, have gained the most from recent ones. The wars have given them a chance to prove their talent in the new technological society.

During World War I, women were urged to enter into many previously male roles, and it is probably no coincidence that they won the right to vote in the United States during the turmoil of the war and the months immediately following it. During World War II, women by the millions took on jobs traditionally held by males.

The upheaval of war also has had the effect of churning the population, separating loved ones, and in general creating an environment for a freer expression of sexual intimacy. And the tensions of hot and cold wars and living in a period when the Bomb or a draft call may strike all tend to contribute to the mood of living for the moment.

Henry David Aiken, Brandeis University philosopher, suggests that "the bomb has created the most extreme of all the predicaments that have ever confronted man" in its constant potential for instant extinction of the human race. This possibility makes it tempting to be unconcerned about tomorrow and to strive today for intensity of experience.

Most of these background forces that have helped create a sexual wilderness in the U.S.A. are at work in many of the world's societies in addition to those of North America and Western Europe. In many parts of the Near East the more worldly prosperous males are likely to join their unveiled monogamously mated wives for strolls. In the urban parts of Greece the arranged marriage is disappearing for all but the quiet rich. Young men and women can be seen in public holding hands, which would have been unthinkable 20 years ago. Some of the bolder Greeks are even appearing on beaches, along with the tourists, in Western-style brief bathing suits. In much of rural Greece it is still considered disgusting for either male or female to expose any flesh beyond hands and face.

Thirty years ago Japan was perhaps the most patriarchal of all societies, and the Japanese head of a family was one of the more awe-inspiring human figures conceivable. He expected and got considerable deference from his family. The most explosive force unleashed in postwar Japan was the Japanese woman, and Americans were at least partly responsible for the unleashing. General Douglas MacArthur, in pressing the adoption of the postwar constitution with its liberating provisions for women, launched a battle of the sexes that is still shaking the nation and causing many husbands to come home later and later at night. Women who were long considered to be little more than chattels by the men gained not only the right to vote but the right to have equal educations and even the right to get divorces. All of this has given them a far greater say about what goes on in the house. They began firmly requesting washing machines, prettier, less inhibiting clothes, and a chance to see more of the world.

Jiro Tokuyama, head of the Nomura Research Institute, advised me that today 80 percent of young Japanese husbands in urban communities turn over their pay envelopes, unopened, to their wives!

There is of course no clear one-to-one relationship between social changes produced by these six background forces and specific new patterns in male-female relationships. The forces that have been cited, furthermore, come to bear at a variety of points in the male-female relationship. The Pill, for example, may affect not only premarital coitus but the power relationships between husband and wife.

At any rate, an awareness of the possible reverberating effect of these six forces may add to our understanding . . . [of] the specific changes in male-female relationships that have been occurring during the past quarter-century.

DISCUSSION QUESTIONS
SUGGESTIONS FOR WRITING

1. Summarize the "six forces in the background" that Packard believes have had the greatest impact and effect on male-female relationships today. Do you agree with his analysis?

2. Would you say that this essay shows little or great influence of the trend toward use of fictional techniques in nonfiction writing?

3. What sources of information does Packard rely on most heavily?

4. Do you agree that "the discrepancy between biological and social maturity may be one of the most fundamental causes of the so-called 'youth problem' besetting so many countries just now"? How could this discrepancy, if it is a problem, be eliminated?

MASTERS AND JOHNSON

THE FEMALE ORGASM

MASTERS and JOHNSON William H. Masters, M.D. (b. 1915), is research director, and Virginia E. Johnson (b. 1925) is research associate of the Reproductive Biology Research Foundation in St. Louis. Together, Masters and Johnson carried out research into the anatomy and physiology of human sexual response that represents a major breakthrough in knowledge of human sexuality.

FEMALE orgasmic experience can be visually identified as well as recorded by acceptable physiologic techniques. The primary requirement in objective identification of female orgasm is the knowledge that it is a total-body response with marked variation in reactive intensity and timing sequence. Previously, other observers have recognized and interpreted much of the reactive physiology of female orgasm. However, definition and correlation of these reactions into an identifying pattern of orgasm per se has not been established.

At orgasm, the grimace and contortion of a woman's face graphically express the increment of myotonic tension throughout her entire body. The muscles of the neck and the long muscles of the arms and legs usually contract into involuntary spasm. During coition in supine position the female's hands and feet voluntarily may be grasping her sexual partner. With absence of clutching interest or opportunity during coition or in solitary response to automanipulative techniques, the extremities may reflect involuntary carpopedal spasm. The striated muscles of the abdomen and the buttocks frequently are contracted voluntarily by women in conscious effort to elevate sexual tensions, particularly in an effort to break through from high plateau to orgasmic attainment.

The physiologic onset of orgasm is signaled by contractions of the target organs, starting with the orgasmic platform in the outer third of the vagina. This platform, created involuntarily by localized vasocongestion and myotonia, contracts with recordable rhythmicity as the tension increment is released. The intercontractile intervals recur at 0.8

second for the first three to six contractions, corresponding in timing sequence to the first few ejaculatory contractions (male orgasm) of the penis. The longer contractions continue, the more extended the inter-contractile intervals. The number and intensity of orgasmic-platform contractions are direct measures of subjective severity and objective duration of the particular orgasmic experience. The correlation between platform contractions and subjective experience at orgasm has been corroborated by study subjects during thousands of cycles. Vaginal spasm and penile grasping reactions have been described many times in the clinical and nonprofessional literature. Orgasmic-platform contrac-tility provides an adequate physiologic explanation for these subjective concepts.

Contractions of the orgasmic platform provide visible manifestation of female orgasmic experience. To date, the precise mechanism whereby cortical, hormonal, or any unidentified influence may activate this and other orgasmic reactions has not been determined (perhaps by creating a trigger-point level of vasocongestive and myotonic increment).

Orgasmic contractions of the uterus have been recorded by both intrauterine and abdominally placed electrodes. Both techniques indi-cate that uterine contractions may have onset almost simultaneously with those of the orgasmic platform, but the contractive intensity of the uterine musculature is accumulated slowly and contractions are too irregular in recurrence and duration to allow pattern definition. Uterine contractions start in the fundus and work through the midzone to termi-nate in the lower uterine segment. With the exception of the factor of contractile excursion (indication of intensity), physiologic tracings of uterine orgasmic contractions resemble the patterns of first-stage labor contractions. Uterine contractile intensity and duration vary widely from orgasm to orgasm. However, there is some early indication that both factors have a positive relation to the parity of the individual and the prior extent of her orgasmic experience, both incidental and cu-mulative.

Involuntary contractions of the external rectal sphincter also may develop during orgasm, although many women experience orgasm without evidencing sphincter contraction. When the contractions do occur, they parallel in timing sequence the initial intercontractile inter-vals of the orgasmic platform. The rectal-sphincter contractions usually terminate before those of the orgasmic platform.

The external urethral sphincter also may contract two or three times in an involuntary expression of orgasmic tension release. The contrac-tions are without recordable rhythmicity and usually are confined to nulliparous premenopausal women.

The breasts evidence no specific response to the immediacy of orgasm. However, detumescence of the areolae immediately subsequent to orgasm is so rapid that its arbitrary assignment purely as a resolution-phase reaction has been cause for investigative concern. Often areolar detumescence is evident shortly after subjective report of orgasmic onset and usually develops simultaneously with the terminal contractions of the orgasmic platform. As a final stage of the rapid detumescent reaction, the areolae constrict into a corrugated state. The nipples remain erect and are turgid and quite rigid (the false-erection reaction).

Rapid detumescence of the vasocongested areolae, resulting in a constricted, corrugated appearance, occurs only with orgasm and is an obvious physical manifestation that provides for visual identification of female orgasmic experience. If orgasm does not occur areolar detumescence is a much slower process, corrugation does not develop, and the false-erection reaction of the nipples usually is reduced in intensity.

The sex flush, a maculopapular rash distributed superficially over the body surfaces, achieves its greatest intensity and its widest distribution at the moment of orgasmic expression. Subsequent to orgasmic experience, the sex flush disappears more rapidly than when resolving from plateau-phase levels of erotic tension.

From a cardiorespiratory point of view, orgasm is reflected by hyperventilation, with respiratory rates occasionally over 40 per minute. Tachycardia is a constant accompaniment of orgasmic experience, with cardiac rates running from 110 to beyond 180 beats per minute. Hypertension also is a constant finding. The systolic pressures are elevated by 30–80 mm. and diastolic pressures by 20–40 mm. Hg.

The clitoris, Bartholin's glands, and the major and minor labia are target organs for which no specific physiologic reactions to orgasmic-phase levels of sexual tension have been established.

Aside from ejaculation, there are two major areas of physiologic difference between female and male orgasmic expression. First, the female is capable of rapid return to orgasm immediately following an orgasmic experience, if restimulated before tensions have dropped below plateau-phase response levels. Second, the female is capable of maintaining an orgasmic experience for a relatively long period of time.

A rare reaction in the total of female orgasmic expression, but one that has been reduplicated in the laboratory on numerous occasions, has been termed *status orgasmus*. This physiologic state of stress is created either by a series of rapidly recurrent orgasmic experiences between which no recordable plateau-phase intervals can be demonstrated, or by a single, long-continued orgasmic episode. Subjective report, together with visual impression of involuntary variation in peripheral myotonia, suggests that the woman actually is ranging with extreme rapidity between successive orgasmic peaks and a baseline of advanced plateau-phase tension. Status orgasmus may last from 20 to more than 60 seconds. . . . The severe tachycardia (more than 180 per minute) and the long-maintained (43 seconds), rapidly recurring contractile patterns of the orgasmic platform are identified easily.

Of interest from both physiologic and psychologic points of view is the recorded evidence of an initial involuntary spasm of the orgasmic platform, developing before the regularly recurring contractions of orgasmic expression. . . . The study subject identified the onset of orgasm and vocalized this subjective experience before the onset of regularly recurrent contractions of the orgasmic platform. However, the initial spasm of the orgasmic platform developed parallel in timing sequence with the subjective identification of the orgasmic experience. To date, preliminary spasm of the orgasmic platform has been recorded only in situations of severe tension increment.

It is investigative impression that the inability to record initial spasm of the orgasmic platform in all orgasmic experiences well may reflect lack of effective experimental technique rather than unimpeachable physiologic fact. Subjectively, the identification of initial spasm of the orgasmic platform is a constant factor in any full orgasmic experience. . . .

No preliminary spastic contraction of the uterine musculature comparable to the initial spasm of the orgasmic platform has been recorded to date. However, the work is in its infancy, and such a preliminary spasm before onset of the regular, expulsive, fundal contractions may, in fact, exist and be recorded in the future.

The subjective identification of orgasmic expression by the human female simultaneously with the initial spasm of the orgasmic platform, but 2 to 4 seconds prior to onset of its regularly recurrent contractions, draws an interesting parallel with the human male's ejaculatory experience. When the secondary organs of reproduction contract, the male feels the ejaculation coming and can no longer control it, but there still is a 2- to 4-second interval before the seminal fluid appears at the urethral meatus under the pressure developed by penile expulsive contractions. Thus the male's psychosensory expression of ejaculatory inevitability may have counterpart in the female's subjective identification of orgasmic onset. The initial spasm of the orgasmic platform, before the platform and the uterus contract with regularity, may parallel the contractions of the prostate and, questionably, contractions of the seminal vesicles before onset of the regularly recurrent expulsive contractions of the penis.

Understandably, the maximum physiologic intensity of orgasmic response subjectively reported or objectively recorded has been achieved by self-regulated mechanical or automanipulative techniques. The next highest level of erotic intensity has resulted from partner manipulation, again with established or self-regulated methods, and the lowest intensity of target-organ response was achieved during coition.

While variations in the orgasmic intensity and duration of target-organ response have been recorded and related to modes of stimulation, there have been no recorded alterations in the basic orgasmic physiology. This finding lends support, at least in part, to many earlier concepts of orgasmic response. The fundamental physiology of orgasmic response remains the same whether the mode of stimulation is heterosexual or artificial coition or mechanical or automanipulative stimulation of the clitoral area, the breast, or any other selected erogenous zone. It follows that orgasm resulting from fantasy also would produce the same basic physiologic response patterns, although a woman capable of fantasying to orgasm has not been available for inclusion in the research population. The ability of women to fantasy to orgasm has been reported by other investigators.

With the specific anatomy of orgasmic-phase physiology reasonably established, the age-old practice of the human female of dissimulating has been made pointless. The obvious, rapid detumescence and corrugation of the areolae of the breasts and the definable contractions of the orgasmic platform in the outer third of the vagina remove any doubt as to whether the woman is pretending or experiencing orgasm. The severe vasocongestive reactions reflecting higher levels of sexual tension cannot be developed other than during involuntary response to sexual stimulation. For example, the transitory but obvious increase in nulliparous breast size, the sex flush, and the minor-labial sex skin reactions are all plateau-phase phenomena that develop only in response to effective sexual stimulation.

DISCUSSION QUESTIONS
SUGGESTIONS FOR WRITING

1. *In their preface to* Human Sexual Response *the authors comment:* "*How can biologists, behavioralists, theologians, and educators insist in good conscience upon the continued existence of a massive state of ignorance of human sexual response, to the detriment of the well-being of millions of individuals? Why must the basis of human sexual physiology create such high levels of personal discomfort among the very men and women who are responsible for guiding our culture?" Can you answer this question?*

2. *Perhaps this shyness (see 1, above), the authors further suggest, in reference to an article of some forty years ago from an important medical journal, is "begotten by the certainty that such study cannot be freed from the warp of personal experience, the bias of individual prejudice, and, above all, from the implication of prurience." In your judgment, based on an analysis of the excerpt in the text, can any of these charges be accurately leveled against the study of human sexual physiology made by Masters and Johnson?*

3. *Given the tone of utter detachment, the emotionless, primarily descriptive diction, the posture of extreme objectivity, what, if anything beyond the subject matter, engages the reader?*

4. *Eliminating the possibilities of parody, would you think this an interesting method to use on some less engaging subject? What would the result be?*

BROWNMILLER

SUSAN BROWNMILLER
(b. 1935) is a frequent
contributor on feminist
subjects to the *Village
Voice, Esquire, Mademoi-
selle,* and the *New York
Times Magazine.* She is a
free-lance writer and
member of the New York
Radical Feminists. In "The
Enemy Within" she raises
issues that ·are crucial to
a serious understanding
of the current widespread
reexamination of and
changing perspectives on
sex roles and stereotypes
and of the movement for
women's liberation.

THE ENEMY
WITHIN

WHEN I was 11 years old and talking in the schoolyard one day with a bunch of girlfriends from class, the discussion came around, as it did in those days, to "What are you going to be when you grow up?" At least three of us wanted to be actresses or models. Two had their sights already set on marriage, motherhood, and a house in the country. But one girl said *she* was going to go to medical school and be a doctor. This announcement was greeted with respectful silence (all those additional years of school!) until Martha, fat, bright, and at the head of the class, said solemnly, "I'd never go to a woman doctor. I just wouldn't have *confidence* in a woman doctor."

"Not even to deliver your baby?" I remember inquiring.

"Nope," Martha replied. "Especially not to deliver my baby. That's too important. Men doctors are better than women doctors."

It has been many years since that schoolyard discussion and I can't even recall the name or the face of the girl who had the ambitions, but I hope she wasn't sidetracked somewhere along the line. But I remember Martha. Calm, the best student, everybody's friend, more advanced physically than the rest of us—she had breasts, we didn't—and utterly positive at that tender age that men did things better than women. I will never forgive her for being the first person of my sex whom I ever heard put down women. I considered it traitorous then in the school-yard, and I consider it traitorous now. Since that time, I have done a lot of observing of that strange phenomenon, have been guilty of it myself, I think, and have come to the conclusion that woman is often her own worst enemy—the enemy within.

One of the hardest things for a woman with aspirations to do in our society is to admit, first to herself and then to others, that she has ambitions that go beyond the routine—a good marriage, clever children. Early on, we learn that men don't take kindly to the notion of a woman entering the competitive lists. It is in the nature of power and position that those who have it do not relinquish it graciously, as all colonial peoples and all minority groups discover at a certain stage in their development. Well, O.K., so be it. But infinitely more damaging to our psyche is the realization that our ambitions are met with equal hostility —pooh-poohed, sniffed at, scoffed at, ignored, or worse, not taken seriously—by mothers, sisters, cousins, aunts and friends, who won't believe that we have set our sights on a different sort of goal than *they* have envisioned, preferring instead to believe that our ambition is merely a "passing phase"—which, unfortunately, it often is because of lack of encouragement.

Psychologists talk a great deal about the importance of the approbation or approval of a peer group upon the individual. It is human nature to want to fit in. The senior at college who sends away for law-school catalogues while her dormitory mates down the corridor are sending away for catalogues of silver patterns is already conscious of swimming against the tide. (How different the atmosphere must be in a man's dormitory!) The magazine researcher who took her job as a stepping-stone to becoming a writer, but discovers that girl researchers are not encouraged to write by the magazine's male editors, will find little sympathy and understanding from other researchers who have taken the job to mark time until their proper engagements are properly announced in *The New York Times*. The peer-group pressure on a young woman in her 20s—as opposed to the pressure on a young man in his 20s—is decidedly against career.

I don't mean to imply that the force is necessarily insidious—although it sometimes is, and I intend to get around to discussing that aspect. I spent a wonderfully noncompetitive, warm, and friendly two years at *Newsweek* in the company of my "fellow" researchers in 1963-64 until I abruptly quit one day, wrenched myself out of the womb, because I finally realized that the warmth, the friendship, the long lunches, the joint shopping excursions to Saks Fifth Avenue, and the pleasant lack of direction among "the girls" had effectively smothered my own sense of direction. I was not the first *Newsweek* girl to break out of the researcher mold, and I will not be the last. But more heartening than individual breakthroughs is the news that has lately reached me from that sunny vineyard on Madison Avenue—the rumblings of insurrection among those very researchers who appeared so content with their lot just a few years ago.

There were two full-fledged women writers at *Newsweek* during the time I was there. One did her job quietly and went about unnoticed, but the other, an attractive, sexy young lady, was rather noticeable. We hated her. Among the grievances we held against this young woman was the fact that she never deigned to talk with us researchers. Considered herself superior, we thought. Got her job through unholy machinations, we believed. Dressed terribly, we agreed. *Couldn't really write*, we fervently hoped. It took me a few years after leaving the magazine to realize what this hostility toward someone we hardly knew was all about. *She was* where *we* wanted to be. When she walked through the halls she was L., the writer, not L., a researcher. There may have been 50 male writers who daily crossed our path at the magazine, but we spared them our collective resentment because, after all, they were men and we weren't. But L. — how dare she! She threatened our collective existence! Two years later, when I was working as a television newswriter at ABC (again, there were only two of us women writers), I experienced some of this collective cattiness from the ABC researchers and understood it perfectly. I also discovered that it's quite natural for writers to pal around with other writers and not with researchers. It has to do with field of interest and not with snobbery at all. L. knew it, and I discovered it.

There was a small item in the news not long ago about the first woman editor-in-chief of the University of Pennsylvania's daily student newspaper. The editor, Judith Teller, a junior at the University's Wharton School of Business, was quoted as saying, "I generally find women basically incompetent, and in general I deal with men." A harsh quote from Miss Teller, to be sure, and not designed to win her any women friends, but at the age of 20 Miss Teller, an obvious careerist, wants to be where the action is, and for that I can't blame her.

Women are *not* "basically incompetent," but so much of their energy goes into pretending incompetence when there are attractive men around who may be watching that the result is often the same. Schooled by their mothers to "let the man win" at Ping-pong or tennis, how can they develop a good game? They can't, of course, and the game becomes not an exercise of skill but a minuet of manners. The Ping-pong-and-tennis syndrome affects a woman's performance in practically all areas of her life. The idea is not to win. "Women is Losers," wails Janis Joplin in a repetitive, powerful lamentation. Losing has been equated with femininity for so long in our culture that it has become a virtual definition of the female role. The way to lose is not to try very hard to win, to convince oneself that personal achievement — if one is a woman — doesn't really matter at all. This peculiar attitude, which flies in the face of every success homily in *Poor Richard's Almanack*, is as unnatural as it is destructive. It has its parallels in the attitudes of the hard-core unemployed who have stripped away personal ambition and belief in their own abilities to a point where they are actually incapable of functioning. We are all familiar with the sexual double standards that men employ, but here is a sexual double standard that women hold on to for dear life: *admire individual achievement in men, but deny it for yourself.* The corollary to this dictum, by the way, is *marry the achiever.* Either way, it is a terrible denial of self-worth.

I have seen women who *admit* to small hankerings of personal ambition (usually expressed by a modest "I'd like to do more at work") throw up unbelievable psychological barriers to their own success. Two conversations I once had in the space of two days with a couple of young ladies who work in television will illustrate what I mean. Both women had neatly resolved their stymied careers with the oddest excuses I have ever heard. One thought she never could rise to a producer because she found the temperature in the film-editing rooms "too cold." The other said she never felt comfortable "near machines." To the first I answered, "Get a sweater." The second rendered me speechless. Of course, what these women were really saying was that their *femininity* — not the fact that they were female — somehow made them unfit for the tough world of television production.

The risk of losing that intangible called femininity weighs heavily on many women who are afraid to compete with men for better jobs. This sad state of affairs has come about because of arbitrary and rigid definitions of what is masculine and what is feminine that our culture has relied on for a variety of complex reasons. We can thank the hippie revolution for knocking down some of the old criteria, particularly external ones like the length of hair and form of dress. But as long as such qualities as self-assertion, decision-making, and leadership are considered masculine — and conversely, unfeminine — a woman who worries about her femininity will never make a go of it in terms of career.

It was men who made the arbitrary rules of masculine/feminine that we suffer under, but it is women who continue to buy the stereotypes. At the early women's-liberation meetings that I attended, I was struck with how all of us were unwilling to assume leadership roles, and how often a sensible comment or brilliant new insight was couched between giggles and stutters or surrounded by self-disparaging phrases and gestures. Clearly, we were women who were unused to speaking forthrightly — without the frills and furbelows of "feminine" roundabout logic designed to make a point as gently as possible for fear of offending. Since we had nobody to offend but ourselves, this namby-pambying ceased to some extent with the passage of time.

But a women's-liberation meeting is a very special crucible. In the world outside, the stereotype of the aggressive, castrating bitch is still posted as a warning to us. If a woman believes in the existence of this mythical creature — and believes in her own potential transmogrification — her case is hopeless. It astounds me that so many women remain convinced that a woman who functions in high gear in business, politics, or in the professions loses something intrinsic that is worth preserving. Personally, I have always felt that true femininity was rather indestructible. One look at the Irish revolutionary Bernadette Devlin should settle the matter once and for all. I suspect that this "castrating bitch" propaganda, a big lie, really, is perpetuated not only by insecure men but also by do-nothing women, the magpies who busy themselves with nothing more than nest-building. There is no getting around the uncomfortable truth that the militant stay-at-homes, the clinging vines, dislike and distrust their liberated sisters. I know exactly what I lost when I gave up pretending that passivity was a virtue and entered the competitive arena—some personality distortions which made me pirouette in concentric circles when I could have simply walked a straight line. And I know what I gained—self-esteem and a stretching of creative muscles and an exercising of a mind which had grown flaccid from disuse since the halcyon days of college.

A major tragedy of the female sex is that friendship and respect between women has never been highly regarded. During the dating years, girls are notoriously quick to ditch an appointment with a girlfriend at the sound of a male voice on the telephone. With marriage and family comes the suspicion that all other women are potentially "the other woman." In an early episode of *The Forsythe Saga* on TV, Irene the adulteress tells Young Jolyon's daughter, "Don't you know that women don't have friends? They have a lover, and they have people that they meet." How pathetic, but how historically accurate.

There is nothing in women's chemical or biological makeup that should preclude deep loyalty to those of the same sex. The sensitivity is certainly there, as is the capacity for warmth and love and fidelity. But until women cease to see themselves strictly in terms of men's eyes and to value men more highly than women, friendship with other women will remain a sometime thing, an expedient among competitors of inferior station that can be lightly discarded. I, for one, would much rather compete *with* men than for them. This affliction of competition between women for the attention of men—the only kind of women's competition that is encouraged by society—also affects the liberated women who manage to secure an equal footing with men in this man's world. Watch a couple of strong women in the same room and notice the sparks fly. Many women who reject the "woman is inferior" psychology for themselves apply it unsparingly to others of the same sex. An ambitious woman frequently thinks of herself as the only hen in the barnyard, to reverse a common metaphor. *She* is the exception, she believes. Women must recognize that they must make common cause with *all* women. When women get around to really liking—and respecting—other women, why then, we will have begun.

DISCUSSION QUESTIONS
SUGGESTIONS FOR WRITING

1. What is your reaction to: "It was men who made the arbitrary rules of masculine/feminine that we suffer under, but it is women who continue to buy the stereotypes"?

2. In the so-called personal essay, of which this is an example, the author expresses his or her personal views of a subject through force of personality, testimonials, personal anecdotes, or appeal to emotions, rather than by reliance on empirical evidence or logical argument. Can you find examples of these methods in this selection?

3. What major issues of the movement for women's liberation are raised by this essay?

4. Does the essay succeed in breaking through your preconceptions, in creating sympathy for, identification with, or greater understanding of the women's liberation movement?

DORIS LESSING (b. 1919) is one of the most influential of those writers whose works have illuminated the role of women in contemporary society. Other important works include *The Golden Notebook* and *Children of Violence.*

A WOMAN
ON A ROOF

|T WAS during the week of hot sun, that June.

Three men were at work on the roof, where the leads got so hot they had the idea of throwing water on to cool them. But the water steamed, then sizzled; and they made jokes about getting an egg from some woman in the flats under them, to poach it for their dinner. By two it was not possible to touch the guttering they were replacing, and they speculated about what workmen did in regularly hot countries. Perhaps they should borrow kitchen gloves with the egg? They were all a bit dizzy, not used to the heat; and they shed their coats and stood side by side squeezing themselves into a foot-wide patch of shade against a chimney, careful to keep their feet in the thick socks and boots out of the sun. There was a fine view across several acres of roofs. Not far off a man sat in a deck chair reading the newspapers. Then they saw her, between chimneys, about fifty yards away. She lay face down on a brown blanket. They could see the top part of her: black hair, a flushed solid back, arms spread out.

"She's stark naked," said Stanley, sounding annoyed.

Harry, the oldest, a man of about forty-five, said: "Looks like it."

Young Tom, seventeen, said nothing, but he was excited and grinning.

Stanley said: "Someone'll report her if she doesn't watch out."

"She thinks no one can see," said Tom, craning his head all ways to see more.

At this point the woman, still lying prone, brought her two hands up behind her shoulders with the ends of a scarf in them, tied it behind her back, and sat up. She wore a red scarf tied around her breasts and brief red bikini pants. This being the first day of the sun she was white, flushing red. She sat smoking, and did not look up when Stanley let out a wolf whistle. Harry said: "Small things amuse small minds," leading the way back to their part of the roof, but it was scorching.

Harry said: "Wait, I'm going to rig up some shade," and disappeared down the skylight into the building. Now that he'd gone, Stanley and Tom went to the farthest point they could to peer at the woman. She had moved, and all they could see were two pink legs stretched on the blanket. They whistled and shouted but the legs did not move. Harry came back with a blanket and shouted: "Come on, then." He sounded irritated with them. They clambered back to him and he said to Stanley: "What about your missus?" Stanley was newly married, about three months. Stanley said, jeering: "What about my missus?"—preserving his independence. Tom said nothing, but his mind was full of the nearly naked woman. Harry slung the blanket, which he had borrowed from a friendly woman downstairs, from the stem of a television aerial to a row of chimney pots. This shade fell across the piece of gutter they had to replace. But the shade kept moving, they had to adjust the blanket, and not much progress was made. At last some of the heat left the roof, and they worked fast, making up for lost time. First Stanley, then Tom, made a trip to the end of the roof to see the woman. "She's on her back," Stanley said, adding a jest which made Tom snicker, and the older man smile tolerantly. Tom's report was that she hadn't moved, but it was a lie. He wanted to keep what he had seen to himself: he had caught her in the act of rolling down the little red pants over her hips, till they were no more than a small triangle. She was on her back, fully visible, glistening with oil.

Next morning, as soon as they came up, they went to look. She was already there, face down, arms spread out, naked except for the little red pants. She had turned brown in the night. Yesterday she was a scarlet and white woman, today she was a brown woman. Stanley let out a whistle. She lifted her head, startled, as if she'd been asleep, and looked straight over at them. The sun was in her eyes, she blinked and stared, then she dropped her head again. At this gesture of indifference, they all three, Stanley, Tom, and old Harry, let out whistles and yells. Harry was doing it in parody of the younger men, making fun of them, but he was also angry. They were all angry because of her utter indifference to the three men watching her.

"Bitch," said Stanley.

"She should ask us over," said Tom, snickering.

Harry recovered himself and reminded Stanley: "If she's married, her old man wouldn't like that."

"Christ," said Stanley virtuously, "if my wife lay about like that, for everyone to see, I'd soon stop her."

Harry said, smiling: "How do you know, perhaps she's sunning herself at this very moment?"

"Not a chance, not on our roof." The safety of his wife put Stanley into a good humour, and they went to work. But today it was hotter than yesterday; and several times one or the other suggested they should tell Matthew, the foreman, and ask to leave the roof until the heat wave was over. But they didn't. There was work to be done in the basement of the big block of flats, but up here they felt free, on a different level from ordinary humanity shut in the streets or the buildings. A lot more people came out onto the roofs that day, for an hour at midday. Some married couples sat side by side in deck chairs, the women's legs stockingless and scarlet, the men in vests with reddening shoulders.

The woman stayed on her blanket, turning herself over and over. She ignored them, no matter what they did. When Harry went off to fetch more screws, Stanley said: "Come on." Her roof belonged to a different system of roofs, separated from theirs at one point by about twenty feet. It meant a scrambling climb from one level to another, edging along parapets, clinging to chimneys, while their big boots slipped and slithered, but at last they stood on a small square projecting roof looking straight down at her, close. She sat smoking, reading a book. Tom thought she looked like a poster, or a magazine cover, with the blue sky behind her and her legs stretched out. Behind her a great crane at work on a new building in Oxford Street swung its black arm across the roofs in a great arc. Tom imagined himself at work on the crane, adjusting the arm to swing over and pick her up and swing her back across the sky to drop her near him.

They whistled. She looked up at them, cool and remote, then went on reading. Again, they were furious. Or rather, Stanley was. His sun-heated face was screwed into rage as he whistled again and again, trying to make her look up. Young Tom stopped whistling. He stood beside Stanley, excited, grinning; but he felt as if he were saying to the woman: "Don't associate with *him*," for his grin was apologetic. Last night he had thought of the unknown woman before he slept, and she had been tender with him. This tenderness he was remembering as he shifted his feet by the jeering, whistling Stanley, and watched the indifferent, healthy brown woman a few feet off, with the gap that plunged to the street between them. Tom thought it was romantic, it was like being high on two hilltops. But there was a shout from Harry, and they clambered back. Stanley's face was hard, really angry. The boy kept looking at him and wondered why he hated the woman so much, for by now he loved her.

They played their little games with the blanket, trying to trap shade to work under; but again it was not until nearly four that they could work seriously, and they were exhausted, all three of them. They were grumbling about the weather, by now. Stanley was in a thoroughly bad humour. When they made their routine trip to see the woman before they packed up for the day, she was apparently asleep, face down, her back all naked save for the scarlet triangle on her buttocks. "I've got a good mind to report her to the police," said Stanley, and Harry said: "What's eating you? What harm's she doing?"

"I tell you, if she was my wife!"

"But she isn't, is she?" Tom knew that Harry, like himself, was uneasy at Stanley's reaction. He was normally a sharp young man, quick at his work, making a lot of jokes, good company.

"Perhaps it will be cooler tomorrow," said Harry.

But it wasn't, it was hotter, if anything, and the weather forecast said the good weather would last. As soon as they were on the roof, Harry went over to see if the woman were there, and Tom knew it was to prevent Stanley going, to put off his bad humour. Harry had grown-up children, a boy the same age as Tom, and the youth trusted and looked up to him.

Harry came back and said: "She's not there."

"I bet her old man has put his foot down," said Stanley, and Harry and Tom caught each other's eyes and smiled behind the young married man's back.

Harry suggested they should get permission to work in the basement, and they did, that day. But before packing up Stanley said: "Let's have a breath of fresh air." Again Harry and Tom smiled at each other as they followed Stanley up to the roof, Tom in the devout conviction that he was there to protect the woman from Stanley. It was about five-thirty, and a calm, full sunlight lay over the roofs. The great crane still swung its black arm from Oxford Street to above their heads. She was not there. Then there was a flutter of white from behind a parapet, and she stood up, in a belted, white dressing gown. She had been there all day, probably, but on a different patch of roof, to hide from them. Stanley did not whistle, he said nothing, but watched the woman bend to collect papers, books, cigarettes, then fold the blanket over her arm. Tom was thinking: If they weren't here, I'd go over and say . . . what? But he knew from his nightly dreams of her that she was kind and friendly. Perhaps she would ask him down to her flat? Perhaps. . . . He stood watching her disappear down the skylight. As she went, Stanley let out a shrill derisive yell; she started, and it seemed as if she nearly fell. She clutched to save herself, they could hear things falling. She looked straight at them, angry. Harry said, facetiously: "Better be careful on those slippery ladders, love." Tom knew he said it to save her from Stanley, but she could not know it. She vanished, frowning. Tom was full of a secret delight, because he knew her anger was for the others, not for him.

"Roll on some rain," said Stanley, bitter, looking at the blue evening sky.

Next day was cloudless, and they decided to finish the work in the basement. They felt excluded, shut in the grey cement basement fitting pipes, from the holiday atmosphere of London in a heat wave. At lunchtime they came up for some air, but while the married couples, and the men in shirt-sleeves or vests, were there, she was not there, either on her usual patch of roof or where she had been yesterday. They all, even Harry, clambered about, between chimney pots, over parapets, the hot leads stinging their fingers. There was not a sign of her. They took off their shirts and vests and exposed their chests, feeling their feet sweaty and hot. They did not mention the woman. But Tom felt alone again. Last night she had asked him into her flat: it was big and had fitted white carpets and a bed with a padded white leather headtop. She wore a black filmy negligée and her kindness to Tom thickened his throat as he remembered it. He felt she had betrayed him by not being there.

And again after work they climbed up, but still there was nothing to be seen of her. Stanley kept repeating that if it was as hot as this tomorrow he wasn't going to work and that's all there was to it. But they were all there next day. By ten the temperature was in the middle seventies, and it was eighty long before noon. Harry went to the foreman to say it was impossible to work on the leads in that heat; but the foreman said there was nothing else he could put them on, and they'd have to. At midday they stood, silent, watching the skylight on her roof open, and then she slowly emerged in her white gown, holding a bundle of blanket. She looked at them, gravely, then went to the part of the roof where she was hidden from them. Tom was pleased. He felt she was more his when the other men couldn't see her. They had taken off their shirts and vests, but now they put them back again, for they felt the sun bruising their flesh. "She must have the hide of a rhino," said Stanley, tugging at guttering and swearing. They stopped work, and sat in the shade, moving around behind chimney stacks. A woman came to water a yellow window box just opposite them. She was middle-aged, wearing a flowered summer dress. Stanley said to her: "We need a drink more than them." She smiled and said: "Better drop down to the pub quick, it'll be closing in a minute." They exchanged pleasantries, and she left them with a smile and a wave.

"Not like Lady Godiva," said Stanley. "She can give us a bit of a chat and a smile."

"You didn't whistle at *her*," said Tom, reproving.

"Listen to him," said Stanley, "you didn't whistle, then?"

But the boy felt as if he hadn't whistled, as if only Harry and Stanley had. He was making plans, when it was time to knock off work, to get left behind and somehow make his way over to the woman. The weather report said the hot spell was due to break, so he had to move quickly. But there was no chance of being left. The other two decided to knock off work at four, because they were exhausted. As they went down, Tom quickly climbed a parapet and hoisted himself higher by pulling his weight up a chimney. He caught a glimpse of her lying on her back, her knees up, eyes closed, a brown woman lolling in the sun. He slipped and clattered down, as Stanley looked for information: "She's gone down," he said. He felt as if he had protected her from Stanley, and that she must be grateful to him. He could feel the bond between the woman and himself.

Next day, they stood around on the landing below the roof, reluctant to climb up into the heat. The woman who had lent Harry the blanket came out and offered them a cup of tea. They accepted gratefully, and sat around Mrs. Pritchett's kitchen an hour or so, chatting. She was married to an airline pilot. A smart blonde, of about thirty, she had an eye for the handsome sharp-faced Stanley; and the two teased each other while Harry sat in a corner, watching, indulgent, though his expression reminded Stanley that he was married. And young Tom felt envious of Stanley's ease in badinage; felt, too, that Stanley's getting off with Mrs. Pritchett left his romance with the woman on the roof safe and intact.

"I thought they said the heat wave'd break," said Stanley, sullen, as the time approached when they really would have to climb up into the sunlight.

"You don't like it, then?" asked Mrs. Pritchett.

"All right for some," said Stanley. "Nothing to do but lie about as if it was a beach up there. Do you ever go up?"

"Went up once," said Mrs. Pritchett. "But it's a dirty place up there, and it's too hot."

"Quite right too," said Stanley.

Then they went up, leaving the cool neat little flat and the friendly Mrs. Pritchett.

As soon as they were up they saw her. The three men looked at her, resentful at her ease in this punishing sun. Then Harry said, because of the expression on Stanley's face: "Come on, we've got to pretend to work, at least."

They had to wrench another length of guttering that ran beside a parapet out of its bed, so that they could replace it. Stanley took it in his two hands, tugged, swore, stood up. "Fuck it," he said, and sat down under a chimney. He lit a cigarette. "Fuck them," he said. "What do they think we are, lizards? I've got blisters all over my hands." Then he jumped up and climbed over the roofs and stood with his back to them. He put his fingers either side of his mouth and let out a shrill whistle. Tom and Harry squatted, not looking at each other, watching him. They could just see the woman's head, the beginnings of her brown shoulders. Stanley whistled again. Then he began stamping with his feet, and whistled and yelled and screamed at the woman, his face getting scarlet. He seemed quite mad, as he stamped and whistled, while the woman did not move, she did not move a muscle.

"Barmy," said Tom.

"Yes," said Harry, disapproving.

Suddenly the older man came to a decision. It was, Tom knew, to save some sort of scandal or real trouble over the woman. Harry stood up and began packing tools into a length of oily cloth. "Stanley," he said, commanding. At first Stanley took no notice, but Harry said: "Stanley, we're packing it in, I'll tell Matthew."

Stanley came back, cheeks mottled, eyes glaring.

"Can't go on like this," said Harry. "It'll break in a day or so. I'm going to tell Matthew we've got sunstroke, and if he doesn't like it, it's too bad." Even Harry sounded aggrieved, Tom noted. The small, competent man, the family man with his grey hair, who was never at a loss, sounded really off balance. "Come on," he said, angry. He fitted himself into the open square in the roof, and went down, watching his feet on the ladder. Then Stanley went, with not a glance at the woman. Then Tom who, his throat beating with excitement, silently promised her in a backward glance: Wait for me, wait, I'm coming.

On the pavement Stanley said: "I'm going home." He looked white now, so perhaps he really did have sunstroke. Harry went off to find the foreman who was at work on the plumbing of some flats down the street. Tom slipped back, not into the building they had been working on, but the building on whose roof the woman lay. He went straight up, with an iron ladder leading up. He emerged onto the roof a couple of yards from her. She sat up, pushing back her black hair with both hands. The scarf across her breasts bound them tight, and brown flesh bulged around it. Her legs were brown and smooth. She stared at him in silence. The boy stood grinning, foolish, claiming the tenderness he expected from her.

"What do you want?" she asked.

"I . . . I came to . . . make your acquaintance," he stammered, grinning, pleading with her.

They looked at each other, the slight, scarlet-faced excited boy, and the serious, nearly naked woman. Then, without a word, she lay down on her brown blanket, ignoring him.

"You like the sun, do you?" he enquired of her glistening back.

Not a word. He felt panic, thinking of how she had held him in her arms, stroked his hair, brought him where he sat, lordly, in her bed, a glass of some exhilarating liquor he had never tasted in life. He felt that if he knelt down, stroked her shoulders, her hair, she would turn and clasp him in her arms.

He said: "The sun's all right for you, isn't it?"

She raised her head, set her chin on two small fists. "Go away," she said. He did not move. "Listen," she said, in a slow reasonable voice, where anger was kept in check, though with difficulty; looking at him, her face weary with anger: "If you get a kick out of seeing women in bikinis, why don't you take a sixpenny bus ride to the Lido? You'd see dozens of them, without all this mountaineering."

She hadn't understood him. He felt her unfairness pale him. He stammered: "But I like you, I've been watching you and . . ."

"Thanks," she said, and dropped her face again, turned away from him.

She lay there. He stood there. She said nothing. She had simply shut him out. He stood, saying nothing at all, for some minutes. He thought: She'll have to say something if I stay. But the minutes went past, with no sign of them in her, except in the tension of her back, her thighs, her arms—the tension of waiting for him to go.

He looked up at the sky, where the sun seemed to spin in heat; and over the roofs where he and his mates had been earlier. He could see the heat quivering where they had worked. "And they expect us to work in these conditions!" he thought, filled with righteous indignation. The woman hadn't moved. A bit of hot wind blew her black hair softly, it shone, and was iridescent. He remembered how he had stroked it last night.

Resentment of her at last moved him off and away down the ladder, through the building, into the street. He got drunk then, in hatred of her.

Next day when he woke the sky was grey. He looked at the wet grey and thought, vicious: "Well, that's fixed you, hasn't it now? That's fixed you good and proper."

The three men were at work early on the cool leads, surrounded by damp drizzling roofs where no one came to sun themselves, black roofs, slimy with rain. Because it was cool now, they would finish the job that day, if they hurried.

DISCUSSION QUESTIONS
SUGGESTIONS FOR WRITING

1. What is this story about? Male chauvinist attitudes? A boy's confrontation of the difference between illusion and reality?

2. Why does the indifference of the woman on the roof make Stanley, Harry, and finally even Tom hostile towards her?

3. Does the woman's attitude toward Tom seem justified in the end, since he has been the one trying to protect her from the vulgarity of the others?

4. How does the setting contribute to the overall effect of the story?

VIII

Revolution in Education

LEONARD

GEORGE B. LEONARD
(b. 1923) is a journalist interested in critical social
problems and senior edi-
tor for *Look* magazine. His
book *Education and Ec-
stasy* is revolutionary in
the sense that it seriously
proposes that education,
at best, should be an ec-
static experience.

THE USES
OF ECSTASY

UNLIMITED amounts of power are coming into human hands, perhaps surpassing what even Huxley could have imagined a few short years ago. For example, the "breeder" reactors now under de-velopment promise to produce more nuclear fuel than they can use. Human control of the death rate already has set into motion a possibly catastrophic population rise, though the means for controlling the birth rate also are available. Both time and distance in the old sense have been annihilated. The whole globe is intimately intertwined with the means for achieving understanding or destruction.

This situation, despite attempts at drawing historical parallels, can-not be viewed simply as more of the same. It is something entirely new, calling for entirely new responses. What is more important, it seems to demand a new kind of human being—one who is not driven by narrow competition, eager acquisition and aggression, but who spends his life in the joyful pursuit of learning. Such a human being, I feel, will result not so much through changed ideologies or economic systems as through changes in the process I have called "education." The idea of education as the most effective human change agent is by no means new. But I have tried to broaden and simplify education's definition, to expand its domain, to link it with the new technology and to alter the relationship between educator and learner. As a chief ingredient in all this, as well as an alternative to the old reinforcers, I have named "ecstasy"—joy, *ananda*, the ultimate delight.

Our society knows little about this ingredient. In fact, every civili-zation in our direct lineage has tended to fear and shun it as a threat to reason and order. In a sense, they have been right. It is hard to imagine a more revolutionary statement for us than "The natural condition of the human organism is joy." For, if this is true, we are being daily cheated, and perhaps the social system that so ruthlessly steals our birthright *should* be overthrown.

How many of us can live through three or four utterly joyful days without feeling, shortly afterwards, that our plane will crash or that we shall be struck with lightning? It is deeply embedded, this societal teaching. And when a highly visible segment of our young people, sometimes through shortsighted means, devotes all its days and nights to the pursuit of joy, how many of us do not feel deeply threatened? Joy *does* threaten things-as-they-are. Ecstasy, like nuclear energy, *is* dangerous. The only thing that may turn out to be more dangerous is shunning it and clinging to the old ways that clearly are dragging us toward destruction.

Perhaps it is time for scholars and pundits to engage in the serious study of delight. What are its dangers? What are its uses? I would suggest three primarily negative considerations as a beginning:

1. Ecstasy is not necessarily opposed to reason. On the other hand, it may help light the way toward relationships, societies and educational systems in which reason and emotion are no longer at odds; in which, in fact, the two are so in tune that the terms themselves, as opposites, will atrophy.

2. Ecstasy is not necessarily opposed to order. On the other hand, it may help us redefine order. In the new definition, a balanced natural ecology in which all creatures grow and act freely represents order. Our free-learning and joyful Kennedy School represents a far higher, more elegant form of order than does a school in which "order" is forced and artificial. Life is an ordering force. Man is an ordering animal. Order will continue to evolve. Ecstasy is implicated in changing not the quantity, but the quality of order.

3. Ecstasy is neither immoral nor moral in itself. At times, forms of ecstasy have powered some of mankind's most destructive movements. The Third Reich, for example, exhibited a certain ecstatic mania. But Hitler's "joy" was used to bolster the old reinforcement system— competition, acquisition and aggression—carried to the most destructive extremes. It was not brought into play as an *alternative* reinforcement system designed to replace the old.

In dealing with ecstasy, as with all powerful forces, context is crucial. The context I have suggested is neither the wantonly Dionysian nor the purely contemplative, but the educational. Ecstasy is education's most powerful ally. It is reinforcer for and substance of the moment of learning.

Knowing this, the master teacher pursues delight. Even those best known as great lecturers have turned their lecture halls into theaters, shameless in their use of spells and enchantments. Great men, as every schoolboy knows, have greeted their moments of learning with crazy joy. We learn how Archimedes leaped, crying, "Eureka!," from his bathtub; how Handel, on finishing the "Hallelujah Chorus," told his servant, "I did think I did see all Heaven before me, and the great God himself"; how Nietzsche wrote *Thus Spake Zarathustra:*

> There is an ecstasy such that the immense strain of it is sometimes relaxed by a flood of tears, along with which one's steps either rush or involuntarily lag, alternately. There is the feeling that one is completely out of hand, with the very distinct consciousness of an endless number of fine thrills and quiverings to the very toes.

What we fail to acknowledge is that every child starts out as an Archimedes, a Handel, a Nietzsche. The eight-month-old who succeeds in balancing one block on another has made a connection no less momentous for him than Nietzsche's. He cannot verbalize it so eloquently and probably would not bother to if he could; such moments are not so rare for him as for Nietzsche. Much of his life at that age, in fact, is learning. The possibility of an endless series of ecstatic moments stretches before him. We quell the ecstasy and the learning, but this is hard work and rarely is it entirely successful. Explaining why he was unable to think about scientific problems for a year after his final exams, Albert Einstein said:

> It is in fact nothing short of a miracle that the modern methods of instruction have not yet entirely strangled the holy curiosity of inquiry. . . . It is a very grave mistake to think that the enjoyment of seeing and searching can be promoted by means of coercion and a sense of duty.

And yet, life and joy cannot be subdued. The blade of grass shatters the concrete. The spring flowers bloom in Hiroshima. An Einstein emerges from the European academies. Those who would reduce, control, quell must lose in the end. The ecstatic forces of life, growth and change are too numerous, too various, too tumultuous.

In the eighteenth century, the Swedish botanist Carolus Linnaeus thought he had catalogued all the species of animals and plants in the world, a total of 4,345. He was wrong. Biologists today estimate they have classified nearly two million different kinds of animals; botanists have identified more than 300,000 kinds of plants. And that is only a beginning. Entomologists believe that, if all forms of insects alone could be counted, they would total from two to ten million. Faced with this profusion, scientists have run out of suitable Latin and Greek names, and now grope for impressive-sounding words that mean nothing whatever in any language. And all this life, the affirmation of development and change, has taken place in the surface film of an average-size planet of an average-size star in one of hundreds of millions of galaxies. If this planet were the size of an orange, the habitat of all living things would be no thicker than a piece of paper.

Life has one ultimate message, "Yes!" repeated in infinite number and variety. Human life, channeled for millennia by Civilization, is only just beginning to express the diversity and range of which it is easily capable. To deny is to swim against the current of existence. To affirm, to follow ecstasy in learning — in spite of injustice, suffering, confusion and disappointment — is to move more easily toward an education, a society that would free the enormous potential of man.

July the Fourth. A lake in the Georgia woods. The soft, still air of afternoon vibrates with a thousand lives: the mad, monotonous trance music of the cicadas rising and falling above the chatter of crickets, the drone of bees; cries of a Cooper's hawk on a dead tree across the lake; birdsong all around, a different blend for every change of sky or air. The acoustics are incredible. Sound floats across the lake, touches me, immediate and eternal. All is one and I am of that one.

I walk slowly toward the lake's edge. A blacksnake whistles away through high grasses. A pair of white herons that have been working their way around the borders of the lake rise with undulating, confident strokes. Disdainful, taking their own time, they fly on to a spot appropriately distant from me. *Perfect.* Over the water, a flycatcher shoots straight upward with wings fluttering fast, then spreading motionless at the apogee — a moment frozen in thin air. A buzzard, an inverted shadow, cruises overhead. And there on a slim pine branch (pine needles spread like star points) a tiny warbler is silhouetted, upside down.

A turtle rests on the bank. I pick it up. Dark brown shell; long, translucent bear claws clawing air. A yellow spotted head lengthens, cranes around. Impersonal eyes see nothing, see everything. I return the turtle to its bank. Squatting down, I watch a dragonfly less than an inch long with wings like amber cellophane quivering on a weed in the burnt gold of late afternoon.

What now? A green grasshopper, disturbed by my movements, has jumped into the lake. He kicks as in a spasm, then lies in the water. Two ripples move out, concentric circles signaling his plight. He kicks again, moving toward the tangled bank. Will he make it? Two more spasmodic kicks and he's in shallow water. The bottom is visible. Almost safe. And the fish is there, a light shadow appearing, fully in position, without movement. Though only as long as a hand, the fish is somehow terribly sinister. *Snakkk!* A sharp report, a mouth sound. Empty water.

Later, just before the sun goes down, blue shadows settle into the spaces beneath the trees across the lake. The sky is a confusion of shifting clouds and colors. With twilight's advance, the colors richen, the sky comes to rest. After sundown, I take a rowboat out onto the water. The air is cooling, the trees are utterly still. White morning glories on the bank are closed for the night. Turtles peep out of the still water, curious rather than predatory. A wood thrush sings, its trill swelling suddenly to fill all the evening like a distended balloon. A wren sings, a cardinal, a warbler — all sweet singers.

Darkness approaches. The songs end. Something is swimming, making steady progress along the shore toward my boat. The swimmer goes into the bank for a moment, curves out again, its ripples making a precise triangle behind it. It sees me, dives. And now I know the night hunters have awakened. Two frogs croak tentatively. A night hawk sweeps across the lake. I can barely make out a possum moving deliberately along the opposite bank. I head the boat back toward the bank. The lake is a faint gleam, the trees black silhouettes.

This world is elegantly interconnected and all-involving. It cannot be compartmentalized. It does not cease.

William Golding's novel of some years back, *Lord of the Flies*, generally has been interpreted as a bitter commentary on man's nature. In it, a group of children, marooned on a deserted island, turn from Ralph, the voice of Civilized reason, and Piggy, his myopic egghead sidekick, to join Jack, who has been interpreted as the villain, the savage, the dark spirit in man that invariably emerges when the Civilized restraints are removed.

But Golding stacked the deck in a way that comments more on Civilization than on "human nature." Ralph is "good," but dull, unimaginative and indecisive. Piggy has "mind," but not much else. He is physically and sensorially inept. Jack, on the other hand, is physically and mentally alert, resourceful, imaginative and creative. He encourages his followers in games and chants, colorful costumes and face paint, ceremonies and a sense of community. He organizes successful pig hunts and provides his meat-hungry children with torchlit feasts. Meanwhile, Ralph and his dispirited followers sicken on their unvarying diet of fruit. What child would not follow Jack? When Golding makes Jack's group evil, he reveals the usual inability in our time to equate the ecstatic with the good. When he makes Civilized Ralph dull and inept, he reveals what he really feels about Civilization as he knows it.

When men must serve as predictable, prefabricated components of a rigid social machine, the ecstatic is not particularly useful and may, in fact, erode the compartments so necessary for the machine's functioning. But when a society moves away from the mechanistic, when an individual may function as a free-roving seeker, when what we now term "leisure" occupies most of an individual's hours, ecstasy may usefully accompany almost every act. Technology is preparing a world in which we may be learners all life long. In this world, delight will not be a luxury but a necessity.

I can recall little of what happened in school the winter I was fifteen. Perhaps that was the year everyone in my English class had to do a chapter-by-chapter synopsis of *Treasure Island*. But the afternoons and nights of that period still are vivid. I was infected with the ham-radio bug. My next-door neighbor, a boy two years older, had got me started, and I lived for months in a state of delicious excitement. I would rush home from school, knowing the day would not be long enough. I would work steadily, practicing code, devouring ham manuals and magazines, poring over catalogues of radio parts, building simple shortwave receivers. I loved everything about it. When later I read Gerard Manley Hopkins' "Pied Beauty," the phrase, "all trades, their gear and tackle and trim," immediately summoned up the coils and condensers, the softly glowing vacuum tubes, the sizzle and smell of hot solder, the shining curls of metal drilled out of a chassis.

One night, my radio experience came to a moment of climax. For weeks I had been working on my first major effort, a four-tube regenerative shortwave receiver. The design was "my own," derived from circuits in the manuals and approved by my knowledgeable friend. Every part was of the highest quality, all housed in a professional-looking black metal cabinet. Every knob and dial was carefully positioned for efficiency and esthetics, and there was an oversized, freewheeling band-spread tuning knob. That particular night I had been working ever since running most of the way home from school. I had skipped dinner, fiercely overriding my parents' protests. And now, at about eleven o'clock, I soldered the last connection.

With trembling hands, I connected the ground and the antenna, plugged in the socket and switched on the set. There was a low, reassuring hum and, after a suspenseful wait, the four tubes lit up. I increased the volume. Dead silence. Nothing. I checked all the switches and dials. No problem there. Perhaps it was the speaker. I plugged in the earphones. Still nothing.

I couldn't imagine what was the matter. For the next hour or so, I went over every connection, traced the circuit until I was dizzy. Since I had splurged on all-new parts, I didn't even consider that one of them might be defective. The mystery, so powerful and unfathomable, could obviously have been cleared up in a few minutes by any well-equipped radio repairman. But, for me, its unraveling was momentous.

The radio's circuit consisted of two stages. The first stage converted radio frequency waves to electrical impulses of an audible frequency; the second stage served as an amplifier for the electrical impulses coming from the first stage. I hit upon the idea of tapping the earphones in at the end of the first stage. Success! Static, code, voices. This seemed to indicate to me that the trouble lay somewhere in the second stage. On an impulse, however, I tied in a microphone at the very beginning of the second stage. Success again. The second stage worked. I could hear my voice coming from the speaker.

At that very instant, the answer was clear: Both stages worked separately. The trouble had to lie in the coupling between them. My eyes went to a little green and silver coil (*the broken connection between subconscious and conscious, the hidden flaw between individual and community*). It *had* to be that impedance coil. With this certainty, I was quite overcome. I would gladly have broken into a radio store to get another one, but my friend, I found, had a spare. I tied it in, not bothering for the moment to solder it. And a universe poured into my room from the star-filled night. I spun the dial: a ham in Louisiana, in California; shortwave broadcasts from England, Germany, Mexico, Brazil. There was no end to it. I had put out new sensors. Where there had been nothing, there was *all of this*.

Ecstasy is one of the trickier conditions to write about. But if there is such a thing as being transported, I was transported that night. And I was, as with every true learning experience, forever afterwards changed.

Every child, every person can delight in learning. A new education is already here, thrusting up in spite of every barrier we have been able to build. Why not help it happen?

DISCUSSION QUESTIONS
SUGGESTIONS FOR WRITING

1. *This essay makes use of the conventions or methods of several of the basic essay types. Can you identify sections of this essay which might be labeled persuasive, personal, autobiographical, informative, biographical, critical? Give explanations for your choices in each case.*

2. *Judging from his attitudes about ecstasy, his criticism of Golding's novel, his reflections on Hitler's use of ecstasy to reinforce competition, acquisition, and aggression, what is Leonard's view of human nature?*

3. *How might he come to terms with the theories of Ardrey and Morris? Are his beliefs necessarily in basic opposition to theirs?*

4. *How is ecstasy "dangerous"? Explore the implications of: "The only thing that may turn out to be more dangerous [than ecstasy] is shunning it and clinging to the old ways that clearly are dragging us toward destruction."*

HOLT

HOW
CHILDREN
FAIL

JOHN HOLT
(b. 1923) is one of the
best-known and most
widely read critics of the
American educational sys-
tem. He has taught En-
glish, French, and math in
elementary and junior high
schools and has done re-
search in several private
schools. His other books
include *How Children
Learn* and *What Do I Do
Monday?*

February 18, 1958

INTELLIGENCE is a mystery. We hear it said that most people never
develop more than a very small part of their latent intellectual capacity.
Probably not; by *why* not? Most of us have our engines running at about
ten percent of their power. Why no more? And how do some people
manage to keep revved up to twenty percent or thirty percent of their
full power — or even more?

What turns the power off, or keeps it from ever being turned on?

During these past four years at the Colorado Rocky Mountain
School my nose has been rubbed in the problem. When I started, I
thought that some people were just born smarter than others and that
not much could be done about it. This seems to be the official line of
most of the psychologists. It isn't hard to believe, if all your contacts with
students are in the classroom or the psychological testing room. But
if you live at a small school, seeing students in class, in the dorms, in
their private lives, at their recreations, sports, and manual work, you
can't escape the conclusion that some people are much smarter part
of the time than they are at other times. Why? Why should a boy or
girl, who under some circumstances is witty, observant, imaginative,
analytical, in a word, *intelligent,* come into the classroom and, as if by
magic, turn into a complete dolt?

The worst student we had, the worst I have ever encountered, was in
his life outside the classroom, as mature, intelligent, and interesting a
student as anyone at the school. What went wrong? Experts muttered
to his parents about brain damage — a handy way to end a mystery that

you can't explain otherwise. Somewhere along the line, his intelligence became disconnected from his schooling. Where? Why?

This past year I had some terrible students. I failed more kids, mostly in French and Algebra, than did all the rest of the teachers in the school together. I did my best to get them through, goodness knows. Before every test we had a big cram session of practice work, politely known as "review." When they failed the exam, we had post-mortems, then more review, then a make-up test (always easier than the first), which they almost always failed again.

I thought I knew how to deal with the problem: make the work interesting and the classroom a lively and enthusiastic place. It was, too, some of the time at least; many of these failing students actually liked my classes. Overcome children's fear of saying what they don't understand, and keep explaining until they do understand. Keep a steady and resolute pressure on them. These things I did. Result? The good students stayed good, and some may have got better; but the bad students stayed bad, and some of them seemed to get worse. If they were failing in November they were still failing in June. There must be a better answer. Maybe we can prevent kids from becoming chronic failers in the first place.

May 10, 1958

Children are often quite frank about the strategies they use to get answers out of a teacher. I once observed a class in which the teacher was testing her students on parts of speech. On the blackboard she had three columns, headed Noun, Adjective, and Verb. As she gave each word, she called on a child and asked in which column the word belonged.

Like most teachers, she hadn't thought enough about what she was doing to realize, first, that many of the words given could fit into more than one column; and secondly, that it is often the way a word is used that determines what part of speech it is.

There was a good deal of the tried-and-true strategy of *guess-and-look*, in which you start to say a word, all the while scrutinizing the teacher's face to see whether you are on the right track or not. With most teachers, no further strategies are needed. This one was more poker-faced than most, so *guess-and-look* wasn't working very well. Still, the percentage of hits was remarkably high, especially since it was clear to me from the way the children were talking and acting that they hadn't a notion of what Nouns, Adjectives, and Verbs were. Finally one child said, "Miss —, you shouldn't point to the answer each time." The teacher was surprised, and asked what she meant. The child said, "Well, you don't exactly *point*, but you kind of stand next to the answer." This was no clearer, since the teacher had been standing still. But after a while, as the class went on, I thought I saw what the girl meant. Since the teacher wrote each word down in its proper column, she was, in a way, getting herself ready to write, pointing herself at the place where she would soon be writing. From the angle of her body to the blackboard the children picked up a subtle clue to the correct answer.

This was not all. At the end of every third word, her three columns came out even, that is, there were an equal number of nouns, adjectives, and verbs. This meant that when she started off a new row, you had one chance in three of getting the right answer by a blind guess; but for the next word, you had one chance in two, and the last word was a dead giveaway to the lucky student who was asked it. Hardly any missed this opportunity; in fact, they answered so quickly that the teacher (brighter than most) caught on to their system and began keeping her columns uneven, making the strategist's job a bit harder.

In the midst of all this, there came a vivid example of the kind of thing we say in school that makes no sense, that only bewilders and confuses the thoughtful child who tries to make sense out of it. The teacher, whose specialty, by the way, was English, had told these children that a verb is a word of action—which is not always true. One of the words she asked was "dream." She was thinking of the noun, and apparently did not remember that "dream" can as easily be a verb. One little boy, making a pure guess, said it was a verb. Here the teacher, to be helpful, contributed one of those "explanations" that are so much more hindrance than help. She said, "But a verb has to have action; can you give me a sentence, using 'dream', that has action?" The child thought a bit, and said, "I had a dream about the Trojan War." Now it's pretty hard to get much more action than that. But the teacher told him he was wrong, and he sat silent, with an utterly baffled and frightened expression on his face. She was so busy thinking about what she wanted him to say, she was so obsessed with that *right answer* hidden in her mind, that she could not think about what he was really saying and thinking, could not see that his reasoning was logical and correct, and that the mistake was not his, but hers. . . .

July 27, 1958

It has become clear over the year that these children see school almost entirely in terms of the day-to-day and hour-to-hour tasks that we impose on them. This is not at all the way the teacher thinks of it. The conscientious teacher thinks of himself as taking his students (at least part way) on a journey to some glorious destination, well worth the pains of the trip. If he teaches history, he thinks how interesting, how exciting, how useful it is to know history, and how fortunate his students will be when they begin to share his knowledge. If he teaches French, he thinks of the glories of French literature, or the beauty of spoken French, or the delights of French cooking, and how he is helping to make these joys available to his students. And so for all subjects.

Thus teachers feel, as I once did, that their interests and their students' are fundamentally the same. I used to feel that I was guiding and helping my students on a journey that they wanted to take but could not take without my help. I knew the way looked hard, but I assumed they could see the goal almost as clearly as I and that they were almost as eager to reach it. It seemed very important to give students this feeling of being on a journey to a worthwhile destination. I see now that most of my talk to this end was wasted breath. Maybe *I* thought the students were in my class because they were eager to learn what I was trying to teach, but they knew better. They were in school because they had to be, and in my class either because they had to be, or because otherwise they would have had to be in another class, which might be even worse.

Children in school are like children at the doctor's. He can talk himself blue in the face about how much good his medicine is going to do them; all they think of is how much it will hurt or how bad it will taste. Given their own way, they would have none of it.

So the valiant and resolute band of travelers I thought I was leading toward a much-hoped-for destination turned out instead to be more like convicts in a chain gang, forced under threat of punishment to move along a rough path leading nobody knew where and down which they could see hardly more than a few steps ahead. School feels like this to children: it is a place where *they* make you go and where *they* tell you to do things and where *they* try to make your life unpleasant if you don't do them or don't do them right.

For children, the central business of school is not learning, whatever this vague word means; it is getting these daily tasks done, or at least out of the way, with a minimum of effort and unpleasantness. Each task is an end in itself. The children don't care how they dispose of it. If they can get it out of the way by doing it, they will do it; if experience has taught them that this does not work very well, they will turn to other means, illegitimate means, that wholly defeat whatever purpose the task-giver may have had in mind.

They are very good at this, at getting other people to do their tasks for them. I remember the day not long ago when Ruth opened my eyes. We had been doing math, and I was pleased with myself because, instead of telling her answers and showing her how to do problems, I was "making her think" by asking her questions. It was slow work. Question after question met only silence. She said nothing, did nothing, just sat and looked at me through those glasses, and waited. Each time, I had to think of a question easier and more pointed than the last, until I finally found one so easy that she would feel safe in answering it. So we inched our way along until suddenly, looking at her as I waited for an answer to a question, I saw with a start that she was not at all puzzled by what I had asked her. In fact, she was not even thinking about it. She was coolly appraising me, weighing my patience, waiting for that next, sure-to-be-easier question. I thought, "I've been had!" The girl had learned how to make me do her work for her, just as she had learned to make all her previous teachers do the same thing. If I wouldn't tell her the answers, very well, she would just let me question her right up to them.

Schools and teachers seem generally to be as blind to children's strategies as I was. Otherwise, they would teach their courses and assign their tasks so that students who really thought about the meaning of the subject would have the best chance of succeeding, while those who tried to do the tasks by illegitimate means, without thinking or understanding, would be foiled. But the reverse seems to be the case. Schools give every encouragement to *producers*, the kids whose idea is to get "right answers" by any and all means. In a system that runs on "right answers," they can hardly help it. And these schools are often very discouraging places for *thinkers*. . . .

DISCUSSION QUESTIONS
SUGGESTIONS FOR WRITING

1. What is Holt's perspective on: the strategies children use to meet the demands made on them, the effect of fear and failure on children, the distinction between real and apparent learning, and the way schools fail to meet the needs of children?

2. How do his conclusions point to ways teachers and parents might make children's daily experiences in school and at home more meaningful?

3. Compare Holt's observations with those of George Leonard. What are the similarities, differences?

4. How does Holt's use of the diary form differ from Kunen's? How does Holt create the sense of fresh insight into what really goes on in the classroom?

MAYA PINES
(b. 1928), a former re-
porter for *Life,* writes about
the social aspects of education and medicine. Her
articles have appeared in
Harper's, The Reporter,
and the *New York Times
Magazine. Revolution in
Learning* came about as
the result of an assign-
ment from *Harper's Maga-
zine*—a report on an ex-
periment in which three-
year-olds were said to be
learning to read and write
by typing on an electric
"talking typewriter." It is
the best existing summary
of important research and
experimentation in the
area of preschool educa-
tion.

REVOLUTION
IN
LEARNING

THE BATTLEGROUND

Millions of children are being irreparably damaged by our failure to
stimulate them intellectually during their crucial years—from birth to
six. Millions of others are being held back from their true potential.

Our severest educational problems could be largely solved if we started
early enough. Yet we recklessly ignore an exciting and persuasive body
of knowledge about how human beings learn.

This knowledge is just beginning to fit together solidly enough to call
for action. Gathered from experimental projects that are scattered about
the country, from research laboratories, and from scholars in various
universities, it comes at a time when—for the first time in man's history
—it makes sound economic sense to invest major efforts in the earliest
years of human life.

Only a century ago, half the world's children died before the age of
five—and this loss was considered inevitable. Through better nutrition
and the control of infection, we now prevent the diseases that used to

kill or cripple vast numbers of preschoolers. At least in the affluent nations, every newborn child stands a good chance of survival. We approve of such public-health measures as putting extra vitamins into milk and flour and teaching mothers to sterilize milk bottles. But we continue to regard the intellectual crippling of young children as largely inevitable or as a private family matter in which nobody should interfere.

The scientists who would raise the nation's intelligence through early learning believe that few educators or parents have yet heard their message. As with public health, their methods could benefit the entire population. They could increase the talents and artistic involvement of all children. Poor children could be given specific training that would bring them up at least to the level necessary for success in school. Middle-class children might gain even more from early stimulation.

Any attempt to stimulate young children's intellectual growth in the United States, however, is likely to run into stiff opposition from the early-childhood Establishment: people trained in early-childhood education or child development and resentful of intrusion by other specialists who, they say, don't really *know* children.

A fierce, though largely undeclared war has been raging since the early 1960's between this Establishment, which is concerned primarily with children's emotional and social development, and the innovators, who emphasize cognitive, or intellectual, growth. The innovators include sociologists, linguists, mathematicians, philosophers and computer technicians, as well as many psychologists, all concerned with how young children learn to think and how best to help them.

The Establishment group believes in educating "the whole child": One should not try to teach specific skills in any organized sequence, but let the child learn from experiences that involve all aspects of his life: his emotions, his relations to other children, his fantasies, his surroundings, his actions. Thus, children are expected to learn color concepts simply by having colored toys around and occasionally hearing the teacher refer to them by color. They are supposed to learn number concepts by playing with blocks. Reading readiness is expected to come from recognizing their first names over their coat hooks. At best, these theories produce a special atmosphere of joy and well-being, from which the children come home all aglow, as after a good party. The Establishment is very indignant about what it calls "the vultures of experimental education poaching on this tender territory, forcing advanced curricula. . . ."

At the opposite pole, the "cognitive" group feels that by failing to take advantage of young children's real drive to know, the Establishment is wasting something very precious. Once past the sensitive period of their earliest years, children will never again learn with the same naturalness and ease. Teachers who prevent children from making the most of this period condemn large numbers of them to a downward spiral of failure. They condemn others to years of drudgery spent laboriously learning skills that might have come with ease at an earlier age, and that they might have been using to explore the world around them. Furthermore, happiness does not come from play alone. As one kindergarten teacher wrote—an exceptional woman who taught her five-year-old pupils to write, count, add, subtract, divide, use a simple microscope, and play the recorder: "'Fun' is too weak a word to describe the elation, satisfaction, and inner peace that come from intellectual accomplishment." The cognitive group believes that such achievement plays a large part in good mental health.

I was unprepared for the violence of some of the experts' reactions. One noted child analyst told me that it was immoral even to write about the experimental programs, since parents might interpret such reports as advice. Others argued vehemently that if children did not learn, it was because of deep emotional problems, that it had nothing to do with teaching methods; accordingly, only therapy and a full spectrum of social services would help.

The two camps read different books, talked about different research problems, and attended different meetings. "Where did you find these people?" exclaimed an Establishment friend of mine when I told her whom I was planning to visit. When brought face to face, the two groups defended themselves with clichés.

"All children, being children, have the same needs," the Establishment asserted when anyone tried to devise special remedial programs for children from the slums. This seemed equivalent to saying that it mattered little whether preschool children were starving or well-fed—what all of them needed was a chance to express themselves through blocks and paint.

"Culturally deprived children need more stimulation," argued the cognitive types, confusing sensory stimulation—sheer amounts of light or sound, for instance—with symbolic stimulation, which implies some intellectual content or meaning.

"Why push them?" the Establishment responded to any attempt at putting some intellectual content into the preschool programs, as if they believed these children were too young to think—or that learning was something unpleasant, to be forced down a child's throat like castor oil.

"The child must learn how to learn," the cognitive psychologists asserted—sidestepping the burning issue of how this would be done (on which they all disagreed).

"They aren't ready to . . . before six," declared the Establishment. (Translation: The teacher isn't ready to teach them.)

It finally dawned on me that the split between these groups reflected more than different professional backgrounds; it revealed the different social classes of children each group most wanted to help. The old-line nursery school people were used to dealing with middle-class children whose parents taught them a great deal at home—or at least enough to cope with the demands of the first grade. The newer, cognitive types, on the other hand, urgently sought ways to arouse the sluggish brains of children raised by parents too poor, harried, or ignorant to teach them much that was relevant to school.

Thus it mattered little, academically, whether or not middle-class youngsters went to the existing nursery schools and kindergartens. Either way, they tended to do well in school; if they failed, the reasons were probably emotional or neurological rather than a lack of preparation. The large-scale failures of the poor, however, had at least one obvious reason: their total lack of preparation at home. Overcoming this lack would require a very different type of school.

A decade ago, Margaret Mead warned against "such fiascos as the application of nursery-school techniques—designed to free the overneat children of middle-class urban homes by letting them mess around with finger paints—to the deprived children from the disorderly, patternless homes of migrant workers. What these children really needed were the satisfying routines of the old kindergarten—itself an institution invented to deal with deprived children and which, when imported into middle-class education, had proved too mechanical and too routinized."

Only a few of the experimental programs dared to break away from the middle-class mold, however. One of the more striking ones I saw was run by two young men at the University of Illinois, in Urbana, who narrowly defined their academic goals for four- and five-year-old slum children, and then proceeded toward these goals one step at a time, in logical sequences.

It surprised me to find how modern and revolutionary the ideas that Maria Montessori first expressed around 1910 still sound—and how applicable they are to problems worrying so many educators today.

Most individualized of all was Omar K. Moore's "responsive environment" method, including his talking typewriter, on which young children could teach themselves to read and write, tracing their own paths to learning.

In various parts of the country, several other exciting pilot projects were going on. They showed how vastly we have underestimated young children's ability to learn, and how much even the brightest middle-class children are missing. Yet nobody was taking advantage of their findings. Their staffs often worked in isolation, hardly aware of what other researchers were doing. The majority of existing preschool programs, and particularly Project Head Start, pointedly ignored them.

The innovators' stiffest hurdle in their conflict with the Establishment was the problem of *proving* that their methods worked better. Unfortunately, the tools with which they tried to measure young children's progress were so crude that such proof was almost impossible. For lack of anything better, most educators fell back on the Stanford-Binet or similar intelligence tests, which they acknowledged to be both too broad and too dependent on verbal ability. Specific achievement tests could be given only *after* a child had learned to read and write. Until then, the various tests that were supposed to measure his ability to think, his reading readiness, his concepts of space, or other traits usually reflected entirely different factors—for example, the kind of speech the child heard at home. They also correlated badly with one another. A truly reliable battery of tests to measure young children's intellectual progress remains to be invented.

The battle also raged around theory. Many of the innovators' ideas seemed based on the work of Swiss psychologist Jean Piaget, who brilliantly described how children construct their changing image of the world out of ingredients supplied by their environment. Though Piaget's major books were first published in the 1930's, they had little impact in the United States at the time, being rediscovered only recently.

Another influential figure is Lev Vygotsky, a Russian psychologist of the same vintage, who died in the Soviet Union in 1934 and whose work has also just been rediscovered. The recent emphasis on children's language development can be traced right back to Vygotsky. American psychologists—relative newcomers to the study of cognitive growth— are only beginning to put their own stamp on the subject, largely through the use of computers.

Though at first I thought the battle would concern mostly children between the ages of three and six, I soon learned that it extended right back to the crib. The hottest area for research right now is not the earliest years, but the earliest *months* of life. Psychologists increasingly believe that the roots of intellectual curiosity are laid during these months. In a rich environment the child begins to get "kicks" out of learning soon after birth. If nothing arouses him, however, or all his attempts at learning are squelched, he will stop seeking this pleasure— to everyone's loss.

As Jerome Bruner wrote recently, "We get interested in what we get good at." Half the children in this country never have a chance to get good at anything, let alone become interested in it. Having failed to master basic skills early in life, they must either beat the system or flee from it, burying whatever talents they might have developed. Other children grow into the kind of college students whose thoughts, Sir Isaiah Berlin noted, "come higgledy-piggledy out of the big, buzzing, booming confusion of their minds."

The cognitive psychologists believe that the lives of all children could be made much richer if their abilities were developed systematically from the moment of birth. The idea is not to forget the other aspects of life—the children's vital emotional and social development, which go on simultaneously—but to give intellectual and artistic growth their proper places. By doing so, and by tailoring each child's intellectual diet to suit his needs, they hope to raise a nation of ever more differentiated, intelligent, adaptable, and creative adults, who will know how to make the best of both work and leisure. . . .

THE AMERICANIZATION OF MONTESSORI

. . . The influence of the Montessori revival has been phenomenal . . . despite violent disagreement on whether the method was fifty years behind the times way back in 1915, or whether it was at least fifty years ahead. Some three hundred Montessori schools have sprung up in the United States in the past few years, surpassing by far the number established during the first wave of American enthusiasm for Montessori in the early part of the century.

"Tell us all about it. Is it really wonderful? Or is it just a fad?" the writer Dorothy Canfield Fisher was asked by her friends in 1912, when she returned from a long visit with Dr. Maria Montessori in Rome. The questions have scarcely changed since then. But few teachers still have open minds on the subject, having learned too well that Montessori was "disproved" years ago by educational philosophers such as William Heard Kilpatrick, who stressed children's social development. Very few teachers of preschool children have actually observed Montessori classes in action. Their training in teachers' colleges, however, leads many of them to reject her method outright, in a sort of neurotic overreaction.

As a result, parents of middle-class children have taken the lead in the Montessori revival. In many cases, the new schools were actually started by parents' groups for their own children. Of all the thousands of Head Start centers around the country, only a handful have been run on Montessori principles, and few of the burgeoning classes for disadvantaged children have used her methods.

Yet Montessori's greatest achievement was her success with children from the slums. This is, in fact, her major relevance today.

She showed how to run model day-care centers for children from three to seven, in districts where no one dared go about unarmed at night, and how to deal with what she called, in 1908, "a new fact which was unknown to past centuries, namely, the isolation of the masses of the poor"—none other than what modern sociologists have rediscovered as alienation.

Dr. Montessori educated these children so well, in an ungraded classroom, that she foresaw that the entire elementary school would have to be changed as a result. The first grade would disappear, since her school would take care of all it taught, and "the elementary classes in the future would begin with children such as ours who know how to read and write . . . who are familiar with the rules of good conduct and courtesy, and who are thoroughly disciplined in the highest sense of the term, having developed, and become masters of themselves, through liberty." Among these children's other virtues, as she described them, they "pronounce clearly, write in a firm hand, are full of grace in their movements . . . and possess the power of spontaneous reasoning."

The chief attraction of Montessori for middle-class parents is the fact that many children in Montessori classes do learn to read, write, and count at a very early age. Nevertheless, this is far from the goal of a Montessori education. Montessori's own aims, as expressed through her books, were much loftier: She wanted her charges to become as powerful in their concentration, as independent of spirit, as strong of will and as clear of thought as the world's greatest geniuses. She noted that many major discoveries stemmed from such virtues as independence and persistence. Newton discovered gravitation by thinking about why an apple fell on him from the apple tree. "The environment sometimes rewards 'small reasonings' of this kind in a surprising manner," said Montessori. "Simplicity is the guide to discovery; simplicity which, like truth, should be naked."

She saw the child of three as carrying within him "a heavy chaos." "He is like a man who has accumulated an immense quantity of books, piled up without any order, and who asks himself, 'What shall I do with them?'" Culture, she said, is not the accumulation of knowledge, but "the prepared order" in the mind which is to receive such knowledge. Her goal, then, was to train children to be like connoisseurs: so sensitive to the specific attributes of things around them, and so expert in classifying them, that everything would possess interest and value for them.

They would learn all this freely—but in a specially "prepared environment." She coined the motto "Things are the best teachers." And she invented the richest array of educational toys seen to this day— hundreds of simple puzzles and games designed to guide the child's progress and make him truly independent, both physically and mentally: buttoning frames; lacing frames; series of pegs with corresponding pieces to develop the concept of numbers; weights to be fitted into progressively deeper or wider holes; map puzzles with small knobs, to develop the kind of dexterity required for writing, while incidentally learning geography; the famous sandpaper letters which a child could trace with his fingers until the movements of forming each letter became permanently engraved in his memory. After playing with these sandpaper letters for a few months, children would often begin writing so naturally that they believed it had come to them just because they had reached the right age. Montessori's fertile mind produced a steady stream of new materials, each serving several purposes at once, each leading from the sensory to the symbolic, each preparing the child for a higher level of understanding.

Her equipment always allowed the child to work at his own pace, though it urged him to perfect himself. The materials were largely self-correcting, requiring a minimum of help from the teacher—usually just a demonstration, at the beginning, of how the materials were to be used. Thus each child could choose from such variety that forty children in the same class might well be occupied with forty different tasks.

Since the children did their own learning, Montessori invented a new role for the teacher. The teacher would no longer dominate the stage with her "patronizing, enfeebling protection." She would not be a substitute mother, or the sole dispenser of knowledge. Instead, she would be a directress, guiding the independent work of her charges, and her chief qualification would be a keen power of observation.

When, in 1912, Dorothy Canfield Fisher visited a Montessori classroom for the first time, this was what struck her most: "There seemed no one there to push the children or to refrain from doing it. That collection of little tots, most of them too busy over their mysterious occupations even to talk, seemed, as far as a casual glance over the room went, entirely without supervision. . . . In our town, where we all know and like the teachers personally, their exhausted condition of almost utter nervous collapse by the end of the teaching year is a painful element in our community life. But I felt no impulse to sympathize with this woman with untroubled eyes who, perceiving us for the first time, came over to shake hands." She also noted that the teacher seemed free of that "lion-tamer's instinct" to keep a hypnotic eye on the "little animals," so marked in the other instructors the author knew; she simply turned away from the children while she spoke, and none of the children appeared to notice that the teacher's back was turned.

In those days it was common school practice for small children to be kept silent and motionless at their desks for hours on end, listening to the teacher. Rows of pupils were confined in this posture for such long periods that physicians began to complain about the extensive curvature of the spine that the schools were producing, and special rehabilitation classes were needed to correct the spinal deformations caused by the desks.

Montessori suggested that children be given instead the right to move about freely, to lie on the floor on little mats if they wished, or to use movable, child-sized tables and chairs. She fought for their right to a free choice of tasks. She fought for their right to make a moderate amount of noise. At a time when discipline and "breaking the child's will" loomed as major issues, she devised ways of developing each child's strength of will—and the children in her classes responded with marvelous self-control.

Children are really patient and gentle creatures, Montessori declared. They have been much maligned. Their overriding aim in life is simply their own self-development—their "autoeducation." In this, Montessori paralleled the progressive educators who later became her bitterest enemies. Yet she differed on several essential points, particularly in her determination not to leave this autoeducation entirely to chance. If the children were to have freedom, she argued, then the environment had to be very carefully planned for them. She spoke of the soaring death rates among small children in the days before rational public-health measures were adopted. Similarly, she said, rational measures were needed to prepare the environment for good mental growth. . . .

"Our emphasis is not so much on social adjustment. Yet I would not go so far as to say there is no opportunity for it."

From the point of view of education for the children of poverty, the Montessori method has at least one extraordinary asset: its peculiar ability to increase the child's span of attention.

Reporting on a Montessori program that included ten Negro children from families receiving Aid to Dependent Children (ADC) in Chicago, Professor Lawrence Kohlberg, of the University of Chicago's psychology department, noted that an obvious fact about the disadvantaged is their defect in attention, due to an environment of constant distractions. They are never alone with any task. At home, their brothers and sisters pounce upon any object they may be trying to play with. The conventional progressive-permissive approach increases these tendencies. But in a Montessori class, he pointed out, the children show long periods of attention, since they are not disturbed. Such attention is easiest to promote in a nongroup context. The preschool years offer a unique opportunity for this kind of solitary, self-directed work.

The IQ's of the ten disadvantaged children jumped an average of 17 points after only three months in the Montessori program, Kohlberg declared, while the IQ's of the same group's middle-class children increased about 10 points. "In our view," he said, "Montessori is useful not for sensory education as such, but for its ordering and labeling activities. However, the sensory activities are pleasurable, and serve as a basis for the development of attention."

Kohlberg also reported on a summer Head Start program run by the same Montessori teacher in the same way. Probably because of its short duration, the children in this group showed no significant changes.

Elsewhere in Chicago, in the city's oldest public-housing project—a nineteen-story development once described as a high-rise slum for low-income Negroes—another Montessori school for disadvantaged children is being run by a young woman named Marcella Morrison.

The whole atmosphere of Cabrini Houses is one of tremendous depression, says Miss Morrison, who was trained at Whitby. It weighs very heavily on the children—almost like being stifled. For instance, there is never anyone at the playground. Thousands of people live in the development, but, except at noon, when children are being dismissed from school, they all stay at home—the world is too threatening. There is no social contact. The Montessori school is the highlight of these children's lives. They begin to find life interesting, and they want to come to terms with it, to get involved.

When they started school, they had almost no span of attention, she recalls. It was bedlam. They were screaming and pushing all the time. Many teachers get stuck right at that spot, and never progress, on the theory that "that's the way they are," she says. Or else teachers become so strict that there is no spontaneity, gaiety, spark, left in the kids; the children conform and just seem to die out. With Montessori, they are not stuck at any one step. Provide an atmosphere that's rich in possibilities—and things really do happen. Although she knows they happen, Miss Morrison has not yet had the opportunity to test the children's progress. She hopes to do so if the OEO provides the money.

As Maria Montessori ran her original school, it was a day-care center, and lasted the whole day. There was time, therefore, for free play, for conversation, for taking care of pets, and for a lot of activities that she did not fully spell out, since they were not too unusual. In her daily program for the first Casa dei Bambini, she allowed only one hour for "intellectual work" with the equipment generally thought of as typically Montessori.

When the program is limited to a half-day, however, the problem of selection becomes more severe. This is especially true in planning for underprivileged youngsters who may have few opportunities to talk or play at home. While the prepared environment leaves little to chance — it was meant that way — it also limits the child's opportunity to make something uniquely his own, except in writing. All the equipment seems to bear the message "There is only one way of doing things — and this is it."

J. McV. Hunt believes that Montessori's materials should be viewed as a beginning, to which modern minds can add many useful inventions. As an example, he cites the work of O. K. Moore.

Clearly, Moore owes much to Montessori in his responsive environments method. Moore himself feels that his approach is essentially different, however, because unlike his talking typewriter, Montessori's materials cannot respond. The Montessori scheme is noninteractional, he told me. The child can't change the Montessori materials; he must adjust to them.

Since the Montessori method remained popular in Europe throughout the half-century when it was forgotten in the United States, I was very interested to hear Jean Piaget's comments about it. Piaget sees Montessori in the stream of educational reformers that includes such progressives as John Dewey and Carleton Washburne. The school with which he is associated in Geneva uses many elements of the Montessori system, he says, but in a more flexible way. The main drawback of the orthodox Montessori schools is that their equipment never changes — it was given once and for all, Piaget points out. He believes there are lots of good ideas there, but equipment should be changed according to need, as one goes along. Those famous weights, for example, are just one type of seriation; one could prepare twenty others along the same lines, using anything at all. He also criticizes Montessori's method on the ground that it provides only fragments of activity, without enabling the child truly to create anything. However, he admits, the Montessori system does promote continuity of effort and a passion for learning.

This half-century of experience in many parts of the world also shows, according to Nancy Rambusch, that the Montessori method is generally benign. At the very least, it doesn't seem to do any harm. One famous graduate was Anne Frank, whose youthful diary showed no signs of stunted creativity.

Mrs. Rambusch has been experimenting with one-hour Montessori classes for youngsters in run-down neighborhoods. Since an early start is particularly important for these children, and Montessori showed how to focus the interests of children as young as two and a half, the method holds great promise for them. Even in 1907, points out Mrs. Rambusch, Montessori worked with children from the age of two and a half years, at a time when American educators were discussing the relevance of her ideas for the four- and five-year-olds in public school kindergartens.

Another advantage of the Montessori system is its reasonable cost. Montessori's first directress was a teen-age girl, the daughter of the superintendent of the housing project in which Montessori established her first Casa dei Bambini. Almost singlehandedly, this girl directed the learning of fifty to sixty children, ranging in age from three to seven. Although this ratio of pupils to teacher seems excessively high, and Montessori teachers must now undergo considerable training, the method certainly requires less personnel than do many of the new techniques. Its equipment, too, is relatively inexpensive.

All this points to the likelihood that the Montessori revival in the United States will continue. The method may become further modified, or Americanized. It may return, at last, to the slums for which it was originally designed. But on its second transplanting, its roots seem to have taken firm hold.

DISCUSSION QUESTIONS
SUGGESTIONS FOR WRITING

1. Summarize the basic ideological differences Maya Pines points out between the "early-childhood Establishment" and the "innovators." How are their fundamental views of human nature at variance?

2. How does a Montessori school differ from a conventional nursery school? What is the historical basis for the lag in development of Montessori principles of early childhood education in America in contrast to Europe?

3. Is Maya Pines an impartial observer whose views are shaped by empirical evidence? Provide examples from the text to substantiate your position.

4. What modifications have come about in Montessori techniques which represent an "Americanization" of Montessori?

UPDIKE

A SENSE OF SHELTER

JOHN UPDIKE (b. 1932) is one of the most talented and widely read writers in America. He attended Harvard College and the Ruskin School of Drawing and Fine Arts in Oxford, England. From 1955 to 1957 he was a staff member of *The New Yorker,* to which he has contributed stories, essays, and poems. He is the author of nine books of fiction—including *Rabbit Run; Pigeon Feathers; The Centaur,* for which he received the National Book Award; *Couples;* and *Bech: A Book*—and three of poetry, as well as a collection of essays and four small juvenile books.

SNOW fell against the high school all day, wet big-flaked snow that did not accumulate well. Sharpening two pencils, William looked down on a parking lot that was a blackboard in reverse, car tires had cut smooth arcs of black into the white, and wherever a school bus had backed around, it had left an autocratic signature of two *V*'s. The snow, though at moments it whirled opaquely, could not quite bleach these scars away. The temperature must be exactly 32°. The window was open a crack, and a canted pane of glass lifted outdoor air into his face, coating the cedarwood scent of pencil shavings with the transparent odor of the wet window sill. With each revolution of the handle his knuckles came within a fraction of an inch of the tilted glass, and the faint chill this proximity breathed on them sharpened his already acute sense of shelter.

The sky behind the shreds of snow was stone-colored. The murk inside the high classroom gave the air a solidity that limited the overhead radiance to its own vessels; six globes of dull incandescence floated on the top of a thin sea. The feeling the gloom gave him was not gloomy but joyous: he felt they were all sealed in, safe; the colors of cloth were dyed deeper, the sound of whispers was made more distinct, the smells of tablet paper and wet shoes and varnish and face powder pierced him with a vivid sense of possession. These were his classmates sealed in, his, the stupid as well as the clever, the plain as well as the lovely, his enemies as well as his friends, his. He felt like a king and seemed to move to his seat between the bowed heads of subjects that loved him less than he loved them. His seat was sanctioned by tradition; for twelve years he had sat at the rear of classrooms, William Young, flanked by Marsha Wyckoff and Andy Zimmerman. Once there had been two Zimmermans, but one went to work in his father's greenhouse, and in some classes—Latin and Trig—there were none, and William sat at the edge of the class as if on the lip of a cliff, and Marsha Wyckoff became Marvin Wolf or Sandra Wade, but it was always the same desk, whose surface altered from hour to hour but from whose blue-stained ink-hole his mind could extract, like a chain of magicians' handkerchiefs, a continuity of years. As a senior he was a kind of king, and as a teacher's pet another kind, a puppet king, who gathered in appointive posts and even, when the moron vote split between two football heroes, some elective ones. He was not popular, he had never had a girl, his intense friends of childhood had drifted off into teams and gangs, and in large groups— when the whole school, for instance, went in the fall to the beautiful, dung-and-cotton-candy-smelling county fair—he was always an odd man, without a seat on the bus home. But exclusion is itself a form of inclusion. He even had a nickname: Mip, because he stuttered. Taunts no longer much frightened him; he had come late into his physical inheritance, but this summer it had arrived, and he at last stood equal with his enormous, boisterous parents, and had to unbutton his shirt cuffs to get his wrists through them, and discovered he could pick up a basketball with one hand. So, his long legs blocking two aisles, he felt regal even in size and, almost trembling with happiness under the high globes of light beyond whose lunar glow invisible snowflakes were drowning on the gravel roof of his castle, believed that the long delay of unpopularity had been merely a consolidation, that he was at last strong enough to make his move. Today he would tell Mary Landis he loved her.

He had loved her ever since, a fat-faced tomboy with freckles and green eyes, she deftly stole his rubber-lined schoolbag on the walk back from second grade along Jewett Street and outran him—simply had better legs. The superior speed a boy was supposed to have failed to come; his kidneys burned with panic. In front of the grocery store next to her home she stopped and turned. She was willing to have him catch up. This humiliation on top of the rest was too much to bear. Tears broke in his throat; he spun around and ran home and threw himself on the floor of the front parlor, where his grandfather, feet twiddling, perused the newspaper and soliloquized all morning. In time the letter slot rustled, and the doorbell rang, and Mary gave his mother the schoolbag and the two of them politely exchanged whispers. Their voices had been to him, lying there on the carpet with his head wrapped in his arms, indistinguishable. Mother had always liked Mary. From when she had been a tiny girl dancing along the hedge on the end of an older sister's arm, Mother had liked her. Out of all the children that flocked, similar as pigeons, through the neighborhood, Mother's heart had reached out with claws and fastened on Mary. He never took the schoolbag to school again, had refused to touch it. He supposed it was still in the attic, still faintly smelling of sweet pink rubber.

Fixed high on the plaster like a wren clinging to a barn wall, the buzzer sounded the two-minute signal. In the middle of the classroom Mary Landis stood up, a Monitor badge pinned to her belly. Her broad red belt was buckled with a brass bow and arrow. She wore a lavender sweater with the sleeves pushed up to expose her forearms, a delicately cheap effect. Wild stories were told about her; perhaps it was merely his knowledge of these that put the hardness in her face. Her eyes seemed braced for squinting and their green was frosted. Her freckles had faded. William thought she laughed less this year; now that she was in the Secretarial Course and he in the College Preparatory, he saw her in only one class a day, this one, English. She stood a second, eclipsed at the thighs by Jack Stephens' zebra-striped shoulders, and looked back at the class with a stiff worn glance, as if she had seen the same faces too many times before. Her habit of perfect posture emphasized the angularity she had grown into. There was a nervous edge, a boxiness in her bones, that must have been waiting all along under the childish fat. Her eye sockets were deeply indented and her chin had a prim square set that seemed in the murky air tremulous and defiant. Her skirt was cut square and straight. Below the waist she was lean; the legs that had outrun him were still athletic; she starred at hockey and cheerleading. Above, she was abundant: so stacked her spine curved backwards to keep her body balanced. She turned and in switching up the aisle encountered a boy's leg thrown into her path. She coolly looked down until it withdrew. She was used to such attentions. Her pronged chest poised, Mary proceeded out the door, and someone she saw in the hall made her smile, a wide smile full of warmth and short white teeth, and love scooped at William's heart. He would tell her.

In another minute, the second bell rasped. Shuffling through the perfumed crowds to his next class, he crooned to himself in the slow, over-enunciated manner of the Negro vocalist who had brought the song back this year:

"Lah-vender blue, dilly dilly,
Lavendih gree-heen;
Eef I were king, dilly dilly,
You would: be queen."

The song gave him an exultant sliding sensation that intertwined with the pleasures of his day. He knew all the answers, he had done all the work, the teachers called upon him only to rebuke the ignorance of the others. In Trig and Soc Sci both it was this way. In gym, the fourth hour of the morning, he, who was always picked near the last, startled his side by excelling at volleyball, leaping like a madman, shouting like a bully. The ball felt light as a feather against his big bones. His hair in wet quills from the shower, he walked in the icy air to Luke's Luncheonette, where he ate three hamburgers in a booth with three juniors. There was Barry Kruppman, a tall, thyroid-eyed boy who came on the school bus from the country town of Bowsville and who was an amateur hypnotist; he told the tale of a Portland, Oregon, businessman who under hypnosis had been taken back through sixteen reincarnations to the condition of an Egyptian concubine in the household of a high priest of Isis. There was his friend Lionel Griffin, a pudgy simp whose blond hair puffed out above his ears in two slick waxed wings. He was rumored to be a fairy, and in fact did seem most excited by the transvestite aspect of the soul's transmigration. And there was Lionel's girl Virginia, a drab little mystery who chain-smoked Herbert Tareytons and never said anything. She had sallow skin and smudged eyes and Lionel kept jabbing her and shrieking, making William wince. He would rather have sat with members of his own class, who filled the other booths, but he would have had to force himself on them. These juniors admired him and welcomed his company. He asked, "Wuh-well, was he ever a c-c-c-cockroach, like Archy?"

Kruppman's face grew intense; his furry lids dropped down over the bulge of his eyes, and when they drew back, his pupils were as small and hard as BBs. "That's the really interesting thing. There was this gap, see, between his being a knight under Charlemagne and then a sailor on a ship putting out from Macedonia—that's where Yugoslavia is now —in the time of Nero; there was this gap, when the only thing the guy would do was walk around the office snarling and growling, see, like this." Kruppman worked his blotched ferret face up into a snarl and Griffin shrieked. "He tried to bite one of the assistants and they think that for six hundred years" —the uncanny, unhealthy seriousness of his whisper hushed Griffin momentarily—"for six hundred years he just was a series of wolves. Probably in the German forests. You see, when he was in Macedonia"—his whisper barely audible—"he murdered a woman."

Griffin squealed in ecstasy and cried, "Oh, Kruppman! Kruppman, how you do go on!" and jabbed Virginia in the arm so hard a Herbert Tareyton jumped from her hand and bobbled across the Formica table. William gazed over their heads in pain.

The crowds at the soda counter had thinned so that when the door to the outside opened he saw Mary come in and hesitate there for a second where the smoke inside and the snow outside swirled together. The mixture made a kind of—Kruppman's ridiculous story had put the phrase in his head—wolf-weather, and she was just a gray shadow caught in it alone. She bought a pack of cigarettes from Luke and went out again, a kerchief around her head, the pneumatic thing above the door hissing behind her. For a long time, always in fact, she had been at the center of whatever gang was the one: in the second grade the one that walked home up Jewett Street together, and in the sixth grade the one that went bicycling as far away as the quarry and the Rentschler estate and played touch football Saturday afternoons, and in the ninth grade the one that went roller-skating at Candlebridge Park with the tenth-grade boys, and in the eleventh grade the one that held parties lasting past midnight and that on Sundays drove in caravans as far as Philadelphia and back. And all the while there had been a succession of boy friends, first Jack Stephens and Fritz March in their class and then boys a grade ahead and then Barrel Lord, who was a senior when they were sophomores and whose name was in the newspapers all football season, and then this last summer someone out of the school altogether, a man she met while working as a waitress in the city of Alton. So this year her weekends were taken up, and the party gang carried on as if she had never existed, and nobody saw her much except in school and when she stopped by in Luke's to buy a pack of cigarettes. Her silhouette against the big window had looked wan, her head hooded, her face nibbled by light, her fingers fiddling on the veined counter with her coins. He yearned to reach out, to comfort her, but he was wedged deep in the shrill booths, between the jingling guts of the pinball machine and the hillbilly joy of the jukebox. The impulse left him with a disagreeable feeling. He had loved her too long to want to pity her; it endangered the investment of worship on which he had not yet realized any return.

The two hours of the school afternoon held Latin and a study hall. In study hall, while the five people at the table with him played tic-tac-toe and sucked cough drops and yawned, he did all his homework for the next day. He prepared thirty lines of Vergil, Aeneas in the Underworld. The study hall was a huge low room in the basement of the building; its coziness crept into Tartarus. On the other side of the fudge-colored wall the circular saw in the woodworking shop whined and gasped and then whined again; it bit off pieces of wood with a rising, somehow terrorized inflection—bzzzzzup! He solved ten problems in trigonometry. His mind cut neatly through their knots and separated them, neat stiff squares of answer, one by one from the long but finite plank of problems that connected Plane Geometry with Solid. Lastly, as the snow on a ragged slant drifted down into the cement pits outside the steel-mullioned windows, he read a short story by Edgar Allan Poe. He closed the book softly on the pleasing sonority of its final note of horror, gazed at the red, wet, menthol-scented inner membrane of Judy Whipple's yawn, rimmed with flaking pink lipstick, and yielded his conscience to the snug sense of his work done, of the snow falling, of the warm minutes that walked through their shelter so slowly. The perforated acoustic tiling above his head seemed the lining of a long tube that would go all the way: high school merging into college, college into graduate school, graduate school into teaching at a college—section man, assistant, associate, *full* professor, possessor of a dozen languages and a thousand books, a man brilliant in his forties, wise in his fifties, renowned in his sixties, revered in his seventies, and then retired, sitting in the study lined with acoustical books until the time came for the last transition from silence to silence, and he would die, like Tennyson, with a copy of *Cymbeline* beside him on the moon-drenched bed.

After school he had to go to Room 101 and cut a sports cartoon into a stencil for the school paper. He liked the building best when it was nearly empty, when the casual residents—the rural commuters, the do-nothings, the trash—had cleared out. Then the janitors went down the halls sowing seeds of red wax and making an immaculate harvest with broad brooms, gathering all the fluff and hairpins and wrappers and powder that the animals had dropped that day. The basketball team thumped in the hollow gymnasium; the cheerleaders rehearsed behind drawn curtains on the stage. In Room 101 two empty-headed typists with stripes bleached into their hair banged away between giggles and mistakes. At her desk Mrs. Gregory, the faculty sponsor, wearily passed her pencil through misspelled news copy on tablet paper. William took the shadow box from the top of the filing cabinet and the styluses and little square plastic shading screens from their drawer and the stencil from the closet where the typed stencils hung, like fragile scarves, on hooks. B-BALLERS BOW, 57-42, was the headline. He drew a tall b-baller bowing to a stumpy pagan idol, labelled "W" for victorious Weiserton High, and traced it in the soft blue wax with the fine loop stylus. His careful breath grazed his knuckles. His eyebrows frowned while his heart bobbed happily on the giddy prattle of the typists. The shadow box was simply a black frame holding a pane of glass and lifted at one end by two legs so the light bulb, fitted in a tin tray, could slide under; it was like a primitive lean-to sheltering a fire. As he worked, his eyes smarting, he mixed himself up with the light bulb, felt himself burning under a slanting roof upon which a huge hand scratched. The glass grew hot; the danger in the job was pulling the softened wax with your damp hand, distorting or tearing the typed letters. Sometimes the center of an *o* stuck to your skin like a bit of blue confetti. But he was expert and cautious. He returned the things to their places feeling airily tall, heightened by Mrs. Gregory's appreciation, which she expressed by keeping her back turned, in effect stating that other staff members were undependable but William did not need to be watched.

In the hall outside Room 101 only the shouts of a basketball scrimmage reverberated; the chant of the cheerleaders had been silenced. Though he had done everything, he felt reluctant to leave. Neither of his parents—both worked—would be home yet, and this building was as much his home. He knew all its nooks. On the second floor of the annex, beyond the art room, there was a strange, narrow boys' lavatory that no one ever seemed to use. It was here one time that Barry Kruppman tried to hypnotize him and cure his stuttering. Kruppman's voice purred and his irises turned tiny in the bulging whites and for a moment William felt himself lean backward involuntarily, but he was distracted by the bits of bloodshot pink in the corners of these portentous eyes; the folly of giving up his will to an intellectual inferior occurred to him; he refused to let go and go under, and perhaps therefore his stuttering had continued.

The frosted window at the end of the long room cast a watery light on the green floor and made the porcelain urinals shine like slices of moon. The semi-opacity of this window gave the room's air of secrecy great density. William washed his hands with exaggerated care, enjoying the lavish amount of powdered soap provided for him in this castle. He studied his face in the mirror, making infinitesimal adjustments to attain the absolutely most flattering angle, and then put his hands below his throat to get their strong, long-fingered beauty into the picture. As he walked toward the door he sang, closing his eyes and gasping as if he were a real Negro whose entire career depended upon this recording:

> "Who—told me so, dilly dilly,
> Who told me soho?
> *Aii* told myself, dilly dilly,
> I told: me so."

When he emerged into the hall it was not empty: one girl walked down its varnished perspective toward him, Mary Landis, a scarf on her head and books in her arms. Her locker was up here, on the second floor of the annex. His own was in the annex basement. A tickling sensation that existed neither in the medium of sound nor of light crowded against his throat. She flipped the scarf back from her hair and in a conversational voice that carried well down the clean planes of the hall said, "Hi, Billy." The name came from way back, when they were both children, and made him feel small but brave.

"Hi. How are you?"

"Fine." Her smile broadened out from the *F* of this word.

What was so funny? Was she really, as it seemed, pleased to see him? "Du-did you just get through cheer-cheer-cheerleading?"

"Yes. Thank God. *Oh* she's so awful. She makes us do the same stupid locomotives for every cheer; I told her, no wonder nobody cheers any more."

"This is M-M-Miss Potter?" He blushed, feeling that he made an ugly face in getting past the *M*. When he got caught in the middle of a sentence the constriction was somehow worse. He admired the way words poured up her throat, distinct and petulant.

"Yes, Potbottom Potter," she said, "she's just aching for a man and takes it out on us. I wish she would get one. Honestly, Billy, I have half a mind to quit. I'll be so glad when June comes, I'll never set foot in this idiotic building again."

Her lips, pale with the lipstick worn off, crinkled bitterly. Her face, foreshortened from the height of his eyes, looked cross as a cat's. It a little shocked him that poor Miss Potter and this kind, warm school stirred her to what he had to take as actual anger; this grittiness in her was the first abrasive texture he had struck today. Couldn't she see around teachers, into their fatigue, their poverty, their fear? It had been so long since he had spoken to her, he wasn't sure how coarse she had become. "Don't quit," he brought out of his mouth at last. "It'd be n-n-n-nuh—it'd be nothing without you."

He pushed open the door at the end of the hall for her and as she passed under his arm she looked up and said, "Why, aren't you sweet?"

The stairwell, all asphalt and iron, smelled of galoshes. It felt more secret than the hall, more specially theirs; there was something magical in its shifting multiplicity of planes as they descended that lifted the spell on his tongue, so that words came as quickly as his feet pattered on the steps.

"No I mean it," he said, "you're really a beautiful cheerleader. But then you're beautiful period."

"I've skinny legs."

"Who told you that?"

"Somebody."

"Well *he* wasn't very sweet."

"No."

"Why do you hate this poor old school?"

"Now Billy. You know you don't care about this junky place any more than I do."

"I love it. It breaks my heart to hear you say you want to get out, because then I'll never see you again."

"You don't care, do you?"

"Why sure I care; you *know*"—their feet stopped; they had reached bottom, the first-floor landing, two brass-barred doors and a grimy radiator—"I've always li-loved you."

"You don't mean that."

"I do too. It's ridiculous but there it is. I wanted to tell you today and now I have."

He expected her to laugh and go out the door, but instead she showed an unforeseeable willingness to discuss this awkward matter. He should have realized before this that women enjoy being talked to. "It's a very silly thing to say," she asserted tentatively.

"I don't see why," he said, fairly bold now that he couldn't seem more ridiculous, and yet picking his words with a certain strategic care. "It's not *that* silly to love somebody, I mean what the hell. Probably what's silly is not to do anything about it for umpteen years but then I never had an opportunity, I thought."

He set his books down on the radiator and she set hers down beside his. "What kind of opportunity were you waiting for?"

"Well, see, that's it; I didn't know." He wished, in a way, she would go out the door. But she had propped herself against the wall and plainly awaited more talking. "Yuh-you were such a queen and I was such a nothing and I just didn't really want to presume." It wasn't very interesting; it puzzled him that she seemed to be interested. Her face had grown quite stern, the mouth very small and thoughtful, and he made a gesture with his hands intended to release her from the bother of thinking about it; after all, it was just a disposition of his heart, nothing permanent or expensive; perhaps it was just his mother's idea anyway. Half in impatience to close the account, he asked, "Will you marry me?"

"You don't want to marry me," she said. "You're going to go on and be a great man."

He blushed in pleasure; is this how she saw him, is this how they all saw him; as worthless now, but in time a great man? Had his hopes always been on view? He dissembled, saying, "No I'm not. But anyway, you're great now. You're so pretty, Mary."

"Oh, Billy," she said, "if you were me for just one day you'd hate it."

She said this rather blankly, watching his eyes; he wished her voice had shown more misery. In his world of closed surfaces a panel, carelessly pushed, had opened, and he hung in this openness paralyzed, unable to think what to say. Nothing he could think of quite fit the abruptly immense context. The radiator cleared its throat; its heat made, in the intimate volume just this side of the doors on whose windows the snow beat limply, a provocative snugness; he supposed he should try, and stepped forward, his hands lifting toward her shoulders. Mary sidestepped between him and the radiator and put the scarf back on. She lifted the cloth like a broad plaid halo above her head and then wrapped it around her chin and knotted it so she looked, in her red galoshes and bulky coat, like a peasant woman in a movie of Europe. With her thick hair swathed, her face seemed pale and chunky, and when she recradled the books in her arms her back bent humbly under the point of the kerchief. "It's too hot in here," she said. "I've got to wait for somebody." The disconnectedness of the two statements seemed natural in the fragmented atmosphere his stops and starts had produced. She bucked the brass bar with her shoulder and the door slammed open; he followed her into the weather.

"For the person who thinks your legs are too skinny?"

"Uh-huh." As she looked up at him a snowflake caught on the lashes of one eye. She jerkily rubbed that cheek on the shoulder of her coat and stamped a foot, splashing slush. Cold water gathered on the back of his thin shirt. He put his hands in his pockets and pressed his arms against his sides to keep from shivering.

"Thuh-then you wo-won't marry me?" His wise instinct told him the only way back was by going forward, through absurdity.

"We don't know each other," she said.

"My God," he said. "Why not? I've known you since I was two."

"What do you know about me?"

This awful seriousness of hers; he must dissolve it. "That you're not a virgin." But instead of making her laugh this made her face go dead and turned it away. Like beginning to kiss her, it was a mistake; in part, he felt grateful for his mistakes. They were like loyal friends who are nevertheless embarrassing. "What do you know about *me?*" he asked, setting himself up for a finishing insult but dreading it. He hated the stiff feel of his smile between his cheeks; glimpsed, as if the snow were a mirror, how hateful he looked.

"That you're basically very nice."

Her returning good for evil blinded him to his physical discomfort, set him burning with regret. "Listen," he said, "I did love you. Let's at least get that straight."

"You never loved anybody," she said. "You don't know what it is."

"O.K." he said. "Pardon me."

"You're excused."

"You better wait in the school," he told her. "He's-eez-eez going to be a long time."

She didn't answer and walked a little distance, toeing out in the childish Dutch way common to the women in this county, along the slack cable that divided the parking lot from the softball field. One bicycle, rusted as if it had been there for years, leaned in the rack, its fenders supporting airy crescents of white.

The warmth inside the door felt heavy. William picked up his books and ran his pencil along the black ribs of the radiator before going down the stairs to his locker in the annex basement. The shadows were thick at the foot of the steps; suddenly it felt late, he must hurry and get home. He was seized by the irrational fear that they were going to lock him in. The cloistered odors of paper, sweat, and, from the woodshop at the far end of the basement hall, sawdust no longer flattered him. The tall green double lockers appeared to study him critically through the three air slits near their tops. When he opened his locker, and put his books on his shelf, below Marvin Wolf's, and removed his coat from his hook, his self seemed to crawl into the long dark space thus made vacant, the humiliated ugly, educable self. In answer to a flick of his great hand the steel door weightlessly floated shut and through the length of his body he felt so clean and free he smiled. Between now and the happy future predicted for him he had nothing, almost literally nothing, to do.

DISCUSSION QUESTIONS
SUGGESTIONS FOR WRITING

1. How does Updike create the atmosphere of the high school and the sense of shelter it provides for William, which is so important to the story?

2. How does Updike combine his physical description and general characterization of Mary Landis with the continuing action of the plot?

3. Does William's confrontation with Mary at the end of the story change his perspective in any way?

4. What is the purpose of this story? What good is it? What emotions did it arouse? Is the failure of communication between William and Mary enough to account for the poignancy of the ending? Does the story offer any insights into the inadequacies of traditional methods of education?

Revolution in Religion

BERRIGAN

DANIEL BERRIGAN
(b. 1921) is a Jesuit priest, poet, educator, and peace activist, who, along with his brother Philip, became the first Roman Catholic priests to receive a federal jail sentence for peace agitation in the United States. With several other Catholics, the Berrigans destroyed draft files in Catonsville, Maryland, in May, 1968, as a protest against the American military involvement in Indochina.

THE BREAKING OF MEN AND THE BREAKING OF BREAD

ON April 1, 1968, the trial of the "Baltimore Four" opened in the federal court of that city. David Eberhardt, Tom Lewis, Jim Mengel, and Phil Berrigan went on trial for pouring of blood on draft files in the Customs House in October of the previous year.

Three days prior to the opening of the trial, the government dropped the most serious of its charges, that of conspiracy. There remained three felony charges: hindering Selective Service operations, disrupting them, and destroying Selective Service records.

The night before the trial opened, President Johnson ordered his bombers home; no more forays over North Viet Nam. I remember how we received the news — as men who were accustomed only to bad news, suddenly and unexpectedly granted a breakthrough. It was as though we had surfaced with bursting lungs after a long and dangerous submersion. Indeed, the hope we were going on was a precarious resource. We seemed to be thrashing about, functioning without organs and limbs, our hearts almost ceasing to beat.

Then suddenly, a strange onset, a new emotion, so long absent from our lives so as to seem almost a myth. The President had stopped the bombing. Could Americans make it after all, racist and bellicose as we were?

Alas, alas. Johnson stalked off, a sullen marauder, recouping his losses as best he might. Kennedy died, McCarthy faded, Nixon came on; last year's Halloween was this year's political charade. The war goes on. For all we know at present writing, the incumbent and his palace court might bequeath the Viet Nam war, a mad national treasure, to a presidential successor in 1972, he to the next in line, and so on. For all we know, for all our scanning of the owlish eyes of Kissinger or the iron scowl of Mitchell, our leaders might see a new thing coming; a war in which the vets of 1965–69 will someday, from wheelchairs, send off their grandsons to bleed and let blood, for the sake of some fictive "finest national hour," under the aegis of some Asian bullyboy, thereafter to be hailed as "one of the two or three finest statesmen of the world."

And what of the impact of the war upon the Church? Officially speaking, in the Catholic instance, the sacred power has quite simply followed the secular, its sedulous ape. Bishops have blessed the war, in word and in silence. They have supplied chaplains to the military as usual and have kept their eyes studiously averted from related questions—ROTC on Catholic campuses, military installations, diocesan investments.

And yet, in a quite astonishing way, the war has shaken the church. Indeed, for the first time in the history of the American church, warfare has emerged as a question worthy of attention. A number of priests are in trouble on this deadly serious and secular issue. Consciences are shaken, the law of the land is being broken.

The good old definition of church renewal (everything in its place, children seen and not heard, virtue its own reward, a stitch in time, a bird in the hand, render unto Caesar) is shattered. The hope for strong, open, affectionate relationships between bishops and communities is dissipated. The war has deepened and widened the chasm; the bishops spoke too late and acted not at all. So the war, along with questions like birth control and the survival of school systems, speech and its unfreedoms, control of properties and income, has made less and less credible official claims to superior wisdom and access to the divine will.

Which is not to say that the older game does not continue. It is merely to suggest that the older game is working badly. Once, when public affairs were more tranquil, peace was more easily kept at home. Grace was intoned at meals, authority was invoked. A common language prevailed. The paterfamilias could assure himself, on whatever occasion, whatever the subject, of a respectful hearing. But then, something happened. An intemperate father sent his son raging from the table. What happened, what in the world happened? A change of style, a trust broken, the difference between candor and the official line, between explaining the truth and explaining it away. Outcome: the family will never again know that easy and thoughtless unity which made it the very joy and pride of the culture.

The trial of the Baltimore Four is over, the sentence has been passed. Six years for Philip Berrigan and Tom Lewis, the chief protagonists. Catonsville followed, raining fire upon the files, a new instrument of destruction. Punishment also descended with all deliberate speed—concurrent sentences for Philip and Tom, 2½- and 3-year sentences for the others.

And the war went on, a Marat-Sade, Johnson-Nixon madhouse farce. There was no letup; we, and others like us, were in for it; a long, long push up Sisyphus Hill.

And yet, something else has happened. Since Catonsville, more hands than ours have stretched out, to block the brute gravity of that boulder. The Boston Two, the Milwaukee Fourteen, the D.C. Nine, the Pasadena Three, the Silver Springs Three, the Chicago Fifteen, the Women Against Daddy Warbucks, the New York Eight, the Boston Eight, the East Coast Conspiracy to Save Lives (the Philadelphia Eleven). Thus goes the current score; Mr. Nixon and his advisers and generals seem determined to extend it. Let the decision be theirs.

If there is one feature common to all the draft-file attacks, it is that they were invariably planned, and in major part executed, by Catholics. The fact is all the more remarkable, in face of the official stance of the church; in face also of the dissolution of the Left, broken by the repeated blows of national policy and factional despair. The Catholic community, that sturdy and well-fashioned hawk's nest, has suffered an invasion of doves; against all expectation, against nature and (they say) grace, a cross-breeding has followed.

Indeed, the Four of the Customs House—Mengel, Eberhardt, Lewis, and Berrigan—got something going. Their hands reached deeply into the springs of existence, cleared away the debris and filth, and set the pure waters running again. Some of us drank there, and took heart once more.

Maybe there was something to this Catholic tradition after all! We used to joke about it, in jail or out, reading our New Testament, breaking the Eucharist, battling to keep our perspective and good humor, trying with all our might to do something quite simple—to keep from going insane. Can it be that in this year, in this age of man, sanity requires so close a struggle? Is sanity so rare a resource on the American scene? Silone said once: It is difficult, but it is necessary, above all, to know who is insane and who is not.

Here are a few criteria.

It is madness to squander the world's resources on lethal military toys, while social misery and despair rise around a chorus of the damned.

It is madness to create the illusion of political or social change, all the while standing firm for spurious normalcy.

It is madness to renege on one's word, by activity which plays out the game one pretended to replace.

It is madness to ignore, with special savagery and determination, the viable and impassioned activists in our midst.

The madness goes on, it proliferates mightily. Behind a facade of sobriety and temperate action, the worst instincts of man are armed, rewarded, and set loose upon the world. An unthinkable Asian war, once a mere canker on the national body, a scratch on the tegument, undergone heedlessly and borne without second thought—it has festered and flowered, a wasting fever, a plague, a nightmare rushing into full day and again into night, and on and on for months and years, until only Jeremiah and Kafka could encompass its irrational horror.

DISCUSSION QUESTIONS
SUGGESTIONS FOR WRITING

1. *Extrapolating from the evidence presented, what generalizations can you make about Daniel Berrigan's view of the religious crisis or crises?*

2. *What is his view of the function of religion in contemporary society? In his view, is that function being adequately served?*

3. *Isn't the essay centrally concerned with "the impact of the war upon the Church"? How do the biographical elements relate to that subject?*

4. *What is your evaluation of the morality of the actions carried out by the "Baltimore Four"—the pouring of blood on draft files? Were their sentences just?*

BERTRAND RUSSELL
(1872–1970), philosopher,
writer, teacher, and
famous pacifist, consid-
ered questions of social
importance with the same
meticulous logic and lofty
wisdom that he used in
his pioneering studies of
mathematics. His usual
approach was closely
reasoned opposition to
any system or dogma
which he believed shack-
led men's minds.

This lecture was deliv-
ered on March 6, 1927,
at Battersea Town Hall
under the auspices of the
South London Branch of
the National Secular So-
ciety.

WHY I AM NOT A CHRISTIAN

AS your Chairman has told you, the subject about which I am going to speak to you tonight is "Why I Am Not a Christian." Perhaps it would be as well, first of all, to try to make out what one means by the word *Christian*. It is used these days in a very loose sense by a great many people. Some people mean no more by it than a person who attempts to live a good life. In that sense I suppose there would be Christians in all sects and creeds; but I do not think that that is the proper sense of the word, if only because it would imply that all the people who are not Christians—all the Buddhists, Confucians, Mohammedans, and so on—are not trying to live a good life. I do not mean by a Christian any person who tries to live decently according to his lights. I think that you must have a certain amount of definite belief before you have a right to call yourself a Christian. The word does not have quite such a full-blooded meaning now as it had in the times of St. Augustine and St. Thomas Aquinas. In those days, if a man said that he was a Christian it was known what he meant. You accepted a whole collection of creeds which were set out with great precision, and every single syllable of those creeds you believed with the whole strength of your convictions.

WHAT IS A CHRISTIAN?

Nowadays it is not quite that. We have to be a little more vague in our meaning of Christianity. I think, however, that there are two different items which are quite essential to anybody calling himself a Christian. The first is one of a dogmatic nature—namely, that you must believe in God and immortality. If you do not believe in those two things, I do not think that you can properly call yourself a Christian. Then, further than that, as the name implies, you must have some kind of belief about Christ. The Mohammedans, for instance, also believe in God and in immortality, and yet they would not call themselves Christians. I think you must have at the very lowest the belief that Christ was, if not divine, at least the best and wisest of men. If you are not going to believe that much about Christ, I do not think you have any right to call yourself a Christian. Of course, there is another sense, which you find in *Whitaker's Almanack* and in geography books, where the population of the world is said to be divided into Christians, Mohammedans, Buddhists, fetish worshipers, and so on; and in that sense we are all Christians. The geography books count us all in, but that is a purely geographical sense, which I suppose we can ignore. Therefore I take it that when I tell you why I am not a Christian I have to tell you two different things: first, why I do not believe in God and in immortality; and, secondly, why I do not think that Christ was the best and wisest of men, although I grant him a very high degree of moral goodness.

But for the successful efforts of unbelievers in the past, I could not take so elastic a definition of Christianity as that. As I said before, in olden days it had a much more full-blooded sense. For instance, it included the belief in hell. Belief in eternal hell-fire was an essential item of Christian belief until pretty recent times. In this country, as you know, it ceased to be an essential item because of a decision of the Privy Council, and from that decision the Archbishop of Canterbury and the Archbishop of York dissented; but in this country our religion is settled by Act of Parliament, and therefore the Privy Council was able to override their Graces and hell was no longer necessary to a Christian. Consequently I shall not insist that a Christian must believe in hell.

THE EXISTENCE OF GOD

To come to this question of the existence of God: it is a large and serious question, and if I were to attempt to deal with it in any adequate manner I should have to keep you here until Kingdom Come, so that you will have to excuse me if I deal with it in a somewhat summary fashion. You know, of course, that the Catholic Church has laid it down as a dogma that the existence of God can be proved by the un- aided reason. That is a somewhat curious dogma, but it is one of their dogmas. They had to introduce it because at one time the freethinkers adopted the habit of saying that there were such and such arguments which mere reason might urge against the existence of God, but of course they knew as a matter of faith that God did exist. The arguments and the reasons were set out at great length, and the Catholic Church felt that they must stop it. Therefore they laid it down that the existence of God can be proved by the unaided reason and they had to set up what they considered were arguments to prove it. There are, of course, a number of them, but I shall take only a few.

THE FIRST-CAUSE ARGUMENT

Perhaps the simplest and easiest to understand is the argument of the First Cause. (It is maintained that everything we see in this world has a cause, and as you go back in the chain of causes further and further you must come to a First Cause, and to that First Cause you give the name of God.) That argument, I suppose, does not carry very much weight nowadays, because, in the first place, cause is not quite what it used to be. The philosophers and the men of science have got going on cause, and it has not anything like the vitality it used to have; but, apart from that, you can see that the argument that there must be a First Cause is one that cannot have any validity. I may say that when I was a young man and was debating these questions very seriously in my mind, I for a long time accepted the argument of the First Cause, until one day, at the age of eighteen, I read John Stuart Mill's Autobiography, and I there found this sentence: "My father taught me that the question 'Who made me?' cannot be answered, since it immediately suggests the further question 'Who made God?' " That very simple sentence showed me, as I still think, the fallacy in the argument of the First Cause. If everything must have a cause, then God must have a cause. If there can be anything without a cause, it may just as well be the world as God, so that there cannot be any validity in that argument. It is exactly of the same nature as the Hindu's view, that the world rested upon an elephant and the elephant rested upon a tortoise; and when they said, "How about the tortoise?" the Indian said, "Suppose we change the subject." The argument is really no better than that. There is no reason why the world could not have come into being without a cause; nor, on the other hand, is there any reason why it should not have always existed. There is no reason to suppose that the world had a beginning at all. The idea that things must have a beginning is really due to the poverty of our imagination. Therefore, perhaps, I need not waste any more time upon the argument about the First Cause.

THE NATURAL-LAW ARGUMENT

Then there is a very common argument from natural law. That was a favorite argument all through the eighteenth century, especially under the influence of Sir Isaac Newton and his cosmogony. People observed the planets going around the sun according to the law of gravitation, and they thought that God had given a behest to these planets to move in that particular fashion, and that was why they did so. That was, of course, a convenient and simple explanation that saved them the trouble of looking any further for explanations of the law of gravitation. Nowadays we explain the law of gravitation in a somewhat complicated fashion that Einstein has introduced. I do not propose to give you a lecture on the law of gravitation, as interpreted by Einstein, because that again would take some time; at any rate, you no longer have the sort of natural law that you had in the Newtonian system, where, for some reason that nobody could understand, nature behaved in a uniform fashion. We now find that a great many things we thought were natural laws are really human conventions. You know that even in the remotest depths of stellar space there are still three feet to a yard. That is, no doubt, a very remarkable fact, but you would hardly call it a law of nature. And a great many things that have been regarded as laws of nature are of that kind. On the other hand, where you can get down to any knowledge of what atoms actually do, you will find they are much less subject to law than people thought, and that the laws at which you arrive are statistical averages of just the sort that would emerge from chance. There is, as we all know, a law that if you throw dice you will get double sixes only about once in thirty-six times, and we do not regard that as evidence that the fall of the dice is regulated by design; on the contrary, if the double sixes came every time we should think that there was design. The laws of nature are of that sort as regards a great many of them. They are statistical averages such as would emerge from the laws of chance; and that makes this whole business of natural law much less impressive than it formerly was. Quite apart from that, which represents the momentary state of science that may change tomorrow, the whole idea that natural laws imply a lawgiver is due to a confusion between natural and human laws. Human laws are behests commanding you to behave a certain way, in which way you may choose to behave, or you may choose not to behave; but natural laws are a description of how things do in fact behave, and being a mere description of what they in fact do, you cannot argue that there must be somebody who told them to do that, because even supposing that there were, you are then faced with the question "Why did God issue just those natural laws and no others?" If you say that he did it simply from his own good pleasure, and without any reason, you then find that there is something which is not subject to law, and so your train of natural law is interrupted. If you say, as more orthodox theologians do, that in all the laws which God issues he had a reason for giving those laws rather than others — the reason, of course, being to create the best universe, although you would never think it to look at it — if there were a reason for the laws which God gave, then God himself was subject to law, and therefore you do not get any advantage by introducing God as an intermediary. You have really a law outside and anterior to the divine edicts, and

God does not serve your purpose, because he is not the ultimate law-giver. In short, this whole argument about natural law no longer has anything like the strength that it used to have. I am traveling on in time in my review of the arguments. The arguments that are used for the existence of God change their character as time goes on. They were at first hard intellectual arguments embodying certain quite definite fallacies. As we come to modern times they become less respectable intellectually and more and more affected by a kind of moralizing vagueness.

THE ARGUMENT FROM DESIGN

The next step in this process brings us to the argument from design. You all know the argument from design: everything in the world is made just so that we can manage to live in the world, and if the world was ever so little different, we could not manage to live in it. That is the argument from design. It sometimes takes a rather curious form; for instance, it is argued that rabbits have white tails in order to be easy to shoot. I do not know how rabbits would view that application. It is an easy argument to parody. You all know Voltaire's remark, that obviously the nose was designed to be such as to fit spectacles. That sort of parody has turned out to be not nearly so wide of the mark as it might have seemed in the eighteenth century, because since the time of Darwin we understand much better why living creatures are adapted to their environment. It is not that their environment was made to be suitable to them but that they grew to be suitable to it, and that is the basis of adaptation. There is no evidence of design about it.

When you come to look into this argument from design, it is a most astonishing thing that people can believe that this world, with all the things that are in it, with all its defects, should be the best that omnipotence and omniscience have been able to produce in millions of years. I really cannot believe it. Do you think that, if you were granted omnipotence and omniscience and millions of years in which to perfect your world, you could produce nothing better than the Ku Klux Klan or the Fascists? Moreover, if you accept the ordinary laws of science, you have to suppose that human life and life in general on this planet will die out in due course: it is a stage in the decay of the solar system; at a certain stage of decay you get the sort of conditions of temperature and so forth which are suitable to protoplasm, and there is life for a short time in the life of the whole solar system. You see in the moon the sort of thing to which the earth is tending—something dead, cold, and lifeless.

I am told that that sort of view is depressing, and people will sometimes tell you that if they believed that, they would not be able to go on living. Do not believe it; it is all nonsense. Nobody really worries much about what is going to happen millions of years hence. Even if they think they are worrying much about that, they are really deceiving themselves. They are worried about something much more mundane, or it may merely be a bad digestion; but nobody is really seriously rendered unhappy by the thought of something that is going to happen to this world millions and millions of years hence. Therefore, although it is of course a gloomy view to suppose that life will die out — at least I suppose we may say so, although sometimes when I contemplate the things that people do with their lives I think it is almost a consolation — it is not such as to render life miserable. It merely makes you turn your attention to other things.

THE MORAL ARGUMENTS FOR DEITY

Now we reach one stage further in what I shall call the intellectual descent that the Theists have made in their argumentations, and we come to what are called the moral arguments for the existence of God. You all know, of course, that there used to be in the old days three intellectual arguments for the existence of God, all of which were disposed of by Immanuel Kant in the *Critique of Pure Reason;* but no sooner had he disposed of those arguments than he invented a new one, a moral argument, and that quite convinced him. He was like many people: in intellectual matters he was skeptical, but in moral matters he believed implicitly in the maxims that he had imbibed at his mother's knee. That illustrates what the psychoanalysts so much emphasize — the immensely stronger hold upon us that our very early associations have than those of later times.

Kant, as I say, invented a new moral argument for the existence of God, and that in varying forms was extremely popular during the nineteenth century. It has all sorts of forms. One form is to say that there would be no right or wrong unless God existed. I am not for the moment concerned with whether there is a difference between right and wrong, or whether there is not: that is another question. The point I am concerned with is that, if you are quite sure there is a difference between right and wrong, you are then in this situation: Is that difference due to God's fiat or is it not? If it is due to God's fiat, then for God himself there is no difference between right and wrong, and it is no longer a significant statement to say that God is good. If you are going to say, as theologians do, that God is good, you must then say that right and wrong have some meaning which is independent of God's fiat, because God's fiats are good and not bad independently of the mere fact that he made them. If you are going to say that, you will then have to say that it is not only through God that right and wrong came into being, but that they are in their essence logically anterior to God. You could, of course, if you liked, say that there was a superior deity who gave orders to the God who made this world, or could take up the line that some of the gnostics took up — a line which I often thought was a very plausible one — that as a matter of fact this world that we know was made by the devil at a moment when God was not looking. There is a good deal to be said for that, and I am not concerned to refute it.

THE ARGUMENT FOR THE REMEDYING OF INJUSTICE

Then there is another very curious form of moral argument, which is this: they say that the existence of God is required in order to bring justice into the world. In the part of this universe that we know there is great injustice, and often the good suffer, and often the wicked prosper, and one hardly knows which of those is the more annoying; but if you are going to have justice in the universe as a whole you have to suppose a future life to redress the balance of life here on earth. So they say that there must be a God, and there must be heaven and hell in order that in the long run there may be justice. That is a very curious argument. If you looked at the matter from a scientific point of view, you would say, "After all, I know only this world. I do not know about the rest of the universe, but so far as one can argue at all on probabilities one would say that probably this world is a fair sample, and if there is injustice here the odds are that there is injustice elsewhere also." Supposing you got a crate of oranges that you opened, and you found all the top layer of oranges bad, you would not argue, "The underneath ones must be good, so as to redress the balance." You would say, "Probably the whole lot is a bad consignment"; and that is really what a scientific person would argue about the universe. He would say, "Here we find in this world a great deal of injustice, and so far as that goes that is a reason for supposing that justice does not rule in the world; and therefore so far as it goes it affords a moral argument against deity and not in favor of one." Of course I know that the sort of intellectual arguments that I have been talking to you about are not what really moves people. What really moves people to believe in God is not any intellectual argument at all. Most people believe in God because they have been taught from early infancy to do it, and that is the main reason.

Then I think that the next most powerful reason is the wish for safety, a sort of feeling that there is a big brother who will look after you. That plays a very profound part in influencing people's desire for a belief in God.

THE CHARACTER OF CHRIST

I now want to say a few words upon a topic which I often think is not quite sufficiently dealt with by Rationalists, and that is the question whether Christ was the best and the wisest of men. It is generally taken for granted that we should all agree that that was so. I do not myself. I think that there are a good many points upon which I agree with Christ a great deal more than the professing Christians do. I do not know that I could go with Him all the way, but I could go with Him much further than most professing Christians can. You will remember that He said, "Resist not evil: but whosoever shall smite thee on thy right cheek, turn to him the other also." That is not a new precept or a new principle. It was used by Lao-tse and Buddha some 500 or 600 years before Christ, but it is not a principle which as a matter of fact Christians accept. I have no doubt that the present Prime Minister, for instance, is a most sincere Christian, but I should not advise any of you to go and smite him on one cheek. I think you might find that he thought this text was intended in a figurative sense.

Then there is another point which I consider excellent. You will remember that Christ said, "Judge not lest ye be judged." That principle I do not think you would find was popular in the law courts of Christian countries. I have known in my time quite a number of judges who were very earnest Christians, and none of them felt that they were acting contrary to Christian principles in what they did. Then Christ says, "Give to him that asketh of thee, and from him that would borrow of thee turn not thou away." That is a very good principle. Your Chairman has reminded you that we are not here to talk politics, but I cannot help observing that the last general election was fought on the question of how desirable it was to turn away from him that would borrow of thee, so that one must assume that the Liberals and Conservatives of this country are composed of people who do not agree with the teaching of Christ, because they certainly did very emphatically turn away on that occasion.

Then there is one other maxim of Christ which I think has a great deal in it, but I do not find that it is very popular among some of our Christian friends. He says, "If thou wilt be perfect, go and sell that which thou hast, and give to the poor." That is a very excellent maxim, but, as I say, it is not much practiced. All these, I think, are good maxims, although they are a little difficult to live up to. I do not profess to live up to them myself; but then, after all, it is not quite the same thing as for a Christian.

DEFECTS IN CHRIST'S TEACHING

Having granted the excellence of these maxims, I come to certain points in which I do not believe that one can grant either the superlative wisdom or the superlative goodness of Christ as depicted in the Gospels; and here I may say that one is not concerned with the historical question. Historically it is quite doubtful whether Christ ever existed at all, and if He did we do not know anything about Him, so that I am not concerned with the historical question, which is a very difficult one. I am concerned with Christ as He appears in the Gospels, taking the Gospel narrative as it stands, and there one does find some things that do not seem to be very wise. For one thing, He certainly thought that His second coming would occur in clouds of glory before the death of all the people who were living at that time. There are a great many texts that prove that. He says, for instance, "Ye shall not have gone over the cities of Israel till the Son of Man be come." Then He says, "There are some standing here which shall not taste death till the Son of Man comes into His kingdom"; and there are a lot of places where it is quite clear that He believed that His second coming would happen during the lifetime of many then living. That was the belief of His earlier followers, and it was the basis of a good deal of His moral teaching. When He said, "Take no thought for the morrow," and things of that sort, it was very largely because He thought that the second coming was going to be very soon, and that all ordinary mundane affairs did not count. I have, as a matter of fact, known some Christians who did believe that the second coming was imminent. I knew a parson who frightened his congregation terribly by telling them that the second coming was very imminent indeed, but they were much consoled when they found that he was planting trees in his garden. The early Christians did really believe it, and they did abstain from such things as planting trees in their gardens, because they did accept from Christ the belief that the second coming was imminent. In that respect, clearly He was not so wise as some other people have been, and He was certainly not superlatively wise.

THE MORAL PROBLEM

Then you come to moral questions. There is one very serious defect to my mind in Christ's moral character, and that is that He believed in hell. I do not myself feel that any person who is really profoundly humane can believe in everlasting punishment. Christ certainly as depicted in the Gospels did believe in everlasting punishment, and one does find repeatedly a vindictive fury against those people who would not listen to His preaching — an attitude which is not uncommon with preachers, but which does somewhat detract from superlative excellence. You do not, for instance find that attitude in Socrates. You find him quite bland and urbane toward the people who would not listen to him; and it is, to my mind, far more worthy of a sage to take that line than to take the line of indignation. You probably all remember the sort of things that Socrates was saying when he was dying, and the sort of things that he generally did say to people who did not agree with him.

You will find that in the Gospels Christ said, "Ye serpents, ye generation of vipers, how can ye escape the damnation of hell." That was said to people who did not like His preaching. It is not really to my mind quite the best tone, and there are a great many of these things about hell. There is, of course, the familiar text about the sin against the Holy Ghost: "Whosoever speaketh against the Holy Ghost it shall not be forgiven him neither in this World nor in the world to come." That text has caused an unspeakable amount of misery in the world, for all sorts of people have imagined that they have committed the sin against the Holy Ghost, and thought that it would not be forgiven them either in this world or in the world to come. I really do not think that a person with a proper degree of kindliness in his nature would have put fears and terrors of that sort into the world.

Then Christ says, "The Son of Man shall send forth His angels, and they shall gather out of His kingdom all things that offend, and them which do iniquity, and shall cast them into a furnace of fire; there shall be wailing and gnashing of teeth"; and He goes on about the wailing and gnashing of teeth. It comes in one verse after another, and it is quite manifest to the reader that there is a certain pleasure in contemplating wailing and gnashing of teeth, or else it would not occur so often. Then you all, of course, remember about the sheep and the goats; how at the second coming He is going to divide the sheep from the goats, and He is going to say to the goats, "Depart from me, ye cursed, into everlasting fire." He continues, "And these shall go away into everlasting fire." Then He says again, "If thy hand offend thee, cut it off; it is better for thee to enter into life maimed, than having two hands to go into hell, into the fire that never shall be quenched; where the worm dieth not and the fire is not quenched." He repeats that again and again also. I must say that I think all this doctrine, that hell-fire is a punishment for sin, is a doctrine of cruelty. It is a doctrine that put cruelty into the world and gave the world generations of cruel torture; and the Christ of the Gospels, if you could take Him as His chroniclers represent Him, would certainly have to be considered partly responsible for that.

There are other things of less importance. There is the instance of the Gadarene swine, where it certainly was not very kind to the pigs to put the devils into them and make them rush down the hill to the sea. You must remember that He was omnipotent, and He could have made the devils simply go away; but He chose to send them into the pigs. Then there is the curious story of the fig tree, which always rather puzzled me. You remember what happened about the fig tree. "He was hungry; and seeing a fig tree afar off having leaves, He came if haply He might find anything thereon; and when He came to it He found nothing but leaves, for the time of figs was not yet. And Jesus answered and said unto it: 'No man eat fruit of thee hereafter for ever' . . . and Peter . . . saith unto Him: 'Master, behold the fig tree which thou cursedst is withered away.' " This is a very curious story, because it was not the right time of year for figs, and you really could not blame the tree. I cannot myself feel that either in the matter of wisdom or in the matter of virtue Christ stands quite as high as some other people known to history. I think I should put Buddha and Socrates above Him in those respects.

THE EMOTIONAL FACTOR

As I said before, I do not think that the real reason why people accept religion has anything to do with argumentation. They accept religion on emotional grounds. One is often told that it is a very wrong thing to attack religion, because religion makes men virtuous. So I am told; I have not noticed it. You know, of course, the parody of that argument in Samuel Butler's book, *Erewhon Revisited.* You will remember that in *Erewhon* there is a certain Higgs who arrives in a remote country, and after spending some time there he escapes from that country in a balloon. Twenty years later he comes back to that country and finds a new religion in which he is worshiped under the name of the "Sun Child," and it is said that he ascended into heaven. He finds that the Feast of the Ascension is about to be celebrated, and he hears Professors Hanky and Panky say to each other that they never set eyes on the man Higgs, and they hope they never will; but they are the high priests of the religion of the Sun Child. He is very indignant, and he comes up to them, and he says, "I am going to expose all this humbug and tell the people of Erewhon that it was only I, the man Higgs, and I went up in a balloon." He was told, "You must not do that, because all the morals of this country are bound round this myth, and if they once know that you did not ascend into heaven they will all become wicked"; and so he is persuaded of that and he goes quietly away.

That is the idea—that we should all be wicked if we did not hold to the Christian religion. It seems to me that the people who have held to it have been for the most part extremely wicked. You find this curious fact, that the more intense has been the religion of any period and the more profound has been the dogmatic belief, the greater has been the cruelty and the worse has been the state of affairs. In the so-called ages of faith, when men really did believe the Christian religion in all its completeness, there was the Inquisition, with its tortures; there were millions of unfortunate women burned as witches; and there was every kind of cruelty practiced upon all sorts of people in the name of religion.

You find as you look around the world that every single bit of progress in humane feeling, every improvement in the criminal law, every step toward the diminution of war, every step toward better treatment of the colored races, or every mitigation of slavery, every moral progress that there has been in the world, has been consistently opposed by the organized churches of the world. I say quite deliberately that the Christian religion, as organized in its churches, has been and still is the principal enemy of moral progress in the world.

HOW THE CHURCHES HAVE RETARDED PROGRESS

You may think that I am going too far when I say that that is still so. I do not think that I am. Take one fact. You will bear with me if I mention it. It is not a pleasant fact, but the churches compel one to mention facts that are not pleasant. Supposing that in this world that we live in today an inexperienced girl is married to a syphilitic man; in that case the Catholic Church says, "This is an indissoluble sacrament. You must endure celibacy or stay together. And if you stay together, you must not use birth control to prevent the birth of syphilitic children." Nobody whose natural sympathies have not been warped by dogma, or whose moral nature was not absolutely dead to all sense of suffering, could maintain that it is right and proper that that state of things should continue.

That is only an example. There are a great many ways in which, at the present moment, the church, by its insistence upon what it chooses to call morality, inflicts upon all sorts of people undeserved and unnecessary suffering. And of course, as we know, it is in its major part an opponent still of progress and of improvement in all the ways that diminish suffering in the world, because it has chosen to label as morality a certain narrow set of rules of conduct which have nothing to do with human happiness; and when you say that this or that ought to be done because it would make for human happiness, they think that has nothing to do with the matter at all. "What has human happiness to do with morals? The object of morals is not to make people happy."

FEAR, THE FOUNDATION OF RELIGION

Religion is based, I think, primarily and mainly upon fear. It is partly the terror of the unknown and partly, as I have said, the wish to feel that you have a kind of elder brother who will stand by you in all your troubles and disputes. Fear is the basis of the whole thing—fear of the mysterious, fear of defeat, fear of death. Fear is the parent of cruelty, and therefore it is no wonder if cruelty and religion have gone hand in hand. It is because fear is at the basis of those two things. In this world we can now begin a little to understand things, and a little to master them by help of science, which has forced its way step by step against the Christian religion, against the churches, and against the opposition of all the old precepts. Science can help us to get over this craven fear in which mankind has lived for so many generations. Science can teach us, and I think our own hearts can teach us, no longer to look around for imaginary supports, no longer to invent allies in the sky, but rather to look to our own efforts here below to make this world a fit place to live in, instead of the sort of place that the churches in all these centuries have made it.

WHAT WE MUST DO

We want to stand upon our own feet and look fair and square at the world—its good facts, its bad facts, its beauties, and its ugliness; see the world as it is and be not afraid of it. Conquer the world by intelligence and not merely by being slavishly subdued by the terror that comes from it. The whole conception of God is a conception derived from the ancient Oriental despotisms. It is a conception quite unworthy of free men. When you hear people in church debasing themselves and saying that they are miserable sinners, and all the rest of it, it seems contemptible and not worthy of self-respecting human beings. We ought to stand up and look the world frankly in the face. We ought to make the best we can of the world, and if it is not so good as we wish, after all it will still be better than what these others have made of it in all these ages. A good world needs knowledge, kindliness, and courage; it does not need a regretful hankering after the past or a fettering of the free intelligence by the words uttered long ago by ignorant men. It needs a fearless outlook and a free intelligence. It needs hope for the future, not looking back all the time toward a past that is dead, which we trust will be far surpassed by the future that our intelligence can create.

DISCUSSION QUESTIONS
SUGGESTIONS FOR WRITING

1. Summarize Russell's formulations and refutations of the following arguments: the first-cause argument, the natural-law argument, the argument from design, the moral arguments for deity, the argument for the remedying of injustice. Do you find any faults in logic in Russell's attempt to refute these arguments for the existence of a deity?

2. Russell concedes that "what really moves people to believe in God is not any intellectual argument at all," but what he calls the "emotional factor." What is the emotional factor? Does he use any methods of persuasion calculated to overcome this factor?

3. Defend one of the following positions by providing evidence from the essay in question: the author of this essay is a well-intentioned but misguided man; the author is a good man with good ideas; the author is an evil man with destructive ideas. Should one's attitude towards a writer's ideas necessarily influence one to make a conclusive judgment about him personally? Is it possible to like a writer but to dislike his ideas, or vice versa?

4. Which characteristics of this essay mark it as an example of the so-called critical essay? (See questions 1 and 2 on "Report on the Federal Civil Defense Booklet.")

COX

RELIGION AND MORALITY

HARVEY COX (b. 1929), clergyman and theologian, is a professor at the Divinity School, Harvard University, and author of *The Secular City,* a best-selling analysis of contemporary urban society and its relation to Christianity. In this work, Cox emphasizes the need for a more socially relevant church, one which is flexible and adaptable enough to meet the changing needs caused by current problems.

L ET'S begin with a concession: religious people are a little mad. So what? If a society built on Miltown, racial neurasthenia and TV commercials is sane, then I gladly line up with the loonies. Which is to say that any religion I am interested in has to be somewhat out of step with its society, even a "great" or decent society. Otherwise, what's the point? Maybe that's why those who envision the ideal society as a smoothly functioning welfare millennium, with circuses and credit cards for all, have begun to see this kind of religion not only as mad but also as a menace. People with one eye on the Kingdom of God have trouble reading billboards. They are also unpredictable. Their bizarre visions make them querulous and insubordinate. A strange belief in *something else* keeps them from lining up docilely for the goodies churned out by the Big Computer. Fanatics, nuts, seers — all are an embarrassment to any society. They don't fit in. May we always have them with us! But granted all that, does religion today have anything positive to offer to our notion of what society should be like? I think so. There is a previous question, however: For the intelligent 20th-Century man, does religion make any sense? Except for antiquarian purposes, why bother with such a Paleozoic fossil? To answer this question, we must first insist that religion cannot be equated with what *churches* do. That is as mistaken as equating education with what schools do or justice with what cops and courts do. Religion is larger than any church, and one can lambaste the churches without jettisoning religion. Isaiah, Jesus and Luther all did. An intelligent man does not fling the whole business overboard because a minister once warned that premarital intercourse lands you straight in Hades.

Neither does the intelligent man equate man merely with intelligence. He knows that in addition to a brain, man has turbulent feelings, powerful fears and glorious fantasies. His hopes soar beyond any rational basis. Religion is founded of these marvelous ingredients—without which life would fade to insipidity. Of course, intelligence has a place in religion; it criticizes and reflects on experience. But reason is only a part of the total man, and the intelligent man knows it. He also knows that life is more than technical know-how. Eons before man carved out tools, he fashioned myths. Before he invented the wheel, he mimed the life forces and the cosmic rhythms. Homo sapiens is the maker of symbols as well as of ideas. A fully conscious man delights in this aspect of his life instead of trying to repress it. He knows religion is a congeries of dramatic symbols and life values, and he swings with it. He has gone beyond both the pious credulity of the peasant and the fastidious disdain of the sophomore atheist.

Our Western religion is a comparatively recent one as religions go. It was preceded by thousands of years of religious development. And it will not last forever. Its central insight, however, remains crucial: that the holy is found not only in fire, thunder and sun but in the ecstasy of love, the angry cry of the poor and the longings of the poets. In recent years, saddled with moralism and empty rites, we had nearly forgotten that religion began with celebration—the dance, the feast, the orgy. Today, however, with jazz masses, agape meals and rock liturgies, people are once again discovering that faith is festivity. Man is celebrating life and hope, despite death and despair. But what does faith's celebration have to do with the decent society?

There are at least three things we must continue to celebrate today, even though there is no strictly empirical basis for any of them. All must be "taken on faith," but each is essential in any society that calls itself decent:

1. *Every single person counts.* This does not mean individualism; it means that man is not just an atom in the natural cosmos. He is a responsible agent, a history maker. Thus, to abscond to some selfless nirvana or exurban grotto, or to turn history over to luck or fate, is a betrayal. Jesus depicted man as a steward placed in charge of the vineyard and fully accountable for what happened. Every person, not just the crowned head or the oil magnate, is intended by God to take part in the decisions that affect his destiny. Our modern idea of democracy rests partially on the old Puritan precept that man has not only the right but the obligation to govern himself. To abdicate by letting someone else do it is to settle for a subhuman state.

As the boxes on great-society organizational charts cramp and suffocate us, the celebration of the personal becomes increasingly necessary.

As technologists design supersonic futures and urban planners cantilever new cities, somebody has to ask what happens to the individual person. This is not just the yelp of a coupon-clipping yeoman who resents the income tax. It is the justifiable insistence that a society that excludes the black and the dispossessed from the fashioning of its future is not a great society at all. It is not even a society; it is a Potemkin village in which plumbing repairs have been allowed to replace the rebuilding of civic life.

The nasty truth is that in emerging urban America, real civic participation is distressingly low. Disaffiliation roams the streets. Fidgety city officials shore up their tottering machines with Federal dollars. Schools become custodial institutions. Garbage reeks in the streets. Those with money flee to suburban enclaves, where their only interest in the city becomes how to avoid its taxes and how to get their loot out in minimum commuting time.

To celebrate the person today, religion will have to become *more*, not less political. Churches will have to expose Governmental programs that increase people's dependency and deepen their sense of powerlessness. To build personal community today, we will have to fashion new types of political structures—first in the neighborhood, but eventually at the metropolitan level. Here, churches can help. They have buildings and personnel located in every slum. They could turn over their property to inner-city residents as the first step in taking over whole blocks of buildings, perhaps through rent strikes, and then rebuild them into model housing. The whole outmoded parochial school system should be abandoned. Then churches could experiment with alternative schooling systems, ones that do not lock youngsters up inside brick and glass tombs. Such church-sponsored model schools might stimulate some action in the calcified public system. Some churches have already begun to support the protest groups that make the voice of the outcasts heard in the councils of power. Admittedly, this infuriates those city fathers who want the clergy to pronounce benedictions at political conventions and then go back to their prayer wheels. But we can expect more Father Groppis and Reverend Coffins in the future.

An emphasis on individual participation in corporate life will also require changes in the church itself. For centuries, we have preached that sin is rebellion against God and all duly constituted authority. Therefore, any questioning of those in charge was condemned. The good believer was obedient and quiescent. Today, most theologians reject this perverted idea of sin, which arose in the period of Christianity's "Constantinian" compromise with Greco-Roman ideologies of sacral state power. Today, we define sin not as insurrection but as indifference, not as the prideful attempt to be more than man but as the slothful refusal to be all that a man should be. This means that the religion of the future cannot be counted on to plaster over the fissures of the great society and solemnly to invoke the Deity's blessings on anything those in charge decide upon. The *protest*ant elements in all churches will undoubtedly become more vociferous. To be *advocatus hominem*, the defense attorney for man, is an age-old task of the church. It should pursue it with vigor in the future.

2. Faith also celebrates the fact that whether we like it or not, *the human family is one*. Take the admittedly somewhat comic figure of the Pope as an example. Of course, his regal finery and Swiss guards seem anachronistic today, but the Pope as a symbol is important. He is a sovereign who sits on land owned by no nation and he reigns over a world-wide spiritual empire. The word is "reigns," not "rules," which the present occupant of Peter's throne seems to have forgotten. But the symbol is still invaluable. It reminds us that despite the artificial and archaic national boundaries we have erected around the world, we all belong together. As out of touch as he often appears, the Pope is closer to the reality of human interdependence than are the waistcoated diplomats who perpetuate the idea of national sovereignty. If you're looking for a really dangerous and outmoded myth, national sovereignty wins over the papacy hands down.

The truth is that no American society can call itself great or decent as long as a single Bengali child gets no breakfast. Admittedly, this pulls the plug on patriotism and national pride. Thinking of V.C.s as brothers rather than as gooks makes it a little harder to fry them in napalm. But that is the price we pay for a faith that claims to be universal rather than merely tribal. This persistent dream of a single world community may explain why Protestant churches got themselves in trouble a few years back for advocating the recognition of Communist China, when the idea was equated with treason. It suggests why the Pope, when he came to America, visited the UN, not the White House. In a century of runaway national jingoism, Christianity is one of the few forces that insists there is no real difference between "Greeks and barbarians." This message must be increasingly emphasized as nervous fingers twitch near nuclear triggers.

But the church has not lived up to its own universal claims. Believers in the same God don helmets and bludgeon one another in the name of this or that great society, classless society or whatever. While some Christians follow a Buddhist example and immolate themselves for peace, others piously pour poisons on rice crops. Even on the home front, the oneness of the human family is denied by hysterical mobs in Alabama and Chicago. But when a bigot's brick hits a nun or a racist's bullet fells Martin Luther King, even the most venomous segregationist is reminded, if only for a moment, that we belong together. To testify to the uncompromising universalism of humankind may cost even more blood in the future. Believers will have to set aside ethnic and racial loyalties and fashion a live model of world citizenship. Our slow-paced ecumenical fumbling must move beyond churchly mergers to the reconciliation of the world, and ultimately to the universe itself. Nothing less will be enough.

3. Finally, faith today celebrates *vision and fantasy*. Our work-

obsessed culture has little time for either. We venerate facts, statistics, probability curves. We dispatch our dreamers to the happy farm and turn the controls of society over to the "realists." It's our sanitary way of stoning the prophets. But realists always have a shrunken sense of what is possible. They are a timid breed. Every society needs seers whose imaginations are not fettered to the presently possible. Prophets peer beyond a guaranteed annual income and color TV in every home to a time of human fulfillment that makes us restive with every present accomplishment. The Bible pulsates with images of men reconciled to nature, lions living with lambs, onyx cities in which there is no more crying, a world of blooming fig trees and discarded spears.

What if we do eventually solve the sheer physical problems of human existence? Does that produce the decent society? Hardly. Then the essential question may press in on us even harder. It is the question prophetic religion always asks: What is really worth doing in life? To generate new answers to that question, and to rethink the old ones, we will need institutions that will enable men to symbolize, play, dream, dance out their fantasies and stretch their aspirations beyond the current constricted horizons. We will need something like religion.

The function of faith is to make a civilization discontent, to rouse it from its complacency and fire it with richer fantasies. This gift of prophecy comes not only to saints. It speaks through artists, dancers, poets. But its nurture and renewal is the very *raison d'être* of religion; for as a prophet of long ago once said, "Where there is no vision, the people perish."

DISCUSSION QUESTIONS
SUGGESTIONS FOR WRITING

1. Does Harvey Cox's view of the function of religion differ fundamentally from that of Daniel Berrigan?

2. What does Harvey Cox see as the "central insight" of Western religion?

3. What "morality" is suggested by this essay?

4. Although "Religion and Morality" is closest to the type of essay frequently referred to as the personal essay—in which the writer expresses his personal views on a subject, relying on eloquence, wit, or some form of emotional appeal rather than verifiable evidence to convince or intrigue his reader—what characteristics of other essay types does it share?

MARK TWAIN (1835–1910), printer and riverboat pilot, newspaperman, lecturer, and writer, is one of the greatest figures in American literature. As a humorist he habitually poked fun at entrenched institutions and traditions. Though philosophically consistent with his early humorous writing, his later works, such as *The Damned Human Race,* were bitterly satiric and sometimes cynical. For this reason and because some of the writings were considered blasphemous, many of the later works were withheld from publication by his executors until 1962, when *Letters from the Earth* was first published, containing a broad sampling from the work of his rich later period.

WAS THE WORLD MADE FOR MAN?

Alfred Russell Wallace's revival of the theory that this earth is at the centre of the stellar universe, and is the only habitable globe, has aroused great interest in the world.—LITERARY DIGEST

For ourselves we do thoroughly believe that man, as he lives just here on this tiny earth, is in essence and possibilities the most sublime existence in all the range of non-divine being—the chief love and delight of God.—Chicago INTERIOR (Presb.)

I SEEM to be the only scientist and theologian still remaining to be heard from on this important matter of whether the world was made for man or not. I feel that it is time for me to speak.

I stand almost with the others. They believe the world was made for man, I believe it likely that it was made for man; they think there is proof, astronomical mainly, that it was made for man, I think there is evidence only, not proof, that it was made for him. It is too early, yet, to arrange the verdict, the returns are not all in. When they are all in, I think they will show that the world was made for man; but we must not hurry, we must patiently wait till they are all in.

Now as far as we have got, astronomy is on our side. Mr. Wallace has clearly shown this. He has clearly shown two things: that the world was made for man, and that the universe was made for the world—to stiddy it, you know. The astronomy part is settled, and cannot be challenged.

We come now to the geological part. This is the one where the evidence is not all in, yet. It is coming in, hourly, daily, coming in all the time, but naturally it comes with geological carefulness and deliberation, and we must not be impatient, we must not get excited, we must be calm, and wait. To lose our tranquillity will not hurry geology; nothing hurries geology.

It takes a long time to prepare a world for man, such a thing is not done in a day. Some of the great scientists, carefully ciphering the evidences furnished by geology, have arrived at the conviction that our world is prodigiously old, and they may be right, but Lord Kelvin is not of their opinion. He takes a cautious, conservative view, in order to be on the safe side, and feels sure it is not so old as they think. As Lord Kelvin is the highest authority in science now living, I think we must yield to him and accept his view. He does not concede that the world is more than a hundred million years old. He believes it is that old, but not older. Lyell believed that our race was introduced into the world 31,000 years ago, Herbert Spencer makes it 32,000. Lord Kelvin agrees with Spencer.

Very well. According to these figures it took 99,968,000 years to prepare the world for man, impatient as the Creator doubtless was to see him and admire him. But a large enterprise like this has to be conducted warily, painstakingly, logically. It was foreseen that man would have to have the oyster. Therefore the first preparation was made for the oyster. Very well, you cannot make an oyster out of whole cloth, you must make the oyster's ancestor first. This is not done in a day. You must make a vast variety of invertebrates, to start with—belemnites, trilobites, Jebusites, Amalekites, and that sort of fry, and put them to soak in a primary sea, and wait and see what will happen. Some will be a disappointment—the belemnites, the Ammonites and such; they will be failures, they will die out and become extinct, in the course of the nineteen million years covered by the experiment, but all is not lost, for the Amalekites will fetch the homestake; they will develop gradually into encrinites, and stalactites, and blatherskites, and one thing and another as the mighty ages creep on and the Archaean and the Cambrian Periods pile their lofty crags in the primordial seas, and at last the first grand stage in the preparation of the world for man stands completed, the oyster is done. An oyster has hardly any more reasoning power than a scientist has; and so it is reasonably certain that this one jumped to the conclusion that the nineteen million years was a preparation for *him;* but that would be just like an oyster, which is the most conceited animal there is, except man. And anyway, this one could not know, at that early date, that he was only an incident in a scheme, and that there was some more to the scheme, yet.

The oyster being achieved, the next thing to be arranged for in the preparation of the world for man was fish. Fish, and coal—to fry it with. So the Old Silurian seas were opened up to breed the fish in, and at the same time the great work of building Old Red Sandstone mountains eighty thousand feet high to cold-storage their fossils in was begun. This latter was quite indispensable, for there would be no end of failures again, no end of extinctions—millions of them—and it would be cheaper and less trouble to can them in the rocks than keep tally of them in a book. One does not build the coal beds and eighty thousand feet of perpendicular Old Red Sandstone in a brief time—no, it took twenty million years. In the first place, a coal bed is a slow and troublesome and tiresome thing to construct. You have to grow prodigious forests of tree-ferns and reeds and calamites and such things in a marshy region; then you have to sink them under out of sight and let them rot; then you have to turn the streams on them, so as to bury them under several feet of sediment, and the sediment must have time to harden and turn to rock; next you must grow another forest on top, then sink it and put on another layer of sediment and harden it; then more forest and more rock, layer upon layer, three miles deep—ah, indeed it is a sickening slow job to build a coal-measure and do it right!

So the millions of years drag on; and meantime the fish culture is lazying along and frazzling out in a way to make a person tired. You have developed ten thousand kinds of fishes from the oyster; and come to look, you have raised nothing but fossils, nothing but extinctions. There is nothing left alive and progressive but a ganoid or two and perhaps half a dozen asteroids. Even the cat wouldn't eat such.

Still, it is no great matter; there is plenty of time, yet, and they will develop into something tasty before man is ready for them. Even a ganoid can be depended on for that, when he is not going to be called on for sixty million years.

The Paleozoic time limit having now been reached, it was necessary to begin the next stage in the preparation of the world for man, by opening up the Mesozoic Age and instituting some reptiles. For man would need reptiles. Not to eat, but to develop himself from. This being the most important detail of the scheme, a spacious liberality of time was set apart for it—thirty million years. What wonders followed! From the remaining ganoids and asteroids and alkaloids were developed by slow and steady and painstaking culture those stupendous saurians that used to prowl about the steamy world in those remote ages, with their snaky heads reared forty feet in the air and sixty feet of body and tail racing and thrashing after. All gone, now, alas—all extinct, except the little handful of Arkansawrians left stranded and lonely with us here upon this far-flung verge and fringe of time.

Yes, it took thirty million years and twenty million reptiles to get one that would stick long enough to develop into something else and let the scheme proceed to the next step.

Then the pterodactyl burst upon the world in all his impressive solemnity and grandeur, and all Nature recognized that the Cenozoic threshold was crossed and a new Period open for business, a new stage begun in the preparation of the globe for man. It may be that the pterodactyl thought the thirty million years had been intended as a preparation for himself, for there was nothing too foolish for a pterodactyl to imagine, but he was in error, the preparation was for man. Without doubt the pterodactyl attracted great attention, for even the least observant could see that there was the making of a bird in him. And so it turned out. Also the makings of a mammal, in time. One thing we have to say to his credit, that in the matter of picturesqueness he was the triumph of his Period; he wore wings and had teeth, and was a starchy and wonderful mixture altogether, a kind of long-distance premonitory symptom of Kipling's marine:

> 'E isn't one o' the reg'lar Line, nor 'e isn't one of the crew,
> 'E's a kind of a giddy harumfrodite—soldier an' sailor too!

From this time onward for nearly another thirty million years the preparation moved briskly. From the pterodactyl was developed the bird; from the bird the kangaroo, from the kangaroo the other marsupials; from these the mastodon, the megatherium, the giant sloth, the Irish elk, and all that crowd that you make useful and instructive fossils out of—then came the first great Ice Sheet, and they all retreated before it and crossed over the bridge at Bering Strait and wandered around over Europe and Asia and died. All except a few, to carry on the preparation with. Six Glacial Periods with two million years between Periods chased these poor orphans up and down and about the earth, from weather to weather—from tropic swelter at the poles to Arctic frost at the equator and back again and to and fro, they never knowing what kind of weather was going to turn up next; and if ever they settled down anywhere the whole continent suddenly sank under them without the least notice and they had to trade places with the fishes and scramble off to where the seas had been, and scarcely a dry rag on them; and when there was nothing else doing a volcano would let go and fire them out from wherever they had located. They led this unsettled and irritating life for twenty-five million years, half the time afloat, half the time aground, and always wondering what it was all for, they never suspecting, of course, that it was a preparation for man and had to be done just so or it wouldn't be any proper and harmonious place for him when he arrived.

And at last came the monkey, and anybody could see that man wasn't far off, now. And in truth that was so. The monkey went on developing for close upon five million years, and then turned into a man—to all appearances.

Such is the history of it. Man has been here 32,000 years. That it took a hundred million years to prepare the world for him is proof that that is what it was done for. I suppose it is. I dunno. If the Eiffel Tower were now representing the world's age, the skin of paint on the pinnacle-knob at its summit would represent man's share of that age; and anybody would perceive that that skin was what the tower was built for. I reckon they would, I dunno.

DISCUSSION QUESTIONS
SUGGESTIONS FOR WRITING

1. Would it be correct to say that this essay succeeds in spite of lies, gross inaccuracies, and deliberate stupidity on the part of the author? Provide examples of these and discuss their function in the essay.

2. What technical insights does an understanding of this essay offer by way of explaining the uses of satire for purposes of persuasion?

3. Was the world made for man?

4. What connections do you see between the subject and treatment in this essay and the crisis of contemporary religious consciousness discussed by Berrigan and Cox?

PART FOUR

INTRODUCTION

THE APOCALYPTICAL character of contemporary experience is embodied in both the form and content of the dominant art forms. While the form and shape of two of the dominant art forms—film and rock—are directly traceable to recent technical-electrical innovations, the ancient technology of literacy, showing few signs of imminent obsolescence, has simply adapted to the apocalyptical influences, absorbed the shock waves from other technologies, and persisted.

An interesting feature of this adaptation has been the increased service and growing vitality of nonfiction prose forms. Meanwhile, fiction writing shows signs of undiminished development into fertile new areas. The "turned on" styles and formal experimentation of much contemporary fiction and nonfiction writing show evidence of strong influences from the electric media.

In terms of content, the dominant art forms are the best expression of the consciousness of the age, which they helped to mold, as well as the most likely enduring repository of cultural data for future ages.

In *2001,* for example, the combined expression of the celebration of technology and the fear of its "taking over" is a characteristic ambivalence of the time. *The Graduate,* as Hollis Alpert points out, as one of the first Hollywood antiestablishment movies, more or less accurately expressed the new values of the youth culture and subsequently became one of the cultural milestones.

Nat Hentoff, in his brief contemporary history of music, outlines the growth and significance of rock: "Growing up . . . under the bomb and packed into schools where conformity and competition were the oppressive norm, . . . [the kids] needed music in which to let go. And that's what the new music was all about—*feeling.* By coming together in liberation, if only in music, a surging youth culture—through music—was rapidly developing." Rock grew to incorporate everything from folk and blues to Indian classical raga, everything from Bach to Cage. Performers became virtuosos, writing their own music and lyrics (e.g., the Beatles), or combining music and literature (e.g., Richard Fariña), or frequently exercising a new role (for musicians) of awakening the consciences of their generation (e.g., Joan Baez).

While writers like Tom Wolfe and Gay Talese were discovering a more subjective "new journalism," while Truman Capote was writing a "nonfiction novel" begun from a newspaper story, and other writers such as Norman Mailer and Vance Bourjaily were turning their novelistic gifts to contemporary history and autobiography, the more general consciousness of the cultural significance of nonfiction forms began to emerge.

For many, the recognition of fiction writers like Joyce Carol Oates and Kurt Vonnegut, Jr.—whose wild imaginations and clear perceptions seem commensurate with the age and necessary for surviving it—has meant a comforting refutation of that earlier foreboding notion that fiction might be a dying form.

Another significant contemporary literary development has been the rediscovery and resurgence of the black American literary tradition, paralleling the civil rights movement of the last decade. Exciting young black writers such as Robert Boles and James Alan McPherson have already written important books.

At a time when reality is frequently stranger than fiction, fiction writers of all kinds have tended to move away from the business of documenting reality—into fantasy and greater subjectivity. A notable instance of this can be seen in the fresh interest in science fiction. Science fiction, long a popular form, has become respectable, in keeping, perhaps, with the fact that more and more of man's fantasies seem to run to a concern for where his technology might be taking him.

A S we move rapidly toward the year 2000, it appears that our civilization is becoming obsessively future-oriented. One explanation for this future orientation is the growing mass popular consciousness that our technological society is determining our futures, rather than we determining the direction in which our exploding technological development will take us.

The peculiar nature of the *Homo sapiens* mind—its evolution as an instrument capable of making projections through time (escaping the animal's eternal present)—may provide another explanation for the fascination of time-obsession in general in human beings—from future-predicting to astrology. Man has learned to worry about the future, hence the attractiveness of any system that seems to establish increased surety and eliminates the randomness, chaos, and unpredictability of upcoming events. But events do not usually occur predictably, no matter how much man wishes they would. Contingencies can be allowed for, arranged for, anticipated, worried about. Man *will* continue to worry (it is part of his successful adaptation). Still, there is a great *freedom* in knowing that events are *not* predictable or determined, that they can be, for one thing, *influenced.*

Yet, the greatest variable in all of man's equations continues to be himself. As Robert Ardrey comments in *African Genesis:* "It is the superb paradox of our time that in a single century we have proceeded from the first ironclad warship to the first hydrogen bomb, and from the first telegraphic communication to the beginnings of the conquest of space; yet in the understanding of our own natures, we have proceeded almost nowhere. It is an ignorance that transcends national or racial boundaries, and leaps happily over iron curtains as if they did not exist. Were a brotherhood of man to be formed today, then its only possible common bond would be ignorance of what man is."

Bertrand Russell, the great pacifist and philosopher, author of the *Principia Mathematica,* one of the greatest works on mathematics in this century, is said to have estimated three-to-one odds *against* survival of the human species by the year 2000. Although that was obviously a debatable sort of pronouncement, it may well be too optimistic. It is difficult to conceive of and harder to accept the fact that *we are truly on the brink of global apocalypse.* We may also be on the threshold of satisfying an ancient and persistent human wish: to choose our futures. Which way we go is still largely within the control of our own enigmatic natures.

Dominant Art Forms

MORGENSTERN

JOSEPH MORGENSTERN (b. 1932) is the film critic of *Newsweek*. He has been a reporter for the *New York Times* and a film and drama critic for the *New York Herald Tribune*. In "Kubrick's Cosmos" Morgenstern comes to terms with what he sees as the positive and negative characteristics of the film *2001*.

KUBRICK'S COSMOS

MOST of the sporadic power and sly humor of *2001: A Space Odyssey* derive from a contrast in scale. On the one hand we have the universe; that takes a pretty big hand. On the other we have man, a recently risen ex-ape in a dinky little rocket ship. Somewhere between earth and Jupiter, though, producer-director Stanley Kubrick gets confused about the proper scale of things himself. His potentially majestic myth about man's first encounter with a higher life form than his own dwindles into a whimsical space operetta, then frantically inflates itself again for a surreal climax in which the imagery is just obscure enough to be annoying, just precise enough to be banal.

The first of the film's four movements deals with man's prehistoric debut. It is as outrageous and entertaining as anything in *Planet of the Apes*, but much more engrossing. Cutting constantly between real apes and actors (or dancers) in unbelievably convincing anthropoid outfits, Kubrick establishes the fantasy base of his myth with the magical appearance of a monolithic slab in the apes' midst. They touch it, dance around it, worship it. The sequence ends with a scene in which one of our founding fathers picks up a large bone, beats a rival into ape-steak tartare with it and thus becomes the first animal on earth to use a tool. The man-ape gleefully hurls his tool of war into the air. It becomes a satellite in orbit around the moon. A single dissolve spans four million years.

With nearly equal flair the second movement takes up the story in the nearly present future. Man has made it to the moon and found another shiny slab buried beneath the surface. By this time the species is bright enough to surmise that the slab is some sort of trip-wire device planted by superior beings from Jupiter to warn that earthmen are running loose in the universe. Kubrick's special effects in this section border on the miraculous—lunar landscapes, spaceship interiors and exteriors that represent a quantum leap in quality over any sci-fi film ever made.

In a lyrical orbital roundelay, a rocket ship from earth takes up the same rotational rate as the space station it will enter. Once again, as in *Dr. Strangelove*, machines copulate in public places. This time, however, they do it to a Strauss waltz instead of "Try a Little Tenderness"—the smug, invariable, imperturbable swoops of "the Blue Danube" juxtaposed with the silent, indifferent sizzling of the cosmos.

Where *Strangelove* was a dazzling farce, *2001* bids fair at first to become a fine satire. We see that space has been conquered. We also see it has been commercialized and, within the limits of man's tiny powers, domesticated. Weightless stewardesses wear weightless smiles, passengers diddle with glorified Automat meals, watch karate on in-flight TV and never once glance out into the void to catch a beam of virgin light from Betelgeuse or Aldebaran.

The third movement begins promisingly, too. America has sent a spaceship to Jupiter. The men at the controls, Keir Dullea and Gary Lockwood, are perfectly deadpan paradigms of your ideal astronaut: scarily smart, hair-raisingly humorless. The computer that runs the ship and talks like an announcer at a lawn-tennis tournament admits to suffering from certain anxieties about the mission (or, more ominously, pretends to suffer from them), but the men are unflappable as a reefed mainsail.

Your own anxieties about *2001* may begin to surface during a scene in which Lockwood trots around his slowly rotating cryptship and shadowboxes to keep in shape. He trots and boxes, boxes and trots until he has trotted the plot to a complete halt, and the director's attempt to show the boredom of interplanetary flight becomes a crashing bore in its own right. Kubrick and his co-writer, Arthur C. Clarke, still have some tricks up their sleeves before Jupiter: pretty op-art designs that flicker cryptically across the face of the instrument display tubes, a witty discussion between Dullea and Lockwood on the computer's integrity.

But the ship is becalmed for too long, with stately repetitions of earlier special effects, a maddening sound of deep breathing on the sound track, a beautiful but brief walk in space and then a long, long stretch of very shaky comedy-melodrama in which the computer turns on its crew and carries on like an injured party in a homosexual spat. Dullea finally lobotomizes the thing and, in the absence of any plot advancement, this string of faintly familiar computer gags gets laughs. But they are deeply destructive to a film that was poking fun itself, only a few reels ago, at man's childish preoccupation with technological trivia.

On the outskirts of Jupiter *2001* runs into some interesting abstractions that have been done more interestingly in many more modest underground films that were not shot in seventy-millimeter Super Pana-vision, then takes a magnificent flight across the face of the planet: mauve and mocha mountains, swirling methane seas and purple skies. But its surreal climax is a wholly inadequate response to the challenge it sets for itself, the revelation of a higher form of life than our own. When Dullea, as the surviving astronaut, climbs out of his space ship he finds it and himself in a Louis XVI hotel suite. Original? Not very. Ray Bradbury did it years ago in a story about men finding an Indiana town on Mars, complete with people singing "Moonlight on the Wabash."

It is a trap, in a sense, with the victim's own memories as bait. The nightmare continues, portentously, pretentiously, as Dullea discovers the room's sole inhabitant to be himself. As he breathes his last breath another slab stands watching at the foot of his deathbed, and when he dies he turns into a cute little embryo Adam, staring into space from his womb. So the end is but the beginning, the last shall be first, and so on and so forth. But what was the slab? That's for Kubrick and Clarke to know and us to find out. Maybe God, or pure intelligence, maybe a Jovian as we perceive him with our primitive eyes and ears. Maybe it was a Jovian undertaker. Maybe it was a nephew of the New York Hilton.

DISCUSSION QUESTIONS
SUGGESTIONS FOR WRITING

1. One major difference between the review and the critical essay is that the reviewer usually assumes the reader has not read the book or seen the movie, play, or whatever the review is about. The author of the critical essay usually assumes that the reader of the essay has read the book or seen the movie or whatever, and that the book, movie, or whatever is worthy of critical attention. The purpose of the critical essay, therefore, is to help us under-stand better something we have already experienced. The purpose of the review is to help us decide whether or not the experience we might be antici-pating is worth having, worth the time, worth spending our money on, etc. For this reason, the review usually states or implies a fairly explicit judg-ment of the work in question. What judgment does Morgenstern make about 2001? Is the movie, though flawed, worth seeing in his judgment?

2. One pitfall the reviewer must avoid is the tendency to give away too many of the situations or secrets of the work in question, so that the reader or viewer will be able to have a fresh experience. At the same time, however, the reviewer must describe what the experience consists of. A compromise is called for. Do you think Morgenstern makes a good compromise with the material of 2001, or does he tell too much?

3. What is the implication and effect of the end of the review, where the reviewer says of the mysterious slab in 2001 that: "maybe it was a nephew of the New York Hilton"?

4. Because of the subjective nature of the reviewing experience, the impossibility of the reviewer's providing empirical evidence to substantiate his claims about a work, the reviewer must resort to eloquence, satire, or invective to persuade his reader. Can you identify examples of these in the Morgenstern review?

HOLLIS ALPERT
(b. 1916) is motion picture
critic for *Saturday Review.*
The author of four novels,
a collection of essays *(The
Dreams and the Dreamer),*
and a biography *(The
Barrymores),* he has
taught at New York Uni-
versity and Pratt Institute.
In "The Graduate Makes
Out" he discusses the
manner in which the film
The Graduate represents
a new departure in "the
Hollywood scheme of
things."

THE GRADUATE MAKES OUT

FROM a window of my apartment I have a view of a movie house on Manhattan's East Side, where, ever since last December, *The Graduate* has attracted long lines of patrons. During some of the coldest winter weekends, the lines extended around the corner all the way down the block, much like those at the Radio City Music Hall during holiday periods—except that the people waiting for the next showing were not family groups but mostly young people in their teens and early twenties. One night when it was eight degrees outside I passed the line and noticed how little they seemed to be bothered by the weather; they stomped their feet, they made cheerful chatter; it was as though they all knew they were going to see something good, something made for *them.* There were other cinemas nearby, but no one waited outside in the cold. *The Graduate* was the film to see.

It still is, although now, with the warm weather, I notice that older people have begun to intermix with the young crowd. Either *The Graduate* has begun to reach deep into that amorphous audience that makes the large hits or the elders have become curious about the movie their offspring have been going to see again and again. For that is what has been happening. *The Graduate* is not merely a success; it has become a phenomenon of multiple attendance by young people.

Letters from youthful admirers of the movie have been pouring in on Dustin Hoffman, the talented thirty-year-old actor who plays the unprepossessing twenty-one-year-old Benjamin Braddock. A strong theme of identification with Benjamin's particular parental and societal hang-ups runs through these letters, as it also does in the letters to Mike Nichols, the director with an uncanny knack for forging hits. They've been writing to Joseph E. Levine, who backed and has been presenting the film. One boy from Dallas wrote Levine, bragging that he had seen *The Graduate* more than any of his friends, no less than fifteen times.

I have seen *The Graduate* three times—once at a preview, twice with audiences—thus satisfying, I hope, the Columbia graduate student who questioned my qualifications to assess the film after only one viewing. "But you must see it at *least* three times," she told me at a brunch given by her literature professor. "You see, it has meanings and nuances you don't get on just one viewing." She, and many others in her age group, cultishly attach all sorts of significance to the most minor of details. In the film's opening moments, for example, Benjamin is seen in the cabin of a huge jet, blank-faced among rows of blank faces. "Ladies and gentlemen," the captain's voice announces, "we are about to begin our descent into Los Angeles." My graduate student interpreted this as symbolic of Benjamin's arrival in purgatory. Close to the end of the film, Benjamin is seen in an antiseptic church, outlined against a glass partition, his arms spread out. Many have interpreted this as suggesting a crucifixion theme, an interpretation, I have it on good authority, that was far from the minds of Mr. Nichols and Mr. Hoffman.

Viewers have made much of the symbolic use of glass and water in the film, signifying Benjamin's inability to get through, to communicate with the generation that has produced him. He peers through the glass of a tank at captive fish. At poolside, and in the pool, he looks out at his parents and their friends through the glass mask of a diving suit. At other times it is through sunglasses that he sees a home environment grown somewhat strange. Surely, Benjamin is alienated, but what is so odd here is that the generation-gappers who love the film regard this sense of estrangement as natural and normal, given the times and the middle-class values espoused by Benjamin's family and friends.

Hollywood has made strenuous attempts to appeal to the young film audience in the past, from Andy Hardy to Elvis Presley. There have been bikini beach parties, rock-'n'-roll orgies, Annette Funicello, and Peter Fonda on LSD, but the coin taken in from these usually cheap and sleazy quickies has been but a pittance compared to the returns from *The Graduate*. I need cite only the fact that *The Graduate* has already taken in more than $35,000,000 at the box office, after playing in only 350 of this country's theaters. Marlon Brando, the revered James Dean, and Presley never came near doing that. But this film, without the so-called stars for security, has now done better, financially speaking, than all but a dozen films of the past, and it still has thousands of drive-ins to play throughout the summer; it has yet to open anywhere abroad; and there are still those lines in front of the theater I see through my window. It is quite possible that *The Graduate* will become one of the three or four most profitable pictures *ever* made, perhaps as profitable as *The Sound of Music*, which has done so sensationally well that some critics renamed it *The Sound of Money*.

But how can these two industry landmarks be equated? *The Graduate* would appear to be squarely attacking all that *The Sound of Music* affirms so prettily: sugary sentiment, the sanctity of vows, whether religious or marital, the righteous rearing of children, melody over the mountains. The one has the well-scrubbed Julie Andrews and a dozen or so cute kids, all of them singing the Rodgers and Hammerstein lush gush as though it were the equal of Handel's *Messiah*. The other has the appealing but unhandsome Dustin Hoffman, Anne Bancroft playing a dissatisfied, alcoholic bitch of a wife, and a musical score by Paul Simon (performed by Simon and Garfunkel) that, contrasted with *The Sound of Music*'s sentimental reverence, chants, "And the people bowed and prayed/To the neon god they made . . . " Yet a somewhat similar pattern of attendance has been noted about both films. The young audiences go to see *The Graduate* again and again. Housewives, matrons, women's clubbers went to see *The Sound of Music* again and again. We must hypothesize, then, that in this period of selective filmgoing there are at least two huge American audiences there for the right picture, one made up of the seventeens to the twenty-fives, the other of the over-thirty-fives. The Motion Picture Association now advertises its more adult fare as "suggested for mature audiences," but one wonders which is the more mature.

I have encountered some members of my generation—let us loosely call it the over-forties—who haven't liked *The Graduate*. More than that, it made them angry. It was almost as though they felt themselves personally attacked, and it has occurred to me that their reaction is less objective and critical than emotional and, possibly, subliminal. These friends do worry about their children, they have brought them up well, given them opportunities of education and aesthetic development, and they are quite certain they have managed to establish communication with their young. Their wives don't drink or seduce the neighbor's son. What's all this business about honesty and truth in *The Graduate*? The cards have been stacked against the middle-class parent and in favor of the rebellious "now" generation. They darkly hint at the commercial motives of Levine, Nichols, and company, who, it's true, hoped to come through at the box office, but had not the faintest notion they would come through so handsomely.

But *The Graduate* was not meant as an attack on a generation; it merely tells a *story*, as effectively as the makers knew how to do it. To understand the story it is necessary, however, to understand that Benjamin Braddock belongs to a milieu that has been termed the affluent society. He has never known financial insecurity—he has grown up among gadgets, among cars and swimming pools—and this he has taken so much for granted that it literally has no meaning for him. His parents, on the other hand, have presumably known hard times; they know the value, for them, of money, of material success, of things. When Benjamin comes of age, literally and symbolically, he finds himself vaguely rejecting all that his parents hold so dear. He finds himself a kind of object, the proud result of proper rearing, a reward of his parents' struggle in his behalf. Somehow, he feels, this is wrong, but he doesn't yet know what is right. What guides and counselors does he have? "Ben, I want to say one word to you, just one word," a friend of the family breathes in his ear at a welcome-home party. Benjamin awaits the word, among clinking glasses holding machine-made ice and good bourbon and Scotch. "Plastics," the fellow says, imparting the great secret to success in our time. "There is a great future in plastics." The young audiences howl, at least they did when I was there, and they're on the side of Benjamin and the movie, which pokes fun at the plastic society and those who believe in it.

It is also interesting that while Benjamin tunes out for a while, he doesn't turn on. He neither joins nor identifies with the hippies, the yippies, or the weirdies; he is still thoroughly middle-class, affluent variety. As he lazes purposelessly in the California sun his thoughts turn heavily to those of sex with Mrs. Robinson, whose frustrating marriage has borne her only one good result, her lovely daughter, Elaine. Elaine will soon have the benefits of her young womanhood, while the mother will sink into her bitter middle age. Unconscious envy on Mrs. Robinson's part turns into willful determination, and she reveals herself in her nudity to Benjamin's unwilling gaze. He first runs from her as from the very devil; after all, there are the proprieties, not to mention the taboos.

But then he backs into the affair with Mrs. Robinson, who uses him for the sex she doesn't get from Mr. Robinson. In only one moment does she allow Benjamin to reach her; their intimacy is, literally, skin deep. When Benjamin stupidly assumes that affection is necessary in a furtive affair, the surprised Mrs. Robinson expels cigarette smoke into his mouth. She too is aware of and insistent on the taboos; Benjamin is never, ever to take Elaine out, for she assumes that by her actions she has cheapened both Benjamin and herself.

And, of course, he does, forced into it by his unaware parents. Some critics have felt that the film breaks in two around this point, that the first half is a "seriocomedy" and the second a kind of campus romance with a chase finale. But this criticism seems to overlook the unifying fact of its all being viewed and experienced through Benjamin, who is in a process of muddle, change, and development. He is a truth-seeker, trying to cut through to some acceptable level of meaning. He even tells the truth to the outraged Mr. Robinson about the affair with Mrs. Robinson: "We got into bed with each other. But it was nothing. It was nothing at all. We might—we might just as well have been shaking hands."

One of the great appeals of the film to the young, and to the young in heart of all ages, is Benjamin's honesty. The most important thing in common between Elaine and Benjamin is that they share the urge to see honestly and clearly. But Elaine's emotions are still unstable. She allows herself to be rushed into a hasty, secret marriage with an available suitor, appropriately enough a medical student, a candidate for surgeondom.

It is the ending of the film that has annoyed some, and delighted many others. If it were not for the ending, I doubt that *The Graduate* would have aroused as much enthusiastic favor as it has among the somewhat inchoately rebellious young. The distraught Benjamin, madly seeking his lost Elaine—the pure, the good, the holy—manages to reach the church, but not (as is invariably the case in a Doris Day movie) in time, upon which his hoarse, despairing appeal causes Elaine to leave her newly wedded groom and the assembled relatives, and to take a bus to nowhere in particular with Benjamin. To hold off the outraged parents, the attendants, and the minister, Benjamin grabs a large golden cross and swings it menacingly, then uses it as a makeshift padlock on the church doors.

Curiously enough, the writer of the novel on which the film is based, Charles Webb, who was not much more than Benjamin's age at the time of writing, had fashioned a different ending—not *very* different, but crucial nevertheless. Benjamin, in the book, did arrive at the church in time, and there was no further "moral transgression" on his part involved, except, perhaps, for that bit of crosswielding. It turns out that Mr. Webb was disturbed by the changed ending. He wrote a letter to *The New Republic*, complaining about critic Stanley Kauffmann's laudatory interpretation of the film, and particularly by what Kauffmann had approvingly termed the "film's moral stance." "As a moral person," Webb wrote, "he [Benjamin] does not disrespect the institution of marriage. In the book the strength of the climax is that his moral attitudes make it necessary for him to reach the girl before she becomes the wife of somebody else, which he does. In the film version it makes no difference whether he gets there in time or not. As such, there is little difference between his relationship to Mrs. Robinson and his relationship to Elaine, both of them being essentially immoral."

However, it does make a great deal of difference that in the film he does not get there in time, and the audiences have taken delight in just that fact. This film-bred, film-loving generation has seen that the ending is aimed, in a double-barreled kind of way, at what might be called general moral complacency in America, and also at Hollywood morality, which, from time immemorial, has felt it necessary to approve only the sexual love that occurs during the state of marriage, and that, up until only a decade ago, took place in twin beds, with at least one foot of the man on the floor.

Not only does Mr. Webb, in his letter, equate morality with marriage licenses, he overlooks the fact that even in his novel Elaine would already have taken out a marriage license by the time Benjamin reached her. And there is a thing called consummation. The Nichols ending (relatively little story tampering was done otherwise) is a bold stroke that not only is effective but gives the story more meaning. We now see clearly Mrs. Robinson's tragedy, that she was unable to break out of the hollow formality, the prosperous smothering surface of her own marriage. "It's too late," she screams at her daughter, who is about to head for Benjamin. Upon which Elaine, seeing it all clearly for the first time, screams triumphantly back, "Not for *me*."

But if that old Production Code has been forsaken, if Doris Day has at last been soundly spanked for her virginal sins, hasn't morality triumphed after all? Of course it has. Mike Nichols, perhaps without fully realizing it, has lined up old Hollywood with avant-garde Hollywood. He has contrived a truly moral ending, and a most positive one at that. Honesty wins the day. Sex without love has been put in its place. Ancient taboos have been struck down. Material values have been shown to be hollow. As uninhibited and refreshing as *The Graduate* is, we are still left in fantasy land. "Most of us," a friend of mine ruefully commented, "still miss the bus."

On the other hand, perhaps the reason this newly mature generation has taken so to *The Graduate* is that it thinks, assumes, imagines it can make the bus. Mike Nichols told of meeting, recently, one of the leaders of the Columbia University rebellion. The student had loved *The Graduate*, as had his associates in rebellion. "In a way," he told Nichols, "it was what the strike was all about. Those kids had the nerve, they felt the necessity, to break the rules."

The Graduate represents a breakthrough of sorts in the Hollywood scheme of things, aside from its fine acting, its technical accomplishment, its vastly entertaining qualities. For it has taken aim, satirically, at the very establishment that produces most of our movies, mocked the morals and values it has long lived by. It is a final irony that it has thereby gained the large young audience it has been seeking and has been rewarded by a shower of gold.

DISCUSSION QUESTIONS
SUGGESTIONS FOR WRITING

1. What is Alpert's argument in favor of the "*truly moral ending*" that he believes Mike Nichols forged for The Graduate, *which Alpert believes is in large part responsible for the success of the film?*

2. Why does Alpert see "*a final irony*" in the fact that through The

Graduate *"the establishment" has gained a large young audience and "been rewarded by a shower of gold"?*

3. *Of what technical significance is the fact that at the beginning of the essay the reviewer comments on seeing—* through his apartment window *— long lines of patrons going to see* The Graduate?

4. *Alpert states that he has it "on good authority"—presumably from Mike Nichols and Dustin Hoffman—that no crucifixion theme was intended in the film. Alpert implies that many of the other attempts at symbolic interpretation of the film are excessive. Does the fact, if it is a fact, that the film-makers did not consciously intend to create such symbolic levels in the film prove conclusively that no such symbolic levels exist in it?*

HENTOFF

SOUL, ROCK'N'ROLL, AND ALL THAT JAZZ

NAT HENTOFF (b. 1925) has served as the New York editor of *Downbeat* and as a staff writer for *The New Yorker*. He has published widely, especially on the subjects of music, civil rights, and poverty, in such magazines as *Commonweal*, *The Reporter*, and *Playboy*. His books include *The Jazz Makers*, *The Jazz Life*, *The New Equality*, *Jazz Country*, *Call the Keeper*, and *Our Children Are Dying*.

WE were waiting for Elvis on a midsummer night in 1969 in Las Vegas' thrustingly new International Hotel. He had chosen this place and this time for his first appearance before a live audience in nine years. So much had happened in music since 1960, and so much more had changed since he initially emerged from Memphis in the mid-1950s as a hip-swiveling, "Hound Dog"-shouting force of nature—an outrage to the old and a source of delightful contagion for the young. We wondered if he would come intact out of the past, a museum piece with no connection to the swirling musical changes which have brought us to the present.

The lights went down, and we didn't wonder long. He came on strong —still a *presence*. More lithe now, with the tensile grace of an Indian, he had lost none of the fierce energy of the old Elvis. But there *were* changes—musical changes. The vocal group backing him was black: the Sweet Inspirations, four crisp girls whose roots are in gospel music. There was also a white, hard-driving rock combo, powered by a Texas drummer, Ronnie Tutt, laying down a walloping beat that reached into your body. And though the songs were partly of the past—the leaping "Hound Dog" and the groaning "Heartbreak Hotel"—there were also Beatles tunes, "Yesterday" and "Hey Jude"; a rhythm-and-blues Ray Charles classic, "What'd I Say"; and a new evocation of what the sociologists call "the inner city," "In the Ghetto."

Watching and listening to Elvis that night was like being in a highly animated kaleidoscope of the radical changes in popular music during the last twenty years. The easy fusion—behind his rocking body—of the white country boys and the Sweet Inspirations. ("They give me my soul," Elvis said in explaining why he'd asked for them to be part of his accompaniment.) And there was also the boundary-crossing diversity of his songs, music created by wanderers from Liverpool and from the white and black South.

By contrast, Americans of earlier generations had grown up within clearly divided sectors of popular music. For young whites in the South and Southwest there had been hillbilly music, sometimes called "country," an amiable mixture of old folk ballads, mountain dance tunes, fundamentalist hymns, and comic turns out of traveling medicine shows. Farther west—and feeding the fantasies of some white youngsters in the East—were tangy Western hollers and laments from the heritage of the cowboys and other frontiersmen. Black youngsters were nurtured by their own rich tradition of Afro-American music with rural blues taking on sharper city rhythms as more and more black people moved off the land. Meanwhile, the more sophisticated black players and listeners turned to jazz, which built on the blues a lineage of subtle shadings and prodigious instrumental virtuosity.

Other youngsters—the majority—with no strong regional or ethnic identifications, listened to Broadway and movie hits played by smooth dance bands and sung by show-wise vocalists. There was, of course, some crossing of the boundaries. A minority of white youngsters cherished black blues and jazz, and black kids as well as Appalachian children went to the movies, too. But the kind of repertory and personnel that Elvis Presley put together at the International Hotel . . . would have been inconceivable in the 1930s. The country was too divided then musically. It still is divided—but not musically.

The first clear signs of change appeared in the early 1950s. Young whites in all parts of the country were moving to different rhythms than even their immediate elders. Wanting, needing a strong beat to dance to, they turned to black rhythm-and-blues groups—the Penguins, the Flamingos, the Orioles, the Chords. Such white musicians as Bill Haley, sensing the winds of change and fortune, began to "cover" the record hits of the rhythm-and-blues combos, and the first primitive "rock" was born—white imitations of the black drive. The beat was heavy and the volume high, but early rock lacked the resiliency and the mocking wit of the originals.

Elvis Presley, however, was different—not only because of the unabashed, sinuous sensuality he projected but also because of the singular mixture in him of so much of the American musical tradition. A truck driver, he had been drawn to deep-country blues by black singers (like Big Boy Crudup) as well as to white-country textures and rhythms. But he was also a city boy, and absorbed rhythm and blues and some jazz. At first attention was focused on the way he moved ("Elvis the Pelvis"), but his black-and-white sound kept getting through, and American pop music was never to be the same.

For the rest of the 1950s white kids throughout the country increasingly found their satisfaction in black singers — Chuck Berry, Little Richard, Fats Domino, Ray Charles — and in those white singers who, like Presley, were creating a fusion of all kinds of influences. Listening, for example, to Carl Perkins, the Everly Brothers, and Buddy Holly, they were getting down into themselves. There was no longer any place on the hit charts for Richard Rodgers, Cole Porter, and those other urbane spinners of fox trots and waltzes which had no connection with the restlessness and rebelliousness of a new generation for whom television and the transistor radio had made the whole world, let alone just this one country, a global village. Growing up, moreover, under the bomb and packed into schools where conformity and competition were the oppressive norm, they needed music in which they could let go. And that's what the new music was all about — *feeling*. By coming together in liberation, if only in music, a surging youth culture — through music — was rapidly developing.

Instead of relying on men of another generation in New York and Hollywood to write their songs for them, the new combos and singers made their own, and anything that moved them was included. The credo was and is that of Larry Coryell, a young guitarist who moves easily between rock and jazz groups: "If music has something to say to you — whether it's jazz, country blues, hillbilly, Indian, or other folk music — take it. Never restrict yourself."

The way was open by the early 1960s for two new liberating forces — Bob Dylan and the Beatles. Dylan, from a small town in Minnesota, had never restricted himself. As a boy he was fascinated by the American folk tradition, ranging from black bluesman Big Joe Williams to the wry, persistently outspoken Oklahoman Woody Guthrie. Coming East, Dylan soon forged his own style, though the many-colored roots were clear; and while he wrote ballads that would not have been unfamiliar in mood and cadence to Kentucky settlers of a century ago, he also became a spokesman for the alliance of the young against forces they felt quite literally threatened their lives. This was the Dylan of "Masters of War" and "The Times They Are A-Changin'." Later, the Jefferson Airplane was to declare the same sense of solidarity: "In loyalty to their kind they cannot tolerate our minds, and in loyalty to our kind we cannot tolerate their obstruction."

In England, meanwhile, contemporaries of Dylan were also finding generational identity in music. But like Dylan, they, too, first dug for roots, for open springs of emotion. While still in Liverpool, the Beatles had been listening to black American music, from old blues singers up to Chuck Berry, as well as to Presley and other white singers of the

1950s who would not let themselves be restricted. Gradually, however, the Beatles were finding out who *they* were, and in the albums *Rubber Soul* (1965) and *Revolver* (1966) they broke through into new, more flexible musical forms as they explored unprecedentedly fresh and evocative nuances of feeling and imagery. In the process they started to experiment with electronics, and also introduced the Indian sitar in several numbers to get exactly the mood they wanted.

It was *Sgt. Pepper's Lonely Hearts Club Band* (1967) which opened up startlingly new possibilities of expression for the Beatles and for scores of American groups. The Beatles had been loosely described as rock performers, but by contrast with the lumpish repetitiveness of Bill Haley's rock ten years before, the *Sgt. Pepper* album was music of a distinctly advanced and venturesome order. It was a celebration of the unexpected, an affirmation of irrepressible possibility. Their first album had been recorded in a day; this one took more than three months, with four to six sessions a week. Technically, they were now masters of the increasingly consciousness-expanding recording equipment itself. There were multiple tracks (layers of over-dubbing) in which percussion, strings, Indian instruments, and other seemingly diverse elements combined into a whirling trip into inner space. On another track, John Lennon on Hammond organ was recorded at different speeds and then overlaid with electronic echoes. But in addition to the technological breakthrough, the music *said* much more than before. So much that listeners found new overtones of meaning with each playing of "A Day in the Life" or "Lucy in the Sky with Diamonds."

Rock had become "art," and for a while the consequence was pretentious chaos. Lured over their heads by *Sgt. Pepper*, many young groups became so fixated on electronic devices that their music was sound without content, a grotesque reflection of the empty technology of the larger society to which they were purportedly opposed. There were lyrics, and they professed to hint at cosmic insights, but the words splintered under close listening, as did the rest of the music. Bob Dylan, unwittingly, had also become an influence on this rush of rock to become fake art. Abandoning the song of social protest, and himself adding electrified accompanying instruments, he was now into eerily expressionistic music, as in the influential album *Blonde on Blonde*. These were pictures, sometimes nightmarish, from a gallery in which the walls were constantly moving as colors and meanings changed before your eyes. It took a composer-lyricist of Dylan's organic originality and unbridled imagination to make these seemingly bizarre journeys meaningful to the initially displaced listener. But the throng of imitation Dylans who subsequently tried to turn free-association scribbling into music were stupefyingly boring. It seemed for a time that the new music was dying prematurely of a ponderous self-consciousness that had removed the very soul of rock — the direct release of emotion, the crackling energy of youth making music to groove with.

[By the early seventies,] however, the emphasis on "art" and "philosophy" happily diminished, and rock was at a natural high again. It is now more diversified than ever before, but it is also much more secure in its intentions and in its satisfactions. What happened was a re-emphasis by players and listeners on roots. After a long period of not recording, Bob Dylan ended his silence with the spare, elemental *John Wesley Harding*, and the even warmer, more basic *Nashville Skyline*. Both signaled a return by Dylan to the ease of country music and to songs that were clear and mellowly personal. Nashville, where the home-grown musicians play "clear as country water," has become a center of revivified popular music. Dylan has recorded there, as have Joan Baez (*David's Album*) and many other performers who have tired of continually straining to be avant-garde. . . .

Simultaneously, country folk themselves have been widening their audiences among the young in all parts of the nation — Glen Campbell, Buck Owens, and, preeminently, Johnny Cash. Part Indian, craggily independent, Cash is the very personification in music of the free-wheeling nonorganization man whose most acutely contemporary manifestation in American myth is the film *Easy Rider*. He professes not to like hippies, but Bob Dylan is a good friend, and I expect the end of *Easy Rider* would move Cash as quickly to shocked rage as it does the throngs of young people who line up to see it — among them, many of Johnny Cash's listeners.

Cash does understand why the country style reaches the young and has transformed many rock groups. "People," he says, "go back to it to find the basic thing, the grass roots. My songs appeal because they have true human emotions as well as being real stories."

Other rock units, however, have now turned to a second source of true human emotions and real stories — the blues. Though white, they try to find a connection between themselves and the black language. So far they have succeeded more as instrumentalists than as vocalists — British guitarist Eric Clapton, for instance, the onetime anchor man of Cream and . . . of Blind Faith. As in other areas, there are hordes of these blues-circuit riders with swiftly changing names. . . .

White blues rockers have simultaneously widened the audience for the real thing — those hard-dues-paying black singers and players who worked for years almost entirely for black audiences. But now all of young America knows their names — men like Muddy Waters, B. B. King, Albert King, and Howlin' Wolf. Theirs is the essence of "soul" music, along with the whiplike drive and the searing sound of such younger black performers as Aretha Franklin and Ike & Tina Turner. This newer black stream is a hurtling combination of old blues, gospel, and the rhythm and blues of the cities.

Less visible, at present, is a third music force — jazz. Never overwhelmingly popular in the sense that *huge* audiences ever supported it, jazz nevertheless used to command a broader section of the young than it does now. The reason for its temporary eclipse is that its quintessence — the pulsating beat and the full-strength emotions — has now pervaded *all* of rock music. But such jazz innovators as Cecil Taylor and Ornette Coleman continue to expand its dimensions; and as black cultural consciousness grows among young blacks, a renaissance of interest in jazz is inevitable. Although it will be black audiences who will be the main support of jazz in the decade ahead, there are already indications that young white rock musicians, and part of their audience, are beginning to turn more to jazz as their developing musical sophistication requires the kind of challenge that this force demands. . . .

Feeling, getting it all out, remains the touchstone of the best of the new music. "To be the real thing," says Peter Townshend of The Who, a British group which . . . created the first authentic rock opera, "a song has to have that undulating rhythm, and, most important, it has to have crammed into it all the poignancy and excitement of youth, because that's what it's really all about. . . ."

That is the core of the new music — it has unlocked the emotions of a whole generation, and of those older listeners who ride with it rather than trying to dissect it. And being free to feel in this music, its players and listeners are unprecedentedly open to all kinds of sounds and life styles. There has never been so releasing a musical phenomenon . . . a music in which so many participate themselves. Across the country there are at least 300,000 rock bands. And the millions more who listen and buy the records have found in this music a way of coming together, a conduit of warmth and humanity at a time of escalating nuclear armament which may deny this generation a future. When more than 300,000 young people gathered in Bethel, New York, . . . for four days of music in mud and rain, the rest of the country marveled that there had been no violence at all. One youngster who had gone two days without sleep grinned: "It's great the way people treated each other. But then, it shouldn't have been a surprise. We were all together . . . the music was together." I don't think, therefore, that Donal Henahan, a classical-music critic for the New York *Times*, was speaking entirely as a musicologist when he said that rock is "the most pervasive and perhaps most historically significant musical idiom of the century to date."

And what of the future? "Communication is getting so good," says Jerry Garcia of the Grateful Dead, "so much music is available on records, and it's so easy to hear anything you want to hear that in another twenty years every musician in the world will be able to sit in with every other musician in the world with no problems at all."

For young listeners rock is already a world music — in Japan, Cuba, wherever there are transistor radios . . . and that *is* everywhere. Gabor Szabo, a Hungarian jazz guitarist who came to America after the 1956 rebellion in his country was smashed, has been moving into rock more and more in the past few years. "This is a really new music," he emphasizes. "The whole world seems to be coming together. Oh, not politically, but in this music. We all used to have our cozy little nests . . . we were Americans and Hungarians, each sticking to our own heritage. But in this music so much of that has gone now. We are now just World, Earth, and the new music definitely reflects this."

The new music has broken all the sound barriers. It has become a common language of affirmation, of how to treat one another. The rest of the world, out there when the music stops, has a long way to catch up.

DISCUSSION QUESTIONS
SUGGESTIONS FOR WRITING

1. What are the central ideas in this selection? What is the organizing principle of the essay?

2. What is the historical connection that Hentoff sees between the growth of the new music and the "surging youth culture"?

3. With the appearance of what important album, in Hentoff's judgment, did rock become "art"? What evidence is presented to substantiate this claim?

4. Notice the manner in which the essay opens — in the same manner, for example, as Tom Wolfe's "O Rotten Gotham." A scene is unfolding. There is immediate dramatic interest, as in a good short story. How does the writer move then from the scenic beginning to the information he wishes to impart? Point out the transition. Practice using the same techniques in an essay of your own.

HUNTER DAVIES
(b. 1936) is a staff writer
for the *Sunday Times* of
London. He is the author
of *The New London Spy,
Here We Go Round the
Mulberry Bush* (novel and
screenplay), and *The
Other Half.* His is the "authorized" biography of the
Beatles from which "noth-
ing is held back."

PAUL
AND
THE QUARRYMEN

A S a child Paul showed no particular interest in music. Both he and his
brother Michael were sent once for a couple of piano lessons, but
nothing happened. "We made the mistake of starting them in the
summer," says Jim. "The teacher used to come to the house and all the
kids would be knocking at our door all the time, wanting them to come
out and play. So I made them go to the teacher's house, but that didn't
last long." Jim also wanted Paul to join Liverpool Cathedral choir.
"I made him go, but he deliberately cracked his voice in the audition.
Later on he did join St. Chad's Choir, near Penny Lane, for a while."

Later still Paul was given an old trumpet by an uncle, on which he
managed to pick out tunes, teaching himself. This talent for picking up
music came from his father. As a boy Jim had taught himself to play the
piano. Of all the Beatles' fathers, Paul's was the only one with any experience of being a musician. . . .

When the Second World War came, and a family, Jim packed in his
playing career, although he often played a bit on the piano at home.
"Paul was never interested when I played the piano. But he loved listening to music on his earphones in bed. Then suddenly he wanted a guitar,
when he was fourteen. I didn't know what made him want it."

His guitar cost £15 and Paul couldn't get anything out of it at first.
There seemed to be something wrong with it. Then he realized it was
because he was left-handed. He took it back and got it altered. "I'd never
been really keen on the trumpet. But I liked the guitar because I could
play it after just learning a few chords. I could also sing to it at the same
time."

He'd followed pop music since he was about twelve, like most of his
friends. The first concert he went to was Eric Delaney's Band's at the

Liverpool Empire when he was twelve. At fourteen he queued up in his lunch hour from school to see Lonnie Donegan. "I remember he was late arriving. He wrote out little notes for the factory girls explaining it was his fault they were late back as he'd kept them waiting. We used to hang around the stage door waiting for anybody and get their autographs. I once queued up for Wee Willie Harriss's autograph."

He also went to the Pavilion. "That was where they had the nude shows. They would strip off absolutely starkers. Some of them were all right as well. It was funny, letting us in at that age. But it was just good clean dirty fun."

Like John and the others, Paul was influenced by the skiffle phase and Bill Haley's early rock numbers, but, like John again, not until Elvis Presley was he really bowled over. "That was the biggest kick. Every time I felt low I just put on an Elvis and I'd feel great, beautiful. I'd no idea how records were made and it was just magic. 'All Shook Up'! Oh, it was beautiful!" When he got his guitar, he tried to play Elvis numbers or whatever else was popular. His best impersonation was of Little Richard.

"I used to think it was awful," says his father. "Absolutely terrible. I couldn't believe anybody was really like that. It wasn't till years later, when I saw Little Richard on the same bill as the Beatles, that I realized how good Paul's impersonation was."

"The minute he got the guitar, that was the end," says Michael. "He was lost. He didn't have time to eat or think about anything else. He played it on the lavatory, in the bath, everywhere."

There was another friend from his class, Ian James, from the Dingle, who also got a guitar about the same time. He and Paul used to go around together, with their guitars. They played to each other, teaching each other bits they'd learned. "We used to go round the fairs," says Paul. "Listening to the latest tunes on the Waltzer and trying to pick them up. We also tried to pick up birds. That never worked. I haven't got the flair for picking them up like that." Both Paul and Ian James wore the same sort of white sports jackets, after the pop song "A White Sports Coat." "It had speckles in it and flaps over the pockets. We used to have black drainies as well. We used to go around everywhere together dressed the same and think we were really flash. We both had Tony Curtis haircuts. It took us hours to get it right."

Jim McCartney tried to stop Paul dressing the way he did, but didn't get very far. "Paul was very clever," says Michael. "When he bought a new pair of trousers, he'd bring them home for Dad to see how wide they were and he would say okay. Then he would take them back and get them altered. If Dad noticed afterwards, he'd swear blind they were what he'd agreed."

"I was very worried he'd turn out a Teddy boy," says Jim. "I had a dread of that. I said over and over again that he wasn't going to have tight trousers. But he just wore me down. His hair was always long as well, even then. He'd come back from the barber's and it would just look the same and I'd say, 'Were it closed, then?' "

Paul was just as interested in girls as the guitar. "I got it for the first time at fifteen. I suppose that was a bit early to get it. I was about the first in my class. She was older and bigger than me. It was at her house. She was supposed to be baby-sitting while her mum was out. I told everybody at school next day, of course. I was a real squealer."

Paul remembers vividly that day in the summer of 1956 when Ivan mentioned that he was going to Woolton Parish Church to see this group he sometimes played with, though he wasn't actually playing with them that day. Paul said yes, he'd come along and see them. Might be a few girls to pick up.

"They weren't bad," says Paul. "John played the lead guitar. But he played it like a banjo, with banjo chords, as that was all he knew. None of the others had even as much idea as John how to play. They were mostly just strumming along. They played things like 'Maggie May,' but with the words a bit different. John had done them up himself as he didn't know them all.

"They were playing outdoors in a big field. John was staring round as he was playing, watching everybody. He told me afterwards that it was the first time he tried sussing an audience — you know, sizing them, seeing whether it was best to twist a shoulder at them or best not to move at all. I was in my white sports coat and black drainies, as usual. I'd just got them narrowed again during the dinner hour from school. They were so narrow they knocked everybody out.

"I went round to see them afterwards in the church hall place. I talked to them, just chatting and showing off. I showed them how to play 'Twenty Flight Rock' and told them all the words. They didn't know it. Then I did 'Bee Bop a Loo,' which they didn't know properly either. Then I did my Little Richard bit, went through me whole repertoire in fact. I remember this beery old man getting nearer and breathing down me neck as I was playing. 'What's this old drunk doing?' I thought. Then he said 'Twenty Flight Rock' was one of his favorites. So I knew he was a connoisseur.

"It was John. He'd just had a few beers. He was sixteen and I was only fourteen, so he was a big man. I showed him a few more chords he didn't know. Ian James had taught me them really. Then I left. I felt I'd made an impression, shown them how good I was." Pete Shotton, however, doesn't recall Paul making any big impression. Pete, being completely unmusical, was a bit harder to impress by "Twenty Flight Rock," however brilliantly executed.

"I didn't really take in Paul that first meeting," says Pete. "He seemed very quiet, but you do when you meet a group of new blokes for the first time. I wasn't really jealous of him, not at first. He was so much younger than us. I didn't think he was going to be a rival. Me and John were still the closest pals. I was always John's friend. 'Cos I loved him, that's why."

"About a week later Paul went over to Menlove Avenue on his bike to see Ivan. He cycled up through the golf course from Allerton. On the way back he met Pete Shotton. Pete said they'd been talking about me. Did I want to join their group? I said okay, right."

John remembers mulling over the meeting with Paul in his mind afterward, before he decided on anything. It was unusual for him to think things out instead of barging on with whatever he wanted. "I was pissed that day," says John. "So I probably wasn't all that clued up. I was very impressed by Paul playing 'Twenty Flight Rock.' He could obviously play the guitar. I half thought to myself 'He's as good as me.' I'd been kingpin up to then. Now, I thought, if I take him on, what will happen? It went through my head that I'd have to keep him in line if I let him join. But he was good, so he was worth having. He also looked like Elvis. I dug him."

Paul's first public performance as a member of the Quarrymen was at a dance at the Conservative Club in Broadway. Paul was going to do his own little solo bit that evening, probably "Twenty Flight Rock," but something happened and he didn't.

But later on, after the dance, he played for John a couple of tunes he had written himself. Since he'd started playing the guitar, he had tried to make up a few of his own little tunes. The first tune he played to John that evening was called "I Lost My Little Girl." Not to be outdone, John immediately started making up his own tunes. He had been elaborating and adapting other people's words and tunes to his own devices for some time, but he hadn't written down proper tunes till Paul appeared with his. Not that Paul's tunes meant much—nor John's. They were very simple and derivative. It was only them coming together, each egging the other on, that suddenly inspired them to write songs for themselves to play. From that day they never stopped.

"I went off in a completely new direction from then on," says Paul. "Once I got to know John it all changed. He was good to know. Even though he was two years older than me and I was just a baby, we thought the same sort of things."

What happened in the subsequent months was that John and Paul got to know each other. They spent all their time together. They both stayed away from school and went to Paul's house, while his dad was out at work, and ate fried eggs and practiced guitar chords. Paul showed John all the ones he knew. John's banjo chords, taught him by Julia, were obviously useless. As Paul is left-handed, after he had shown John what to do, John had to go home and do it in the mirror on his own, then get it the right way round.

Pete Shotton began to feel a bit out of it. "My days with the group soon came to an end," says Pete. "We were playing at someone's party in Smithdown Lane. It was a right pissup really. John and I got hilarious, laughing like mad at each other's jokes. Then he broke my washboard over my head. I lay there, in tears, with it framed round my neck. That was the end of me with the Quarrymen. It wasn't the life for me any more, playing in a group. Apart from feeling no good, I didn't like standing up there. I was too embarrassed."

Ivan Vaughan had long since left the group, though he was still a friend of John's at home and of Paul's at school. Paul began to think more and more of the possibility of another great friend of his from his school joining the group. He had taken up skiffle and rock and Elvis about the same time, but was coming on even better than most people at the guitar. He thought he would bring him along to see John. He was even younger than Paul, but he didn't think that would matter, he was so good.

Ivan Vaughan was annoyed when he did. Ivan had taken along first of all Len Garry and then Paul McCartney from the Institute to meet John. He looked upon the procuring as his prerogative. He didn't like the idea of Paul taking someone else along. This new friend was not just much younger, but he didn't even make any pretense at being an intellectual, the way Paul did. George Harrison, as the friend was called, was a real out-and-out Teddy boy. Ivan couldn't understand why the Quarrymen should be interested in him.

DISCUSSION QUESTIONS
SUGGESTIONS FOR WRITING

1. The biographer's task is to recreate a flesh-and-blood human being, one who reveals himself through his actions and words. What differences are there between the biographer's task of characterization and the novelist's?

2. A relevant distinction is the difference between factual biography and fictional biography. In factual biography, the dominant type, the biographer limits himself in what he says about his subject to verifiable "facts," to the letters, autobiography, reminiscences of the subject or of those who knew the subject, etc. In fictional biography, the writer frequently invents, out of his knowledge of the subject, dramatic details that would be impossible to document. Which type of biography is Hunter Davies' The Beatles?

3. Some critics believe that biographers should adopt an impersonal and objective point of view (usually referred to as "distance") toward their subjects, permitting the reader to draw his conclusions from the selected detail. Does Davies do this? Compare the Davies selection with the Baez, "Smith," and Berrigan selections. Which has the most "distance"?

4. Though this biography was written before the Beatles split up as a group, are there any indications in this section of possible friction or personality conflicts even at this stage that may have led to the split?

OATES

THE NATURE OF SHORT FICTION

In this selection Joyce Carol Oates discusses the nature of art as well as some of the reasons why writers write.

Why do you write?

It is sometimes another writer who asks this question of me, and therefore a serious, even doomed person, but most of the time it is a man twice my size who has found himself seated next to me at dinner and can't think of anything else to say. *Why do you write?* he says, though I don't ask him *Why do you work so hard?* or *Why do you dream?* I don't even ask him *Why must you ask that question?* When I am being polite my mind goes blank, and at such times I am most feminine; I usually reply, *Because I enjoy writing.* It is a harmless answer, and perfectly correct; it satisfies the kind of bullies who are always bothering me (on the average of once a week this past year) with questions designed to 1) suggest the writer's general inability to cope with the real world 2) suggest the questioner's superiority because *he,* certainly, need not resort to fantasy in order to survive.

Why do you write?

A fascinating question. Though I never explain or defend myself in public, in private I am obsessed with the motives behind writing or behind any kind of artistic creation. I am obsessed with the deeps of the mind, of the imagination, particularly of the semi-conscious imagination, which throws up to us bizarre and lovely surprises daily and nightly —I am not so different from the skeptic who asks me sardonically why I write, for he too "writes," he creates, he dreams every night and perhaps during the day, and his dreams are legitimate artistic creations.

We write for the same reasons we dream—because we cannot not dream, because it is in the nature of the human imagination to dream. Those of us who "write," who consciously arrange and re-arrange reality for the purposes of exploring its hidden meanings, are more serious dreamers, perhaps we are addicted to dreaming, but never because we fear or despise reality—as Flannery O'Connor said (in her excellent book of posthumously-collected essays *Mystery and Manners*) writing is not an escape from reality, "it is a plunge into reality and it's very shocking to the system." She insists that the writer is a person who has hope in the world; people without hope do not write.

We write in order to give a more coherent, abbreviated form to the world, which is often confusing and terrifying and stupid as it unfolds about us. How to manage this blizzard of days, of moments, of years? The world has no meaning; I am sadly resigned to this fact. But the world has meanings, many individual and alarming and graspable meanings, and the adventure of being human consists in seeking out these meanings. We want to figure out as much of life as we can. We are not very different from scientists, our notorious enemies, who want also to figure things out, to make life more coherent, to set something in order and then go on to something else, erasing mysteries. We write in order to single out meanings from the great confusion of the time, or of our lives: we write because we are convinced that meaning exists and we want to fix it in place.

"Art hallucinates Ego mastery," says Freud, who was as concerned with the mysterious symbolic (and therefore artistic) dimension of the mind as anyone who ever lived. This sentence amazes me. Everything is in it, everything is there. Art "hallucinates" as a dream; it is a dream made conscious and brought into the daylight, occasionally published in hard-cover and no doubt over-priced. If it is a really marketable dream it will be sold to the movies, that marvelous modern art-form that simulates our dreams for us, moving flatly across a screen in the dark, exaggerating images, faces, gestures, wonderfully suited for the conveyance of all kinds of nightmares. . . . If it is a not especially marketable dream it may never be published but, like most of human attempts, it will lie in some out-of-the-way place, harmless and ignored but still valuable. No dream is without value. It is a "hallucination" and all hallucinations, like all visions, are of inestimable value.

We must be true to our dreams, Kafka wrote.

When people "begin" writing (though the notion of "beginning" to write is odd to me, like "beginning" to breathe) they are buoyed up by energy, the sense that they have something unique to say and that only they can say it. This energy, this mysterious conviction, is the basis of all art. But, in entering a craft that appears from the outside to be so formalized, so professional, perhaps even in 1969 so decadent, they are soon terrorized by the fear of not being technically proficient. Therefore they attend writers' conferences. They take courses in Creative Writing. They buy books to instruct them in the "nature of fiction." And none of these activities are misleading, for a writer can use any information he can get, but the basis of the writer's art is not his skill but his willingness to write, his desire to write, in fact his inability *not* to write. I always instruct my students to write a great deal. Write a journal. Take notes. Write when you are feeling wretched, when your mind is about to break down . . . who knows what will float up to the surface? I am an unashamed believer in the magical powers of dreams; dreams enhance us. Even nightmares may be marketable—there is something to be said for the conscious, calculating exorcism of nightmares, if they give to us such works as those of Dostoyevsky, Celine, and Kafka. So the most important thing is to write, and to write nearly every day, in sickness and in health. In a while, in a few weeks or a few years, you can always make sense of that jumble of impressions . . . or perhaps it will suddenly reveal its sense to you. Theodore Roethke would jot down a striking line of "poetry" and carry it around with him for years before it made its way into a poem. Or perhaps the line generated a poem around it. What difference does it make? Energy is sacred; we write because we have an excess of energy, because we are more nervous or lively or curious about life than other people; why not make the best of it?

And so it is true that art "hallucinates." Because, of course, art is not "real." You don't find your way around any terrain by means of art, but by means of maps that are faithful to the surfaces of the world; you don't locate human beings by reading, but by looking in the telephone book. Art is not "real" and has no need to be real, artists scorn mundane reality, they are fond of making statements (I like to think they make them at dinner parties, refusing to be bullied as I am always bullied) like "So much the worse for reality!" Reality—real life—the newspapers and the newsmagazines and what goes on across the street—these are the materials of great art, but not art itself, though I am conscious of the semantic difficulties inherent in the word "art." Let us say that "art" points to a cultural, and not aesthetic, phenomenon: that a wilted spider put inside a picture frame somehow, magically, becomes a work of "art," but that the same spider, untouched, unnoticed, is still a work of "nature" and will win no prizes. This is a definition of art that greatly angers traditionalists, but it pleases me because it suggests how Gestalt-like and shapeless life really is and how necessary we writers (and scientists, and map-makers, and historians) are to make it sane.

Why do you write?—To seek out the meanings of life, which are hidden. This is a possible answer, a pleasing, optimistic answer, though perhaps Faustian. I always take my materials from ordinary life. I am greatly interested in the newspapers and in the Ann Landers' columns and in *True Confessions* and in the anecdotes told under the guise of "gossip." Amazing revelations! The world is filled with revelations, with tragedies —go at once to the newspaper and look at page five or page nineteen and let your eye become drawn to a headline, any headline; here is a story. I can't begin to count the stories I have written that are based on the barest newspaper accounts . . . it is the very skeletal nature of the newspaper, I think, that attracts me to it, the need it inspires in me to give flesh to such neatly and thinly-told tales, to resurrect this event which has already become history and will never be understood unless it is re-lived, re-dramatized. From the fragment of someone's life that is represented in a newspaper story the writer is drawn to reconstruct the entire object. It is like finding a single piece of a jigsaw puzzle on the floor . . . with a little effort you can reconstruct the whole, why not? Or perhaps you will imagine a better whole than the "real" one. Why not?

Therefore, art "dreams" or hallucinates, broods, upon what is given in reality. An overheard remark, a sudden stabbing emotion, a sense of dismay, a sense of anger, a story in *True Confessions* that reads exactly like a nightmare: these are our materials. I don't want to write anything that couldn't have been written, first, for *True Confessions*. I don't want to write anything that couldn't have been sung, in some form, as a ballad, that barest and most dramatic of art forms, a dream hardly made into art. Critical writing intrigues me just as intellectual men intrigue me, perhaps to folly, and I can't resist matching my wits with those of other writers, analyzing and exploring their works, trying to make sense of them—but the gravest and most sacred task is not criticism, but art, and art may be easier to achieve.

"Art hallucinates Ego mastery." What is the Ego? It is my Ego that is writing this, it is your Ego, your self, that is reading this. You are like protoplasm within a certain confinement—your *self* is not fixed but fluid, changeable, mysterious. It is never quite the same self, and yet it is never another self. When you die no one will take your place. When I die my particular being, my personality, will vanish forever—it may be a good thing—but it is an irreparable fact. Our Egos desire control; we desire "mastery." Reality always eludes us because, like ourselves, it is fluid and mysterious and vaguely terrifying . . . it is always beyond our grasp, even those we love and who love us and whom we imagine we control, a little, are ultimately beyond our grasp, very noble in their independence, doomed to private lives and deaths. But we want, we want desperately this mastery. And, wanting it, we must therefore create it; we dream; we create a world (let us say a short story) which is populated by people we have made, whose thoughts we direct, and whose fates we make sure add up to some sense.

Freud tells us what we need to know, economically, about ourselves as writers—we write in order to pretend mastery of the world. Unlike the typical skeptic who dislikes art because it is "not real," I find this immensely pleasing. I think it is a noble task. To attempt "Ego mastery" of the world, or of some bitten-off chunk of the world, seems to me noble. There is a sacred air about the lightest, most delicate of short stories (let's say Eudora Welty's—or Chekhov's) just as there is a sacred air, though a more profound one, about those monstrous works of the nineteenth-century, novels like *Moby Dick* and *The Brothers Karamazov*, written by men who wanted to get everything down on paper, everything!—because the artist is a kind of priest, or a kind of magician, or even a kind of scientist, fascinated by the meanings that lay beneath the surface of the world. To explore these meanings is a noble task.

All art is meaningful. Its meaning may be in the violent, rather vicious *process* by which it is created—let us say the paintings of de Kooning or Pollock—or it may be in the more traditional texture of the work itself, spelled out, so that a student may underline *Live all you can; it's a mistake not to* (in James' *The Ambassadors*) and feel that he is getting the "meaning" of the work, without double-talk. The "meaning" of *Moby Dick* is located not just in the famous chapter on the White Whale, but in all the chapters—the tedious ones as well as the dramatic ones—the entire work adding up to its meaning, which is the exploration of reality by Melville.

And so, *Why do you write?* To answer this distinguished question once again: we write because we are ordained to a noble task, that of making clear mysteries, or pointing out mysteries where a numbing and inaccurate simplicity has held power. We write to be truthful to certain facts, certain emotions. We write to "explain" apparently crazy actions . . . why does an intelligent young man go berserk and kill, why does a happy woman ruin her life by running away with someone, why does a well-adjusted person commit suicide? I confess that I am old-fashioned, conventional. I look and behave in a conventional manner and the stimulus behind my writing is conventional, not weird. I am fascinated by weird structures and points of view, and if I could I would tell a story hanging upside-down, or in three columns at once, but really behind all my meek extravaganza is a simple desire to make sense . . . I want to know the *why* behind human emotions, even if I can only say again and again that human emotions are our deepest mystery and there is no understanding them. I am less interested in technical gimmicks that explore the flat surface of the page, emphasizing its unreality (the works of Beckett, for instance, which mock the very process of writing), though certainly cubist and abstract artists have made beautiful things out of the canvas as canvas instead of the canvas as mirror. But mere intellect to me, as a woman, is quickly tiring; if a story is only intelligent, might it not be better as an essay or a letter to the editor? I am preoccupied with verbs that go nowhere except to suggest the fluid nature of the world we inhabit.

If a story is well done there is no need to emphasize its meaning or its bewilderment before the fact of meaninglessness: the story *is* its meaning, that is all. Any story of Chekhov's is its meaning. It is an experience, an emotional event, usually of great beauty and occasionally of great ugliness, but it is pure in itself, needing no interpretation. "The Lady with the Pet Dog," a typical Chekhov story, tells of a hopeless love affair between a very experienced man and inexperienced woman, the wife of a dull, well-to-do man. They meet, they fall in love, they continue to meet . . . she weeps, he is helpless, they cannot marry because of their families, their social obligations, etc. That is all the story "means." Chekhov gives us a sense of dilemma, an unforgettable sense of their anguish, and the story need have no meaning beyond that. Surely they are not being punished for adultery!—nor are they being punished for not being daring enough to run away together, for not being romantic enough. They are ordinary people trapped in an extraordinary situation; "The Lady with the Pet Dog" is a record of their emotional crises, and we respond to it because, reluctantly perhaps, we see ourselves in such traps, deceiving ourselves, hopeless in spite of our cunning and intelligence.

As to the nature of short fiction? There is no nature to it, but only natures. Different natures. Just as we all have different personalities, so the dreams of our personalities will be different. There are no rules to help us. There used to be a rule—"Don't be boring!"—but that has been by-passed; today writers like Beckett and Albee and Pinter are deliberately boring (though perhaps they succeed more than they know) and anything goes. Outrageous exaggeration. Outrageous understatement. Very short scenes, very long scenes . . . cinematic flashes and impressions, long introspective passages in the manner of Thomas Mann: anything. There is no particular length, certainly, to the short story or to the novel. I believe that any short story can become a novel, and any novel can be converted back into a short story or into a poem. Reality is fluid and monstrous; let us package it in as many shapes as possible. Let us declare that everything is sacred and therefore material for art—or, perhaps, nothing is sacred, nothing can be left alone.

The amateur writer wants to write of great things, serious themes. Perhaps he has a social conscience! But there are no "great" things but only great treatments. All themes are serious, or foolish. There are no rules. We are free. Miracles are in the wings, in the ink of unopened typewriter ribbons, craving release. I tell my students to write of their true subjects. How will they know when they are writing of their true subjects? By the ease with which they write. By their reluctance to stop writing. By the headachy, even guilty, joyous sensation of having done something that must be done, having confessed emotions thought unconfessable, having said what had seemed should remain unsaid. If writing is difficult, stop writing. Begin again with another subject. The true subject writes itself, it cannot be silenced. Give shape to your dreams, your day-dreams, cultivate your day-dreams and their secret meanings will come out. If you feel that sitting blankly and staring out the window is sinful, then you will never write, and why write anyway? If you feel that sitting in a daze, staring at the sky or at the river, is somehow a sacred event, that your deepest self is pleased by it, then perhaps you are a writer or a poet and in time you will try to communicate your feelings.

Writers write, eventually; but first they feel.

A marvelous life.

DISCUSSION QUESTIONS
SUGGESTIONS FOR WRITING

1. How does Freud's statement, "Art hallucinates Ego mastery," relate to the function of art or the artist?

2. This essay, though clearly autobiographical, also shares some characteristic elements of essays that have been discussed as informative, critical, persuasive, personal, etc. What are these various elements?

3. What is art?

4. What does Joyce Carol Oates mean by: "The amateur writer wants to write of great things, serious themes. Perhaps he has a social conscience! But there are no 'great' things but only great treatments. All themes are serious, or foolish"?

LOUIS D. RUBIN, JR.
(b. 1923), is a well-known
literary critic whose interests are primarily in the
novel and in the southern
literary tradition in America. He is currently pro-
fessor of English at the
University of North Caro-
lina. His books include
The Golden Weather (a
novel), *The Faraway
Country: Writers of the
Modern South,* and *The
Curious Death of the
Novel.*

THE CURIOUS DEATH OF THE NOVEL: OR, WHAT TO DO ABOUT TIRED LITERARY CRITICS

I. FABLE

Once upon a time there was a group of very talented writers known as Modern Novelists, who wrote books known as Modern Novels. The writers known as Modern Novelists were named Joyce and Proust and Dreiser and Mann and Faulkner and Fitzgerald and Hemingway and Wolfe. While no one of these writers wrote books like those of any of the others, they were all considered to be very good Modern Novelists.

At the same time there was another group of people, some of them very talented and some of them not so very talented, who were known as Literary Critics. They read the books of the Modern Novelists, and they thereupon said to each other, "Aha! Now we know what a Modern Novel is." This was a very astute observation and they were most satisfied with it.

Time Passed, and after a long while every one of the group of people known as Modern Novelists was dead. There were now some new people around who also wrote books, and who kept insisting that the books were Novels and that therefore they too were Modern Novelists. "Heavens, no!" replied the people known as Literary Critics. "How can *you* be Modern Novelists? Modern Novelists are writers who write Modern Novels, and we all know what a Modern Novel is; it is a book written by Joyce or Proust or Dreiser or Mann or Faulkner or Fitzgerald or Hemingway or Wolfe."

"But we are not *those* Modern Novelists," said the new people; "we are Bellow and Malamud and Styron and Barth and Salinger and So Forth and So On."

"Don't be silly," the people known as Literary Critics declared. "Unless you write the same kind of books as those written by Modern Novelists, they can't be Modern Novels and you can't be Modern Novelists."

"But those people are all dead," the new people objected.

"True," admitted the people known as Literary Critics, "and so is the Novel."

"Then what do you call the books that *we* have written?" the new people asked.

"I couldn't say," the people known as Literary Critics told them, "because, now that the Novel is dead, I don't keep up with current fiction any more."

Moral: Nothing is quite so dead as a dead definition, unless it is a dead critic.

II. EXPLICATION

One hears it all the time, and one gets tired of listening to it. The Novel is Dead. It has passed on into history with the Epic Poem and the Volstead Amendment. The Great Age of Prose Fiction which began with Fielding and Richardson and reached its flowering in the first several decades of the twentieth century is drawing to a tawdry close. Novels continue to be written, but they have nothing new to communicate, because the possibilities of the literary form have been exhausted, and without discovery there can be no survival.

Sometimes I wonder who it was who first discovered that the novel was dead. I suspect that it was some English literary critic who, having read *Pamela* and *Tom Jones*, happened upon *Tristram Shandy* and immediately afterward announced that the form had now been fully explored and that therefore no more works in that genre could be written. When someone offered to lend him the new work by Jane Austen titled *Sense and Sensibility*, he refused to look at it, declaring instead that the genius of his age lay in works of non-fiction such as Charles Lamb's *Recollections of Christ's Hospital*, or perhaps in the throbbing vitality of magazine journalism as exemplified in *Blackwood's* and the *Edinburgh Review*. But on second thought it was probably not an Englishman who discovered that the novel was dead; doubtless it was a Frenchman, for that is the sort of thing that the French are constantly discovering. Perhaps it was some Parisian seer of the early nineteenth century who deduced that no one would ever want to write a novel any more, because no one would ever be able once again to bring himself to say, "The little town of Verrières may be regarded as one of the most attractive in the Franche-Comté."

So the novel is dead. Who killed the novel? There has been no lack of answers. We are told that the Age of Prose Fiction is over, that the Novel was a nineteenth-century phenomenon which depended for its life on the breakdown of the traditional class structure. Now that the class structure is permanently fluid (try that one at the Belle Meade Country Club), there is no place for the novel. The bewildering cacophony of modern times, with its continual crises, its everyday reality more weird than anything formerly portrayed in the most visionary works of fiction, has left no room for the mere loveliness of the belles lettres. Actual events boggle the imagination; this is the age of non-fiction, of the quest for meaning involved in interpretive reportage. Furthermore, television and journalism have provided our culture with art forms that mirror contemporary reality far more accurately and faithfully than the leisurely prose of the novel could ever do. And, besides, the discoveries of modern physics and of behavioral psychology have all but destroyed the old certainty of the human ordering of experience, so that there can be no solid basis, whether in finite matter or human reason, upon which the novelist can erect his commentary. The vast terror of the atomic bomb has rendered individual tragedy inconclusive and unimportant. And of course the helplessness of the modern human being, caught in the play of mass forces and the gigantic wheelings and evolutions of whole societies and cultures, is such that the distraught single citizen cannot of himself achieve the personal meaning necessary to art. All these things together spell the death of fiction. So the story goes.

The trouble with most of these arguments is not that they are implausible but that they are no more true now than during those past times when the novel was supposedly in its heyday. The class structure, for example, is constantly breaking down and regrouping itself. Can anyone contend for example, that the social hierarchy was not dealt a colossal, and to contemporaries what surely was apparently a mortal, blow by the French Revolution? Yet the very regrouping of the supposedly obsolete class structure provided Stendhal with some of his best subject matter. Besides, to what extent do class and clique help account for, say, Melville? (It will not do to invoke the old distinction between the novel and the romance; if *Moby Dick* is not a novel, then we would gladly settle for the survival of the romance.) It is quite true that modern times seem bewildering, but surely no more bewildering than the early seventeenth century must have seemed to a religious traditionalist like Donne or a religious dissenter such as Milton; alas, the times are *always* chaotic and bewildering. And, as always, the apparent lure of non-fiction — naked "truth" — over art is specious; in the eighteenth century everyone used to read another kind of "truth" — journals, instead of fiction; in the mid-nineteenth century came the rise of the daily newspaper. As for television doing the trick, not long ago it was movies that were blamed; a few decades ago the magazines and book clubs were destroying literature. Something is *always* destroying literature, but good books have managed to come along. (The truth is that the only thing that can destroy literature is *bad* books, and surely these are no more common now than in previous eras.) So it will do no good to attribute the alleged death of the novel to our crass times; Hawthorne's times seemed pretty crass to everyone concerned, and so did Proust's. It is not very original to blame the situation on the exploding universe theory and behavioral psychology, either; I would suggest that neither has had anything like the potential for shock that Newtonian physics and the Darwinian hypothesis had in their time; and, anyway, writers are notoriously myopic about such matters. The only really new phenomenon we have to offer to the cataclysmic hypothesis is the atomic bomb; but I suggest that it is probably no more a menace than the Black Death seemed to fourteenth-century Europeans; imaginative literature did not die out then. The truth is that obviously we *do* live in difficult and demanding times, but that the response of novelists to difficult and demanding times will doubtless continue to be what the response of writers to difficult and demanding times always has been: namely, difficult and demanding works of literature.

So I do not accept the theory that the alleged death of the novel is due to the lamentable condition of the cosmos. Times have *changed* some; but they are not necessarily any worse. What I suggest instead is that, if the novel is at present in a kind of slump, in all probability we are roughly in the plight that, say, a devotee of the art of English poetry might have experienced in the year 1790 or so. Pope was dead. Swift was dead. Gray was dead. Dr. Johnson was dead. What more was there to look forward to? The current reigning practitioners seemed competent enough, but were obviously not of the stature of the titans of eighteenth-century verse. How could such a person have heard of the existence of William Blake, or have known that Wordsworth and Coleridge would be growing up in a few years? Surely such a person would have thought that the upheaval of the French Revolution and the swarming confusion of the growing industrial revolution in England had killed off all future possibility of poetry for the generations of mankind. Yet the art of poetry managed to survive, and even to take on a new excitement that quite outdid the Augustan achievement.

Or let us think of a devotee of American poetry who looked around him in the year 1890, and perceived such giants of verse as James Russell Lowell, Bliss Carman, Richard Hovey, and Edmund Clarence Stedman. Could anything have convinced him that hope resided in the fact that persons named T. S. Eliot and Robert Frost and John Crowe Ransom and Ezra Pound were growing up?

What I would propose, by inference, is that what we have been experiencing with the novel during the past decade or two is a time of the rearrangement and replenishment of literary energies. We have many good and interesting novels, and we apparently have no Faulkners, Hemingways, Fitzgeralds, Prousts, Manns, Joyces, and the like. Is this, after all, odd? Since the post-World War II years, we have lived in a period immediately following one of the richest and most imposing in the history of literature. The first four decades of this century saw the publication of some literary work of almost incredible brilliance. It is no accident that our writers of criticism still devote great attention to this work, that our curricula in colleges and universities is dominated by this work. We are all still trying our best to savor the full flavor of so rich a harvest. This work has dominated our imagination in the way that the drama of Shakespeare, say, dominated the imagination of early seventeenth-century English literature, and that of Milton dominated the imagination of late seventeenth-century literature. The chief impact of this sort of domination, as Eliot remarked of Milton, is on the writers who follow along immediately afterward. A whole way of using language — which is to say, a whole way of giving order to experience — is imposed on the sensibility of the times. This kind of situation is tough on the newer writers, because try as they will they find themselves writing in other men's modes, which can never be a satisfactory arrangement. They are impeded in the process of self-discovery; try as they may, they see their own experience through Proust's or Joyce's or Faulkner's eyes — which is to say, through the language of those writers — and there is very little they can do except struggle against it. What is produced is work of great technical competence; after all, the immediate problems have been detailed for them already. But what is missing are new perceptions and new discoveries.*

Let me put this in more specific terms. What has been the chief formal problem of the Southern writers who came along in the 1940s and 1950s? It has been, to *not* write about their experience as Faulkner or Warren or Wolfe would do it. It cannot be said that they have greatly succeeded in avoiding this peril, for the example of the great Southern writers of the 1920s and 1930s is so massive and so persuasive that one cannot simply will oneself to look the other way. And it is not just that the language and perceptions of the Faulknerian mode (to call a richly varied literature after the name of its greatest practitioner) no longer suffice to apprehend experience; the difficulty is that to a large extent this mode *still* suffices, and yet the times *are* changing and have changed since the years when those writers were learning how to see their world, and their eyes will not quite do any more. But their vision is still so temptingly available that one can hardly avoid using it.

We see approximately the same kind of thing going on in France, except that the French have a way of reasoning their problems out in abstract terms that tempts them into all manner of odd extremes of posture and position. The whole business of the *nouveau roman*, it seems to me, is an elaborate and intensive attempt on the part of an entire literary generation to get out from under the massive example of the greatest of twentieth-century novelists, Marcel Proust, and, to a lesser

---

*In retrospect, five years after composing the above paragraph, I must say that it seems a pretty fatuous and condescending statement to make about a body of writing that includes *The Sot-Weed Factor* and *The Confessions of Nat Turner.*—L.D.R.

extent, that of Gide and Camus. It would be next to impossible to carry introspective examination and psychological analysis in depth any further than Proust did; very well, said the young Frenchmen, we will move in the opposite direction and write only of what is personally seen and felt. The result is the *nouveau roman*, in which, as Susan Sontag remarks of Nathalie Sarraute, "the novel must record without comment the direct and purely sensory contact with things and persons which the 'I' of the novelist experiences."

This of course is palpable nonsense; the very act of writing involves interpretation, and, as Miss Sontag rightly points out, there is nothing wrong with looking from the outside in as well as from the inside out. The important thing to remember, however, is that aesthetic philosophizing almost always represents attempts to rationalize and to articulate the ruling psychological needs of writers. While the French have a knack for convincing themselves and others that it is the theory that is triumphant, they are actually no more skilled than any other group of writers in adapting their actual literature to abstract theoretical demands—which is to say, not very good at all. The pure *nouveau roman* is impossible; just as the pure *roman expérimental* of Zola was impossible, and the *unités* of the seventeenth century. Much of the true art, then as now, consists of the struggle of the creative impulse against the theoretical dogma, and Nathalie Sarraute, for example, is a fine novelist in the traditional French vein of lucidly analytical fiction.

Over here we have had nothing so determined as the *nouveau roman*. There was a period, a few years back, when Jack Kerouac seemed determined to lead us out of the wilderness into a new promised land (located, so far as one could tell, on a highway somewhere in the vicinity of Denver, Colorado), and so uneasy were we that we tended to give him rather more attention than he merited. But the Beat version of the New Freedom turned out to be nothing more than a word game involving the repetition of a few quickly minted clichés, and it has since been more or less abandoned.

Instead, what we have done is to mark time while a group of highly talented writers—Styron, Bellow, Malamud, Barth, others—explores the already discovered ground to see whether anything important has been overlooked. This has, all in all, proved to be a fairly sensible and rewarding thing to do, and there is evidence that several of them have found ample room in which to write well. It is an indication of the capabilities of these four, I think, that while each has published at least three novels—and Bellow has, I believe, six to his credit—we are quite prepared to believe that each of them may with his very next book produce something more exciting than ever before. None of them is really a known quantity. Bellow has gone right along exploring and widening his range from novel to novel; his best book was his most recent. Malamud is capable of almost anything. Styron is a very powerful writer. Barth is just beginning to be fully appreciated; his next novel may well be of first-class quality. We simply do not know what these writers can do, and this of itself ought to be enough to dispel any premature talk of the death of the American novel in our time.

Yet promise is not fulfilment; and we cannot deal entirely in terms of possibilities. I would instead insist that even if it happens that not one of these novelists, and not one of their immediate contemporaries, produces fiction worthy to stand alongside that of Faulkner and Hemingway, this would hardly be unexpected. It has been, after all, less than five years since the death of both of those writers; apparently there is even now some unpublished Hemingway fiction remaining. Both men were, after all, *our* contemporaries. Their times are still largely *our* times, and it would not be wholly strange if it took the writers who come immediately after them, and so must write in their shadow, a little while longer to disengage themselves from their example. What we are quite likely to have, it seems to me, is a period lasting as long as a full generation or more in which our better writers are more or less engaged, however unintentionally, primarily with learning to see things in their own right again, or at any rate sufficiently in their own right so that what they produce is no longer importantly compromised by the version of reality afforded them by their great immediate predecessors. Among the most valuable services that the immediate post-Faulkner and post-Hemingway generation of novelists can perform is that which they are, I think, busily involved in performing, however without their meaning to: searching out the resources at their command, discovering new vantage points, finding where the barriers lie, and so on. They are keeping the spirit of the novel alive and flourishing, and writing some highly excellent books in the process, some few of which, I am convinced, will hold up very well in succeeding years.

Meanwhile they are undoubtedly, all unwittingly perhaps, turning up the clues that will serve a new day and the new literary generation when the time is again propitious. When that generation comes to write its books, it will not lack for models when needed. For just as, in a sense, it was Sherwood Anderson who prepared what Mark Twain had discovered for its use by Faulkner and Hemingway, and just as Proust needed Anatole France and the Goncourts to adapt for him what Stendhal and Balzac and Zola had developed in the art of the novel, so the role of the novelists who followed the great writers of the first several decades of the twentieth century may well turn out to be that of interpreting the lessons of Proust and Faulkner and Joyce and so forth for a new and changed kind of experience. . . .

III. CODA

Capote on the "non-fiction novel," Norman Mailer on Viet Nam and the White House, Norman Podhoretz on the greater realism of journalism in our time, Susan Sontag on the jewel-speckled paintings of Carlo

Crivelli—what do they have to signify for the state of the novel in our time? What does such counsel mean for the novelist of today, trying to write his *Herzog* and *Sot-Weed Factor* and *Set This House on Fire?* Marcel Proust knew the answer quite well, for he heard many similar pronouncements in his own iron time. It was to look within his own life for signs of the meaning concealed therein:

> To read the subjective book of these strange signs (signs standing out boldly, it seemed, which my conscious mind, as it explored my unconscious self, went searching for, stumbled against and passed around, like a diver groping his way), no one could help me with any rule, for the reading of that book is a creative act in which no one can stand in our stead, or even collaborate with us. And therefore how many there are who shrink from writing it; how many tasks are undertaken in order to avoid that one! . . . But in art excuses count for nothing; good intentions are of no avail; the artist must at every instant heed his instinct; so that art is the most real of all things, the sternest school in life and truly the Last Judgment. This book, the most difficult of all to decipher, is also the only one dictated to us by reality, and the only one the "imprinting of which on our consciousness was done by reality itself.

And William Faulkner knew it too: "the young man or woman writing today has forgotten the problems of the human heart in conflict with itself which alone can make good writing because only that is worth writing about, worth the agony and the sweat." And, to disagree with Faulkner, I think that the best of our own day's novelists know that, too. They know that there is no substitute in our time for the novel, and that the task of the novelist remains what it has always been: to depict the way things are, which is an act of the highest intelligence.

Surely there are times when this seems easier to do than at other times, and ours appears not to be such a time, among other reasons because of the existence, right up to the edge of our own day and even into it, of some highly convincing and revealing models of literary perception which, however, no longer quite illuminate and yet can get in the way of our own attempts to see. But there is only one thing to do about this; it is to write novels, without worrying about the cries and demands of the market place, all of which must necessarily grow silent when confronted with the genuine article.

Is the best of today's fiction up to that of a generation ago? How can one say, finally? I only know that there are novels being written each year that I find greatly interesting and enjoyable; I am not disposed to spend much time looking around for what they do not provide when they so obviously provide so much. I suggest, then, that we stop worrying so much over whether the novel is dead, and spend more time reading living novels. And if, just around the corner, there are coming new novels which will be for our own time what *The Sound and the Fury* and *The Sun Also Rises* and *Ulysses* and *The Remembrance of Things Past* were for the generation before ours, one of the ways whereby we will be able to recognize them is that they most assuredly will not start out

"Through the fence, between the curling flower spaces, I could see them hitting," or "Robert Cohn was once middleweight boxing champion of Princeton," or "Stately, plump Buck Mulligan came from the stairhead," or "For a long time I used to go to bed early." They will be their own selves, and because they are they will speak for all of us as well.

DISCUSSION QUESTIONS
SUGGESTIONS FOR WRITING

1. Though the writer of the critical essay may be more concerned with presenting convincing evidence than with providing dramatic or entertaining illustrations, in the less formal sort of critical essay, of which "The Curious Death of the Novel" is an example, a writer with the right kind of wit and intelligence can obviously be highly entertaining as well as convincing. Compare this essay with "Report on the Federal Civil Defense Booklet." In what instances is the personality, the individuality, of the writer more apparent in "The Curious Death of the Novel"?

2. Is the following an accurate summary of what this piece accomplishes: Louis D. Rubin, in his essay "The Curious Death of the Novel," refutes all the arguments given to support the theory of the death of the novel as well as offering plausible explanations for why the death of the novel was ever hypothesized in the first place"?

3. What forms of evidence are used by Rubin to substantiate his thesis?

4. What is the technical function of the "Fable" at the beginning of "The Curious Death of the Novel"?

PODHORETZ

THE ARTICLE
AS ART

NORMAN PODHORETZ
(b. 1930) is editor of
Commentary and a fre-
quent contributor to *Par-
tisan Review, The New
Yorker, Harper's,* and *The
New Republic.* As a literary critic, he has dealt with
literary achievement in
areas ordinarily regarded
as outside the critic's
range of interest—in political speeches, memoirs,
television drama, and
magazines. His books in-
clude *Doings and Undo-
ings: The Fifties and After
in American Writing* and
Making It, an interesting,
controversial autobiogra-
phy.

ANYONE who has given much attention to postwar American fiction
is likely to have noticed a curious fact. Many of our serious novelists
also turn out book reviews, critical pieces, articles about the contemporary world, memoirs, sketches—all of which are produced for magazines and which these writers undoubtedly value far lower than their
stories and novels.

Indeed, some novelists (and this applies to many poets too) tend to
express their contempt or disdain for discursive prose in the very act of
writing it. You can hear a note of condescension toward the medium
they happen to be working in at the moment; they seem to be announc-
ing in the very construction of their sentences that they have no great
use for the prosy requirements of the essay or the review, that they are
only dropping in from Olympus for a brief, impatient visit. But just as
often—and this is the curious fact I am referring to—the discursive
writing of people who think of themselves primarily as novelists turns
out to be more interesting, more lively, more penetrating, more intelligent, more forceful, more original—in short, *better*—than their fiction,
which they and everyone else automatically treat with greater respect....

I am not one of those who talk about the death of the novel, but I do think that it has fallen on bad days. I also think that the fault lies at least partly with these rarefied and incense-burning doctrines of the imagination, which have had the effect of surrendering the novel—to apply a remark of F. R. Leavis on Shelley's theory of inspiration—"to a sensibility that has no more dealings with intelligence than it can help." My own criticism of much contemporary fiction would be precisely that it lacks the only species of imagination worth mentioning—the kind that is vitalized by contact with a disciplined intelligence and a restless interest in the life of the times. And what the novel has abdicated has been taken over by discursive writers. Imagination has not died (how could it?) but it has gone into other channels; these channels are not by any means commensurate with the novel: they are, in fact, *channels* and not the sea. But there is living water in them nevertheless.

What I have in mind—and I cheerfully admit that the suggestion sounds preposterous—is *magazine articles*. I won't call them essays, even though to do so would make the point seem less disreputable and silly, because the type of thing I am referring to is not an essay in the old sense. Strictly speaking, the essay requires an audience that has no doubts about where the relevant subjects of discussion are to be found, and it is therefore written without any need to persuade the reader that he ought to concern himself with this particular question. The magazine article, as they say in the trade, always hangs on a peg; it takes off from an event in the news, a book recently published, a bill in Congress. And even then, with its relevance established in the most obvious way conceivable, it still has to sell itself to a reader who wants to be told why he should bother pushing his way through it when there are so many other claims on his attention. This is a tyrannical condition which can, of course, result in the reduction of all thought to the occasional and the newsworthy. But now and then a writer whose interests and talent go beyond the merely journalistic can be forced into very exciting pieces of work by the necessity to demonstrate the continuing importance of his special concerns by throwing them into the buzz and hum around him. . . .

Why should the magazine article, of all things, have become so important and fertile a genre in our day? Why have so many writers—both "critics" and professional journalists—found it possible to move around more freely and creatively within it than within fiction or poetry? No doubt it has something to do with the spiritual dislocations of the cold war period, but the essence of the answer, I think, lies in an analogy with architecture. It has often been pointed out that functionalism is more an idea than a reality: the products of functional architecture aren't purely functional at all, since they always contain "useless" elements that are there for aesthetic rather than practical reasons. Yet the fact remains that our sense of beauty today is intimately connected with the sense of usefulness: we consider a building beautiful when it seems to exist not for anyone to enjoy the sight of or to be impressed by, but solely and simply to be used. We think of those glass structures like Lever House in New York or the United Nations or the Manufacturers Trust Company building on Fifth Avenue as practical, in the sense that women call walking shoes practical; they have a kind of no-nonsense look about them, they seem to be stripped down to essentials, purged of all superfluous matter.

The same is true of the way we furnish our homes—Scandinavian efficiency is our idea of handsomeness; foam rubber rather than down our idea of comfort; stainless steel rather than silver our notion of elegant cutlery. I would suggest that we have all, writers and readers alike, come to feel temporarily uncomfortable with the traditional literary forms because they don't *seem* practical, designed for "use," whereas a magazine article by its nature satisfies that initial condition and so is free to assimilate as many "useless," "non-functional" elements as it pleases. It is free, in other words, to become a work of art.

This is not, of course, an ideal situation for literature to be in, but nothing can be gained from turning one's eyes away in horror. Certainly the rigid distinction between the creative and the critical has contributed to the growth of a feeling that the creative is "useless." Curiously enough, the very concept of imagination as a special faculty—and of novels and poetry as mysteriously unique species of discourse subject to strange laws of their own—itself implies that art is of no use to life in the world. What we need, it seems to me, is a return to the old idea of literature as a category that includes the best writing on any subject in any form. We need a return to this idea and we need it, I should add, most urgently of all for the sake of fiction and poetry.

DISCUSSION QUESTIONS
SUGGESTIONS FOR WRITING

1. What is the central idea or main thesis of Podhoretz's essay?

2. In what ways, if any, is Podhoretz in fundamental disagreement with Louis D. Rubin in "The Curious Death of the Novel"?

3. In what ways, if any, is Podhoretz in disagreement with Joyce Carol Oates in "The Nature of Short Fiction"? Would they agree, for example, on the nature and uses of "imagination"?

4. Can you offer any other explanations—in addition to the "functionalism" mentioned by Podhoretz—to account for the phenomenon of the magazine article, its having become "so important and fertile a genre in our day"?

ROBINSON, WOLFE,
TALESE, AND HAYES

LEONARD W. ROBINSON
(b. 1912) is a professor at
the Columbia Graduate
School of Journalism. In
the following interview
with writers Tom Wolfe
and Gay Talese and with
Esquire editor Harold
Hayes—all proponents of
the so-called "new jour-
nalism"—he explores the
genesis, meaning, and
distinguishing character-
istics of the "new journalism."

THE NEW
JOURNALISM

rofessor Leonard Wallace Robinson: Last year Professor Lawrence Pinkham here at the Columbia Graduate School of Journalism created a course called Subjective Realism for the winter and spring term. During the course of those sessions, the following remarks got made: "The so-called Outside Reality you are generally asked to accept as true is under suspicion today. There is a general conviction we are being lied to, by politicians, by TV, by advertising, by magazines, by mothers and fathers, and by professors. All external reality as it's being presented in the multimedia of today seems less and less like reality as we individuals experience it. Now, what does one do when he finds out the world does not correspond to the world as described by authority? He is forced back on his own subjective reactions, for one thing, or he's apt to be. He may do any number of things, he may just explode, or he may go mad. But as a writer he's forced inward, to some extent."

Here's something else that was said by the *New American Review* last year, and it seems to me very pertinent: "The role of many American writers today is that of a witness. This does not necessarily mean that they provide a firsthand account of the political and cultural warfare of today, though many more write about events and demonstrations and trials than was formerly the case; it *does* mean that they provide a firsthand account of their involvement in what has been happening in and to America. This is true of fiction, poetry and drama, as well as of

355

the essay; in all of them one senses a movement toward 'bloody cross-roads,' as Lionel Trilling puts it, 'where art and politics meet.' Similarly, the contemporary essay tends toward reportage, or interior journalism, which at its best places the writer's own values on the line and turns the merely topical piece into a form of testimony."

I think these words describe better than I could, the New Journalism. It represents man in a deep quandary, man trying to define himself in the world about him. Now would you, Mr. Wolfe, tell how you would describe the New Journalism — because I suppose we'll have many different ways of expressing the matter.

Tom Wolfe: I think the New Journalism is the use by people writing nonfiction of techniques which heretofore had been thought of as confined to the novel or to the short story, to create in one form both the kind of objective reality of journalism and the subjective reality that people have always gone to the novel for.

Professor Robinson: Mr. Hayes, what do you, as an editor, think?

Harold Hayes: What interests me is the promise that the very best literary form offers for reportage. And it seems to me what has been going on in the last ten years has been a greater tendency on the part of magazines and book publishers to encourage nonfiction writers, particularly to extend themselves into forms which were not previously seen as nonfiction. Len Robinson, a managing editor of *Esquire* back at the time when this whole movement was just beginning, knows from his own past experience that the magazine article was a form very largely taken for granted among editors and writers. They knew precisely what we required of the writer on any given assignment. The magazine article was a convention of writing, and those who were successful at it were those who understood the convention in the same way that a reporter understands the demands of a news story. There was an anecdotal lead opening into the general theme of the piece; then some explanation, followed by anecdotes or examples. If a single individual was important to the story, some biographical material was included. Then there would be a further rendering of the subject, and the article would close with an anecdote. Now that's a crude expression of the form, but it was a form up until that time; it was a form that was commercially successful in almost all the consumer magazines with the exception of the *New Yorker*, with *Esquire* to some extent, the *Atlantic* and *Harper's*. With these magazines, there was some feeling that the possibilities of nonfiction were greater. This conventional form could be seen regularly in *Collier's, Saturday Evening Post, Redbook, The American*, the works, right across the board. And writers were interchangeable for those magazines; it *was* a time when there was a profession of freelance writers, because they all thought alike and the magazines ordered the same kind of work from them, and the magazines thrived on it. At the other magazines I mentioned, there was a greater willingness to experiment. It's really fascinating to go back and look up, I think, some of the things that appeared in the *New Yorker* in the Forties in this area, and perhaps back even into the Thirties. In *Esquire*, F. Scott Fitzgerald was writing through a form that was hard to categorize—it was nonfiction, it was revelatory, it dealt with his emotional experiences, it wasn't reporting exactly. Hemingway was writing his letters at the time; discursive letters, which kept him in the center of events and he described the events that he saw, and he did it on a very high level of literary writing. So again I think that the distinction I would raise is that if there's been any great change to accelerate the possibility of writers dealing more flexibly with the language and with form, it's not because of the birth of a new journalistic form, but because there is a commercial disposition among magazines to see that imaginative writing now is more appealing to their readers.

Their magazines express themselves better because the writers are expressing themselves better. Now I don't think a writer can sit down and say, I'm going to be a New Journalist. Many of them are trying to do that today, and I think that it's one of the by-products, and a bad one, of this tendency of ours to find a label for everything that comes along. I don't think Tom Wolfe started as a New Journalist; I don't think Gay Talese started as a New Journalist. I think they started as marvelously original writers. There was an opportunity for them to express this unique way they had towards their materials, and they took it. The great premium is not upon the existence of a form, but on originality. And a writer's own personal sense of deciding precisely what he should respond to, and how he will go about it.

Professor Robinson: Mr. Talese, would you describe your entry into New Journalism?

Gay Talese: Well, I started as a newspaperman, as Tom did. And what got me into this so-called New Journalism was a realization on my part that I couldn't tell through the old journalism the whole story. Or maybe it wasn't so old. I'm from the *New York Times* school, the fundamental old school of journalism, that's the citadel of old-fashioned reporting. Granted this was daily reporting but I found I was leaving the assignment each day, unable with the techniques available to me or permissible to the *New York Times*, to really tell, to report, all that I saw; to communicate through the techniques that were permitted by the archaic copy desk. So I don't know at what point I got into another form of journalism, more ambitious, more suspect. The heroes that I had certainly were not journalists. They were two fiction writers, short story writers, John O'Hara and Irwin Shaw. Right out of the Forties and Fifties. Irwin Shaw was my favorite writer of the short story because of his style, mood, and economy of words. Both of these writers, I so much admire because of their ability to convey so much, with so few words, and with an almost artless style. I started with trying to use the techniques of the short story writer. In some of the *Esquire* pieces I did in the early Sixties. I remember one particularly on the director Joshua Logan. Underlying all of what I did then and do now and will do in the future is one fundamental thing, and that is care in reporting. It may read like fiction, it may give some critics the impression that it was made up, faking quotes or faking scenes, or over-dramatizing incidents for the effect those incidents may cause in the writing, but without question in my own case and I'm sure this is true of Tom and other people we admire, there is reporting. There is reporting that fortifies the whole structure. Fact reporting, leg work. In the Joshua Logan incident, I was just trying to write a piece for Harold about this once famous and now somewhat obscure theatrical director who was trying to make a new success of an old play on Broadway, and his failure to do so. I was writing really about failure. It is a subject that intrigues me much more than success. Here you have in Tom and myself two people about the same age, who in reporting have gone off in quite different directions, although admiring many of the same things, including my admiration for him. But Tom is interested in the new, the latest, the most current; Tom is way ahead in knowing these things, and relays them to those who read him, including myself. What is so contemporary, or what will be. I'm more interested in what has held up for a long time and how it has done; I'm more interested in old things, the Joshua Logan trying to make a comeback, the Joe DiMaggio become an old hero, how his life is, a Frank Sinatra, who seems to symbolize, at least to me, fame and how a man lives with it. I keep getting off the point. The point was to try to say something about how I got into New Journalism. Or old journalism. Para-journalism is Dwight MacDonald's description of it.

Professor Robinson: Parajournalism?

Gay Talese: Parajournalism. He is one of the critics who believes that we are fake artists. There was a scene during a rehearsal of his play Logan was directing in which he and the star, an actress named Claudia McNeil, got into a great argument. This was an afternoon rehearsal and I was one of the three people in the theatre watching these two people battle one another on the stage, she calling him various names, he calling her names, threatening to walk off, close the production. I just got my pencil and with some of the light that was left (it was a seat on the aisle), started writing down the dialogue; remembering what I couldn't write. I don't use a tape recorder, never will. And I thought, this is a marvelous scene, it revealed so much more of those characters, Logan and his actress, than I could have done by reporting it with the techniques of journalism as taught me in the journalism department. The scene as it read in that magazine article reads just like fiction. And yet every fact is verifiable. And that's been true, I think, of everything that I've written since then. And in the *New York Times* book, it's New Journalism on the old journalism. If I may take the liberty again of considering this new. There is not one fact in that book that I think is not verifiable. And yet verifiable facts aren't enough for me. I'm sure they're not enough for Tom. Not enough to get a fraction of the truth. Or not even that we are getting at the whole truth, but we are closer to the telling on a much broader scale, with the techniques of fiction: the dialogue, the scenes, than we could do with the more restricted form allowed us by the traditional journalism as expressed in some of the old magazines. And the last point, what I'm doing now is to try to carry this New Journalism further, I'm trying to use interior monologue in reporting. Things that I've gotten away from are direct quotations. I rarely if ever will use a direct quotation any more. I'll use dialogue, but I would never, if someone that I may be interviewing, and following around, should say something, I would never quote as an old *New Yorker* profile might quote some fisherman for 8,000 words in a row. Never do I use direct quotations. I always take it out of the direct quotation and use it without quotations but always attribute. And very often, now, if I were interviewing Tom Wolfe, I would ask him what he *thought* in every situation where I might have asked him in the past what he did and said. I'm not so interested in what he did and said as I am interested in what he *thought*. And I would quote him in the way I was writing as that he *thought* something. Throughout *The Kingdom and the Power* I have people thinking things. And critics have said, "Now, how does Talese know that people are thinking that?" Talese just asked them what they were thinking. And you must know your characters well enough (that, of course, is important). Underlying that is great research, enough research to write almost a book about any one character that you're going into depth on. In the new book that I'm doing, I'm going to be using almost entirely interior monologue. No quotes. Scenes, and interior monologue.

Tom Wolfe: One example of the use of interior monologue that has intrigued me was in John Sack's book about Vietnam. Here was a man who followed this company through practically its whole tour of duty in Vietnam. He also came to the point where it became absolutely necessary to be able to tell what people were thinking, because so many soldiers when they go through a battle do it with absolutely stolid faces, and even by watching their faces and listening to what they have to say, you're not going to get what really goes on in a battle. What goes on in a battle is terror, mainly. I mean, if you've ever been in the presence of gunfire, the flashes and the sound doesn't really seem very real, and it all happens so fast, it's the terror that's the real thing. The reality of most police stories is the terror. And that doesn't come through in the account that you get. You have to project the terror into it. Sack started going around to each one of these soldiers after something would happen, and also asking them, as Gay was saying, "What were you thinking at that instant?" Now there is a valid criticism of this, which is simply the fact that it's very hard to remember what you were thinking thirty seconds ago really faithfully. But I think you can get an approximation of the mood, and I think it's justifiable to do it to at least try to get inside of the psyche somehow, and to be able to report on the interior of the skull in some way. The whole Freudian revolution is not about sex, it's about the effect of subjective reality on people's actions. And that's why I think it is a tremendous breakthrough to be able to have people writing in nonfiction to get into that. The other point that Gay just mentioned that I'd like to stress, too, is that in this kind of reporting you're really reporting scenes; that's what you're looking for constantly. You start following somebody or a group around, and you really have to end up staying with them for a day, sometimes weeks, sometimes months even. And you are waiting for things to happen in front of your eyes, because it's really the scene that brings the whole thing to life, that's where you get the dialogue. The old kind of reporting which I also went through ten years of you'd usually have only an hour to do something anyway, or maybe two hours, when you're on general assignments, you're going out to get something, so you're always going from the direct quote, What did you do at this point? and this kind of thing. And you are dependent upon that. And any time you asked a politician a question, you'd get this numbing response. The words start pouring out, but under the old system you're sort of duty bound to take them and you transfer his words from his desk back to your city desk, or from his desk back to a cable office, you're just a courier, that's all you are; you're not really reporting.

Gay Talese: Let me interject something. This form cannot succeed, I do not believe, unless the old style of reporting precedes it. I believe that the old style reporting has to be done too — I mean the constant interviewing of your subject or subjects, getting to know everything that you can about this person, so that later on when you follow them around, as Tom said, you wait like a fisherman for something to happen. You wait, sometimes weeks, months, of waiting; months, for something to happen. When this thing does happen, you should be able to recognize the significance of it inasmuch as you know your character by that point. You couldn't just go out and be with your character, your theatrical director, your beautiful girl, your whatever it is you're writing about, unless you have begun with the direct interviewing approach. Interviewing from time of birth right through, and interviewing lots of other people who know your subject. And then having finished that, that work, the interviewing and understanding of your character, then you start. You start to follow the person around. And in the old form of magazine writing, they would have stopped at that point. They would have interviewed, asked the direct questions, throw it all together and do the piece. Well, that's where the old ended, and that's where now I would begin. With all that background just as an understanding of character, so that if something happened on the Broadway stage, I would know how that might have related to something in a person's career earlier or in childhood, or I would have an understanding of that.

When I was a newspaperman reporting was such as Tom mentioned — you go out, at two o'clock in the afternoon, you get your quotes or whatever it is of the alleged happening, most of which you didn't see, incidentally. The old journalism was never eye-witness, except in sports writing. I think a sportswriter was actually the only reporter who sees with his own eyes what he's reporting the next day in a newspaper. But most of us went out, and we got the police sergeant's version of the thing, together with the social workers, or the bombardier's, or the press agent's or the PR man's. And in any case, we were not able to report how things changed, because the newspaper business is just a one-shot business.

Harold Hayes: I want to go back to something that Tom said, which I think is very important too, as I have observed it; and that is the importance of scene. Which I think also bears on Gay's point of research. Did not someone say that Character is action? Isn't that sort of a homily (sic) about fiction, that if you're trying to develop something dramatically, something has to happen to define character. The weak point in this kind of writing seems to me often comes when a writer knows the material that he wants to get out to the reader, but dramatically it's not working. He's telling the reader rather than having his material unfold, through some sequence of events. I can't agree that necessarily a magazine article is restricted to showing the kind of truth that many of these writers are after by this kind of total research. Of course it can only build to your picture. On the other hand, if you're fortunate, if you're where a scene occurs, and if you're deep enough into your story, it's entirely conceivable that you can get it within a day, and get it within two hours, if that magic thing happens before you. It certainly has happened to Gay, and it certainly has happened to Tom, and in a short time. So I would very much argue that. Certainly I would in terms of Norman Mailer.

Gay Talese: Now what Mailer does, that I'm not doing, is using himself as a character. The red balloon moving around. That's all right. I'm using a third person; I always try to use people.

Harold Hayes: That's for you. But, with the increased possibilities of nonfiction writing today, I think that Norman Mailer can decide, all right, I'll take five days in Chicago, and I will observe this as carefully as I can, and then with everything I have as a writer, I will try to tell this *my way.*

Gay Talese: You take on the moon reporting he did for *Life* a month ago. If you would have taken from that section of his coming book all that Mailer had written about himself, you would have no piece there, except some very good reporting about the technology, about science, insofar as the space program is concerned. But what he's doing is just writing from his own familiarity with his own past, beginning the moon thing with his relationship with Hemingway, and his stuff for *Harper's* about his four wives, and all the rednecks that his wife knew, and all that. That's wonderful, and it related very much to what he was covering, the steps of the Pentagon, and also the Chicago convention. But if you took Mailer's right to write about himself away from him, indeed, if Mailer tried to intrude into the skull, as Tom said, of his major characters —

Harold Hayes: That's essentially my point. Why should he? That's his great art. All I'm saying is that the range is broad enough to allow Norman Mailer to do something which absolutely nobody else can do.

Gay Talese: When he was writing shorter pieces for the *New Yorker*, you got the sense that Joe Liebling had established himself as sort of the fat man on the scene; it was, The Fat Man Goes to a Fight, The Fat Man Is in Parie Restaurants, or The Fat Joe Liebling is down in New Orleans with Huey Long. Liebling had established himself to a lesser degree than Mailer to be sure, established himself as a character so that he did not have to re-introduce himself every time he reported on an event, be it boxing or politics. Mailer does that now, and he has done it, through himself as a celebrity and himself as a superb writer, developed over the years, has introduced the public to *him*. Now he can ride on that; he can coast on that. He can assume a knowledge on the reader's part that I, for example, cannot; I must do the reporting, and that's why it takes me much more time than it would someone like Mailer.

Professor Robinson: But there is a relationship between you and Mailer, Gay, isn't there, insofar as you're both interested in the interior monologue. He's interested in his own inner monologue, which he can be an expert on, without the kind of profound research you have to do; you have to become an expert from the outside looking in. He's in a powerful position — already inside himself, and able to use himself as his own subject. A strong position, the position of the novelist, omniscient and omnipotent. But you both conceive a reality as inside basically — he inside himself, you inside your interviewees.

Harold Hayes: I think an interesting point as far as the two writers that are here today, is the question of impulse. What is it that gets them into a story, what is it causes them to start to see things their own way? With Tom, the thing that was absolutely fascinating for us at *Esquire*, was the point when he decided to write good stuff, but fairly conventional stuff. And suddenly, on a weekend, Tom discovered a voice for himself, absolutely unique, and it is now perhaps one of the most copied voices in all of magazine reporting. He's ruined a whole generation of journalists, I think.

Tom Wolfe: Well, I've written about the way this thing happened; I was doing a story about custom cars for *Esquire* and I went to California, did all the reporting, and I came back and I just got a total block on it. And *Esquire* has many ingenious ways for making you either turn out some copy or relinquish your material; they told me that they had $10,000 worth of plates on the press and that if I didn't get the story in it would be down the drain. Ten thousand dollars seemed like the end of the world or something. Anyhow, I tried and tried to write this thing, but the subject was so new to me, the custom cars, I ran into a whole world I hadn't seen before, that I just couldn't do it. Finally, Byron Dobell who was Harold's second-in-command at that point, told me to just type up my notes and hand them in and they'd get a "competent" writer to write them up.

Harold Hayes: An old journalist?

Tom Wolfe: So one day about eight o'clock I started typing up the notes in a very straightforward way, but I did it as kind of a memo to Byron, whom I got to know pretty well in all the time he'd had to nag me to get the story in. I started off, writing a letter about what I had seen on the custom cars. My only intent was just to write down in black and white all of my notes. But I had them here in front of me, and I started to type "The first place that I saw custom cars was at————," and that's the way this story actually begins. Well anyway, I ended up writing all night long, finally by about six in the morning, I had typed up 48 pages of what in effect was a letter to Byron Dobell. At the end of that he just knocked the Dear Byron off and ran the letter. Well now the thing that this proved to me about style was, (a), that most people end up all of their lives doing their best writing in letters. Especially to a friend, or somebody you think understands you, and somebody you're not inhibited with, because you don't have all of those forty or fifty or seventy people looking over your shoulder that most of us feel like are there when we actually start writing for public consumption. We think that all of our professors, teachers, other writers, and all sorts of terrific people are looking on. (In fact, they're not; they're not ever looking.) But in a letter to a friend you just start letting it all roll out; you don't hold back the little random comments.

Of course the second time around it's a little hard to do this, because the second time around you're fooling yourself; you know, you're saying, well I'm going to write this as if I'm writing a letter to a friend, only you're really not. But nevertheless, you do find something, once you've done that. You start to see what your own voice is.

DISCUSSION QUESTIONS
SUGGESTIONS FOR WRITING

1. What are the distinguishing characteristics of the "new journalism"? How does it differ from conventional journalism?

2. Do you agree that "All external reality as it's being presented in the multimedia of today seems less and less like reality as we individuals experience it"?

3. Describe in detail the convention of the magazine article as it used to be practiced. Is this convention now totally obsolete?

4. What is the significance of Tom Wolfe's statement: "I think it's justifiable to . . . try to get inside of the psyche somehow, and to be able to report on the interior of the skull in some way" to the current revolution in nonfiction forms?

XI

People

JOAN BAEZ
(b. 1941), famous folk
singer and peace activist,
writes in her autobiography
Daybreak of her sister Mimi and Mimi's husband,
Richard Fariña. A writer
as well as one of the leading folk-rock composers
and performers in the
United States, Richard
Fariña was killed in a
motorcycle accident two
days after the publication
of his first novel, *Been
Down So Long It Looks
Like Up to Me.*

CHILD
OF
DARKNESS

I'LL tell you what he was in my eyes. He was my sister Mimi's crazy husband, a mystical child of darkness—blatantly ambitious, lovable, impossible, charming, obnoxious, tirelessly active—a bright, talented, sheepish, tricky, curly-haired, man-child of darkness.

Remember that he was my brother-in-law—husband to one sister Mimi, close friend to the other sister, Pauline, and mystical brother to me. He'd won me full over by the end, from a hostile, critical in-law of Dick the intruder to a fond friend. By the end we sisters and many other people had some of Dick's blood running in our veins, and mad Irish Cuban thoughts in our heads.

Dick worried about the monkey-demon on the night of the full moon, and kept a little stash of pot in a cut-away hole in the center of an old book on the Irish Revolution. He carried in his wallet a tiny leather box from India which held a hair and a piece of paper with two words written on it in a strange language, and which mustn't be opened until just before its carrier was to die. He talked by candlelight late late into the night with Mimi—all about the cards. And then he cut the deck for himself and drew the King of Hearts. Happy in the strange night, he made Mimi cut a card for herself, and she drew the Queen of Hearts. And they were close and certain and frightened and "Mimi," he said, "you do one for Joanie. Come on, one for Joanie." And Mimi cut me the Jack of Dia-monds. And this too . . . that out of all the angles and candles and king purple and gold and burgundy red and hushed magnificence of the ancient cathedral at Chartres, Dick spied a tiny black alcove, and as he whispered toward it he saw that it had in it, among other miniature statues, strange little demon figures, the same demons he felt he knew by heart.

But Dick's thorny demons of the night hid themselves during the day from the sun which shone on a fairyland of beauty. A fairyland of thoughts and images of swallows and rose petals and new love and the eternal blossoming springtime of another land. In this other land he took his friends by the hand, and strutted and bowed and doffed his hat, and played a million roles, wrote a million songs and a million poems, swished his dulcimer from under a tree and sang and talked before a million people. Also in this land he was a writer, which was not such grand fun all the time, which was hard work and which no one seemed to understand, and which tested Dick as a young man and Mimi as his second wife.

I knew Dick then, in that odd world for those few years, those typewriter and spaghetti years which got a little plusher toward the end. And he and Mimi never went under. They never really thought about going under because it was too much fun treading water. And besides, they liked each other lots, and Dick and Mimi had a most extraordinary and rare capacity for having fun. . . .

A dinner at home. At Dick's house. Yes, I remember. Dick would cook with garlic. Tons of garlic. All other foods were secondary. There would be music. Loud music — Gospel, or Vivaldi, or the Beatles. I can remember a Beatles night. Dick was an automatic host, and that evening as friends began to wander in the door he waved his onion-cutting knife, turned the music up past the pain threshold and began salad directing Mimi. Mimi made exasperation faces as she began to labor over the greens. The house was at a low rumble. No mustard. Over the Beatles everyone must understand no mustard. Dick would die in a flash from mustard allergy. Simply clog up somewhere in the pipes and smother to death. Someone poured the wine and more guests came and the house was heavy with spice smells. Small talk about Carmel and big talk about Vietnam. Carmel had been beautiful that day and Johnson was a monster and had terrible-looking ears. Also, shouted Dick, he prayed on Sundays and killed Orientals all week and that was pretty revolting by itself. Everyone agreed. One more round of wine and a record change and dinner was on. A last guest knocked and was admitted. He was new. A glass for the new guest. Bring him to the table. Hello, hi, hi, groovy, sit down. And that night the new guest said it by chance. There was always an opening line. The new guest, by chance, over the clapping and stomping of the Birmingham Back Home Gospel Choir, offered unwittingly, "It's been a splendid day . . ."

"Yes!" said Dick. "A splendid day. Splendid. Splendid day for grouse!"

And he raised his wine glass high to the roars of laughter. The new guest was initiated and blushing and on his own, and we teased Dick for his timing and began to eat. Dick held his fork European style and mashed bits of food onto it with his knife. I watched him heap it to overweight, raise it halfway to his mouth and then pause with great drama. One of the regulars to his right was gulping milk. He turned toward her.

"Agatha."

Agatha. It was her name for the evening and it was delivered in high English. "Must you drink your milk with such an incredible amount of onomatopoeia?"

The regular didn't know what onomatopoeia was but laughed anyway. Dick nodded to his wife and commenced eating. All right. If Dick would be high English, I would be low English. Not only would I be low English, I'd be blind and in a wheelchair. I was interrupted in the middle of my fantasies.

"Samantha." That was me. "I believe I heard you belch. I do prefer my own gastronomical fluids. We all do choose our savories to our own tastes. Eat up, dear. Chew each bite succulently." I burped and was preparing a comment.

"Eloise, you're beginning to perspire. Would you like a Phillips tablet? Would you like the pukka boy? Shall I ring for Rob?"

The laughing was steady from that point on with pauses for eating and changes of character. Dick commanded and directed the show, swaying the tide of nonsense, starring but always tugging at the quiet ones to try out the fun — to laugh. Before a night was over he would have gone German officer, gone Festus Turd from Texas, gone Indian foreign exchange student, gone paralyzed, gone weightless, gone blind, and gone mad. I would go with him because I loved it. It was crazy and it was fun, and the night roared by as we laughed ourselves teary-eyed.

That dinner ended with a salad fight, when a piece of sliced tomato knocked a Mexican plate off the wall from directly over my head. The house was rented and so was the plate, of course, so we felt dampened and all gave serious thought as to how to glue up fifty pieces of crumbly plaster. We gave up, had a plate funeral, talked about politics for a while, lingered, felt good, and finally went home.

I laughed to myself, reflected upon the evening and felt enormously grateful and happy. Those nights of fun, hosted by the Black Irish Mad Hatted Rose — those nights are what I miss most of all since Dick died.

Dick died before he ever figured out how he felt about "making it." What he meant when he said "making it" was the Hollywood thing — having money and fame and a public image. Dick and I knew when we talked how stupid the whole concept was — that a public image was based upon some truths, some half-truths, some innocent rumors, and a few nasty lies. It meant general overexposure and self-consciousness (as opposed to self-awareness) and the constant danger of accepting someone else's evaluation of you in place of your own—your own being practically impossible to make already. Money meant power, an irresistible prestige value, and lots of extra attention—all of which could be used, almost in spite of themselves, for good things if you kept your head. We also knew the meaning of the word temptation, and what a smart thing it was for Jesus to say, "Lead us not into temptation," because He knew well that once we got there we were all so very weak.

Sometime, not too long before the carnival ended, Dick's wild carrousel slowed down long enough for him to write these words in a song to Mimi—

> Now is the time for your loving, dear,
> And the time for your company.
> Now when the light of reason fails
> And fires burn on the sea,
> Now in this age of confusion
> I have need for your company.

DISCUSSION QUESTIONS
SUGGESTIONS FOR WRITING

1. Daybreak *is an example of the recent movement towards autobiography —writers, a long way from old age, writing autobiographies that might just as well be novels, as they borrow the conventions of realistic fiction, except for the fact that the writer leaves in his own name and that, presumably, the events recounted are autobiographical and not invented. In the case of a known personality such as Joan Baez writing an autobiography, however, the promise of character interest and revelation is present, as in the usual conception of autobiography, even before the book is opened. What does this selection reveal about Joan Baez's personality?*

2. Since Richard Fariña is the subject of this section of Daybreak, *the section may be viewed as biographical as well as autobiographical. How is the piece enhanced by the fact that the biographer is a participant-observer?*

3. What details of Joan Baez's characterization of Richard Fariña make him seem most vivid and exceptional and alive?

4. What accounts for the poignancy of the ending?

VANCE BOURJAILY (b. 1922) is a well-known novelist and teacher of writing at the Writers Workshop of the University of Iowa. He has also been a newspaperman, a television dramatist, and a playwright and has contributed to *The New Yorker* and many other magazines. His books include *The End of My Life, The Hound of Earth, The Violated, Confessions of a Spent Youth, The Unnatural Enemy, The Man Who Knew Kennedy,* and *Brill among the Ruins.*

CONFESSIONS OF A SPENT YOUTH

SINCE you are going to read about me as a lover my appearance is probably relevant; I will treat it as a permanent thing. For so it is, really—aging is the treatment our looks receive, once we are grown, not a real revision of them.

I am five feet six and a half inches tall; do not believe my driver's license which reads five feet seven. I have never developed the erect and bristling carriage with which many short men manage to disguise their lack of height and am, in fact, a sloucher and not tidy. My hair is a very ordinary shade of brown and very ordinarily in need of cutting, but seldom to the point of defiant unconventionality; as I approach that point I often have it all chopped down army style. I am, at this moment, while writing, wearing a mustache, but those I have raised in the past have never been of lasting satisfaction to me, and I doubt that this one will; safer to think of me as clean-shaven.

I am neither ill-co-ordinated nor am I graceful, quite strong in the legs and back, limber, able to catch most kinds of ball if they aren't thrown too fast, so that I am inclined to ascribe my lack of notable athletic achievement to mental rather than physical characteristics. I have insufficient drive to win at games, but enjoy playing; I like to fish small streams alone, and I shoot well enough with a shotgun but in streaks, sometimes missing every easy shot for a month. I mention these activities because I want you to see my movements as neither quick nor slow, deteriorating under pressure, but not always without skill.

My weight varies a good deal; once, four or five years ago, I did enough neurotic eating, in reaction to some problems I couldn't seem to solve, to get up close to 170 pounds, and at that weight I looked bloated. Normally, though, I stay within a few pounds of 150 and am not fat, whatever young Quincy says. However, along with the strong back I mentioned I have the hips, trunk, and shoulders of a slightly larger man set on my somewhat stubby legs; smile, enemies. Friends, regard my face.

At times I recall having had the notion that I could identify with those secondary creatures in detective stories one of whose assets is the ability to appear entirely usual, to blend with crowds and so on — perhaps that is my type in terms of features in repose, but I do not have the inexpressiveness that must complete the type unless I remember to compose it. Most of the time I suspect I am quite transparent, and that you would like or dislike my appearance on the basis of what showed through the face at the time we met, well-being or weariness, or sullenness or joy. Suspect this? Boast. When there were no lines, when the flesh upon the face was young, wasn't transparency my most effective, because least conscious, charm?

About the flesh itself, it is sallow, a word more precise than pleasant; the dark, Levantine skin of my father, the fair English of my mother, are, whatever a geneticist might say of the possibility, too exactly met halfway in me. But it isn't really that bad, being sallow, except towards the end of a city winter when an overlying pallor gives me the skin tone of a scaled fish. I avoid city winters and in summer tan well enough, and my beard shows less.

The rest is fretting: sometimes I think my nose too heavy, my teeth crooked, and my chin too slight. At other times they look normal enough, and I grant myself that I have a decent set of brows and lashes and that the general modelling of my face and forehead will do, though they are nothing exceptional.

When I lived in the South, where girls are taught the value of flirtation by physical compliment, the feature they always spoke of, when one happened to find herself flirting with me, was my eyes; these are blue and fairly bright.

That will do to sum up; if you are complimented on your eyes by a Southern girl, it's a giveaway that she has looked you over, considered all she comprehends about you, and found nothing in particular worth mentioning. Anyone can be made to believe that he or she has lovely eyes for, in fact, everyone does.

DISCUSSION QUESTIONS
SUGGESTIONS FOR WRITING

1. One of the main difficulties of self-characterization — necessary to autobiography — is creating sympathy for oneself as a character and avoiding the appearance of conceit or egotism that would alienate the reader. How does Vance Bourjaily accomplish this result in this selection?

2. Is it always necessary to be self-effacing in such a writing situation? How does one express what one is accurately?

3. What types of descriptions suggest deeper levels of personality?

4. How would you characterize yourself if you were writing your own autobiography? Attempt such a characterization on paper, using the Bourjaily piece as a model.

BELLAMY

AN INTERVIEW WITH ROBERT BOLES

ROBERT BOLES (b. 1943) is the author of two highly praised novels, *The People One Knows* and *Curling,* and has contributed stories to *The New Yorker* and to the Langston Hughes anthology *Best Short Stories by Negro Writers.* The *New York Times Book Review* recently listed him among a handful of contemporary black writers with "substantial reputations." The following interview took place on December 4, 1969, in Mansfield, Pennsylvania, where Mr. Boles had come to read, lecture, and meet with students in conjunction with a new English course at Mansfield State College entitled "20th Century Black Fiction in America."

Interviewer: One thing that some of the students in my class noted, as I did — we've read Wright, we've read Baldwin and Ellison and Jim McPherson and now your book *Curling* — and it really is different. It seems to have a different purpose from the other books. Maybe the difference is related to what you were saying about fiction becoming more like poetry. The way I explained it to them was: It seemed to me your concern was not with plot and not much with Victorian conventions that are still being used in a lot of novels (Wright certainly used them) but with capturing consciousness, capturing the fabric of the way the mind functions — in each moment. Would you say that's an accurate description of what you're trying to do?

Boles: Yes, I guess so. I'm not really wild about plot. I believe that fiction is changing — for a lot of reasons. Time in novels, for instance, isn't being used the way it has been. People don't want to read the old kind of novel where time flows evenly; they want to be sort of punched again and again and again.

Interviewer: What do you think accounts for such a change?

Boles: I really think it's due to a lot of things—but, for instance, television. Like, if you watch television, if you notice how many different settings you absorb, say, in a given two hours, how many different settings, how many different situations, that is, how many different *pictures* are really sort of bombarding you, you can't help being amazed. I think people are expecting fiction to do some of the things television does. People want more variety—faster, sharper images—things that are going to hit them, you know. That's what poems do, and fiction is getting more like that, it seems to me—in lots of books. It's apparent, for instance, that people are writing shorter scenes, more powerful scenes; they're isolating moments and writing about them; and more and more books are, like, collections of these.

Interviewer: You go to almost any movie; you watch Simon and Garfunkel on their TV special; in almost every aspect of current popular art and even art that isn't predominantly popular there seems to be an effort to explain what's happening with America. It seems to me that since the assassination it's been that way. Do you think it has to be everyone's purpose? Do you have to write *the* American novel every time you write a novel—or make some statement about the way it is in America?

Boles: Hm. You're absolutely right about that. For instance, right up to the change in administration, especially on television, things were either left or right.

Interviewer: It's like a big identity crisis.

Boles: Things were either really left-wing or right-wing. Name any show, and I'll tell you if it's right-wing or left-wing. I really think that's unfortunate. Well, music is that way, too. Rock is generally left-wing. I really think it's too bad that art should be. . . . Well, you see, I don't think current American politics are valuable enough. I think it can only make art sort of worse—as bad as the politics. I really think it's unfortunate. I try to keep politics out of things—the Negro thing especially. I try to keep politics out of it. But it's very difficult because everything now is a political symbol. People, the ways people dress, are political symbols. I wonder where it will end? It seems to be getting, you know, worse and worse.

Interviewer: What was your purpose in making Chelsea in *Curling*? He seems to be constantly trying to remember. Was that an expression of your own trying to remember? Or did you have some other purpose in mind?

Boles: He was very hard to write. I worked with him a long, long time. I just wanted him to be uncertain, so uncertain that he would lose the capability of thinking, of making judgments. I guess that's why some people thought it was an existentialist novel. But I don't think it was because with him, you know, every experience did carry a different weight.

Interviewer: You mentioned in one of your earlier sessions that Chelsea was a man without a history — that he was cut off from his history and *that* was one of his vital concerns. Could you say more about that?

Boles: I think that history is really an important thing — to have. Just as I think, for instance, that people should know their sources. For instance, do you know how much more comfortable you said you felt, like, eating the apples you had from your own tree? It's like if you go pheasant hunting or something like that, you're actually responsible for what you eat, and it's close to you. You find you're more comfortable. I think old attitudes of people, like, *change* because they eat packaged food. I think that the farther and farther people get from their sources — well, take pheasant hunting or killing a chicken — you know, if everyone had to do it for himself, I think people would be more sensitive to life. And the farther they get away from it, the less they care about — life, killing in general. I think if everyone hunted — hunted his own food, I don't think we'd be in Vietnam. But that might sound like a strange thing to say.

Interviewer: It seems to me that it's related to — the kind of senseless murder that is committed by Chelsea. How do you account for the necessity of that act — and how it seems to purge him?

Boles: Well, he's concerned because he doesn't have a history. And he's really in a very strange situation, a very strange world that doesn't really have any relation to him. I think what he learns at the end, is that an act such as he commits, you know, killing the guy, doesn't at all give him the kind of history that he's after. The wrong way to solve problems is with that kind of action.

Interviewer: It's almost as if he wants to be part of the history, or wants to know the history, of the man he kills?

Boles: He does. He even likes him.

Interviewer: Do you think Chelsea is a figure who is meant to be, either consciously or unconsciously, more than one person? Is he more than an individual? I mean, are you writing about modern alienated man — or the plight of the black man in America — as well as about Chelsea Burlingame?

Boles: Both. You see, one thing about Negroes is that — great numbers of them — their histories have been denied them and — that's bound to affect a person. Then too, there are a lot of people who are generally, I guess, urban—and just choose not to recognize their histories. They are the kinds of people—this is too broad a generalization—imagine the people who live in cities, who work at jobs, people whose jobs and lives are so superfluous. Just imagine someone, well let's say, in advertising in New York, or some other job in New York, someone who's so far away from any source that is sustaining him—and whose work is so superfluous that if he were cast out of the city, he couldn't survive. I don't know—it's kind of hard to talk about. Basically, I guess, I just want people to stop killing people. And I really want to find out why they do. And—why it's tolerated.

Interviewer: Your first book was described by one reviewer as the story of "a fully dimensioned Negro fighting more than a color problem." How do you feel about that?

Boles: Well, I would say that that's right. There's always more than a color problem in anyone's life. And my character is not obsessed with the color problem. It's there, you know, it's evident; but his problems deal with other things too, which are also very important. It was strange when the novel came out because a few reviewers reviewed it strictly as a—as a race novel and were disappointed, you know, because it wasn't.

Interviewer: What is your picture of a "fully dimensioned Negro"?

Boles: A man. In lots of fiction—well, it's growing less and less so— Negroes always had a function, which was to be—Negro, you know. And, well, people are just not quite that simple, and it would be lying if I wrote characters that way.

Interviewer: What do you mean that Negroes always had a function?

Boles: In novels, in plays, in protest literature, the black man was either servile, or protesting, or angry, but the whole crux of his character was always that this was a black.

Interviewer: As one of my students might say—isn't that a very understandable reaction to American society which tries to make the Negro white?

Boles: Let me say first that—I'm an integrationist, and I'm an American; I'm a man; I'm a Negro; I'm all sorts, you know, I'm all sorts of things. I think that being black, the way that most people think of it, is—is a state of mind really. I think anyone can be black. I've known white people who were black. And I think it has less and less to do with race at all. I don't believe—I don't believe in racism.

Of course, it's a very complicated question. In some places, for instance the South, banding together is really necessary to gain economic power, political power, other kinds of power. But then too *that* kind of banding together, for those reasons, I don't think of as generally racist. I mean it's something that is necessary, but it's not—glorification of race as a way of life.

Interviewer: What do you think about the kind of course I'm teaching now? Do you think it's legitimate? Do you think it's filling a need that should have been filled before?

Boles: I don't know, I'm really sort of touchy about—black literature. Mostly because, you know, I think it's unfair. If I were going to teach a black literature course, aside from using, like only black American writers, I would use, like, African writers, and also use, like, Pushkin, who was black, and Alexandre Dumas, who was black. It really is true art. You see, it's coming much too late. Black literature should have been included in American literature from the first. And I think that's generally where it belongs.

Interviewer: Do you resent being invited to come to a place to speak as a "young black writer"?

Boles: Strangely enough, no. It doesn't really bother me any*more*. I guess that's because of what I ultimately say to people. What does offend me very much is—being a black writer, if I wrote something about—name the subject—in the library it would be classified under black writers, regardless of what it was about; and I think that's unfortunate. There are so many things I want to write about, just lots and lots of things. And lots of things I want to write about don't have anything to do with—with race. But black writers are expected to be concerned with race—and only that. And I'm not and I think it would be wrong for me, you know, to live that way. It wouldn't be fair to me, you know, as a writer. It wouldn't be fair. I want to get the most I can out of life and out of working and—I just can't devote my life to racism—or else I'd become a racist. I'm challenged an awful lot by lots of black people who say I'm copping out, who say I should be writing to tell people where the problems are; but people *know* where the problems are. Lots of people think black writers should write, you know, propaganda. That's really bad. I've always thought, if I'm going to be writing seriously, just about race, propounding an argument to say what to do, who's going to read it but the people who are already sold? There are enough black protest novels, I think. The only thing I could do in that line would be sort of, you know, to copy. And I don't want to do that. Just like with *Curling*, like, the *New York Times* reviewer said in his review "the author gives the reader the option of coloring the hero," you know, "either black or white"; and the reason he said that was, like, he was reading the book and at times didn't think of the character as a Negro but sort of—just a man; and, like, that's the kind of character I want to write. I don't want to write cardboard people. And if people can, if white people, white readers, can identify with black, like, a Negro character, as a constant thing, I think I can do much more that way. I want to make my characters human.

Interviewer: So you sometimes wish that people would let you out of black literature courses and into the mainstream of the culture so that you could be a significant *American* writer?

Boles: Yeah, yes. I don't want to use race to get ahead because I think, you know, that's a lousy way of doing things, nor do I want it to hold me back.

Interviewer: Are you worried about the death of the novel?

Boles: . . . No.

Interviewer: Or the death of writing, the death of language, written language?

Boles: No. Are you worried about it?

Interviewer: I'm worried about it a little bit. There was a time there when I was reading Susan Sontag and McLuhan and Norman Podhoretz that I was getting kind of worried. Susan Sontag wasn't saying the novel was going to disappear, but that it would become so specialized that only specialists could understand it; so it wouldn't be a mass medium anymore. Does that seem likely to you? As fiction writers become more sophisticated, more like poets, their audiences become smaller and more sophisticated. . . .

Boles: I really tend to disagree with that—because I don't think the audiences are becoming smaller.

Interviewer: Percentagewise or something?

Boles: Not even percentagewise really. Maybe the day will come when we're at that time. Then writers will be doing the same things they're doing in another way.

Interviewer: You know, novels that look like novels *may* be diminishing in number. Critics keep writing that the novel is dying because the novel is not doing so many of the things that novels are supposed to do. And then you say the novel is not moribund at all, but your own books might confirm some of the critics' worst fears. What do you think the novel *is*?

Boles: Oh, that's a good question. That's a good question. We were talking in an earlier session about the differences between fiction and poetry. The major difference, I think, is that novels rely on middlemen. Novelists always intersperse characters between the reader and the writer—for the reader to identify with. I think that's probably, for me at any rate, the major distinction. And you can use characters in lots and lots and lots of ways. Novels can take almost any shape or form, I think.

Interviewer: Say you received a package in the mail, and it was a total environment kit and was going to give you the consciousness of a character or a group of characters, and it had filmstrips, and it had tape recordings and all sorts of things you could do to recreate the states of mind of the characters, and maybe, say, only a fourth of it was actual linear writing — would you consider that a novel?

Boles: Probably. I even know a novelist who wants to write books that people can actually eat.

Interviewer: (laughter)

Boles: Really and truly.

DISCUSSION QUESTIONS
SUGGESTIONS FOR WRITING

1. *Do you see any evidence of the influence of the electronic media — of the type Robert Boles points out — in the fictional selections in this anthology? Or in the nonfiction selections? In the increasing currency, for example, of the interview form itself?*

2. *What is Boles' attitude toward the recommendation that black writers should concern themselves chiefly with race, and therefore with protest literature? What alternative mode does he suggest? Why?*

3. *What does Boles mean by: "I think that the farther and farther people get from their sources . . . the less they care about — life, killing in general"?*

4. *Until recently, the interview has not been taken as seriously as it might have been, perhaps because it seems, on the surface, too easy — just a lot of talking written down. In actual practice, a good interview requires considerable preparation and research on the part of the interviewer. In addition to the requirement of asking informed questions, what skills must the interviewer exercise?*

JOHN CASEY (b. 1939) is a writer, lawyer, and reviewer for such magazines as the *New York Times Book Review.* His fiction has appeared in *The New Yorker, Sports Illustrated,* and *Redbook.* The following interview with Kurt Vonnegut, Jr., was conducted in the winter of 1968 during a visit by Vonnegut to the Iowa Writers Workshop.

AN INTERVIEW WITH KURT VONNEGUT, JR.

Vonnegut: I know you'll ask it.

Interviewer: Are you a black humorist . . . ?

Vonnegut: You asked it. One day in solitude on Cape Cod, a large bell-jar was lowered over me by Bruce Friedman, and it said "black humor" on the label; and I felt around a bit and there was no way I could get out of that jar—so here I am and you ask the question. At the time, I didn't know what "black humor" was, but now because the question must be asked, I have worked up what is called a "bookish" answer.

In the Modern Library edition of *The Works of Freud,* you'll find a section on humor in which he talks about middle European "gallows humor," and it so happens that what Friedman calls "black humor" is very much like German-Austrian-Polish "gallows humor." In the face of plague and Napoleonic wars and such things, it's little people saying very wry, very funny things, on the point of death. One of the examples Freud gives is a man about to be hanged, and the hangman says: "Do you have anything to say?" The condemned man replies: "Not at this time."

This country has made one tremendous contribution to "gallows humor," and it took place in Cook County Jail (you'll have to ask Nelson Algren who said it). A man was strapped into the electric chair and he said to the witnesses, "This will certainly teach me a lesson."

Anyway, the label is useless except for the merchandisers. I don't think anybody is very happy about the category or depressed about being excluded from it—Vance Bourjaily was, and took it very well, I thought.

Interviewer: And the science-fiction label . . . ?

Vonnegut: If you allow yourself to be called a science-fiction writer, people will think of you as some lower type, someone out of the "mainstream," great word isn't it? The people in science-fiction enjoy it—they know each other, have conventions and have a hell of a lot of fun. But they are thought to be inferior writers, and generally are, I think, at least the ones who go to conventions.

When I started to write, I was living in Schenectady, working as a public relations man, surrounded by scientists and machinery. So I wrote my first book, *Player Piano*, about Schenectady and it was published. I was classified as a science-fiction writer because I'd included machinery, and all I'd done was write about Schenectady in 1948! So, I allowed this to go on, I thought it was an honor to be printed anywhere. And so it was, I suppose. But I would run into people who would downgrade me. I ran into Jason Epstein, a terribly powerful cultural commissar, at a cocktail party. When we were introduced, he thought a minute, then said, "Science-fiction," turned and walked off. He just had to place me, that's all.

But I continued to include machinery in my books and, may I say in *confidence*, in my life. Most critics, products of humanities and social science departments, have felt fear of engineers. And there used to be this feeling amongst reviewers that anyone who knew how a refrigerator works can't be an artist too! Machinery is important. We must write about it.

But I don't care if you don't; I'm not urging you, am I? To hell with machinery.

Interviewer: Are there science-fiction writers you admire?

Vonnegut: Yes. Ray Bradbury, Ted Sturgeon, Isaac Asimov, among others.

Interviewer: One of the sections of *Sirens of Titan* I'm very fond of is the chapter on harmoniums. But most of the book is so sardonic that I was surprised by the lyricism of the section. Did you mean this as relief? The way Shakespeare has comic relief?

Vonnegut: I hope my relief is more helpful than Shakespearean comic relief.

Interviewer: Did you intend . . . ?

Vonnegut: Yes, I can say it probably was because at one point I used to talk about what I was going to do to lighten it up for a while. . . . well, I don't think that way anymore. There was a time when I was a very earnest student writer and had a teacher, Kenneth Littauer, an old-time magazine editor, agent, and splendid old gentleman. And we would talk about things like that, that is, after dark passages you have a light one . . .

Interviewer: . . . and there should be large and small shapes and in-between shapes . . .

Vonnegut: . . . and use short sentences with short words when people are running, and long sentences and long words when people are sleeping. Those things are all true, the things I learned from Littauer about pace and point of view, things that are discussed in *Writer's Digest,* decent and honorable things to know. We must acknowledge that the reader is doing something quite difficult for him and the reason you don't change point of view too often is so he won't get lost and the reason you paragraph often is so that his eyes won't get tired, is so you get him without him knowing it by making his job easy for him. He has to re-stage your show in his head, costume and light it. His job is not easy.

Interviewer: Is this still the way you . . . ?

Vonnegut: I don't know. I have this strong sense of merely unfolding. I let the old ghost use me when he feels he can.

Interviewer: This girl I know says that Kurt Vonnegut dislikes women. . . .

Vonnegut: You know, I think I get along with women quite well. In my life, in my actual life, I hope I don't treat them disparagingly. It has never worried me, but is puzzling, that I've never been able to do a woman well in a book. Part of it is that I'm a performer when I write. I am taking off on different characters and I frequently have a good British accent and the characters I do well in my books are parts I can play easily. If it were dramatized I would be able to do my best characters on stage, and I don't make a very good female impersonator.

And also there is the resentment I had against my wife. Everybody gets pissed off at his wife, and when I'd be angry at her and there's a houseful of kids and so forth—you know there *were* these shattered realities in my life—I'm working in a houseful of diapers and my wife wanting money and there not being enough and so forth. I was angry with my wife for the same reason everybody is angry with his wife. And I'm not anymore. The children are all grown up. Maybe I can write better about it now.

Interviewer: Is Winston Niles Rumford in *Sirens of Titan* a verbal portrait of FDR? There are hints, the cigarette holder, high Groton tenor, and details like that. Was FDR part of the impulse to write the book?

Vonnegut: You know, no one else has ever commented on that. The fact is Roosevelt is the key figure in the book, although the impulse was to write about what FDR had been to me as a young man during the Depression and the Second World War and so forth. Roosevelt took the lead in the book, however, not me. I wrote that book very quickly. I hadn't written a book for maybe eight years, and a friend of mine, Knox Burger, an editor, saw me one day and said, "Write me a book!" I had an idea, he liked it. I went home and very cheerfully and very quickly produced it. Almost automatic.

Interviewer: Are there any other people . . . ?

Vonnegut: Well. Eliot Rosewater, for instance, in *God Bless You, Mr. Rosewater*, there really is a man who is that *kind*. Except he's poor, an accountant over a liquor store. We shared an office and I could hear him comforting people who had very little income, calling everybody "dear," and giving love and understanding instead of money. And I heard him doing marriage counseling and I asked him about that and he said that once people told you how little money they'd made they felt they had to tell you everything. I took this very sweet man and in a book gave him millions and millions to play with.

Interviewer: In *Cat's Cradle*, where did you get the idea for Ice-9?

Vonnegut: Irving Langmuir, a Nobel Prize winner in Chemistry, told H. G. Wells as an idea for a science-fiction story about a form of ice that was stable at room temperature. Wells wasn't interested. I heard the story, and as Langmuir and Wells were both dead, considered it my legacy, my found object.

At a cocktail party once, I was introduced to a famous crystalographer and I told him about Ice-9. He just dropped out of the party, went over to the side of the room and sat down while everybody was chatting away, for a long time, then he got up and came over to me and said, "Uh unh, not possible."

Interviewer: . . . Childhood. . . .

Vonnegut: Here are two things that ruined my earlier life: life insurance and envy.

When I became a writer, I quit General Electric, had a family and moved to Cape Cod, which was an alarming thing to do. It frightened me so much about what might happen to my family that I bought a perfect bruiser of a life insurance policy. Every nickel I made went into this, until it was obvious I could make a hell of a lot of money by merely dying. I became obsessed with this idea. I talked to a scientist I knew about life insurance (you should have some scientists among your friends, they think straight); this guy (his name is Dr. John Fisher) was a well-known metallurgist (and his wife's name is Josephine). I said, "John, how much life insurance have you got?" He said, "None." And I said, "What, you don't have *any* insurance," and he said, "Hell no, what do I care what happens to Jo after I'm dead: I won't feel anything." It was release. I let my policy lapse.

On envy, well, I was nearly consumed with it, like being shot full of sulphuric acid. I have beaten it pretty well. I was put to the test recently when a young man dropped by (young people *do* seem to like me a lot) in a Lincoln Continental, and he was nineteen years old and had kept a diary of the Columbia riots which he had sold along with the movie rights. He said, "So far, I've made $27,000 from the riots." And I took it beautifully, I said, "Isn't that nice."

I'm richer now than I used to be. I'm a lot happier too.

Interviewer: What about your newest novel, *Slaughterhouse 5*?

Vonnegut: It's . . . it's very thin . . . about as long as *The Bobbsey Twins*. This length has been considered a fault. *Ramparts* (*Ramparts* is serializing the novel) called to ask if they had received all the manuscript. I said, "Yeah, that's it." I'm satisfied. They're satisfied. They just wanted to make sure they had all the paper they were entitled to.

But I think this is what a novel should be right now. I'd like, for example, to write books that *men* can read. I know that men don't read, and that bothers me. I would like to be a member of my community and men in our society do not customarily value the services of a writer. To get their attention, I should write short novels.

The reason novels were so thick for so long was that people had so much time to kill. I do not furnish transportation for my characters; I do not move them from one room to another; I do not send them up the stairs; they do not get dressed in the mornings; they do not put the ignition key in the lock, and turn on the engine, and let it warm up and look at all the gauges, and put the car in reverse, and back out, and drive to the filling station and ask the guy there about the weather. You can fill up a good size book with this connective tissue. People would be satisfied too. I've often thought of taking one of my thin books (because people won't pay much for one) and adding a sash-weight to it, just to give someone the bulk he needs to pay seven or eight dollars for the thing which is what I need to really eat and stuff.

There's the *Valley of the Dolls* solution which is the Bernard Geis solution which is to print the book on ¾ inch plywood, each page, and to print the type in the width of a newspaper column down the middle of the plywood. Then you've got a good size book. But there're no words in it. Incidently nobody's really complained yet.

Interviewer: What about your newest novel, *Slaughterhouse 5*?

Vonnegut: . . . was to treat a disaster. I was present in the greatest massacre in European history, which was the destruction of Dresden by fire-bombing. So I said, "OK, you were there."

The American and British air forces together killed 135,000 people in two hours. This is a world's record. It's never been done faster, not in the battle of Britain or Hiroshima. (In order to qualify as a massacre you have to kill *real* fast). But I was there, and there was no news about it in the American papers, it was so embarrassing. I was there—so say something about it.

The way we survived—we were in the stockyards in the middle of Dresden. How does a firestorm work? Waves and waves of planes come over carrying high explosives which open roofs, make lots of kindling, and drive the firemen underground. Then they take hundreds of thousands of little incendiary bombs (the size had been reduced from a foot and a half to a shotgun shell by the end of the war) and scatter them. Then more high explosives until all the little fires join up into one apocalyptic flame with tornadoes around the edges sucking more and more, feeding the inferno.

Dresden was a highly ornamented city, like Paris. There were no air-raid shelters, just ordinary cellars, because a raid was not expected, and the war was almost over.

We got through it, the Americans there, because we were quartered in the stockyards where it was wide and open and there was a meat locker three stories beneath the surface, the only decent shelter in the city. So we went down into the meat locker, and when we came up again the city was gone and everybody was dead. We walked for miles before we saw anybody else; all organic things were consumed.

Anyway, I came home in 1945, started writing about it, and wrote about it, and wrote about it, and WROTE ABOUT IT. This thin book is about what it's like to write a book about a thing like that. I couldn't get much closer. I would head myself into my memory of it, the circuit breakers would kick out; I'd head in again, I'd back off. The book is a process of twenty years of this sort of living with Dresden and the aftermath. It's like Henrik Boll's book, *Absent Without Leave*—stories about German soldiers with the war part missing. You see them leave and return, but there's this terrible hole in the middle. That is like my memory of Dresden, actually there's nothing there. It's a strange book. I'm pleased with it.

Interviewer: One last question. . . .

Vonnegut: I'll give you a disturbing answer. People are programmed, just like computers with this tape feeding out. When I was teaching student writers, I suddenly realized in most cases what I was doing was reaching into the mouth, taking hold of the piece of tape, pulling gently to see if I could read what was printed on it.

There is this thing called the university and everybody goes there now. And there are these things called teachers who make students read this book with good ideas or that book with good ideas, until that's where we get our ideas. We don't think them, we read them in books.

I like Utopian talk, speculation about what our planet should be, anger about what our planet is.

I think writers are the most important members of society, not just potentially but actually. Good writers must have and stand by their own ideas.

I like everything there is about being a writer, except the way my neighbors treat me. Because I honor them for what they are, and they really do find me irrelevant on Cape Cod. There's my state representative. I campaigned for him, and he got drunk one night and came over and said, "You know, I can't understand a word you write and neither can any of your neighbors . . . so why don't you change your style, so why not write something people will like?" He was just telling me for my own good. He was a former English major at Brown.

Interviewer: Did he win?

Vonnegut: He went crazy. He really went bug-house finally.

DISCUSSION QUESTIONS
SUGGESTIONS FOR WRITING

1. Though he eschews the label of black humorist, Kurt Vonnegut, Jr., is certainly some sort of humorist. What humorous responses in the interview strike you as particularly Vonnegutian and why?

2. What is your reaction to Vonnegut's statement: "People are programmed, just like computers with this tape feeding out . . . "?

3. Examine Vonnegut's use of language. Note especially its general informality and lack of pretentiousness. Would you say these same traits characterize his fiction, as in "Harrison Bergeron," for example?

4. Why do you think Vonnegut says: "I think writers are the most important members of society, not just potentially but actually"? What important functions do writers perform for a society?

The Future

KAHN AND WIENER

HERMAN KAHN
(b. 1922) is director of the
Hudson Institute and one
of the founders of the
"new science" of strategy
games and predicting for
policy for decision-mak-
ers. His previous books,
*On Thermonuclear War,
Thinking about the Un-
thinkable,* and *On Escala-
tion: Metaphors and Sce-
narios,* have shaped the
national defense planning
and public policy-making
of the United States for
over ten years—not only
through their specific rec-
ommendations, but also
through the general
methodology that Mr.
Kahn, and others in cen-
ters like the RAND Corpo-
ration, created after World
War II.
ANTHONY J. WIENER
(b. 1930) is chairman of
the Research Manage-
ment Council of the Hud-
son Institute and one of
the institute's founding
members.

ONE HUNDRED TECHNICAL INNOVATIONS VERY LIKELY IN THE LAST THIRD OF THE TWENTIETH CENTURY

IN order to provide a quick impression of science and technology (with an emphasis on technology) in the last third of the twentieth century, we list [below] one hundred areas in which it is probable that technological innovation will occur in the next thirty-three years. . . .

Each item in the list has the following characteristics:

(1) It is important enough to make, by itself, a significant change in the next thirty-three years. The difference might lie mainly in being spectacular (e.g., transoceanic rocket transportation in

twenty or thirty minutes rather than supersonic in two or three hours); in being ubiquitous (e.g., widespread use of paper clothes); in enabling a large number of different things to be done (e.g., super materials); in a general and significant increase in productivity (e.g., cybernation); or simply in being important to specific individuals (e.g., convenient artificial kidneys).

(2) A responsible opinion can be found to argue a great likelihood that the innovation will be achieved before the year 2000 — usually long before. (We would probably agree with about 90-95 per cent of these estimates.)

(3) Each warrants the description technological innovation, revolution, or breakthrough. None is simply an obvious minor improvement on what currently exists.

The list is deliberately eclectic and disordered because this communicates a more accurate description of what we know about these future possibilities than the superficial appearance of order and understanding that would be given by a somewhat differently ordered list. Indeed since . . . serendipities and unexpected synergisms play an important role, reading this eclectic and disordered list is almost a simulation of the process of innovation and diffusion.

We should also note that the one hundred areas are not entirely randomly ordered. Most people would consider the first twenty-five as (largely) unambiguous examples of progress or human benefit. A few would question even these. The first item, for example, lasers and masers, might make possible a particularly effective kind of ballistic missile defense, and thus, some believe, could accelerate the Soviet-American arms race. Or the expansion of tropical agriculture and forestry, as suggested in the eighth item, could mean a geographical shift in economic and military power as well as a dislocation of competitive industries. Indeed nearly all the areas of innovation could involve adjustment difficulties of this kind. Nevertheless there probably would be a consensus among readers that the first twenty-five areas do represent progress — at least for those who are in favor of "progress."

The next twenty-five innovations would clearly have controversial consequences; many would argue that government policy might better restrain or discourage innovation or diffusion here. . . . These twenty-five "controversial areas" raise issues of accelerated nuclear proliferation; of loss of privacy; of excessive governmental and/or private power over individuals; of dangerously vulnerable, deceptive, and degradable overcentralization; of decisions becoming necessary that are too large, complex, important, uncertain, or comprehensive to be left to mere mortals (whether acting privately or publicly, individually or in organizations); of new capabilities that are so inherently dangerous that they are likely to be disastrously abused; of too rapid or cataclysmic change for smooth adjustment, and so on.

The last fifty items are included in part because they are intrinsically interesting and in part to demonstrate that it is fairly easy to produce a long list of items of innovation that entail nontrivial consequences.

One Hundred Technical Innovations Very Likely in the Last Third of the Twentieth Century

1. Multiple applications of lasers and masers for sensing, measuring, communication, cutting, heating, welding, power transmission, illumination, destructive (defensive), and other purposes
2. Extreme high-strength and/or high-temperature structural materials
3. New or improved superperformance fabrics (papers, fibers, and plastics)
4. New or improved materials for equipment and appliances (plastics, glasses, alloys, ceramics, intermetallics, and cermets)
5. New airborne vehicles (ground-effect machines, VTOL and STOL, superhelicopters, giant and/or supersonic jets)
6. Extensive commercial application of shaped-charge explosives
7. More reliable and longer-range weather forecasting
8. Intensive and/or extensive expansion of tropical agriculture and forestry
9. New sources of power for fixed installations (e.g., magnetohydrodynamic, thermionic and thermoelectric, and radioactivity)
10. New sources of power for ground transportation (storage battery, fuel cell, propulsion [or support] by electro-magnetic fields, jet engine, turbine, and the like)
11. Extensive and intensive worldwide use of high altitude cameras for mapping, prospecting, census, land use, and geological investigations
12. New methods of water transportation (such as large submarines, flexible and special purpose "container ships," or more extensive use of large automated single-purpose bulk cargo ships)
13. Major reduction in hereditary and congenital defects
14. Extensive use of cyborg techniques (mechanical aids or substitutes for human organs, senses, limbs, or other components)
15. New techniques for preserving or improving the environment
16. Relatively effective appetite and weight control
17. New techniques and institutions for adult education
18. New and useful plant and animal species
19. Human "hibernation" for short periods (hours or days) for medical purposes
20. Inexpensive design and procurement of "one of a kind" items through use of computerized analysis and automated production
21. Controlled and/or supereffective relaxation and sleep

22. More sophisticated architectural engineering (e.g., geodesic domes, "fancy" stressed shells, pressurized skins, and esoteric materials)

23. New or improved uses of the oceans (mining, extraction of minerals, controlled "farming," source of energy, and the like)

24. Three-dimensional photography, illustrations, movies, and television

25. Automated or more mechanized housekeeping and home maintenance

26. Widespread use of nuclear reactors for power

27. Use of nuclear explosives for excavation and mining, generation of power, creation of high-temperature–high-pressure environments, and/or as a source of neutrons or other radiation

28. General use of automation and cybernation in management and production

29. Extensive and intensive centralization (or automatic interconnection) of current and past personal and business information in high-speed data processors

30. Other new and possibly pervasive techniques for surveillance, monitoring, and control of individuals and organizations

31. Some control of weather and/or climate

32. Other (permanent or temporary) changes — or experiments — with the overall environment (e.g., the "permanent" increase in C-14 and temporary creation of other radioactivity by nuclear explosions, the increasing generation of CO_2 in the atmosphere, projects Starfire, West Ford, and Storm Fury)

33. New and more reliable "educational" and propaganda techniques for affecting human behavior — public and private

34. Practical use of direct electronic communication with and stimulation of the brain

35. Human hibernation for relatively extensive periods (months to years)

36. Cheap and widely available central war weapons and weapon systems

37. New and relatively effective counterinsurgency techniques (and perhaps also insurgency techniques)

38. New techniques for very cheap, convenient, and reliable birth control

39. New, more varied, and more reliable drugs for control of fatigue, relaxation, alertness, mood, personality, perceptions, fantasies, and other psychobiological states

40. Capability to choose the sex of unborn children

41. Improved capability to "change" sex of children and/or adults

42. Other genetic control and/or influence over the "basic constitution" of an individual

43. New techniques and institutions for the education of children

44. General and substantial increase in life expectancy, postponement of aging, and limited rejuvenation
45. Generally acceptable and competitive synthetic foods and beverages (e.g., carbohydrates, fats, proteins, enzymes, vitamins, coffee, tea, cocoa, and alcoholic liquor)
46. "High quality" medical care for undeveloped areas (e.g., use of medical aides and technicians, referral hospitals, broad spectrum antibiotics, and artificial blood plasma)
47. Design and extensive use of responsive and supercontrolled environments for private and public use (for pleasurable, educational, and vocational purposes)
48. Physically nonharmful methods of overindulging
49. Simple techniques for extensive and "permanent" cosmetological changes (features, "figures," perhaps complexion and even skin color, and even physique)
50. More extensive use of transplantation of human organs
51. Permanent manned satellite and lunar installations—interplanetary travel
52. Application of space life systems or similar techniques to terrestrial installations
53. Permanent inhabited undersea installations and perhaps even colonies
54. Automated grocery and department stores
55. Extensive use of robots and machines "slaved" to humans
56. New uses of underground "tunnels" for private and public transportation and other purposes
57. Automated universal (real time) credit, audit and banking systems
58. Chemical methods for improving memory and learning
59. Greater use of underground buildings
60. New and improved materials and equipment for buildings and interiors (e.g., variable transmission glass, heating and cooling by thermoelectric effect, and electroluminescent and phosphorescent lighting)
61. Widespread use of cryogenics
62. Improved chemical control of some mental illnesses and some aspects of senility
63. Mechanical and chemical methods for improving human analytical ability more or less directly
64. Inexpensive and rapid techniques for making tunnels and underground cavities in earth and/or rock
65. Major improvements in earth moving and construction equipment generally
66. New techniques for keeping physically fit and/or acquiring physical skills
67. Commercial extraction of oil from shale

68. Recoverable boosters for economic space launching
69. Individual flying platforms
70. Simple inexpensive home video recording and playing
71. Inexpensive high-capacity, worldwide, regional, and local (home and business) communication (perhaps using satellites, lasers, and light pipes)
72. Practical home and business use of "wired" video communication for both telephone and TV (possibly including retrieval of taped material from libraries or other sources) and rapid transmission and reception of facsimiles (possibly including news, library material, commercial announcements, instantaneous mail delivery, other printouts, and so on)
73. Practical large-scale desalinization
74. Pervasive business use of computers for the storage, processing, and retrieval of information
75. Shared time (public and interconnected?) computers generally available to home and business on a metered basis
76. Other widespread use of computers for intellectual and professional assistance (translation, teaching, literature search, medical diagnosis, traffic control, crime detection, computation, design, analysis and to some degree as intellectual collaborator generally)
77. General availability of inexpensive transuranic and other esoteric elements
78. Space defense systems
79. Inexpensive and reasonably effective ground-based BMD
80. Very low-cost buildings for home and business use
81. Personal "pagers" (perhaps even two-way pocket phones) and other personal electronic equipment for communication, computing, and data processing program
82. Direct broadcasts from satellites to home receivers
83. Inexpensive (less than $20), long lasting, very small battery operated TV receivers
84. Home computers to "run" household and communicate with outside world
85. Maintenance-free, longlife electronic and other equipment
86. Home education via video and computerized and programmed learning
87. Stimulated and planned and perhaps programmed dreams
88. Inexpensive (less than one cent a page), rapid high-quality black and white reproduction; followed by color and high-detailed photography reproduction — perhaps for home as well as office use
89. Widespread use of improved fluid amplifiers
90. Conference TV (both closed circuit and public communication system)

91. Flexible penology without necessarily using prisons (by use of modern methods of surveillance, monitoring, and control)
92. Common use of (longlived?) individual power source for lights, appliances, and machines
93. Inexpensive worldwide transportation of humans and cargo
94. Inexpensive road-free (and facility-free) transportation
95. New methods for rapid language teaching
96. Extensive genetic control for plants and animals
97. New biological and chemical methods to identify, trace, incapacitate, or annoy people for police and military uses
98. New and possibly very simple methods for lethal biological and chemical warfare
99. Artificial moons and other methods for lighting large areas at night
100. Extensive use of "biological processes" in the extraction and processing of minerals

The following are areas in which technological success by the year 2000 seems substantially less likely (even money bets, give or take a factor of five), but where, if it occurred, it would be quite important, are these:

Some Less Likely but Important Possibilities

1. "True" artificial intelligence
2. Practical use of sustained fusion to produce neutrons and/or energy
3. Artificial growth of new limbs and organs (either in situ or for later transplantation)
4. Room temperature superconductors
5. Major use of rockets for commercial or private transportation (either terrestrial or extraterrestrial)
6. Effective chemical or biological treatment of most mental illnesses
7. Almost complete control of marginal changes in heredity
8. Suspended animation (for years or centuries)
9. Practical materials with nearly "theoretical limit" strength
10. Conversion of mammals (humans?) to fluid breathers
11. Direct input into human memory banks
12. Direct augmentation of human mental capacity by the mechanical or electrical interconnection of the brain with a computer
13. Major rejuvenation and/or significant extension of vigor and life span—say 100 to 150 years
14. Chemical or biological control of character or intelligence
15. Automated highways
16. Extensive use of moving sidewalks for local transportation
17. Substantial manned lunar or planetary installations
18. Electric power available for less than .3 mill per kilowatt hour

19. Verification of some extrasensory phenomena
20. Planetary engineering
21. Modification of the solar system
22. Practical laboratory conception and nurturing of animal (human?) foetuses
23. Production of a drug equivalent to Huxley's soma
24. A technological equivalent of telepathy
25. Some direct control of individual thought processes

We list below ten radical possibilities, some of which hardly make sense. We do not believe that any of them will occur by the year 2000, or perhaps ever. But some of them are discussed today; and such a list does emphasize the fact that some dramatic and radical innovation must be expected. The list may suggest how surprising and exciting (or outrageous) such an event might prove.

Ten Far-Out Possibilities

1. Life expectancy extended to substantially more than 150 years (immortality?)
2. Almost complete genetic control (but still homo sapiens)
3. Major modification of human species (no longer homo sapiens)
4. Antigravity (or practical use of gravity waves)*
5. Interstellar travel
6. Electric power available for less than .03 mill per kw hour
7. Practical and routine use of extrasensory phenomena
8. Laboratory creation of artificial live plants and animals
9. Lifetime immunization against practically all diseases
10. Substantial lunar or planetary bases or colonies

* As usually envisaged this would make possible a perpetual motion machine and therefore the creation of energy out of nothing. We do not envisage this as even a far-out possibility, but include antigravity, even though it annoys some physicist friends, as an example of some totally new use of a basic phenomenon or the seeming violation of a basic law.

And finally there is the possibility—more far-fetched than popular science fiction would have it, but impossible to exclude—of a discovery of extraterrestrial life; or, much more extreme, of communication with extraterrestrial intelligence.

These lists make only the obvious point that as a result of the long-term trends toward accumulation of scientific and technological knowledge and the institutionalization of change through research, development, innovation, and diffusion, many important new things are likely to happen in the next few decades. It is worth while asking specifically what the consequences of each item—and their synergistic interactions—might be.

DISCUSSION QUESTIONS
SUGGESTIONS FOR WRITING

1. The second twenty-five innovations in the authors' list of innovations represent, they say, changes that "would clearly have controversial consequences." What are some of the issues they predict, arising from these twenty-five "controversial areas"? Speculate about other possible issues you foresee as consequences of these innovations.

2. This piece is made up primarily of pure information. The validity of the information is established solely on the strength of the authority of the authors to arrive at such conclusions. Since their authority to make such predictions is well established, the reader is reasonably convinced that such information is worth reading, that chances of accurate information are fairly good. What techniques could a layman use if he wished either to question such information or to develop further evidence for it?

3. What do the authors mean by: since "serendipities and unexpected synergisms play an important role, reading this eclectic and disordered list is almost a simulation of the process of innovation and diffusion"?

4. What are the implications of the authors' prediction of "decisions becoming necessary that are too large, complex, important, uncertain, or comprehensive to be left to mere mortals (whether acting privately or publicly, individually or in organizations)"?

CLARKE

THE OBSOLESCENCE OF MAN

In this selection Arthur C. Clarke speculates about future life-forms.

ABOUT a million years ago, an unprepossessing primate discovered that his forelimbs could be used for other purposes besides locomotion. Objects like sticks and stones could be grasped — and, once grasped, were useful for killing game, digging up roots, defending or attacking, and a hundred other jobs. On the third planet of the Sun, tools had appeared; and the place would never be the same again.

The first users of tools were *not* men — a fact appreciated only in the last year or two — but prehuman anthropoids; and by their discovery they doomed themselves. For even the most primitive of tools, such as a naturally pointed stone that happens to fit the hand, provides a tremendous physical and mental stimulus to the user. He has to walk erect; he no longer needs huge canine teeth — since sharp flints can do a better job — and he must develop manual dexterity of a high order. These are the specifications of Homo sapiens; as soon as they start to be filled, all earlier models are headed for rapid obsolescence. To quote Professor Sherwood Washburn of the University of California's anthropology department: "It was the success of the simplest tools that started the whole trend of human evolution and led to the civilizations of today."

Note that phrase — "the whole trend of human evolution." The old idea that man invented tools is therefore a misleading half-truth; it would be more accurate to say that *tools invented man.* They were very primitive tools, in the hands of creatures who were little more than apes. Yet they led to us — and to the eventual extinction of the ape-men who first wielded them.

Now the cycle is about to begin again; but neither history nor prehistory ever exactly repeats itself, and this time there will be a fascinating twist in the plot. The tools the ape-men invented caused them to evolve into their successor, Homo sapiens. The tool we have invented *is* our successor. Biological evolution has given way to a far more rapid process — technological evolution. To put it bluntly and brutally, the machine is going to take over.

This, of course, is hardly an original idea. That the creations of man's brain might one day threaten and perhaps destroy him is such a tired old *cliché* that no self-respecting science-fiction writer would dare to use it. It goes back, through Capek's *R.U.R.*, Samuel Butler's *Erewhon*, Mary Shelley's *Frankenstein* and the Faust legend to the mysterious but perhaps not wholly mythical figure of Daedalus, King Minos' one-man office of scientific research. For at least three thousand years, therefore, a vocal minority of mankind has had grave doubts about the ultimate outcome of technology. From the self-centered, human point of view, these doubts are justified. But that, I submit, will not be the only—or even the most important—point of view for much longer.

When the first large-scale electronic computers appeared some fifteen years ago, they were promptly nicknamed "Giant Brains"—and the scientific community, as a whole, took a poor view of the designation. But the scientists objected to the wrong word. The electronic computers were not *giant* brains; they were dwarf brains, and they still are, though they have grown a hundredfold within less than one generation of mankind. Yet even in their present flint-ax stage of evolution, they have done things which not long ago almost everyone would have claimed to be impossible—such as translating from one language to another, composing music, and playing a fair game of chess. And much more important than any of these infant *jeux d'esprit* is the fact that they have breached the barrier between brain and machine.

This is one of the greatest—and perhaps one of the last—breakthroughs in the history of human thought, like the discovery that the Earth moves round the Sun, or that man is part of the animal kingdom, or that $E = mc^2$. All these ideas took time to sink in, and were frantically denied when first put forward. In the same way it will take a little while for men to realize that machines can not only think, but may one day think them off the face of the Earth.

At this point you may reasonably ask: "Yes—but what do you mean by *think?*" I propose to sidestep that question, using a neat device for which I am indebted to the English mathematician A. M. Turing. Turing imagined a game played by two teleprinter operators in separate rooms—this impersonal link being used to remove all clues given by voice, appearance, and so forth. Suppose one operator was able to ask the other any questions he wished, and the other had to make suitable replies. If, after some hours or days of this conversation, the questioner could not decide whether his telegraphic acquaintance was human or purely mechanical, then he could hardly deny that he/it was capable of thought. An electronic brain that passed this test would, surely, have to be regarded as an intelligent entity. Anyone who argued otherwise would merely prove that he was less intelligent than the machine; he would be a splitter of nonexistent hairs, like the scholar who proved that the *Odyssey* was not written by Homer, but by another man of the same name.

We are still decades—but not centuries—from building such a machine, yet already we are sure that it could be done. If Turing's experiment is never carried out, it will merely be because the intelligent machines of the future will have better things to do with their time than conduct extended conversations with men. I often talk with my dog, but I don't keep it up for long.

The fact that the great computers of today are still high-speed morons, capable of doing nothing beyond the scope of the instructions carefully programmed into them, has given many people a spurious sense of security. No machine, they argue, can possibly be more intelligent than its makers—the men who designed it, and planned its functions. It may be a million times faster in operation, but that is quite irrelevant. Anything and everything that an electronic brain can do must also be within the scope of a human brain, if it had sufficient time and patience. Above all, it is maintained, no machine can show originality or creative power or the other attributes which are fondly labeled "human."

The argument is wholly fallacious; those who still bring it forth are like the buggy-whip makers who used to poke fun at stranded Model T's. Even if it were true, it could give no comfort, as a careful reading of these remarks by Dr. Norbert Wiener will show:

> This attitude (the assumption that machines cannot possess any degree of originality) in my opinion should be rejected entirely. . . . It is my thesis that machines can and do transcend some of the limitations of their designers. . . . It may well be that in principle we cannot make any machine, the elements of whose behaviour we cannot comprehend sooner or later. This does not mean in any way that we shall be able to comprehend them in substantially less time than the operation of the machine, nor even within any given number of years or generations. . . . This means that though they are theoretically subject to human criticism, such criticism may be ineffective until a long time after it is relevant.

In other words, even machines *less* intelligent than men might escape from our control by sheer speed of operation. And in fact, there is every reason to suppose that machines will become much more intelligent than their builders, as well as incomparably faster.

There are still a few authorities who refuse to grant any degree of intelligence to machines, now or in the future. This attitude shows a striking parallel to that adopted by the chemists of the early nineteenth century. It was known then that all living organisms are formed from a few common elements—mostly carbon, hydrogen, oxygen, and nitrogen—but it was firmly believed that the materials of life could not be made from "mere" chemicals alone. There must be some other ingredient—some essence or vital principle, forever unknowable to man. No chemist could ever take carbon, hydrogen, and so forth and combine them to form any of the substances upon which life was based. There was an impassable barrier between the worlds of "inorganic" and "organic" chemistry.

This *mystique* was destroyed in 1828, when Wöhler synthesized urea, and showed that there was no difference at all between the chemical reactions taking place in the body, and those taking place inside a retort. It was a terrible shock to those pious souls who believed that the mechanics of life must always be beyond human understanding or imitation. Many people are equally shocked today by the suggestion that machines can think, but their dislike of the situation will not alter it in the least.

Since this is not a treatise on computer design, you will not expect me to explain how to build a thinking machine. In fact, it is doubtful if any human being will ever be able to do this in detail, but one can indicate the sequence of events that will lead from H. sapiens to M. sapiens. The first two or three steps on the road have already been taken; machines now exist that can learn by experience, profiting from their mistakes and — unlike human beings — never repeating them. Machines have been built which do not sit passively waiting for instructions, but which explore the world around them in a manner which can only be called inquisitive. Others look for proofs of theorems in mathematics or logic, and sometimes come up with surprising solutions that had never occurred to their makers.

These faint glimmerings of original intelligence are confined at the moment to a few laboratory models; they are wholly lacking in the giant computers that can now be bought by anyone who happens to have a few hundred thousand dollars to spare. But machine intelligence will grow, and it will start to range beyond the bounds of human thought as soon as the second generation of computers appears — the generation that has been designed, not by men, but by other, "almost intelligent" computers. And not only designed, but also built — for they will have far too many components for manual assembly.

It is even possible that the first genuine thinking machines may be *grown* rather than constructed; already some crude but very stimulating experiments have been carried out along these lines. Several artificial organisms have been built which are capable of rewiring themselves to adapt to changing circumstances. Beyond this there is the possibility of computers which will start from relatively simple beginnings, be programmed to aim at specific goals, and search for them by constructing their own circuits, perhaps by growing networks of threads in a conducting medium. Such a growth may be no more than a mechanical analogy of what happens to every one of us in the first nine months of our existence.

All speculations about intelligent machines are inevitably conditioned — indeed, inspired — by our knowledge of the human brain, the only thinking device currently on the market. No one, of course, pretends to understand the full workings of the brain, or expects that such knowledge will be available in any foreseeable future. (It is a nice philosophical point as to whether the brain can ever, even in principle, understand itself.) But we do know enough about its physical structure to draw many conclusions about the limitations of "brains" — whether organic or inorganic.

There are approximately ten billion separate switches — or neurons — inside your skull, "wired" together in circuits of unimaginable complexity. Ten billion is such a large number that, until recently, it could be used as an argument against the achievement of mechanical intelligence. About ten years ago a famous neurophysiologist made a statement (still produced like some protective incantation by the advocates of cerebral supremacy) to the effect that an electronic model of the human brain would have to be as large as the Empire State Building, and would need Niagara Falls to keep it cool when it was running.

This must now be classed with such interesting pronouncements as, "No heavier than air machine will ever be able to fly." For the calculation was made in the days of the vacuum tube (remember it?), and the transistor has now completely altered the picture. Indeed—such is the rate of technological progress today—the transistor itself is being replaced by still smaller and faster devices, based upon abstruse principles of quantum physics. If the problem was merely one of space, today's electronic techniques would allow us to pack a computer as complex as the human brain on to a single floor of the Empire State Building.

Interlude for agonizing reappraisal. It's a tough job keeping up with science, and since I wrote that last paragraph the Marquardt Corporation's Astro Division has announced a new memory device which could store inside a six-foot cube *all information recorded during the last 10,000 years.* This means, of course, not only every book ever printed, but *everything* ever written in *any* language on paper, papyrus, parchment, or stone. It represents a capacity untold millions of times greater than that of a single human memory, and though there is a mighty gulf between merely storing information and thinking creatively—the Library of Congress has never written a book—it does indicate that mechanical brains of enormous power could be quite small in physical size.

This should not surprise anyone who remembers how radios have shrunk from the bulky cabinet models of the thirties to the vest-pocket (yet much more sophisticated) transistor sets of today. And the shrinkage is just gaining momentum, if I may employ such a mind-boggling phrase. Radio receivers the size of lumps of sugar have now been built; before long, they will be the size not of lumps but of grains, for the slogan of the micro-miniaturization experts is "If you can see it, it's too big."

Just to prove that I am not exaggerating, here are some statistics you can use on the next hi-fi fanatic who takes you on a tour of his wall-to-wall installation. During the 1950's, the electronic engineers learned to pack up to a hundred thousand components into one cubic foot. (To give a basis of comparison, a good hi-fi set may contain two or three hundred components, a domestic radio about a hundred.) . . . At the beginning of the sixties, the attainable figure [was] around a million components per cubic foot; [in the] 1970['s], when today's experimental techniques of microscopic engineering have begun to pay off, it may reach a hundred million.

Fantastic though this last figure is, the human brain surpasses it by a thousandfold, packing its ten billion neurons into a *tenth* of a cubic foot. And although smallness is not necessarily a virtue, even this may be nowhere near the limit of possible compactness.

For the cells composing our brains are slow-acting, bulky, and wasteful of energy—compared with the scarcely more than atom-sized computer elements that are theoretically possible. The mathematician John von Neumann once calculated that electronic cells could be ten billion times more efficient than protoplasmic ones; already they are a million times swifter in operation, and speed can often be traded for size. If we take these ideas to their ultimate conclusion, it appears that a computer equivalent in power to one human brain need be no bigger than a matchbox.

This slightly shattering thought becomes more reasonable when we take a critical look at flesh and blood and bone as engineering materials. All living creatures are marvelous, but let us keep our sense of pro-portion. Perhaps the most wonderful thing about Life is that it works at all, when it has to employ such extraordinary materials, and has to tackle its problems in such roundabout ways.

As a perfect example of this, consider the eye. Suppose *you* were given the problem of designing a camera—for that, of course, is what the eye is—which *has to be constructed entirely of water and jelly*, without using a scrap of glass, metal, or plastic. Obviously, it can't be done.

You're quite right; the feat is impossible. The eye is an evolutionary miracle, but it's a lousy camera. You can prove this while you're reading the next sentence.

Here's a medium-length word:—photography. Close one eye and keep the other fixed—repeat, *fixed*—on that center "g." You may be surprised to discover that—unless you cheat by altering the direction of your gaze—you cannot see the whole word clearly. It fades out three or four letters to the right and left.

No camera ever built—even the cheapest—has as poor an optical performance as this. For color vision also, the human eye is nothing to boast about; it can operate only over a small band of the spectrum. To the worlds of the infrared and ultraviolet, visible to bees and other insects, it is completely blind.

We are not conscious of these limitations because we have grown up with them, and indeed if they were corrected the brain would be quite unable to handle the vastly increased flood of information. But let us not make a virtue of a necessity; if our eyes had the optical performance of even the cheapest miniature camera, we would live in an unimaginably richer and more colorful world.

These defects are due to the fact that precision scientific instruments simply cannot be manufactured from living materials. With the eye, the ear, the nose—indeed, all the sense organs—evolution has performed a truly incredible job against fantastic odds. But it will not be good enough for the future; indeed, it is not good enough for the present.

There are some senses that do not exist, that can probably never be provided by living structures, and that we need in a hurry. On this planet, to the best of our knowledge, no creature has ever developed organs that can detect radio waves or radioactivity. Though I would hate to lay down the law and claim that nowhere in the universe can there be organic Geiger counters or living TV sets, I think it highly improbable. There are some jobs that can be done only by vacuum tubes or magnetic fields or electron beams, and are therefore beyond the capability of purely organic structures.

There is another fundamental reason living machines such as you and I cannot hope to compete with nonliving ones. Quite apart from our poor materials, we are handicapped by one of the toughest engineering specifications ever issued. What sort of performance would you expect from a machine which has to grow several billionfold during the course of manufacture—and which has to be completely and continuously rebuilt, molecule by molecule, every few weeks? This is what happens to all of us, all the time; you are not the man you were last year, in the most literal sense of the expression.

Most of the energy and effort required to run the body goes into its perpetual tearing down and rebuilding—a cycle completed every few weeks. New York City, which is a very much simpler structure than a man, takes hundreds of times longer to remake itself. When one tries to picture the body's myriads of building contractors and utility companies all furiously at work, tearing up arteries and nerves and even bones, it is astonishing that there is any energy left over for the business of thinking.

Now I am perfectly well aware that many of the "limitations" and "defects" just mentioned are nothing of the sort, looked at from another point of view. Living creatures, because of their very nature, can evolve from simple to complex organisms. They may well be the only path by which intelligence can be attained, for it is a little difficult to see how a lifeless planet can progress directly from metal ores and mineral deposits to electronic computers by its own unaided efforts.

Though intelligence can arise only from life, it may then discard it. Perhaps at a later stage, as the mystics have suggested, it may also discard matter; but this leads us in realms of speculations which an unimaginative person like myself would prefer to avoid.

One often-stressed advantage of living creatures is that they are self-repairing and reproduce themselves with ease—indeed, with enthusiasm. This superiority over machines will be short-lived; the general principles underlying the construction of self-repairing and self-reproducing machines have already been worked out. There is, incidentally, something ironically appropriate in the fact that A. M. Turing, the brilliant mathematician who pioneered in this field and first indicated how thinking machines might be built, shot himself a few years after publishing his results. It is very hard not to draw a moral from this.

The greatest single stimulus to the evolution of mechanical—as opposed to organic—intelligence is the challenge of space. Only a vanishingly small fraction of the universe is directly accessible to mankind, in the sense that we can live there without elaborate protection or mechanical aids. If we generously assume that humanity's potential *Lebensraum* extends from sea level to a height of three miles, over the whole Earth, that gives us a total of some half billion cubic miles. At first sight this is an impressive figure, especially when you remember that the entire human race could be packaged into a one-mile cube. But it is absolutely nothing, when set against Space with a capital "S." Our present telescopes, which are certainly not the last word on the subject, sweep a volume at least a million million million million million million million million million million times greater.

Though such a number is, of course, utterly beyond conception, it can be given a vivid meaning. If we reduced the known universe to the size of the Earth, then the portion in which *we* can live without space suits and pressure cabins is about the size of a single atom.

It is true that, one day, we are going to explore and colonize many other atoms in this Earth-sized volume, but it will be at the cost of tremendous technical efforts, for most of our energies will be devoted to protecting our frail and sensitive bodies against the extremes of temperature, pressure, or gravity found in space and on other worlds. Within very wide limits, machines are indifferent to these extremes. Even more important, they can wait patiently through the years and the centuries that will be needed for travel to the far reaches of the universe.

Creatures of flesh and blood such as ourselves can explore space and win control over infinitesimal fractions of it. But only creatures of metal and plastic can ever really conquer it, as indeed they have already started to do. . . .

It may well be that only in space, confronted with environments fiercer and more complex than any to be found upon this planet, will intelligence be able to reach its fullest stature. Like other qualities, intelligence is developed by struggle and conflict; in the ages to come, the dullards may remain on placid Earth, and real genius will flourish only in space—the realm of the machine, not of flesh and blood.

A striking parallel to this situation can already be found on our planet. Some millions of years ago, the most intelligent of the mammals withdrew from the battle of the dry land and returned to their ancestral home, the sea. They are still there, with brains larger and potentially more powerful than ours. But (as far as we know) they do not use them; the static environment of the sea makes little call upon intelligence.The porpoises and whales, which might have been our equals and perhaps our superiors had they remained on land, now race in simpleminded and innocent ecstasy beside the new sea monsters carrying sixteen megatons of death. Perhaps they, not we, made the right choice; but it is too late to join them now.

If you have followed me so far, the protoplasmic computer inside your skull should now be programmed to accept the idea—at least for the sake of argument—that machines can be both more intelligent and more versatile than men, and may well be so in the very near future. So it is time to face the question: Where does that leave man?

I suspect that this is not a question of very great importance — except, of course, to man. Perhaps the Neanderthalers made similar plaintive noises, around 100,000 B.C., when H. sapiens appeared on the scene, with his ugly vertical forehead and ridiculous protruding chin. Any Paleolithic philosopher who gave his colleagues the right answer would probably have ended up in the cooking pot; I am prepared to take that risk.

The short-term answer may indeed be cheerful rather than depressing. There may be a brief golden age when men will glory in the power and range of their new partners. Barring war, this age lies directly ahead of us. As Dr. Simon Remo put it recently: "The extension of the human intellect by electronics will become our greatest occupation within a decade." That is undoubtedly true, if we bear in mind that at a somewhat later date the word "extension" may be replaced by "extinction."

One of the ways in which thinking machines will be able to help us is by taking over the humbler tasks of life, leaving the human brain free to concentrate on higher things. (Not, of course, that this is any guarantee that it will do so.) For a few generations, perhaps, every man will go through life with an electronic companion, which may be no bigger than today's transistor radios. It will "grow up" with him from infancy, learning his habits, his business affairs, taking over all the minor chores like routine correspondence and income-tax returns and engagements. On occasion it could even take its master's place, keeping appointments he preferred to miss, and then reporting back in as much detail as he desired. It could substitute for him over the telephone so completely that no one would be able to tell whether man or machine was speaking; a century from now, Turing's "game" may be an integral part of our social lives, with complications and possibilities which I leave to the imagination.

You may remember that delightful robot, Robbie, from the movie *Forbidden Planet*. (One of the three or four movies so far made that anyone interested in science fiction can point to without blushing; the fact that the plot was Shakespeare's doubtless helped.) I submit, in all seriousness, that most of Robbie's abilities — together with those of a better known character, Jeeves — will one day be incorporated in a kind of electronic companion-secretary-valet. It will be much smaller and neater than the walking jukeboxes or mechanized suits of armor which Hollywood presents, with typical lack of imagination, when it wants to portray a robot. And it will be extremely talented, with quick-release connectors allowing it to be coupled to an unlimited variety of sense organs and limbs. It would, in fact, be a kind of general purpose, disembodied intelligence that could attach itself to whatever tools were needed for any particular occasion. One day it might be using microphones or electric typewriters or TV cameras; on another, automobiles or airplanes—or the bodies of men and animals.

And this is, perhaps, the moment to deal with a conception which many people find even more horrifying than the idea that machines will replace or supersede us. It is the idea, already mentioned in the last chapter, that they may combine with us.

I do not know who first thought of this; probably the physicist J. D. Bernal, who in 1929 published an extraordinary book of scientific predictions called *The World, the Flesh and the Devil*. In this slim and long out-of-print volume (I sometimes wonder what the sixty-year-old Fellow of the Royal Society now thinks of his youthful indiscretion, if he ever remembers it) Bernal decided that the numerous limitations of the human body could be overcome only by the use of mechanical attachments or substitutes—until, eventually, all that might be left of man's original organic body would be the brain.

This idea is already far more plausible than when Bernal advanced it, for in the last few decades we have seen the development of mechanical hearts, kidneys, lungs, and other organs, and the wiring of electronic devices directly into the human nervous system.

Olaf Stapledon developed this theme in his wonderful history of the future, *Last and First Men*, imagining an age of immortal "giant brains," many yards across, living in beehive-shaped cells, sustained by pumps and chemical plants. Though completely immobile, their sense organs could be wherever they wished, so their center of awareness—or consciousness, if you like—could be anywhere on Earth or in the space above it. This is an important point which we—who carry our brains around in the same fragile structure as our eyes, ears, and other sense organs, often with disastrous results—may easily fail to appreciate. Given perfected telecommunications, a fixed brain is no handicap, but rather the reverse. Your present brain, totally imprisoned behind its walls of bone, communicates with the outer world and receives its impressions of it over the telephone wires of the central nervous system—wires varying in length from a fraction of an inch to several feet. *You would never know the difference if those "wires" were actually hundreds or thousands of miles long, or included mobile radio links, and your brain never moved at all.*

In a crude way—yet one that may accurately foreshadow the future—we have already extended our visual and tactile senses away from our bodies. The men who now work with radioisotopes, handling them with remotely controlled mechanical fingers and observing them by television, have achieved a partial separation between brain and sense organs. They are in one place; their minds effectively in another.

Recently the word "Cyborg" (cybernetic organism) has been coined to describe the machine-animal of the type we have been discussing. Doctors Manfred Clynes and Nathan Kline of Rockland State Hospital,

Orangeburg, New York, who invented the name, define a Cyborg in these stirring words: "an exogenously extended organizational complex functioning as a homeostatic system." To translate, this means a body which has machines hitched to it, or built into it, to take over or modify some of its functions.

I suppose one could call a man in an iron lung a Cyborg, but the concept has far wider implications than this. One day we may be able to enter into temporary unions with any sufficiently sophisticated machines, thus being able not merely to control but to *become* a spaceship or a submarine or a TV network. This would give far more than purely intellectual satisfaction; the thrill that can be obtained from driving a racing car or flying an airplane may be only a pale ghost of the excitement our great-grandchildren may know, when the individual human consciousness is free to roam at will from machine to machine, through all the reaches of sea and sky and space.

But how long will this partnership last? Can the synthesis of man and machine ever be stable, or will the purely organic component become such a hindrance that it has to be discarded? If this eventually happens —and I have given good reasons for thinking that it must—we have nothing to regret, and certainly nothing to fear.

The popular idea, fostered by comic strips and the cheaper forms of science fiction, that intelligent machines must be malevolent entities hostile to man, is so absurd that it is hardly worth wasting energy to refute it. I am almost tempted to argue that only *un*intelligent machines can be malevolent; anyone who has tried to start a balky outboard will probably agree. Those who picture machines as active enemies are merely projecting their own aggressive instincts, inherited from the jungle, into a world where such things do not exist. The higher the intelligence, the greater the degree of cooperativeness. If there is ever a war between men and machines, it is easy to guess who will start it.

Yet however friendly and helpful the machines of the future may be, most people will feel that it is a rather bleak prospect for humanity if it ends up as a pampered specimen in some biological museum—even if that museum is the whole planet Earth. This, however, is an attitude I find impossible to share.

No individual exists forever; why should we expect our species to be immortal? Man, said Nietzsche, is a rope stretched between the animal and the superhuman—a rope across the abyss. That will be a noble purpose to have served.

DISCUSSION QUESTIONS
SUGGESTIONS FOR WRITING

1. Arthur C. Clarke maintains that the argument that "no machine can show originality or creative power or the other attributes which are fondly labeled 'human' " is "wholly fallacious." This might be called argument by assertion. He further maintains that those who make such an argument are "like buggy-whip makers who used to poke fun at stranded Model T's." This might be called argument by invective or argument using a questionable analogy. Does Clarke use any but wholly emotional methods of persuasion? Analyze the arguments carefully.

2. Note the manner in which the author presents his thesis—that the machine is going to take over—in the first four paragraphs of the essay. How does the clever use of analogy tend to increase the plausibility of his thesis?

3. What is a Cyborg, and why should people find such a conception, in Clarke's words, "even more horrifying than the idea that machines will replace or supersede us"?

4. What is the effect of the author's disclaimer concerning speculation about intelligence eventually discarding matter that "this leads us in realms of speculation which an unimaginative person like myself would prefer to avoid"?

ANGELL

YOUR HOROSCOPE: MORE UNSOLICITED GUIDANCE FROM OUT THERE

In this selection Roger Angell parodies the familiar form of prediction by horoscope.

TAURUS (Apr. 21-May 21)

With Venus ascendant and frozen pork-belly futures holding firm, this is a week for modest household chores. Unkink and clean all shoe-laces, not overlooking the lacing on your football. Recaulk the dog's water dish, the tank on the Water Pik, etc. Toward the end of the week, chair casters may be inspected in relative safety. Because of an enigmatic (or quietly amused) aspect of Mercury, it would be wiser not to get dressed before nightfall.

GEMINI (May 22-June 21)

Sorry, Gemini people, but still no advice for you. Eleven weeks now and still not a word from the Stars for this dormant house! Oh, well, things are bound to start popping soon. Meantime, try not to do anything at all.

CANCER (June 22-July 23)

A confused period for you normally ebullient Crabs. Purely social occupations will help keep your mind off insomnia, erasers, and east-bound watercraft. Damp bathing suits may prove annoying on Tuesday, but try to keep your composure at all costs. Some rumpling of the eye-brows may be observed upon arising. An elderly terrier will be thinking about you over the weekend.

LEO (July 24-Aug. 23)

Your best week of the entire year for sheer recklessness. Obey that wiggy impulse! Vault subway turnstiles, dress up in your wife's clothes, tell off a policeman, coat yourself in peanut butter—it doesn't matter, for the Stars say this is your time to howl! A meditative period will descend late in the week, when you may wish to consult legal and medical experts.

VIRGO (Aug. 24-Sept. 23)

Those not born under this sign would do well to visit all their Virgo friends before 4:20 P.M. on Monday, but to stay well away thereafter. As for you Virgos—well, astrology is still a difficult science, and maybe we're reading these signs wrong, ha, ha! Good luck to you all.

LIBRA (Sept. 24-Oct. 23)

A time for inwardness and mental housecleaning. Try to rid your mind of excess baggage. Forget about the Diet of Worms. Forget factoring, the cambium layer, Deanna Durbin, and Sibyl Colefax. Get rid of the Rock of Chickamauga, the color of Ventnor Avenue, and the words of "Bibbidi-Bobbidi-Boo." Throw out Gantner Wikies, Engine Charlie Wilson, and "anent." Try never to think about tundra. What a lot of trash you've been carrying around in the old bean! No wonder you can't make any money.

SCORPIO (Oct. 24-Nov. 22)

Mars will be entering this house shortly after lunch on Tuesday, so you Scorpios, already habitually suspicious, would do well to double your guard in this period. If your friends have been whispering about you in the past, just think what they're saying now! Laundrymen and Celts may try to bilk you, possibly through the mails. An agent of a Balkan power, perhaps posing as a close relative, will try to blow nerve gas through your telephone receiver while you sleep. Next week will be worse.

SAGITTARIUS (Nov. 23-Dec. 21)

All you Archers—so good-looking, so impetuous, so lovably harum-scarum—have been making a perfect hash of your lives ever since the moon slipped off your cusp way back in March, 1964. Time to come down to earth! This week, try to study some modest, everyday object and appreciate its true nature. Study one of your thumbs, for instance. Not the handsomest of all your fingers, perhaps, but one that does its job, day in and day out, without fanfare or vaingloriousness. See how wrinkled it has grown around the knuckle, but with never a word of complaint. You are lucky to have stubby Mr. Thumbkin (a typical Gemini) working for you, and you might do well to emulate his patience. If you were a dog or a fox, your thumb would be way up by your wrist somewhere, and absolutely useless. What a lesson for us all!

CAPRICORN (Dec. 22-Jan. 20)

Pablo Casals, Senator Dirksen, Renata Tebaldi, Willie McCovey, Howard Hughes, Ava Gardner, President Nasser, and President Nixon were all born under this sign, which rules the knees. The best guide to your week is to watch these fellow-Capricorns closely, for if things go well for them they will go well for you, too. If they all have a terrible week—broken cello strings, blocked legislation, tonsillitis, popups, etc.— so will you, in your own tiny way. You may find it difficult to discover much in common with each and every one of these Goat people, but that's the way astrology works, so stop complaining.

AQUARIUS (Jan. 21-Feb. 19)

Persons born under Aquarius are restless, indolent, fond of water sports, pleasing, and agreeable. Their greatest fault is procrastination. This will be a fine week for you to mooch around the house quietly, smoothing over family arguments and making friends with the milkman. Take a nap or look out the window for a while. Maybe you could get in a little surfing. On the other hand, why don't you wait and go surfing *next* week? What the hell.

PISCES (Feb. 20-Mar. 20)

This week climaxes a series of highly favorable indications for fish and Fish people. Go to the aquarium, take up fly-tying, buy a pair of guppies. Try codfish balls for breakfast—delicious! On Friday, before the onset of your coming counter-period of drought, why not throw a mammoth "Fish Fry"? Invite Hamilton Fish, Bob Trout, Ben Pollack, Dick Bass, Jean Shrimpton, Aldo Ray, Hulan Jack, Bishop Pike, etc. How they will laugh when they all "get it"!

ARIES (Mar. 21-Apr. 20)

The Stars tell us that during the coming six to eight weeks the Indonesian government will be overthrown by a Mormon clique; two European chiefs of state will be unmasked as C.I.A. agents; Liverpool will be ravaged by locusts; Akron, Ohio, will slide into the Atlantic Ocean (you can't argue with the Stars); the International Monetary Fund will be rocked by a Profumo-type scandal; and an oil slick will imperil the Wollman Memorial Rink. In view of the world-shaking nature of these impending events, how can you pushy, invariably selfish Rams keep asking astrologists for help with your petty personal affairs? Enough, already! Can't you see we're busy?

DISCUSSION QUESTIONS
SUGGESTIONS FOR WRITING

1. The horoscope is related to the diary in that both make use of a chronological record, the diary to record passing events, the horoscope to attempt to predict events before they come to pass. Both forms acquire their primary significance as a result of the development of the Homo sapiens mind as an instrument capable of making projections through time. Man has learned to worry about the past and the future; hence the attractiveness of any system that seems to establish surety and eliminate the randomness, chaos, and unpredictability of events. What attitude toward horoscopes does Roger Angell express in "Your Horoscope"?

2. What values are generally held up for ridicule in this piece?

3. Some observers have offered the idea that the increase in interest in astrology in contemporary culture is an expression of a desire for a return to the tribal state. How does this relate to the ideas of Morris and McLuhan?

4. What futures are possible for the human species? Think seriously about this question.